APPLYING ECONOMICS TO THE ENVIRONMENT

APPLYING ECONOMICS
TO THE ENVIRONMENT

Clifford S. Russell

Vanderbilt University

New York • Oxford

OXFORD UNIVERSITY PRESS

2001

Oxford University Press

Oxford   New York
Athens   Auckland   Bangkok   Bogotá   Buenos Aires   Calcutta
Cape Town   Chennai   Dar es Salaam   Delhi   Florence   Hong Kong   Istanbul
Karachi   Kuala Lumpur   Madrid   Melbourne   Mexico City   Mumbai
Nairobi   Paris   São Paulo   Shanghai   Singapore   Taipei   Tokyo   Toronto   Warsaw

and associated companies in
Berlin   Ibadan

Published by Oxford University Press, Inc.
198 Madison Avenue, New York, New York, 10016
http://www.oup-usa.org

Oxford is a registered trademark of Oxford University Press

Library of Congress Cataloging-in-Publication Data

Russell, Clifford S.
  Applying economics to the enivornment / by Clifford S. Russell
      p.   cm.
    ISBN 0-19-512684-X
    1. Environmental economics.   2. Macroeconomics.   3. Microeconomics.   I. Title.
  HC79.E5 R87   2001
  333.7—dc21   00-069298

Printing number: 9 8 7 6 5 4 3 2

Printed in the United States of America
on acid-free paper

CONTENTS

Preface   xi

CHAPTER 1
WHAT DOES ENVIRONMENTAL ECONOMICS HAVE TO DO WITH
THE ENVIRONMENT?   1

Some Historical Problems   2

Analyses of Causes and Solutions   4

Getting Closer to Specifics   6

A Sketch of Environmental Policy Choices   7

Development and the Environment   11

A Concluding Theme   13

CHAPTER 2
BACKGROUND ON ACTUAL POLICY CHOICES   16

A Little History   16

Efforts to Deal Legislatively with the Environment in the United States   18

The 1970s—A Decade of Environmental Legislation   19

Summarizing the Place of Economics in Environmental Legislation in the
United States   25

A Few Comments on International Comparisons and Global Concerns   26

Things to Keep in Mind   28

CHAPTER 3
MICROECONOMICS: REVIEW AND EXTENSIONS   32

Demand, Willingness to Pay, and Surpluses   32

Supply/Marginal Cost   38

Social Welfare Notions: Prices and Optimality   41

Notes on Optimization and the Choice of Environmental Policy   50

Optimization in Microeconomics   52

Reminders   56

APPENDIX 3.I SOME BASICS   57

Rationality   57

Demand Functions and Willingness to Pay   60

Time and Uncertainty   61

Ignorance of the Future   64

Risk and Uncertainty   65

APPENDIX 3.II EXTENSIONS   67

Correcting Market Failures: Is Partial Correction Better Than Nothing?   67

Optimizing with Inconveniently Shaped Functions   68

When Available Future Decisions Are Changed by Present Decisions   70

CHAPTER 4
AN INTRODUCTION TO THE "ENVIRONMENTAL" PART OF ENVIRONMENTAL ECONOMICS   74

Functions of the Environment Relevant to Environmental Economics   77

Models of the Natural World   79

More About Space, Time, and Randomness   88

Ignorance   91

Concluding Comments and Reminders   92

CHAPTER 5
COST-BENEFIT ANALYSIS AND THE MANAGEMENT OF THE ENVIRONMENT   94

Going Beyond the Simplest Optimizing Problem   96

A More Formal and Complex Model of the Optimizing Problem   100

Doing Less Than Basin-Wide Net Benefit Maximization   112

Conclusion   118

CHAPTER 6
DAMAGE AND BENEFIT ESTIMATION: BACKGROUND
AND INTRODUCTION   121

Practical Arguments   121

Ethical Objections and Counter Considerations   124

Some Important Misunderstandings About Economics   126

Some Possible Bases for Valuing Environmental Goods and Services   128

The Heart of the Economic Approach   129

Benefit "Routes": A Brief Review   134

Conclusion and Reminders   137

CHAPTER 7
INDIRECT BENEFIT ESTIMATION   140

Demand Shifts: Complementarity   140

Cost Shifts: Averting, Replacing, or Curing Expenditure   150

Travel Cost and Its Relation to Environmental Quality   155

General Comments on Indirect Methods of Benefit Estimation   159

Conclusions and Reminders   163

CHAPTER 8
DIRECT METHODS OF BENEFIT ESTIMATION   166

Strategic Responses   167

Cognitive Difficulties and Lack of Knowledge   173

Some Other Challenges for Direct Questioning Methods   175

Conjoint Analysis   176

Three Final, Practical Problems   182

An Attempt at a Bottom Line on Direct Questioning Techniques   183

CHAPTER 9
POLICY INSTRUMENTS I: SOME BASIC RESULTS
AND CONFUSIONS   188

Narrowing Down   188

Bases for Judging Among Instruments   192

Static Efficiency   192

Contrasting the Static and Dynamic Cases   201

A Word About Subsidies   204

A Summary to This Point   205

Chapter 10
POLICY INSTRUMENTS II: OTHER CONSIDERATIONS AND
MORE EXOTIC INSTRUMENTS   210

Comparing Instruments: Other Considerations   210

General Institutional Demands   210

Prices, Ethics, and Politics in Environmental Policy   212

Other Dimensions of Judgment   216

Beyond Administered Prices and Straightforward Regulations   220

Liability Provisions   220

The Provision of Information   226

Challenge Regulation   233

Concluding Comments and Reminders   235

Chapter 11
MONITORING AND ENFORCEMENT   240

Characteristics of Various M & E Settings   241

Elements of a Monitoring and Enforcement System   244

Some Simple Economics of Monitoring and Enforcement   245

Monitoring and Compliance as a Decision Under Uncertainty   250

Conclusion and Reminders   255

Chapter 12
DEALING WITH RISK: THE NORMATIVE MODEL
AND SOME LIMITATIONS   257

Rational Models for Dealing with Risk   258

Cognitive Problems with Risky Decisions   265

Some Conclusions   277

CHAPTER 13
RISK ANALYSIS AND RISKY DECISIONS: SOME APPLICATIONS　279

Risk Analysis and Risk Management　279

Irreversible Decisions, Ignorance, and the Techniques for
Informing Decisions　285

Concluding Comments　294

CHAPTER 14
DEVELOPMENT AND ENVIRONMENT: DESCRIPTIVE STATISTICS AND
SPECIAL CHALLENGES　297

Trying to Understand Economic Growth and Sustainability　298

Describing Countries and Their Health and Environmental Problems　304

Back to the Question of Special Challenges　314

Does Rising Income Lead to Better Environment and Thus
to Sustainability?　316

Concluding Comments　319

CHAPTER 15
ESTIMATING ENVIRONMENTAL QUALITY BENEFITS OR DAMAGES IN
DEVELOPING COUNTRIES　322

Benefit Estimation Methods for the Developing Country Setting　323

Direct, Hypothetical, or "Stated Preference" Methods　327

Some Evidence on Contrasts Between Developing and
Developed Countries　330

Conclusion　336

CHAPTER 16
CHOOSING INSTRUMENTS OF ENVIRONMENTAL POLICY
IN THE DEVELOPING COUNTRY CONTEXT　340

The Institutional Setting in Developing Countries　341

Are Market-based Environmental Policy Instruments the Best Answer for
Developing Countries? Observations and Suggestions　344

Some Evidence on the Actual Choices of Environmental Policy Instruments
Being Made in Latin America　351

Concluding Comments   356

APPENDIX 16.I INSTITUTIONAL CAPABILITIES AND MARKET
CONFIGURATIONS IN LATIN AMERICA   357

Industrial and Commercial Configurations in Latin America   358

Rural Configurations   360

CHAPTER 17
DEVELOPING COUNTRY ENVIRONMENTS AND OECD COUNTRY
TASTES: AN ASYMMETRIC RELATION   364

Some Possibilities for Cross-Border Influence   365

Where Does This Leave Us?   368

Index   371

PREFACE

This text is designed for and has been successfully used in upper-level undergraduate courses in environmental economics and in environment and development. "Upper-level" in practice means that the students are presumed to have had some version of an intermediate microeconomics course and to have been exposed to a course in the calculus. However, in my experience, the contents of "prerequisite" courses, certainly the retained contents, are highly variable. With that in mind the third chapter and its appendices concentrate on reviewing the microeconomic tools and concepts most relevant to environmental problems and to introducing a few extensions from that base. One appendix contains some simpler material for those without much background in economics. The other goes into a few more advanced topics that will interest some readers. As far as the calculus is concerned, minimal demands on the students are made, almost all being in the line of the use of differentiation in the context of optimization.

The topics covered are arranged as implied by the following view of the policy process, broadly construed but economically motivated:

Introduction and Background
- to the subject (Chapter 1)
- to the actual choices of environmental policy (Chapter 2)
- to the required microeconomics (Chapter 3) including appendices
- to the environment itself and models of its role (Chapter 4)

First: The choice of environmental targets
- Cost-benefit analysis (Chapter 5)
- Benefit and damage estimation (chapters 6–8)

Leading to:
- The choice of policy instruments for achieving the targets (chapters 9, 10)

Implying the need for:
- Monitoring to check on compliance with the instruments and enforcement to punish noncompliance (Chapter 11)

Finally, and somewhat asymmetrically, as one finds it in the real policy world:
- Dealing with uncertainty (chapters 12, 13)

The next three chapters of the book take up environmental problems in the context of development:

• Descriptively (Chapter 14)
• Special benefit and damage challenges (Chapter 15)
• Special policy instrument challenges (Chapter 16)
• A brief wrap-up (Chapter 17)

Throughout, I have tried to keep the writing style and presentation informal, along the lines of a conversation with the student. And I have tried to anticipate where in that conversation the student might have an objection or a difficulty with the intuition. I have also made an effort to suggest where the student could usefully spend some time thinking about possibilities that relate to (sometimes that contrast with) the major line of results reported.

The first draft of the book was written during the spring and summer of 1997, while I was Valfrid Paulsson Visiting Professor of Environmental Economics at the Beijer Institute, Royal Swedish Academy of Sciences, Stockholm, a position generously funded by the Swedish Environmental Protection Agency. I owe a great debt of gratitude to Karl-Göran Mäler, director at Beijer, for making this visit possible; to Carl Folke, Professor of Systems Ecology of Stockholm University, whose invitation to teach in his course at Stockholm University pushed me to really get started; and to Peter Bohm, Professor of Economics at Stockholm University, with whom I had many, many stimulating conversations during my months in Stockholm. I am also grateful to the students in my environmental economics course in 1997, 1998, and 1999 and to Mats Bohman, Professor at the Royal Technical College in Stockholm who has used the draft text book in classes and supplied feed back, by taking the time to point out problems, errors, and possibilities for improvement. Finally, I want to thank several anonymous reviewers who pointed out places that needed work. I revised the draft during the summers of 1998 and 1999 and again at the end of 1999. Both the first draft and the revisions were produced by VIPPS' desk-top publishing expert, Rebecca Brewington, who worked her magic with graphics and page layout.

APPLYING ECONOMICS TO THE ENVIRONMENT

1

What Does Environmental Economics Have to Do with the Environment?

The short answer given to the question in the title is often "nothing." This seems to be true both for people with a passionate commitment to environmental ("green") causes and those who could, as it is said, care less.

On a little reflection, some of these people might admit that knowing something about the costs of environmental policy decisions is useful. But others, even if they admit that these costs are part of reality, would see their estimation, and thus the role of economists, as just another obstacle to doing the "right" thing. These people are apt to refer to economists as "bean counters," obsessed with markets and profits and heedless of larger, longer term concerns such as the "sustainability" of human society within the context of the environment. Said more simply, many environmentalists, if they think about economics and economists at all, see them as selling out the future for present increases in frivolous use of resources to support "western" lifestyles.

If there can be said to be a single, overarching purpose to this text it is to persuade you the reader that this view is as narrow in its own way as that attributed, wrongly, to economists. Properly understood and practiced, economics has no antienvironment bias. Indeed, as we shall see when considering techniques of benefit estimation (chapters 6–8), probably a better case exists for seeing current methods as biased toward preservation, or higher environmental quality, or less disruption of nature.

But at the same time, we have to be careful not to put economics on some sort of pedestal—to think of the contributions of environmental economics as uniquely important to the collective choice problem posed by human society's interaction with the natural world. Environmental economics can be helpful, but the information it provides is only one of the several sorts useful in the public choice process. And economics is more helpful the better it integrates and is integrated into the insights that come from other relevant disciplines, such as ecology, hydrology, sanitary engineering, psychology, and political science. A second aim of the text, then, is to introduce the notion of such integration where it seems most useful, while recognizing that this is a book about economics and that it cannot succeed if it tries instead to be about everything that could possibly be relevant.

By way of getting on with all this, let us consider a variety of examples of environmental problems. Then we can discuss alternative ways of explaining the occurrence of these problems; which leads quite naturally to general prescriptions for their solution. We will then be in a better position to understand where environmental economics is coming from and can set out an agenda of topics on which it has, I believe, something useful to say.

SOME HISTORICAL PROBLEMS

Environmental problems have existed for as long as people have interacted with the natural environment. For example:

• Ancient civilizations developed irrigation systems that resulted in salinization of soils over long periods of use (evaporation of water leaving salts behind).

• Greece and other parts of the Mediterranean world were deforested and, indeed, "desoiled," very early in their histories by sheep and goat grazing.

• Rome brought water to some of its major cities in lead-lined aqueducts and gave itself a lead-poisoning problem.

• London polluted itself and the Thames, creating not only aesthetic but public health damages.

    The reasons for these problems vary. Salinization might be thought of as "caused by" ignorance, both of causal mechanism and of potential cures. Similarly for the Roman water-supply mistake.
    Mediterranean deforestation, on the other hand, was very likely the result of open-access patterns of resource use. That is, no one had the right or responsibility to manage the land for the long run. On the contrary, each family had the incentive to "use" the land to the greatest extent possible. If they cut back on use—had smaller herds—other families would simply move in on the "space" they vacated.[1]
    The Thames River, seen as a receptor of (a "sink" for) human, animal, commercial, and industrial waste, also could be said to have suffered from open access—lack of ownership power and responsibility. No single person or small group was in a position to protect the Thames by forcing waste discharges to behave differently. And no one person (or group) could make a dent in the problem by voluntarily cutting back his or her own discharges.[2]
    More recently, in mid-twentieth-century industrial societies, there were both nagging, chronic problems and dramatic events that, taken together, convinced a large number of people that something was going wrong—probably seriously wrong. Examples include:

• Killer fogs (or smogs) in London and other European cities and in the United States (e.g., Donora, Pa.). These events, triggered by unusual meteorological conditions, involved the trapping of air pollution discharges, especially sulfur dioxide (SO_2) and particulates, at ground level with resulting buildups in concentrations.

The high concentrations, in turn, led to "epidemics" of respiratory disease-like symptoms and higher than normal hospital admissions and death rates.

• A river catching fire. The Cayuhoga River, running through downtown Cleveland, Ohio, "caught fire" when the load of oil and grease (pollution) floating on its surface ignited.

• Contamination of waterways. More generally, it became unpleasant and dangerous to swim in natural watercourses because of upstream sewage and chemical discharges. Some rivers at some times were so heavily loaded with sewage that they lost the ability to support normal forms of aquatic life (algae, fish, insects, . . .) because their dissolved oxygen (DO) was used up in the biochemical reactions involving the components of the pollution (Chapter 4). When this happened, a different population of basic bacteria would take over the work of breaking down the sewage—so-called anaerobic bacteria, tolerant of zero-DO conditions. These tend to produce as their own by-products foul-smelling compounds involving sulfur, most notably hydrogen sulfide (H_2S) that smells like rotten eggs. This condition was found especially in rivers in the eastern United States where population and industrial activity were concentrated and flows small in many summers. (Examples include the Charles River through Cambridge and Boston, Mass., and the Delaware River in the vicinity of Philadelphia, Camden, N.J., and Wilmington, Del.).

• Heavy-metal poisoning. In Japan two forms of heavy-metal poisoning occurred because of the casual use of the environment as a sink for mercury and cadmium. Industrial emissions of mercury, the element, were first involved in a chemical reaction in the anaerobic sediment of the bay into which discharges occurred. The product was an organic and poisonous mercury compound, which then entered the aquatic food chain. The process called bioaccumulation resulted in quite high concentrations of mercury compounds in the flesh of the fish that the population around the bay ate as a staple. (In bioaccumulation, a compound, such as the organic mercury in this case, is successively ingested along a food chain as organisms graze plants or prey on other organisms. At each succeeding level, the concentration of the compound in the organisms flesh may be higher, until at some level it is high enough to be damaging to *that* organism.) More than 200 people were seriously affected, and about a quarter of them died. The symptoms of mercury poisoning involve loss of motor and other kinds of control, and the poisoning of people working in the felt-hatmaking trade who were exposed to mercury compounds gave rise to the expression, "mad as a hatter." The Japanese version was called Minamata disease after the bay into which the mercury was discharged around which the victims lived and in which they fished. The cadmium case involved water contaminated by a mine and used to irrigate rice and soybean crops. Again, the metal accumulated, this time in the plants; and again local populations suffered. In this case, the cadmium caused skeletal damage and extreme sensitivity to any pressure on the body. The disease became known as "itai-itai," or "ouch ouch."

• Poisoning of wildlife. Aerial spraying of the pesticide DDT on wetland areas of Long Island, New York, and Michigan to control mosquito populations in the vicinity of suburban developments, again via bioaccumulation, was seen to be wiping out populations of predator birds and producing high concentrations of the breakdown products of DDT in predator fish. The flesh eaters, such as ospreys and trout, had concentrations high enough to cause noticeable effects on reproduction and even to cause deformity and death in current generations.

ANALYSES OF CAUSES AND SOLUTIONS

It would not be hard to go on with the catalog—soot falling in industrial cities such as Pittsburgh, regular smog alerts in Los Angeles, loss of salmon runs on the rivers of the northwestern United States attributable to the building of dams for production of electricity and storage of irrigation water, are just a few more of many examples. But now let us ask the question: Why? Why were these events happening to our society? Leaving aside such far-fetched explanations as claims that we were experiencing a set of biblical plagues arranged by an angry god, or that alien invaders were engaged in weakening the earth's societies prior to taking us over, several answers have been suggested. Some of the major competitors were (and are):

• Ignorance. Just like the Romans and the ancient Middle Eastern societies, we interfere with nature without having any idea what the total effects will turn out to be.

• Growth in population and incomes, and development of exotic technology. More people; driving more cars; demanding more, and more exotic, food; using more, and more complex, machinery in every phase of life; and looking for new products such as nylon and human-concocted pesticides, are bound to harm the natural world.

• Moral failure. Pollution and other forms of environmental damage simply reflect the selfishness of humans, especially the humans inhabiting Western, industrialized societies. In effect, we are all violating the "golden" (or Kantian) rule and are not treating each other as we wish to be treated. We are harming each other by not individually refraining from polluting actions, directly or, more often, indirectly through our consumption habits.

• Institutional weakness or failure. The characteristics of environmental assets, and of the goods and services they produce, mean that many of the most important are treated as open-access resources, which results in destructive overuse. In addition, it is difficult to mobilize the collective will to change the situation, because no person or firm can sell the resulting beneficial effects. (They are "public goods," as explained in Chapter 3.) And because the workings of the environment often act to take the detrimental effects of one's own actions somewhere else, to affect someone else, the incentive is to disregard those effects in private decision making. (They are "externalities," as explained in Chapter 3.)

Not surprisingly, the prescriptions for solutions to environmental problems differ across the imputed causes (explanations).

• Those who stress ignorance tend to think that more knowledge is the key to solution. Once society sees the problem it will act to pursue technically correct policies and strategies.

• If environmental insults are really the inevitable result of the pressures of growing population and incomes, and increasingly exotic technology, the prescription must be to reduce population growth to zero (maybe even to try to have population decline for a while); to aim for a steady state in terms of per capita income; and to make sure that technological "advances" are environmentally friendly rather than damaging.

• The failure of individual morality cries out for some combination of education and more formal, collective reinforcement via legal prohibitions of bad, or requirements for good, behavior. So we should make pollution discharge illegal; similarly for indiscriminate use of pesticides, irresponsible logging practices, and construction of dams that block salmon runs. People should be vigorously educated about environmentally friendly consumption.

• If environmental problems result from institutional failure, it is necessary to repair or add to the set of available institutions. If, for example, rivers are polluted because no one owns them or the services they provide (such as recreational fishing and boating; beauty as part of the landscape; homes and food supplies for other species valued in other contexts, such as ospreys and sea-going fish that spend some time as youngsters in freshwater) then we should figure out either how to act as collective owners (make the rivers common, rather than open access) or how to make their outputs private property so that owners will act to protect them.[3]

At this point the reader may be muttering that this whole discussion seems a bit phony. Surely most real environmental problems can be argued to arise from more than one of the "causes." And therefore most solutions must involve a bit of this and a pinch of that. True enough. But the fact is that past policy debate and the solutions proposed and written into law have tended to be dominated by the moral and "knowledge" viewpoints. The flavor of the laws we shall discuss in Chapter 2 has tended to be condemning and prohibiting, and a major route to solutions has been seen to be better knowledge and hence better technology. At the same time, a vigorous strain in the public debate has been that captured by the title of the book *The Population Explosion* (Ehrlich and Ehrlich, 1990). This analysis and the prescriptions that flow from it have tended to come from ecologists, who see very clearly the finiteness of the world and its resources—including under that head its ability to deal with the waste from human societies. They also believe, based on their studies of natural systems, that populations simply cannot go on increasing forever; and that, if they attempt it, the end is likely to be a crash rather than a smooth "landing" at an equilibrium. (This phenomenon arises from the complex interactions of populations that are interdependent, as in predator-prey relations. For example, reproduction can "get ahead of" food supply and not be correctable in time to prevent mass starvation when something happens to reduce or interrupt that supply.)

By now, if there was previously any doubt, you will have figured out that the last prescription, institutional analysis, is characteristic of the economist's approach to the environment. The stress is on the failure of the markets we depend on to organize provision of other goods and services, on the need for collective decisions to do something about those failures, and on analysis of alternative ways to "do something." In choosing this path, the economist offends nearly everyone else in the debate. The economist's too ready assumption that the necessary knowledge and technology exist is not accepted by the hard-core "ignorance" analyst; and the too-optimistic view about the adjustment capabilities of human society displeases the proclaimers of inevitable doom.

To point out these differences is not to say that the other analyses and their advocates must be absolutely wrong. It has already been noted that elements that justify each view can be found in every significant problem. The differences should therefore be seen as differences of degree, of emphasis. Economists, for example, are likely to favor policies that provide incentives that push in the desired direction but that leave the specifics of responses to the individual actors in the economy (consumers, firms, farms). They are likely to think about how to live in the presence of ignorance rather than to say that knowledge must be obtained before action should be taken. They see absolute views as potentially dangerous, since achieving zero pollution is very likely impossible and pushing toward that goal is bound to require enormous commitments of resources. As we shall see, there is also a tendency of the moralist view to reduce incentives for economic actors to look for better knowledge and technology by viewing such activity as no more than their duty and failing to reward it. (See Chapter 10 on the "rachetting down" provision of U.S. water legislation.)

GETTING CLOSER TO SPECIFICS

The last section may have seemed very abstract. Even though real problems were cataloged, the analyses were characterized and put in very broad terms—ignorance, population (and wealth), moral negligence, institutional failure. Similarly, the prescriptions were not exactly ready for use off the shelf—get smarter, have fewer babies (and drive less), be "better" people, design new institutions. These sketches (some might call them caricatures) may help us see where economists are coming from but not where society might think about going when it faces a particular environmental problem. Let us therefore try to outline the questions that have to be answered in the process of dealing with such a problem, be it pollution or some other interaction of human society and nature.

The discussion does assume there is at least enough agreement on the existence of a problem that some people are seeking a solution. One fascinating and challenging feature of the environmental setting is that individuals and groups often disagree on this. One group's disaster in the wings is another's green hysteria.

A very real example here is the current debate over global climate change. On the one hand, many people, scientists included, think it is obvious that the world environment will warm quickly and substantially (compared with historical experience) over the next 50 to 100 years. They foresee large rises in sea levels (disasters for low-lying countries); dramatic shifts in average rainfall and temperature patterns; increases in violent storm activity; loss of species and even whole ecosystems as these are unable either to move themselves or adjust their makeup quickly enough; and perhaps worst of all, a reinforcing feedback via human society, as higher average temperatures increase the demand for air conditioning and hence energy inputs. Another group sees no evidence in the record of global temperatures for anything other than "normal" long-term fluctuation. This group sees the predictive global climate models, on which much of the case for change rests, as too simple to be taken seriously or even as biased by the preconceptions of their makers. These skeptics want proof before they will be willing to talk solutions.

Those who see the problem as clear and immediate (or nearly so) think action should have been taken yesterday, with tomorrow being almost certainly too late. Those who see the whole thing as the product of overheated imaginations rather than an overheated global atmosphere see no point in hypothetical chat about policies to prevent climate change. While each year sees additional evidence that many of us see adding to the case for concern and action, there remain enough skeptics in important enough positions to keep the political debate at the level of "Is there really a problem?," rather than deciding on the best ways to respond.

A SKETCH OF ENVIRONMENTAL POLICY CHOICES

In the following paragraphs, for simplicity, four choices are distinguished and discussed as though they could, in fact, be made separately. These choices are:

- What *goals* to set for the environment
- What mix of *enforceable requirements*, such as specified limits on levels of pollution discharge, and *open-ended incentives*, such as a price per unit of such discharge, to impose in seeking to achieve the goals (what *instruments* to use)
- How much and what sorts of effort to expend in *monitoring* what actually happens, and in *penalizing* bad behavior or *rewarding* good behavior
- How to deal with the inevitable *uncertainty*

Unfortunately, these are not really separable decisions, and, in fact, the choices are usually mixed up in a complicated stew of debate. This complexity was hinted at in the box just above dealing with global climate change. Because there is still no full agreement on whether this is a real problem, it is very difficult to have a clear debate on what we ought to do about the *possibility* that it is real. This, in turn, makes deciding on even conditional goals extremely difficult. And without goals, discussions of implementation methods become somewhat abstract, though for every possible method there can be debate about how easy or hard it may be to monitor compliance and enforce required actions.

Nonetheless it will continue to be convenient to use these choices as organizing principles for the book. And, for starters, let us consider what, if anything, environmental economics might have to say by way of informing the debate on each choice.

1. Setting goals. While the choice of environmental goals is inherently a political problem, for reasons we take up in chapters 2 and 3 especially, there is nonetheless a role for economic analysis in providing information about the choices open in any particular problem setting. This role can be given the shorthand label cost-benefit analysis (CBA); in it the aggregate (total across all the actors in society) effects of alternative choices are compared in money terms. The first contribution of economics here has been to clarify the definitions of costs and benefits so that they are sensible and consistent with the entire conceptual foundation that underlies our view of free markets as desirable institutions, consumers and firms as participants in those markets, and environmental goods and services as prime examples of the "failure" of markets to lead society to "optimal" situations when "public goods," such as air quality, and "externalities," such as pollution, are involved (chapters 3, 5, and 6).

The second contribution, and in some ways the most interesting and challenging part of environmental economics, is and has been the development of practical (albeit complex and controversial) ways of estimating the benefits associated with alternative environmental goals. These techniques are the subject of chapters 6 through 8.

Further, economics provides consistent rules for dealing with time in the context of environmental policy decisions. Most simply, comparing alternatives usually involves comparing different patterns of benefits and costs over some chosen time period. Thus, for one way of dealing with a problem, initial costs may be high and benefits low, while in the future benefits may grow and costs decline. Another policy alternative might have the opposite pattern. Comparing two different patterns requires deciding how valuable the future is compared with the present.[4]

2. Choosing policy instruments (chapters 9 and 10). In general, attaining any chosen environmental goal requires affecting the decisions and behavior of many independent economic actors (firms, farms, consumers, even government agencies). These actors will, also in general, have to incur different costs for changing their behavior (discharging less pollution, for example). And the effects on attainment of the goal of the changes at each actor's location will also be different. So, for example, if a goal is chosen for the quality of the air in a region ("ambient air quality") as measured at certain places, the polluters whose discharges have to change to obtain an improvement in air quality will all be located differently with respect to the measurement places. This is important because the actions of the environment itself, especially wind and weather, mean that, in general, differently located sources produce different effects on ambient quality for similar changes in pollution discharges (Chapter 4).

Beyond the current situation, as captured by "static" models, there will be opportunities for actors to try to change their own costs by investing in finding and installing different technology. And, over the same time span, changes that have nothing to do with environmental policy, such as changes in consumer tastes, communication technology, even the organization of firms, will be changing the set of actors, their locations, and relative sizes (Chapter 9).

Further complicating this choice among alternative policy instruments is that some will produce government revenue while others will not. Recently, this distinction has received a great deal of attention because some environmentally oriented charges or taxes, such as one on the carbon content of fuels burned in utility boilers or auto engines, or used up in industrial process units, will produce large amounts of money. How to take into account the effect of these revenues on the government's general tax requirements is a complex and still somewhat cloudy question (Chapter 10).

What are these "alternative ways" to meet chosen goals? Well, over a dozen approaches or instrument types are distinguished in various parts of the policy and environment literatures. The now-defunct U.S. Office of Technology Assessment used a catalog of thirteen in one of its last reports to Congress (1995). These range from quite specific orders and prohibitions (such as, do not make and sell this chemical; do not use this type of input; do use these measures to prevent soil erosion from construction sites) through limitations on the amount of pollution that may be emitted per week or month, charges on each unit of emission, all the way to the provision of information about what is being emitted by particular companies or plants.

3. Deciding about monitoring and enforcement methods and level of effort (Chapter 11). In general, though not invariably, choosing a goal and a method (or methods) by which to try to accomplish it implies that some government agency has put itself in the position of forcing firms, farms, or consumers (or all three simultaneously) to do things they would, selfishly, be better off not doing. There may be prohibitions on actions or input use, requirements for particular equipment installation, limits on discharges or other actions, or payments for the privilege of discharging or dumping. Even if the policy instrument chosen is simply provision of information to the public on the behavior of sources, the only practical way to get that information in the first place is (usually) to require the polluters to provide it.

It is perhaps sad, but it seems unquestionably true, that firms, farms, consumers, even government agencies, put in such a position will be tempted to ignore the order—unless they fear the consequences of being caught at it. This is, after all, why we have radar speed traps, why liquor stores ask for age proof, and why the IRS audits some fraction of taxpayers every year.

Intuitively, it is probably clear that the different policy instrument choices imply different problems for finding cheaters (monitoring). For example, checking whether a piece of equipment has been installed or a report filed gives those responsible for monitoring lots of chances. The absence of the machine or report is easy to discover. But checking up on a limit on discharge of pollution per month turns out to be much harder because the actual discharges do in effect disappear immediately after emission in the same way that a gallon of tea poured into a lake would "disappear" in a short time through mixing with the water already there. Finding out where the dispersed molecules came from, and how much tea there was after twenty-four hours, would be difficult if not impossible. The first problem (checking up on the presence of something) is closer to that facing the IRS. The second (measuring a quantity while it is measurable) is the speed-cop's problem.

Further considerations affecting monitoring include: how good the measurement equipment is (its accuracy and precision); how quickly the source can adjust to look as though it is in compliance if it receives a warning of an impending check; and how expensive the monitoring effort is.

Beyond monitoring—following from it—are the enforcement actions taken, usually in the form of penalties applied to those who misbehave. Much of the economics literature talks about fines as the penalties of choice. But a few analysts have looked at jail time as an alternative with certain useful properties. And, more generally, there is the possibility that the common law of torts (civil wrongs) or specially structured liability laws can move the whole problem of enforcement into the private sector by making it possible for those injured by pollution to go after the cause directly. Finally, there are some interesting ideas for bringing monitoring effort and enforcement together by making use of the data gathered in previous monitoring of a regulated firm, say to decide either on future monitoring probabilities or penalties to be applied for future detected violations.

4. Dealing with uncertainty (chapters 12 and 13). Economics, and its relative, decision analysis, provides both prescriptive guidance for (you should do . . .) and descriptive observation on (people actually do . . .) dealing with uncertainty.[5] The former takes the form:

> *Here is the way to use the available information to arrive at a choice of strategy in the face of the unknown and unknowable future. For any situation there will be several possible ways, and in general they will produce different "best" strategies. But the good news is that these different ways to identify a "best" strategy can themselves often be categorized as conservative ("risk averse," in the jargon), neutral, or aggressive ("risk seeking"). If it is possible to decide in advance among those general mind sets, then one or another of the choice techniques may seem most appropriate.*

On the descriptive side, the lessons of the literature are generally that:

People, even quite sophisticated people, do not use the prescribed methods when actually making "risky" decisions (decisions with uncertain outcomes). Indeed, they have trouble with every facet of the problem, from understanding probabilities, to deciding on a stance from the averse-neutral-seeking set of choices, to actually picking a strategy when everything is laid out clearly. These observations about actual choices are both interesting in themselves and helpful in understanding some of the actual behavior we see in the world. (We may even recognize some of our own foibles.)

Chapters 12 and 13 deal with both aspects of the risk literature and include discussion of some clever ways economists have suggested for dealing with gaps in our knowledge.

So, there is a very quick and dirty summary of one answer to the question in the title of this first chapter. That answer, spelled out more carefully, constitutes the guts of the rest of the book. An effort will be made as we go along to tie the arguments and (inevitable) abstractions to real problems and policies. You may find the whole enterprise more interesting, however, if you keep an eye open for news items that bring uncertainty, goals, instruments, and enforcement to life. Once you start looking, you'll be surprised how much material appears every month in newspapers and magazines and on TV.

DEVELOPMENT AND THE ENVIRONMENT

Environmental economics as a subdiscipline and environmental policy as an activity of governments have to a very large extent grown up together over the second half of the twentieth century in the context of the so-called developed nations. These nations are conveniently thought of as those of Western Europe and North America plus Japan.[6] They display high education levels and per capita incomes, long life expectancies for citizens, and generally good health status during those long lives. Their institutions, both public and private, tend to be reasonably efficient, well organized, and free of at least gross corruption. Their infrastructure, as in roads, rail lines, communications systems, and water supply and waste disposal conduits, tend to be in good physical condition and adequate to the tasks imposed on them.

During the same half century, another subdiscipline has grown up in economics, one that is concerned with how to encourage and facilitate the economic growth of the countries that are now relatively poor in income terms. These nations, as both cause and effect of poverty, tend to have lower education levels and health status; less adequate infrastructure; and less capable and reliable institutional resources, both government and private. They also often display some very serious local environmental problems, such as severe air and water pollution in the vicinity of cities and industrial areas. In addition, these nations often happen to be the owners of environmental assets that are deemed by people in the developed nations to be of global significance. Examples include the huge forests of the Amazon Basin in South America, of Central America, and of the large islands of Southeast Asia; the animals of the East African savannah; and the mangrove wetlands, with their associated ocean fish nurseries, along many tropical coast lines.

Roughly over the past twenty-five years, concerns about economic development and about the environment have become more frequently linked, both in public debate over international development policies and in academic discussions. The noisiest and most public of these discussions tend to involve some version of the claim by developing countries that environmental protection is a rich nation's game and that the poorer nations should not have to play. Rather they should be left alone and allowed to develop economically at whatever environmental cost—just as, they point out, the OECD countries did for almost 200 years. In the late 1990s, this argument is seen in the context of the global climate change negotiations.

Implicit in this position is the notion that growing per capita incomes ("developing") must be bad for the environment and vice versa. But in opposition to this view is the notion of "sustainability," which, to oversimplify a bit, points out that all human economic activity, indeed life itself, rests ultimately on the environment. Development that ignores this and destroys its environment destroys itself in the long run. Those who stress sustainability say that nations cannot choose *between* growth and environment but must work at reconciling the two. Then there are those who say to developing countries, in effect, "Forget the long run. Your people are suffering badly right now from the ravages of unchecked pollution. Fix these problems or you'll never see the long run."

The resulting disagreements, particularly the public and political ones, often suffer from a lack of clarity about what sort of environmental problem is the motivation. At one extreme, there may be a concern about the local pollution problems that pose serious public health threats, even in the context of generally poorer health status and shorter life expectancies. Examples include the threat of intestinal disease (a major cause of infant deaths) due to inadequate attention to keeping people and their wastes separated; and the threat of lead poisoning due to high levels of lead used in gasoline to increase octane, coupled with increasing auto populations and traffic congestion. It seems clear that even poorer nations should give some attention to these matters, though there is no reason to expect that the policies they choose for dealing with them will match decisions taken in the OECD world.

At the other extreme, citizens of the OECD world have become more and more concerned about the way some of the environmental assets referred to above—those of apparently global significance because of size or uniqueness—are being treated by their "owners." Here the identification of self-interest on the part of the poorer nations becomes much trickier. For example, it may suit Brazil very well to reduce the area of its Amazonian forests in exchange for obtaining room to settle parts of its growing population. In the long run, the world at large may suffer because of a loss of carbon-fixing trees (global warming again) and loss of plant, insect, and animal species that might have had genes we would find useful if we but knew about them (uncertainty again). But trying to get Brazil to behave differently merely by pointing this out is likely to be a fruitless exercise.

Chapters 14 through 16 of the book are designed to add some light to the heat of the resulting debates about development and environment. First, in Chapter 14, an attempt is made to make the notion of relative poverty a bit more three dimensional by reproducing data on how the OECD and less-developed nations differ. Along the way, the extent of the local and immediate environmental threats will become clearer. Then the hugely complex questions of development itself, its causes, the extent to which it really can be influenced by national policy, and how it may be linked to environmental policy will be touched on.

Chapter 15 reconsiders the matter of damage and benefit estimation from chapters 6 through 8 in the developing nation context. Both methods—which of the available ones seem likely to prove most useful in the developing nation context—and results are dealt with.

In Chapter 16, an analogous exercise is pursued in the business of choosing environmental instruments. The stress there is on the differential importance of institutional capabilities in the successful application of different possible instruments. The conclusion, perhaps not very surprising to the noneconomist reader is that instrument choices that may arguably be "best" for OECD settings may not be so for developing countries.

Chapter 17 deals with the asymmetric relationship involving OECD tastes for how the developing countries manage their environments, unmatched by significant concern running the other way.

A CONCLUDING THEME

A theme that might be said to tie together the problems of internal, domestic environmental policy choices and the international environment-development debate is the notion of the "principal-agent" problem, or how one party (the principal) who wants to achieve a particular goal, can best motivate another party or parties (the agent(s)) to act as though he, she, or they share that same goal even though they may not. That this is a fundamental conundrum for human society, not just in the environmental policy arena, should be clear after a little reflection. It is certainly a problem for the work place, where owners, managers, and employees may all have different objectives but where none will achieve what he or she wants unless somehow all manage to come together in at least a minimal way to cooperate on some tasks. A little more thought may persuade the reader that even the classroom is a principal-agent problem setting. Most teachers and most students are not after exactly the same ends when they embark on a course, and the set of motivating tools available to the former for influencing the latter is quite limited.

In the world of environmental policy, a full description of principals and agents reveals the great complexity of the problem. Ultimately, everyone has a stake in higher environmental quality, though every person's "stake" is slightly different, depending on location, tastes, habits, and even beliefs about the uncertain future. Almost every person also has a stake in environment-threatening activities, for example as owner, manager, or employee of a firm that pollutes or as citizen of a local government unit that does the same. This same complexity applies in the global context, and in the development-environment debate specifically. Here it is useful to think of OECD countries or groups of their citizens as principals and the developing nations as agents. Rather than shouting at each other about principles, we should get on with designing and putting in place ways of motivating desired policies. This, it seems to me, is the great challenge for environmental economics in the twenty-first century.

NOTES

1. This phenomenon has become associated in much popular environmental writing with a name given it by Garrett Hardin, an ecologist. It is known as "the tragedy of the commons" after his 1968 paper by that title in *Science*. However, as becomes clear after reading Dan Bromley's work (e.g., *Environment and Economy: Property Rights and Public Policy,* 1991), a more accurate name would be the tragedy of open access. This keeps alive a useful distinction between common property, which is managed by collectively set and enforced rules and restrictions on access; and open-access land or water, in which both rules and access restrictions are lacking. Commons are fascinating ancient institutions and are still recreationally important in England.
2. That this was true is almost certainly in good part due to the size of the river and the number of dischargers. A case at the other end of both scales—a tiny stream in the countryside near Cambridge, England—is described in the book *The Common Stream* by Rowland Parker. Note the word "common." This stream was long subject to rules limiting timing, quantities, and types of waste discharge that were imposed on those living along it, by ancient institutions blending democracy and feudal power in complex ways.
3. This is far-fetched for landscape services but not for recreational fishing. The right to do such fishing for trout and salmon is a private property right in Wales, England, most of Scotland, Norway, and Sweden. These rights may be bought, sold, and rented, and the rivers are protected rather aggressively from pollution by associations of owners.
4. A more difficult problem arises with time when current decisions change the set of possible decisions available at future times. We shall call this the "dynamic" problem and will introduce it and talk informally about its solution in Appendix 3.II.
5. There is an old distinction, which remains in much of the literature, between risk—situations in which the probabilities of possible outcomes are known—and uncertainty—in which these probabilities are not known. If, however, we take seriously the proposition that probabilities are always available, even if only from expert subjective judgments, then the need for the distinction disappears. In this text "risk" and "uncertainty" are used as synonyms. More about all this in Chapter 12.
6. The "club" of rich nations is the Organization for Economic Cooperation and Development (OECD). This now includes South Korea. The initials provide a convenient way to refer to the developed world.

REFERENCES

Bromley, Daniel W. 1991. *Environment and Economy: Property Rights and Public Policy.* Oxford: Basil Blackwell.

Ehrlich, Paul, and Anne Ehrlich. 1990. *The Population Explosion.* New York: Simon and Schuster.

Hardin, Garrett. 1968. "The tragedy of the commons." *Science* 162 (Dec): 1243–1248.

Parker, Rowland. 1975. *The Common Stream.* London: Collins.

U.S. Congress, Office of Technology Assessment. 1995. *Environmental Policy Tools, a User's Guide.* OTA-ENV 634. Washington, D.C.: U.S. Government Printing Office (Sept.).

2

BACKGROUND ON ACTUAL
POLICY CHOICES

This text, in common with the rest of microeconomics, will stress the economic efficiency aspects of human society's dealings with the environment—particularly the environment as receptor for the "residuals" of our production, transportation, and consumption activities, and as provider of services to individuals and households, such as recreation. The resulting catalog of concerns, techniques, and recommendations has only recently had any impact on actual environmental policy. And even now it would be a stretch to call economics central to most of the environmental policy debate. So it seems worthwhile to spend a little time at the beginning on what actual policies look like and even on why they look that way. As background to this background, we'll try to get a sense for the longer history of environmental problems and solutions, which will give us some notion of the links among scientific understanding, technological abilities, and the scope and content of efforts to reduce the inconvenience (and more serious harm) caused by human polluting activities.

A LITTLE HISTORY

At low population densities and with the unsophisticated technologies of peasant agriculture, human society makes quite a small impact on the natural environment seen in the large. The waste by-products of farming, cooking, clothes making, and eating are low volume, "natural," and degradable.[1] The smell might offend modern noses, but the extra contribution to human misery would be tiny, except in isolated cases, such as the bad siting of a privy relative to a well. Such efforts as were necessary to keep things in hand might take the form of restrictions on when or where certain activities could go on. As noted already, for example, the book *The Common Stream* (Rowland, 1975), lists ancient rules for using a small stream running through a village in the English countryside. An attempt was made to segregate *in time* such activities as doing laundry and watering animals.

    The concentration of population in towns and cities creates an obviously different situation. Food and other products of farms, mines, and forests have to be brought in. And much more human and animal waste is generated per unit area than can be absorbed into what remains of the natural system. This waste has to be taken out. There are also cooking and heating fires, and at least some wastes from "industry" (forges, tanneries, and bakeries, for example). This could lead to both unpleasant and unhealthy conditions.

The concentration of people and their wastes also makes the possibilities for the spread of certain diseases much greater. The classic story of early epidemiology—the study of the spread of epidemics, or more generally, of the nature and extent of health risks—involves a water pump in a neighborhood in London. This pump was pinpointed as the source of a localized typhoid epidemic by plotting new cases on a map and inferring where the people involved must be getting their household water. The underground water the well was drawing from had somehow become contaminated by human waste.

Still, the problems of pollution in the sense we use the word today were limited by the size, concentration, and technological capabilities of human population. Outside of cities, most of that population lived, until very recently, much as people had done for thousands of years, so close to the natural world as to almost be part of it. (If you think that sounds healthy and even romantic, read a book on what peasant life was like. You don't have to have industrial pollution to suffer from toothache, pneumonia, tuberculosis, arthritis, and many other acute and chronic diseases.) The cities themselves, their air and their waterways, could be very dirty indeed.

The set of events that began to change the scale and nature of human impacts on the environment we call the Industrial Revolution. Its beginning is generally taken to be in the last few decades of the eighteenth century. At that time, some serious progress was made in human ability to harness the power of steam and to make large quantities of iron from iron ore using coal instead of wood as the energy source. There followed changes in transportation, agriculture, and industry, which together transformed at least Europe and North America in the nineteenth century. These changes in turn laid the foundation for further advances in technology—electricity, artificial fertilizers, railroads, the internal combustion engine, organic chemistry, nuclear fission, the vacuum tube and then the transistor. From the point of view of this text there were several environmental consequences:

- Life expectancy increased and infant mortality decreased—more people.

- Higher concentrations of people became possible and seemed desirable.

- The burning of fossil fuels—first coal, then oil, now much natural gas—became the energy foundation for a great deal of human activity.

- Huge numbers of new molecules were created and came into use as pesticides, fabrics, refrigerants, solvents, even structural materials.

- Real incomes increased dramatically for almost every stratum of society. This increase was taken partly in goods (money) and partly in leisure (shorter work weeks, longer vacations, and earlier retirement).

- These income and leisure effects, in turn, helped increase the demands for travel and for outdoor recreation, which put new stresses on remote environments at the same time that it created a larger and larger group sensitive to these environments.

- Among the increases in scientific knowledge was to be found a better understanding of environment-to-health links—not only disease transmission but direct health effects such as the threat posed by breathing chronically high concentrations of particulates in combination with sulfate (SO_4) aerosols.

On the whole, however, the belching industrial smokestack and even the dirty river tended to be seen as symbols of industrial progress rather than as threats to the quality (or length) of life right up to the middle of the twentieth century. But after the convulsion of World War II and the smaller Korean conflict, people began to have time to reflect, rather than simply reacting to crisis and pushing the production system toward its physical limits. There began to develop a sense, at least among the better off and better educated, that all might not be for the best in this "best of all possible worlds." This nagging doubt was eventually to become a full-blown conviction that itself fueled an activist environmental movement that is still in existence and still working to affect policy. Several events were especially influential in this shift.

- "Killer" air pollution episodes in London and in the small Pennsylvania town of Donora (1948) gave evidence that air pollution could actually kill people directly and fairly quickly.
- Rachel Carson's 1963 book, *Silent Spring*, dealt with human impacts on nature, such as the loss of populations of birds of prey that seemed to be traceable to the effects of pesticides on the birds' reproductive systems. The pesticides in turn were being sprayed in large quantities to keep down mosquito populations.
- Lake Erie, one of the Great Lakes and touching Michigan, Ohio, Pennsylvania, and New York, was said to be "dying" because of inputs of organic material and fertilizers—especially phosphates from the newer whitening detergents. The lake might more accurately have been said to be dangerously "alive," with massive growth of the tiny plants called algae, which were making the water turbid (preventing light from penetrating to help other aquatic vegetation grow) and making for large fluctuations in dissolved oxygen (up as the plants grew and "breathed out"; crashing to low levels, even to zero in small areas, when the plants died off and the resident microbes started breaking down their organic materials, using up oxygen in the process).

EFFORTS TO DEAL LEGISLATIVELY WITH THE ENVIRONMENT IN THE UNITED STATES

General concern and specific incidents began generating pressure for government intervention well before the environmental decade of the 1970s. These early responses did not produce much improvement on the ground, though they did spur some activity that would later prove useful. One such effort was the setting of state ambient (in-stream) water quality standards for interstate rivers and lakes. This got the states thinking about what uses these water bodies *should* be fit for and, with federal guidance, about quality levels along various quality dimensions that would be consistent with those uses. But unfortunately, a related part of the 1960s water quality legislation, through the failure of the water quality improvement institutional process it contained, set the stage for some of the least defensible features of the 1970s legislation.

The key ideas in the early efforts were that the states should take the lead, and that river basin conferences should be convened to decide on how the effort at discharge reduction required to meet the chosen ambient standards in a basin should be shared out across the states, and ultimately across the individual dischargers within those states.[2] In hindsight it is perhaps not very surprising that these conferences came to nothing. The states had little incentive to agree to costs that would be imposed on their industries for the benefit of downstream populations in other states. Nonetheless, disappointment with this process and frustration with the states were important elements in the design of the federal clean water legislation of 1972, which largely turned its back on ambient quality standards and sharing of discharge reduction burdens in order to meet such standards. Rather, as we shall see below, the approach became one of specifying what each discharger should do by way of reduction on the basis of what available technology appeared to make feasible.

THE 1970s—A DECADE OF ENVIRONMENTAL LEGISLATION

Exactly why the decade of the 1970s saw the dam break and a flood of environmental laws spill out of the U.S. Congress is not for a mere economist to try to say. Certainly, as sketched above, the pressure had been building, albeit slowly, from the mid-1950s. And the attempts to fix things with "minimally invasive procedures" in the 1960s seemed to have come to nothing. Then there was the debacle of Vietnam, creating massive tensions between young and old, government and citizens, executive and legislature. Someone had to be thinking that it would be politically invaluable to find a policy area that promised to heal, even if only temporarily, some one of these divisions. There was also Senator Edmund Muskie, who very much wanted to be President Muskie and who appeared to see the environment as an issue he could ride into the White House. (As chairman of the powerful Senate Public Works Committee he was in a position to strongly influence what legislation survived to arrive on the floor of the Senate, even if he could not guarantee its passage there or, even more obviously, in the House.) For an excellent and contemporary discussion of the wave of environmental legislation and its background in earlier policy experiments, see Davies and Davies, 1975.

Whatever explanations are eventually agreed on by political historians, the facts speak for themselves. Between 1970 and 1980, seven major pieces of environmental legislation, some new, some amending existing laws, were passed and signed by

TABLE 2.1 Major Environmental Legislation for the Decade of the 1970s

1. National Environmental Policy Act, 1969
2. Clean Air Act (CAA), 1970 (originally passed in 1963; amendment of 1970 began the decade of environmental legislation; subsequently amended in 1977 and 1990)
3. Clean Water Act (CWA), 1972 (originally amendments to the Federal Water Pollution Control Act of 1948; amended and renamed in 1977; further amended in 1981 and 1987)
4. Federal Insecticide, Fungicide, and Rodenticide Act (FIFRA), 1972 (originally passed in 1947; amended in '64, '72, '78, and '88)
5. Noise Control Act, 1972 (amended 1978)
6. Marine Protection, Research, and Sanctuaries Act, 1972
7. Safe Drinking Water Act (SDWA), 1974 (amended 1977, 1979, 1980)
8. Toxic Substances Control Act (TSCA), 1976
9. Resource Conservation and Recovery Act (RCRA), 1976 (amended 1984)
10. Comprehensive Environmental Response, Liability, and Compensation Act (CERCLA, or more simply, Superfund), 1980 (amended 1986 [SARA])

Note: The main date given is that usually attached to the major policy initiative, even where that was technically embodied in amendments to older legislation.

presidents Nixon, Ford, and Carter. (Two Republicans and one Democrat, it is worth noting, given the terms of the debate in Washington thirty years later, which tend to have Democrats taking on the pure environmental role and Republicans complaining about the costs and restrictions imposed on private parties by the existing laws.)

Table 2.1 summarizes the laws passed. For purposes of this text I want to concentrate on just a few central dimensions of the design of these laws and to look at how various of the laws compare on those dimensions. The dimensions are keyed to some of the book's major themes, and a list of them is given in Table 2.2. In the commentary that follows I will attempt to look both at the original act and at subsequent changes or additions, but I do not guarantee completeness. In particular, I will not comment on every law along every dimension but will concentrate on not-

TABLE 2.2 Some Dimensions on Which to Compare Environmental Laws

What concerns drive the legislation; for example: human health, recreation, or integrity of ecological systems?

What role, if any, is given to estimated costs or benefits, and is a balancing of costs and benefits required or even allowed?

How are concerns and goals translated into enforceable regulations governing "discharges"? (In particular, are ambient quality goals the basis for discharge standards?)

What role does technology play, if any; and how are new technological possibilities dealt with?

Do payments, charges or markets play a role in implementation? (These are usually referred to as "economic incentives.")

Are any other, more unusual, implementation methods introduced?

What are the implications for monitoring and enforcement problems?

TABLE 2.3 Air (Clean Air Act) and Water Pollution Control (Clean Water Act) Legislation Contrasted

	Air (CAA)	Water (CWA)
Driving concerns	Health (primary); materials, "general welfare" (secondary); acid rain (added later)	Recreation (fishable, swimmable). Ecosystems (zero discharge goal).
Costs/benefits	Cannot be used in decisions (presidents have nonetheless required estimation).	Cost concern built into definitions of technology-based discharge standards. Balancing, of a kind, implied.
Defining enforceable rules	In principle, AEQ (NAAQS)[a] drives discharge permit terms for existing sources. New sources get technology-based standards. New source standards are quite strict.	New and existing sources get technology-based standards. New source standards are tougher.
Role of technology	See above.	See above. Also "ratchetting down" of technology-based definitions aimed at taking advantage of exogenous technical advances.
Economic incentives	None in original; introduced later by EPA and then ratified by amendment to law. New acid rain amendments have marketable permit approach.	None in original. Experiments have been carried out with marketable permits, but these have not led to extensions.
Other implementation innovations	Penalties for not attaining NAAQS in a region.	If state water quality standards not met, further discharge reductions could be ordered.
Monitoring and enforcement	Heavy emphasis on proving that a source *could* meet its permit terms (initial compliance); monitoring instruments not well suited to checking on later (continuing) compliance.	Point source monitoring straightforward. Nonpoint sources, such as farms, not amenable to monitoring by current technology—but not seriously regulated in any case.
Other contrasts and problems	Private, point sources most important except for CO and ground level O_3, where vehicles dominate.[b]	Publicly owned waste water treatment plants and nonpoint sources (esp. farms) are very important.

[a]AEQ = ambient environmental quality; NAAQS = national ambient air quality standards. [b]CO = carbon monoxide; O_3 = ozone (major constituent of "smog")

ing what I think are interesting contrasts. The idea here is to set the stage, not to make you an expert in the law.

First, let me contrast the air and water pollution control legislation (see Table 2.3). The importance of health as the primary driving force behind the 1970 Clean Air Act (CAA) no doubt helps explain some of the contrasts here. For example, that law does not allow for cost of implementation to be taken into account in deciding on the National Ambient Air Quality Standard levels (NAAQS) for the "criteria" pollutants.[3] These NAAQSs in turn are supposed to drive the setting of discharge permit terms for sources. In the clean water legislation (The 1972 Federal Water Pollution Control Act Amendments, later renamed the Clean Water Act), on the other hand, discharge standards are defined source by source on the basis of what is deemed technologically and economically "achievable" through a complex and lengthy process of engineering study (and legal challenge). Cost, therefore, is considered. But costs and benefits are not balanced in any formal way, and technology rather than ambient environmental quality (AEQ) drives the system. (AEQ enters the regulatory picture for streams if the technology-based standards fail to produce quality at least as good as the standards set under the earlier legislation referred to above.) Both acts, the water act especially so, treat technological advance as something entirely outside the influence of the law's provisions—as though better technology will appear at the same pace independent of the provisions of laws. And neither act, as originally written, contemplated the use of what are called "economic incentives." These were introduced later by EPA as a way around some of the rigidities of CAA that threatened to create a fire storm of political opposition that could have killed or crippled the effort to improve air quality. The incentives took the form of a restricted system of "tradable discharge permits." (We will come back to these in chapters 9 and 10, which deal with policy instruments.)

Another contrast between the situations the acts sought to address is the relative importance of publicly owned and "nonpoint" sources in the air and water. In air pollution, nonpoint sources, especially cars and trucks (nonpoint both because they move and because there are too many to monitor individually in a continuing way) are central to carbon monoxide and ground-level ozone concerns. The other criteria pollutants tend to be dominated by point sources ("smokestacks"). On the water side, nonpoint sources—farms and feedlots, golf courses, managed forests, construction sites—are very important in determining the quality of many water bodies. And among the point sources (discharge pipes), publicly owned (usually municipal) sewage treatment plants are often quite important. This creates rather direct conflicts for a federal system—the "feds" telling cities and towns, through the states, what they must do. But some version of this approach is necessary to get beyond the upstream-cost/downstream-benefit problem mentioned above.

Let's look next at the Resource Conservation and Recovery Act (RCRA) (Table 2.4), a 1976 law aimed at *preventing* "solid-waste pollution"—in particular, the pollution of groundwater and surface water via the unrestricted disposal in landfills of hazardous substances. This I will contrast with the Comprehensive Environmental Response, Liability, and Compensation Act (CERCLA), better known as "Superfund," which became law in 1980 and is aimed at cleaning up existing sites where such contamination has already occurred or may be about to occur.

Together these two laws provide a powerful incentive for firms (especially) to cut back the use of compounds defined as "hazardous," whether as inputs that are transformed or as solvents that simply become less effective with use. But the several routes by which this incentive effect is achieved are complex and to some ex-

TABLE 2.4 Resource Conservation and Recovery Act and Comprehensive Environmental Response, Liability, and Compensation Act (Superfund)

	RCRA	CERCLA
Driving concerns	Groundwater protection (human health).	Exposure to existing hazardous wastes in environment by whatever route (human health).
Costs/benefits	Balancing ruled out for many decisions. But see under incentives.	Balancing ruled out.
Defining enforceable rules	• Technology specifications for operating and closed landfills. • Manifest requirements to trace shipments. • Rules for incinerator capabilities for the destruction of hazardous compounds.	Unclear, except that "safety" is defined in terms of cancer risks. Each site involves negotiation of method of cleanup and goal for results.
Role of technology	See above; quite central.	None specified.
Economic incentives	Liability insurance required. Natural Resource Damage Assessments as the basis for after-the-fact recovery of damages caused.	For future actions: "Joint and several liability" for costs of cleanup. Natural Resource Damage Assessments.
Other implementation innovations		Toxics Release Inventory (TRI) as part of "community right to know" (see Chapter 10).
Monitoring	Catching determined violators is hard because "sources" are transportable.	Monitoring here is an ex post "discovery" problem: Who dumped waste into this particular landfill?
Other contrasts and problems	• Defining "hazardous wastes." • How to deal with minimally contaminated waste streams.	• Defining reasonable future possible uses for sites. • Secondary disposal of cleaned up waste. • Incentives for "potentially responsible parties" to tie process up in court.

tent indirect; and when you add in the Toxics Release Inventory (TRI), an innovation of the late 1980s, the whole tangle takes on a very ad hoc quality—a wonderful example of sequential efforts at design by committee. From the point of view of background for a look at environmental economics, though, notice the following:

• "Safety," defined in terms of human health, is the goal of both RCRA and CERCLA. It is to be defined in some "scientific" way involving human health risk. But the value of added safety is not to be balanced against the cost of achieving it.

• Technology plays a central role, especially in RCRA, where landfill technology is specified in great detail, including the design and operation of required groundwater monitoring schemes.

• A "manifest" system was imposed by RCRA, designed to track hazardous materials "from cradle to grave" and to make "midnight dumping" detectable via the paper trail. But this assumes the trail is ever begun. If someone wanted to break the rules, the first step would be to deal with a transporter/disposer who is willing to take material without a manifest.

• Liability—prospective and, at least in theory, insurable, under RCRA and both retrospective and prospective under Superfund—sends the message of society's concern with these hazards in a way that at least roughly complements the onerous technology and reporting requirements. The extent of liability can be approximated by the size of prospective "natural resource damage assessments" (NRDA)—the other side of the benefit estimation coin. Both RCRA and CERCLA provide for efforts to estimate, in money terms, the extent of the damages to natural resources (surface water, wildlife, underground water, for example) caused by the actions of some firm or municipality (or group of firms). The "trustees," usually state or federal agencies for the resources involved, are authorized to go to court to recover these damages from the responsible parties.

• Superfund, especially, has been very controversial. In part this is because it has encouraged a lot of legal sparring rather than a lot of cleanup; and in part it is because the extent of required cleanup appears to be unreasonably stringent, assuming, in effect, that every site will in future years have a preschool or a housing development put on top of it, and requiring that the resulting lifetime addition to cancer risk should be extremely small for the exposed individuals. But finally, Superfund imposes ex post liability for the costs involved in correcting *society's* mistake—allowing the dumping of toxics for many years.

• The Toxics Release Inventory adds to the incentive not to use "toxics" by making public every plant's discharges of over 600 compounds (at least what the plants *say* their discharges are). This can be seen as a massive experiment in the use of public information as a policy tool. (Again, we will be returning to this innovation in Chapter 10.)

Finally, let's look at two laws that are designed to stop *introduction* of hazardous substances into human society and the environment. These substances might be used in manufacturing and ultimately be candidates for "discharge," as residuals, to landfills or via incineration; or they might be "discharged" as a necessary part of use, as are insecticides and herbicides. The laws are the Toxic Substances Control Act (TSCA) and the Federal Insecticide, Fungicide, and Rodenticide Act Amendments (FIFRA) of 1972. Table 2.5 outlines their similarities and contrasts. Notice that there are more of the former than the latter.

There are two interesting features highlighted by this table, I think. One is that both laws permit a balancing of costs and benefits (or risks and benefits depending on the definition of the status quo). This marks a contrast from the CAA and CWA

TABLE 2.5 Toxic Substances Control Act and Federal Insecticide, Fungicide, and Rodenticide Act Amendments Compared

	TSCA	FIFRA
Driving concerns	Human health and environmental effects.	Human health and environmental effects.
Costs/benefits	Balancing of risks and benefits is encouraged by legislative history.	Balancing officially sanctioned in the amendments.
Defining enforceable rules	Rule making under these acts tends to be of the on/off variety. Either some compound can be manufactured and used or it cannot, though some permissions specify uses that are allowed.	
Role of technology	Not central.	Not central.
Economic incentives	None.	None.
Other implementation innovations	Burden of proof on introducer of new chemical or proposer of new use.	Burden of proof on introducer of new chemical or proposer of new use.
Monitoring	Possible problem of checking up on safety data submitted by proposer.	Difficult to detect nonpermitted uses (e.g., spraying on wrong crop or at wrong time).
Other contrasts and problems	• Sheer number of new and existing compounds. • Difficulty of finding subtle or long-term exposure effects.	• Difficulty of finding subtle or long-term exposure effects.

and, for the most part, from RCRA. It is not clear why Congress took this different tack, particularly since we are talking here about "toxics," with all the emotional baggage that it involves. If anything, I would have expected these acts to be *more* explicitly antibalancing.

The second feature of great interest is the assignment of the burden of proof. As we shall see in Chapter 13, assigning the burden to the proponent of a new chemical or new use usually implies that approval will be less likely than it would have been if the burden had been on the agency. So this approach can be seen as providing additional protection and to work in the opposite direction from the allowance of balancing (where the benefits of the proposed introduction or new use can offset the human and ecological risks foreseen).

SUMMARIZING THE PLACE OF ECONOMICS IN ENVIRONMENTAL LEGISLATION IN THE UNITED STATES

For whatever combination of reasons, it seems that economic concerns have played a small, and we might even say a haphazard, role in the policies written into U.S. laws over the period since 1970. In general, the goals of the acts are defined in such terms as the protection of human health or of the environment's ability to provide such services as recreation. The implication is clearly that society, speaking through its elected representatives, finds these goals worth whatever costs are involved. There are exceptions: TSCA and FIFRA, in particular, allow for the prospective benefits of introduction of new compounds to be balanced against prospective damages. At the other extreme, the CAA discourages even considering the costs of achieving the mandated goals. But neither the CAA nor the CWA contemplates cost-benefit analysis as a guide to choosing ambient quality standards.

A second feature of these laws that has offended many environmental economists is their reliance on traditional regulatory approaches—that is, on the writing of permits to do something or prohibitions of doing something else. Economists have generally been enthusiastic about charging regulated parties some price per unit of an activity that is to be discouraged (an effluent or emission charge). They have demonstrated to their own satisfaction that this approach can dramatically lower the costs of achieving whatever ambient quality improvements are contemplated. More recently, there has been more interest among economists in making the permits to emit pollution marketable. This has likely been driven by, rather than leading, a readiness among, first bureaucrats and then politicians to contemplate the use of such an approach. It is now to be found very much at the center of air pollution control laws and policy.

Finally, there seem to be common threads in the new versus old technology question in these laws. First, technological advance of a kind that is "environment saving" is taken as given and unrelated to anything in the laws. That is, production processes and end-of-pipe treatment technology are assumed to be more or less constantly improving in the sense of leading to lower discharges of pollution per unit of production. The legislation is written to take advantage of this by mandating tougher standards for new sources (e.g., new power plants or oil refineries). The CWA even establishes a process for making standards tougher for *existing* sources when technological progress makes that feasible. This all seems perverse to many economists, who see technological progress as being driven by features *of* the system—by the advantages for firms, farms, and even municipalities of finding and applying cleaner technologies.

Altogether, it appears to environmental economists that U.S. legislation has been driven too much by the moralistic forces described in Chapter 1 and not nearly enough by the institutional insights developed by the field we are examining in this text.

A FEW COMMENTS ON INTERNATIONAL COMPARISONS AND GLOBAL CONCERNS

There has long been a thread in the U.S. environmental economics literature that pictures Europe as the home of logical and efficient environmental policies. This was encouraged—probably created—by the early praise heaped on the German system of emission charges that had been used in the Ruhr River basin for decades before environmental economists were even there to comment. It was further encouraged by the adoption of a national emission charge system in Germany (before unification) and by the observation that several other countries, including France and the Netherlands, also seemed to be using such charges as an instrument of policy. And many of the early environmental economists believed charges to be the sine qua non of intelligent policy.

I would not go so far as to say that this view is completely without merit, but I do think it is overblown. For starters, most of the charging schemes pointed to so enthusiastically by economists are just money-raising arrangements, not incentive systems in the sense discussed in chapters 9 and 10 below, on policy instruments. The revenue raised is used to support the administration of water quality programs and, more importantly, for the building of regional sewers and treatment plants, with the idea of taking advantage of economies of scale. This might be clever, both politically and economically, where populations and industry are quite closely packed, but it is not a breakthrough or model for the rest of the world—certainly not for most of the United States where everything tends to be strung out over huge areas, making the necessary wastewater collection systems very expensive.

Another feature of Europe—the close grouping of many separate nations—also influences the region's policy, for many problems are necessarily international. The negotiation of solutions involves a process more like the basin conferences in the 1960s in the United States than the top-down imposition of policies that occurred in the 1970s. While it is true that the European Union sets broad policy goals and restrictions, there is still a great deal of leeway in the country-by-country implementation. And one has the strong impression that the countries of the EU vary in their environmental zeal at least as widely as in their enthusiasm for monetary union or a new structure for voting weights. Finding out what is actually going on "in the trenches" is also complicated by the number of languages in which the real regulations appear and by the traditional secretiveness of these governments.

The British are as secretive as anyone else, but at least the commentary on their failures and successes is accessible in English. And the lesson I take from such of the commentary as I have read is that they have only recently gotten even modestly serious about holding polluters' feet to the fire. This was signaled by the formation of an integrated environmental agency, built on the bones of separate water and air pollution agencies. That water agency was itself formed only within the past decade, as the National Rivers Authority. Prior to that, water quality was the responsibility of the large regional "Water Authorities," who supplied both water and sewer service to households and firms in their regions. As they owned and operated the major wastewater treatment plants, they were also often the largest polluters along their rivers. It is telling that they wanted, and were able, to keep secret for a decade the results of the monitoring of pollution sources, results that made it clear they were not meeting their own discharge permit terms.

One other feature of the European scene seems worth a note: the difference in the routes by which citizen interest in environmental quality improvements can be channeled and harnessed. In the United States, much of what has happened since

1970 has been driven by national environmental organizations such as the Sierra Club and Audubon Society, the Natural Resources Defense Council (NRDC), and the Environmental Defense Fund (EDF). These groups have successfully leveraged quite modest amounts of (tax deductible) contributions through skillful use of litigation and of lobbying in front of executive agencies where the guts of laws are spelled out as enforceable rules. Often the groups can be used by the responsible agencies as an excuse for making a decision that is not going to be politically popular. (It is an interesting feature of the U.S. system that the Congress creates the decision requirements for EPA but then may criticize the agency for actually trying to follow the law.) In Europe it is harder to use the courts, but, in the parliamentary nations with some version of proportional representation, "greens" might actually hold the balance of power in the legislature. This can make it possible to exact an environmental policy price for supporting nonenvironmental initiatives. (See Box 2.1.)

THINGS TO KEEP IN MIND

The above quick review and discussion of actual environmental policy is intended to give you a rough picture of the policy reality against which we shall be setting the concerns, techniques, and prescriptions of environmental economics. Here are a few broad guideposts to keep in mind.

1. Economists have almost unanimously criticized U.S. environmental policy for failing to be "efficient" in the sense of finding levels of environmental quality, across space and even time, that maximize the difference between the benefits of reductions in pollution levels and the costs of achieving those reductions. You have seen enough in this chapter to know that several major laws even forbid this sort of balancing and that their prescriptions for discharges are based on technological capabilities (water), or efforts to protect health absolutely (air). But you should think, as we proceed, about at least the following related questions:

a. What are the prospects for aggregate efficiency as a basis for policy in a democracy?

b. Do the available techniques for benefit estimation seem to you to be sufficiently sound to be defensible in such an important role? These techniques will be discussed in chapters 6 through 8.

c. If efficiency (in the sense the word is used above) is not sought, is (are) there any other role(s) for benefit and damage estimation in money terms that might be useful in the policy world?

2. Another line of economists' criticism of U.S. policy has been the failure to use economic incentives—emission charges or marketable permits. Again, you have seen that, while a version of a marketable permit system has been developed, particularly on the air pollution side, such incentives as were originally built into the laws tended to be of the legalistic variety—liability for past actions and required in-

Box 2.1

American Environmental Regulation Compared with That of Other Major OECD Countries[4]

A study of the experience of multinational firms with environmental regulations in the U.S. and in four other OECD countries (Japan, Holland, Germany, and the United Kingdom) concludes that U.S. processes are "more detailed, intrusive, complex, punitive, unpredictable and costly to comply with." Further, U.S. regulatory regimes are "quicker to impose legal penalties for violations," and "the sanctions tend to be more severe." This does not reflect a difference in the severity of the substantive regulations themselves (such as required discharge reductions or cleanup efforts).

The U.S. approach, according to the study, imposed higher costs for similar environmental outcomes by forcing the firms to spend more on lawyers and on reports and documentation, and to delay desirable actions and investments while waiting longer for regulator approval.

These differences are observed despite the fact of broad agreement across countries on the notion that central government ought to set standards and lower levels of government ought to do the detailed implementation and enforcement. The differences arise because American federalism has some distinctive features;

- The political parties are less cohesive, and elections to Congress tend to hinge on local issues.
- Traditions of state and local government control over many environmentally important functions are strong.
- Environmental interest groups have relatively easy access to the court system to force local, state, and federal agencies to comply with laws and regulation.
- Those same groups, through their political leverage, have encouraged the writing of quite detailed laws, leaving less discretion to the regulatory agencies.
- But national legislators have both reason and freedom to try to insert exceptions that benefit their constituents.

The result is highly specific, yet not necessarily internally consistent law, and several overlapping levels of enforcement, including the possibility of private (environmental group) enforcement to back up or "egg-on" the bureaucrats.

surance purchase against future liability. In the chapters (9 and 10) on policy instruments, keep your eye on the following:

a. How strong a case do economists make for the use of charges and marketable permits, and where does the strength come from?

b. What are the downsides to the use of these instruments?

3. The ability to enforce policies is crucial. But the susceptibility of different environmental problems and approaches to measurement of results (monitoring) and sanctions for poor performance (or rewards for good) is highly variable. Be alert for differences between the characteristics of the common, garden-variety, point-source pollution problem and some other equally important ones such as nonpoint sources (farms for example) and movable sources (such as barrels of liquid hazardous waste). One size solutions do not fit all problems. (Monitoring and enforcement are the subjects of Chapter 11.)

4. There have been a few quite interesting "experiments" with regulatory approaches during the past twenty years or so. (For example, retrospective liability (Superfund), shifting the burden of proof between agency and "source," and the use of information as a tool as in the Toxics Release Inventory).

a. What can we say about these experiments?

b. Do you see other opportunities for trying out new ideas, or have we seen all there is to see?

5. Finally, nothing—or almost nothing—has been said so far in this chapter about *ignorance*—our ignorance of environmental processes of how exposure to toxics actually leads to chronic or acute disease, of how future technology and tastes will develop, and so on. How does or should this pervasive ignorance affect our environmental policy recommendations? (This is discussed in chapters 12 and 13.)

NOTES

1. This is not to say that no effects would be visible. In local situations a concentration of population using badly chosen techniques could do some serious damage by destroying forests, encouraging soil erosion, or even, through excessive irrigation, salinating otherwise useful soil.

2. It seems that this approach owed something to two earlier experiments in river basin management that, at least on the basis of the testimony of their enthusiasts, were successful: negotiations about raising dissolved oxygen minimums in the Delaware River Estuary (N.Y., N.J., and Pa.) to protect migratory fish and other recreational opportunities; and, in the Ohio, about reducing chloride concentrations raised by various chemical plant discharges.

3. The Clean Air Act singled out air pollution as an especially prominent threat to public health and required EPA to set "primary" standards for the quality of the ambient air—the air we are all exposed to outside our homes and other inside spaces. These standards were to protect the health of the most sensitive part of the population, for example asthmatics. The pollutants for which these standards have been set are: particulate matter (originally the total amount of particulate matter suspended in the air; now focused on very small particles), sulfur dioxide, carbon monoxide, nitrogen oxides, ozone, hydrocarbon vapors, and lead. Because of the requirement in the act that these standards be based on scientific studies summarized in "criteria documents," these pollutants are often referred to as the "criteria pollutants." A second level of ambient standards was to be set based on

the vaguer notion of "welfare," encompassing such effects as those on materials (e.g., the deterioration of tires caused by ground-level ozone concentrations) and visibility.

4. Based on Robert A. Kagan, "Local Discretion, Central Control," 1998.

REFERENCES

Carson, Rachel. 1963. *Silent Spring*. London: Hamish Hamilton.

Davies, J. Clarence, and Barbara S. Davies. 1975. *The Politics of Pollution*. 2d ed. Indianapolis: Pegasus.

Kagan, Robert A. 1998. "Local discretion, central control." *Public Affairs Report* 39(4):12, 13.

3

MICROECONOMICS
Review and Extensions

One assumption behind the level of material presented in this text is that the reader has survived and profited from exposure to some version of intermediate-level microeconomics. This allows me to take as mastered many basic concepts and techniques, such as definitions of rationality, the logic of demand curves for normal consumer goods, and how the passage of time affects the value in the present of future benefits and costs. But, in my experience, there is a great deal of variation in what even students who share intermediate microeconomics can dredge up out of working memory. Further, and just as important, I have hopes that some of you will come to this book out of environmental engineering or other backgrounds. If so, you will likely have a reasonably strong math background but not necessarily much economics. To try to cater to the range of resulting needs, this chapter concentrates on the material most useful in the rest of the book and least likely to have been covered carefully in an intermediate microeconomics course. Attached to the chapter are two appendices: the first (Appendix 3.I) contains some material that may provide helpful background to the reader without such intermediate microeconomics, material such as that mentioned above as assumed. The second (Appendix 3.II) includes extensions that are not crucial for the book but that may help readers see beyond the examples in the text—to begin to see the structure of some of the frontier problems in the discipline. These extensions are: the problems for optimization created by "badly shaped" functions, the problem of the general lack of a "second-best" solution to a situation in which two or more market failures interfere with the necessary equating of marginal cost to marginal willingness to pay, and what characterizes a really dynamic problem.

DEMAND, WILLINGNESS TO PAY, AND SURPLUSES

One of the two fundamental building blocks of microeconomics is the demand function, the relation between the price of a good and the amount purchased at that price by either a single consumer or a group (all consumers in a nation, for example). The common way of displaying a demand function has price on the vertical axis and quantity purchased on the horizontal.

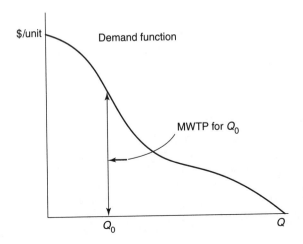

Figure 3.1 The Height of the Demand Function as "Marginal Willingness to Pay" for the Particular Quantity, Q

Notice that economists have chosen to *talk* about quantity as a function of price but to *graph* the relation unconventionally, with quantity on the horizontal axis as though the major interest were in price as a function of quantity.

But it is important to remember that either way of thinking about the relation is equally legitimate. And in environmental settings we shall often look at the relationship as one between the quantity of a good and a consumer's (or many consumers') marginal willingness to pay (MWTP) for that quantity, as in Figure 3.1.

SURPLUSES

Price and MWTP are identical for any consumer where choice of quantity at a given price is open to that consumer, as it is for private goods. In an unrestricted market situation, your MWTP for "the last unit" you buy must be no less than and no greater than the price being asked. Of course your MWTP is not what you actually pay for more than one unit. You pay the price times the quantity you buy. But your *total willingness* to pay for those units will generally be greater than what you actually have to pay. The difference, for an ordinary demand curve, is called "consumer surplus." The simplest version is shown in Figure 3.2. This concept of a surplus is usefully generalized in several ways, some of which will have to wait a bit. But for now, just observe that we can talk about total WTP[1] and consumer surplus for a change in the market price (Figure 3.3) or for a change in quantity available at a given price, as when some sort of rationing is relaxed (Figure 3.4). If price falls from P_0 to P_1, as in Figure 3.3, ΔCS_1 is added to CS_0. The total area under D out to Q_1 is the new WTP. The area out to Q_0 is the original WTP. Forgetting price, if the availability of a good increases, as in Figure 3.4, from Q_0 to Q_1, WTP increases by ΔWTP.

So far the discussion has involved only the observation that, with demand curves sloping down (MWTP falling with increasing optimal quantity purchased), the con-

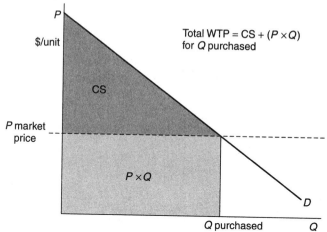

Figure 3.2 Consumer Surplus (CS) for a Private Good, Q. WTP, willingness to pay; D, demand.

sumer enjoys a surplus of total WTP over total cost for whatever she or he consumes. But what does this have to do with consumer utility, which is, after all, the basis for statements about welfare? Figure 3.5 relates WTP to utility through the device of asking: How big would the transfers of income to or from the consumer have to be to maintain his or her utility level at a constant in the face of a price change?

First, the figure should remind you of how an ordinary demand curve is derived, something you saw in intermediate microeconomics, if not before. The points

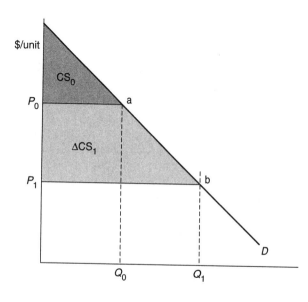

Figure 3.3 Willingness to Pay Price P for a Lower Price for a Good, Q (Increase in Consumer Surplus [CS])

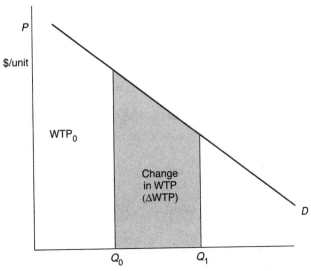

Figure 3.4 Willingness to Pay Price P for a Larger Quantity of a Good, Q. D, demand.

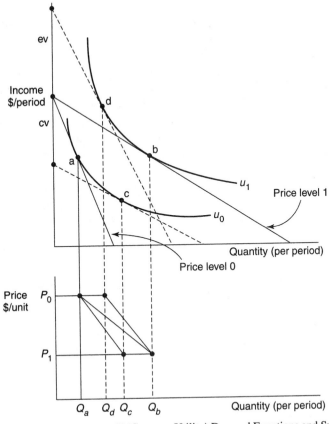

Figure 3.5 Deriving "Compensated" (Constant Utility) Demand Functions and Surpluses Associated with Price Changes. ev, equivalent variation; cv, compensation variation (see text).

a and b in the indifference curve graphic at the top are the points of optimal choice, for the consumer depicted, as prices fall from level 0 to level 1, in the absence of compensation. The quantities represented by a and b are shown as Q_a and Q_b in the bottom part of the graphic. The line connecting them, with associated prices, P_0 and P_1, is an approximation to a piece of the ordinary demand function for this good and this consumer. Notice that there is an increase in surplus, seen in the lower graphic, associated with this change in price; and that to this point Figure 3.5 is just an elaboration of Figure 3.3.

But economists are uncomfortable with the fact that the consumer's utility changes (continuously) between points a and b (quantities Q_a and Q_b). Since the idea of WTP is to connect money to utility, there is something to be said for trying to make the connection using fixed benchmarks. Hence the extra lines and points in Figure 3.5 that involve the same two prices and indifference curves, but in different combinations. Thus, point c (and Q_c) is defined by the optimal choice of quantity under the new lower price, but also with a new lower income as well—the new lower income that just allows the consumer to attain U_0, the utility level attained in the beginning with the original price and income. The amount of income that can be taken away, when the price falls, while still allowing for attainment of U_0 is another measure of the value of the price fall to the consumer—another measure of the surplus generated. This measure is shown on the lower graphic as the area between P_0 and P_1 to the left of the demand function (approximation) connecting Q_a and Q_c. It is an income length labeled cv in the upper part of the graphic.

By a similar line of argument a third measure of the value of the price change can be constructed. This one asks what amounts to the opposite question: How much would have to be given to this consumer to make her or him as well off with the old (higher) price as with the new lower one? This amount is labeled ev in the upper graphic and is the area to the left of the demand function (approximation) between Q_d and Q_b in the lower graphic. The labels cv and ev stand for "compensating variation" and "equivalent variation" respectively; but rather than the labels, concentrate on the concepts. As you will see just below, the notions of cv and ev translate into situations in which quantity varies, when the consumer has no choice but to live with the given quantity—a situation common in analyzing the value of providing environmental "goods" such as clean air.

First, however, let me set out a couple of algebraic expressions that capture the content of Figure 3.5. For the points actually found, involving price-level lines P_0 and P_1, the "compensation" works as follows:

1. Starting with P_0 and income, M, a price decrease to P_1, coupled with a "tax" of cv, would leave the consumer on u_0. I use $V(\ )$ here to indicate that the function that relates income and prices to utility level is not the same as the function relating income and consumption quantities to utility. The former is commonly called the "indirect" utility function.

$$V(M, P_0) = V((M - \text{cv}), P_1) = u_0 \tag{3.1}$$

2. For the other compensated curve, the compensation can be thought of as the payment to the consumer required to reconcile her or him to giving up the price decrease.

$$V(M, P_1) = V((M + ev), P_0) = u_1 \qquad (3.2)$$

In this context, cv is perhaps more clearly seen as the WTP for P_1 as opposed to P_0 (with utility held constant); and ev as the total willingness to accept (WTA) compensation for *not* getting P_1.

To check your understanding of the graphical technique, explain to yourself why, as price falls, the "price lines" get flatter. Also make sure you understand that the transformation of the price line slopes into the price levels in the lower graph is essentially arbitrary in the absence of quantities to scale things from.

More interesting in environmental economics than WTP for changes in prices is WTP for changes in quantities, when price is irrelevant and there is no consumer choice. Similar benchmarks can be defined in this situation, as shown in Figure 3.6.

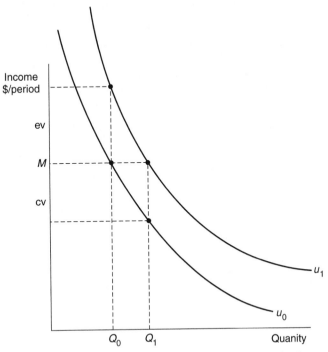

Figure 3.6 Willingness to Pay (cv) and Willingness to Accept (ev) for Imposed Quantity Changes (the consumer has no choice about quantity; there is no price to react to). cv, compensation variation; ev, equivalent variation; M, income; u, utility.

cv is defined by $u(M, Q_0) = u(M - cv, Q_1) = u_0$; and ev by $u(M + ev, Q_0) = u(M, Q_1) = u_1$. The interpretations of ev and cv are the same, except that higher quantity replaces lower price. (Benefit estimation, departing from these benchmarks, is the subject of chapters 6 through 8.)

In my experience, students find these quantity change benchmarks in some way harder to come to grips with than the ones discussed just above for prices. This is, I think, because of the lack of price lines, which are part of so many indifference-curve-based derivations in microeconomics. Here, price is effectively zero, but only a given amount of the good is available. So the equilibrium points are defined by intersections—of horizontal lines representing income plus or minus transfers and vertical lines representing quantities of the good in question. The indifference curves that are relevant are the ones that go through the pairs of intersections, that is, through Q_0, $M + ev$, and Q_1, M; and through Q_0, M and Q_1, $M - cv$.

How can we be so sure that there are *indifference curves connecting the points as drawn?*

SUPPLY/MARGINAL COST

In intermediate microeconomics courses, marginal cost functions are derived from information on input prices and production technology (the production function and its associated "isoquants," connecting points in the space of inputs that are capable of producing, at most, a given amount of output).

Again, if memory fails you, check it out in a textbook.

You also learn why the marginal cost (MC) function, whether short or long term, is the firm's supply function (short or long run): a schedule of amounts that will be supplied by the firm at various possible prices for the good. The aggregate supply function for a market is the horizontal sum of the MCs for the constituent firms. (Pick a price, add up all the amounts that would be supplied by the constituent firms at that price.)

More generally, marginal cost means marginal sacrifice or commitment. So when supply equals demand in a private-goods market, marginal sacrifice equals marginal WTP—what goes into the last unit produced equals the satisfaction derived from that unit by its consumer. (For a brief discussion of how actual demand and supply functions are obtained, and why the process is problematic, see Box 3.1.)

One consumer per private good unit is the usual assumption. Though everyone can think of examples of sharing—sandwiches, condos, CDs—if the purchase is commonly shared the units just have to be redefined to get back to one person or family per unit.

Box 3.1

A Note About Finding Demand and Supply Functions Empirically

The raw material for finding ("estimating") demand and supply functions is all around us—the price and quantity data generated by (though not necessarily easily available from) markets for private goods. A moment's thought should suggest to you at least one problem, however: The data from markets represent the intersections of demand and supply functions for particular periods of time. We do not observe values for either the demand or supply functions other than these market equilibria. And from just the pairs (*PQ*) of price and quantity observations, there is no way to tell what relations led to the data. As an illustration, what can you see in the plot of such points below?

At one extreme, each point could be the equilibrium for a different *D*, *S* pair (small dashes). Or, at the other extreme, a single demand curve with shifting supply might apply (the solid lines). This source of measurement difficulty is called the "identification problem"—deciding what functions generated the observed *P*, *Q* pairs. Solving this problem depends on achieving some understanding of the market and its underlying technologies and conditions so one can make reasonable assumptions about what is shifting and why and find data that capture those shifts.

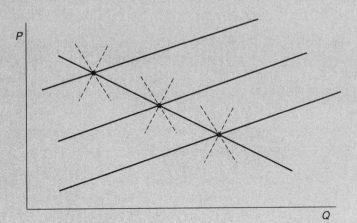

Figure 3.7 The "Identification" Problem

SURPLUSES

Because demand curves usually slope down to the right and supply curves up to the right, there will usually be a range of production/consumption levels for which MWTP > MC. As just discussed, the accumulation of MWTP minus price paid amounts equals consumer surplus for the market in question. Analogously, the ac-

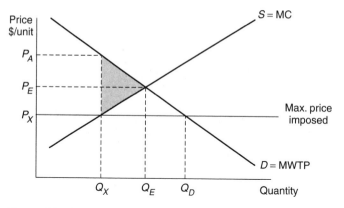

Figure 3.8 The Loss in Surplus (S) Caused by Imposing a Maximum Price. MC, marginal cost; MWTP, marginal willingness to pay (see text).

cumulation of price minus marginal cost amounts equals producer surplus.[2] The sum of the two is the surplus associated with having that market in its free state as opposed to not having it at all. Also, as just discussed, surpluses measured using compensated demand curves are the real benchmarks for the net benefits of policies and projects.

If the market is distorted, as by the imposition of a maximum price that can be charged or of a maximum amount that can be sold, the total surplus is reduced. The reduction is the loss attributable to the imposition of the distortion. So, for the case of an imposed maximum price P_X, we have the loss as shown in Figure 3.8, where

$$Q_E = \text{free-market equilibrium quantity at } P_E \text{ price.}$$

$$Q_X = \text{amount produced at } P_X \text{ price}$$

$$\text{Shaded area} = \text{minimum lost surplus} = \int_{Q_x}^{Q_E} (\text{MWTP} - \text{MC})dQ$$

$$Q_D - Q_X = \text{excess of demand over supply at } P_X$$

A question that remains is how the Q_X gets shared out, since there are willing buyers for much more than Q_X at P_X. If P_A were charged in a "black market," defying the maximum pricing rule, those for whom MWTP $\geq P_A$ would get the good. But if P_X is actually enforced, some extramarket method such as a lottery or a first-come/first-served system (a queue) would have to be put in place. With a well-designed lottery, those who obtained some of the good would constitute a random sample of the people with MWTP $> P_X$. This means that the actual loss of surplus would be greater than that shown.[3]

SOCIAL WELFARE NOTIONS: PRICES AND OPTIMALITY

Free competitive markets are quite remarkable institutions, especially when compared with the alternative—a centrally managed economy in which benevolent planners try to find out what consumers want and to arrange for its production in the "right" quantity at the "right" cost. The massive centralized flows of information into and out of the planning office, and the matching massive calculating task required to massage inflow into the outgoing orders to producers, transporters, and so on, are mind boggling. And the evidence from the experiments of the middle portion of the twentieth century is not encouraging as to the likelihood of success.

For these centralized flows and computations, markets substitute prices, as decentralized carriers of information. Usually the process by which prices are used is modeled in theoretical work as an elaborate, multigood, multiperiod auction in which offers to buy and sell particular goods are eventually "matched," with the spur being the competition among the would-be sellers and buyers.

Without getting entangled in even the "simple [graphical] analytics" of social welfare maximization that can be used to show why freely competitive markets, *under ideal conditions*, can move society to its welfare frontier (explained below), I just want to make sure you understand the nature of this benchmark; in particular, how it is defined by economists. (A classic graphical derivation of the result was provided by Francis Bator in "The Simple Analytics of Welfare Maximization," in the *American Economic Review* of March 1957.) And then I want to talk about some problems with prices that lead to what is known as "market failure" (to attain the welfare frontier). The problems I will concentrate on are those most relevant to environmental economics: externalities and public goods.

THE SOCIAL WELFARE FRONTIER

Economists almost always define social optimality in an efficiency sense. That sense is called "Pareto optimality" after an early Italian economist, Vilfredo Pareto, deemed responsible for the idea. It is easy enough to state: Society is on its efficiency frontier if no one person or group can be made better off without, in the process, making some other person or group worse off. For a two-person society, the utility frontier is usually represented as in Figure 3.9. The shape, concave to the origin, falls out of the usual assumptions made about the available production technologies and the shapes of the personal utility functions of the citizens.

The first thing to understand here is that, by the definition of the frontier, the point F is not a *feasible* outcome for society. It is outside the frontier. Second, movements *along* the frontier (such as from A to B) necessarily involve making one person better off *at the expense of* the other. The frontier is *not* an indifference curve. Rather, it shows a transformation or exchange along the *production possibility frontier* for the economy, taking into account the tastes of the consumers (two in this simple graph).

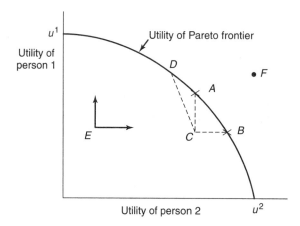

Figure 3.9 The Social Utility Frontier and Associated Possibilities for Movements

Movements *from within* the frontier *to* the frontier may involve making both people (all people in the general case) at least as well off as before the move. A set of such moves, called "Pareto optimal moves," is indicated by the cone of possible moves from point C to any place on the frontier from A to B. Other movements from C to the frontier, such as the one from C to D, make one person better and one person worse off. And general movements within the *feasible space*, the area under the frontier, may result in making both people at least as well off (one being better off and neither worse off) or they may not. (Starting, for example, from E, moves to the northeast are Pareto optimal. Moves to the northwest or southwest are not. You do not have to move all the way to the frontier to have made a Pareto optimal move.)

Now, as already said, the decentralized, free, competitive market system can be shown formally to be capable of putting society on the Pareto frontier. Prices, as decentralized signaling devices, are the key to this benchmark ability. In particular, the prices that inspire production and ration consumption must contain the correct and only the correct information about marginal sacrifices (costs) and marginal WTP (demands). When they do, and the market is not distorted in *any* of a number of possible ways, $MC_i = MWTP_i$ for all goods, i, and the frontier is attained.

It will not surprise you to learn that the strict assumptions about the underlying conditions are never fully satisfied in practice. And environmental economics would not exist as a useful and interesting field if they were. To get the feel of the thing, let's look first at something nonenvironmental but possibly familiar from other general microeconomics courses: monopoly. As you almost certainly learned at some time in your career, a monopolist (single seller facing no competitors) takes account of his or her effect on price rather than taking a market price as given and reacting to it. This means that a new function, called the "marginal revenue function," is "created" by the monopolist, and that the monopolist maximizes net revenue—profit—where MR = MC—*not* where P = MC. The simple algebra looks like this:

The monopolist's problem is simple optimization,

$$\text{Max [revenue} - \text{cost]} \equiv \underset{Q}{\text{Max}} \; [P(Q) \cdot Q - C(Q)] \qquad (3.3)$$

where $P(Q)$ is the market demand function with price as a function of quantity purchased, and $C(Q)$ is the total cost of producing Q.

This maximization is accomplished, for well-behaved functions, by selecting Q such that:

$$\text{Marginal revenue} = \text{marginal cost}$$

or

$$\frac{d(P \cdot Q)}{dQ} = \frac{dC(Q)}{dQ}$$

or

$$P(Q) + Q \cdot \frac{dP}{dQ} = \frac{dC}{dQ} \qquad (3.4)$$

Notice that for the competitive firm, assumed to take price as given, independent of its quality decision, $dP/dQ = 0$.

Since $dP/dQ < 0$, however for the monopolist, the demand function sloping down to the right, the monopolist picks Q so that marginal cost equals something less than the price he or she charges (P_M in Figure 3.10); thus marginal sacrifice is less than MWTP. Graphically, for a linear demand function, the result is a loss of surplus, as in Figure 3.10. Then the quantity the monopolist produces, QM, is less than the competitive market quantity for the same supply and demand relations (Q_C).

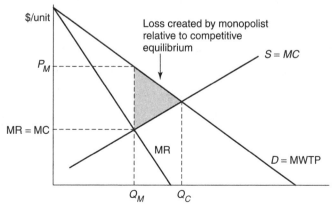

Figure 3.10 The Monopoly Problem. See text for explanation of symbols.

Can you convince yourself that, if the demand function is linear, the MR function will also be linear, with slope two times that of the demand function (twice as steep) and quantity intercept one-half that of the demand function?

MARKET FAILURE

This little review example leads on to a thread more closely related to the market failure literature—"natural monopoly." In this setting, the MC function is downward sloping in the region of its intersection with the demand function. Now, when MC is declining in Q, MC is below average cost.[4] So if a competitive firm tried to produce where MC = P, it would make a loss, because AC (average cost) > P and AC · Q > P · Q—total cost would exceed total revenue.

Only a monopolist (or, more complexly, some other market-sharing arrangement that does away with competition) can survive.[5] Price fails as a signaling device because of the nature of the technology that leads to falling MC. That technology is *not consistent* with P = MC. The situation is shown graphically in Figure 3.11. An attempt to operate as in competition, where MC = MWTP (demand = supply), leads to the quantity Q_C and the price P_C (C for competition). But at Q_C, (AC$_C$ − P_C) · Q_C = loss, so Q_C is not sustainable. Notice, however, what happens when a monopolist operates the technology. P_M can be greater than AC$_M$ when MC = MR, and the quantity produced is Q_M.

Where is the loss of surplus to be found here?

Two other causes of price signal (or market) failure are especially important to environmental economics: externalities and public goods. These are defined in the

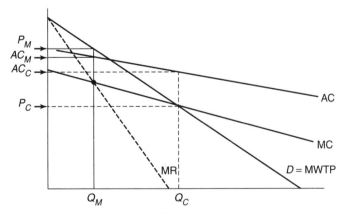

Figure 3.11 Declining Marginal Cost and "Natural Monopoly." See text for explanation of symbols.

next subsections but for the moment, just notice that for externalities price signals *fail to contain* the *socially* appropriate information. In the second, price signals that simultaneously equate MC to social MWTP *and* correctly ration the available quantity of the good *fail to exist*.

EXTERNALITIES: MARKET FAILURE

An externality exists when one (or more) economic actor(s) affect(s) another actor (or group) directly without the intervention of a market transaction. The classic examples involve such direct interactions as smoke (from one barbecue into another suburban yard or from a giant power plant into a neighboring region), noise (a party in the apartment below or the roar from a busy highway), smells (a pig farm or a petrochemical complex affecting its neighbors).

Before looking at the graphical analysis of price signals in the presence of externalities let me follow up a few ideas that are implicit in this list of examples.

• Consumers can create externalities for other consumers.

• Externalities can, in effect, be created by the dynamism of the economy. If suburban development spreads up to and around a pig farm it seems fair to say that the externality has been created by the development, not the mere existence of the farm. This observation becomes relevant when "rights" are at issue. Who has the right in this example? The farmer to farm or the new homeowners to be free of pig?

• It may be possible to negotiate a solution to an externality if it involves only two or a few parties. These negotiations may or may not be easy; they will not often involve money payments; and they will often involve assertions of rights. But the point is that government intervention is not automatically made necessary by the mere existence of an externality. (See Box 3.2.)

Now about the graphics and prices in the presence of externalities. Figure 3.12 shows the simplest sort of situation, where a host of simplifying assumptions—and assumptions about the knowledge available to the analyst—have been made. It involves a single producer of a private good. (Let's start using X for the private good, anticipating a need to reserve Q for "quality" and public goods in much of the rest of the text.) In this setting, we introduce marginal "external costs," e_x, which, to keep things really simple, are assumed constant per unit of production of X. (That is, each additional unit of X produced subtracts the same amount from the welfare of other consumers or producers.) The essence of the externality is that our producer does not take account of it in making her production decision. Rather, she looks at MC_{PR}, private marginal costs, and produces X_P in response to market price, P_C. But society as a whole would prefer that the producer look at MC_{SOC}, and produce at X_S, the socially optimal quantity, because then all the costs are reflected in the decision. The loss from failing to do this is the shaded area.

Coase and the "Coase Theorem"

Ronald Coase (1960) made a profound impact on the world of externalities and policy by pointing out that in many cases these could be solved by negotiation between (among) the parties (Coase, 1960). His "theorem" amounts to the result that the physical results of such negotiations can be expected to approximate the efficient resolution of the externality. That is, *at the margin*, what is given up by the party who must reduce an activity is likely to be valued as much as what is gained by the party who wants to see that activity reduced. This result will be arrived at whatever the initial assignment of "rights." That assignment will, however, tend to govern who actually pays. Thus, if the pig farmer is deemed to have the right to continue farming because he was there first, the suburbanites will have to pay him to reduce his scale or to install odor control equipment on his barns and manure pits. If the suburbanites have the "right" to be free of certain kinds of farms because of a political zoning decision, the farmer will have to absorb the cost of adjustment. But the level of adjustment, according to the Coase theorem, is expected to be the same.

This result does have the effect of encouraging us to look for negotiation possibilities in many common externality situations. (Though, in the U.S., "negotiation" often means "lawsuit.") But I think that those who dislike "big government" on principle have made rather too much of the Coase result. Even Coase himself admitted that his theorem applied when the costs of negotiation were small. Real pollution problems of the sort this text concentrates on do not usually satisfy that condition. There are many polluters and many "pollutees." These parties are spread across several political jurisdictions. Often the *only* way to deal with an externality of this sort is to have rights and duties assigned by legislation at the level of jurisdiction that includes all the affected parties.[6] This is why so much U.S. environmental legislation is national, even though many duties are devolved on state governments as agents.

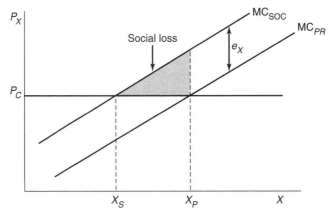

Figure 3.12 A Very Simple Example Showing the Social Loss from an Externality Caused by a Single Competitive Producer. See text for explanation of symbols.

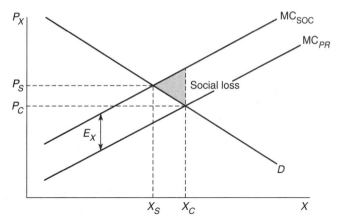

Figure 3.13 A Simple Industry Externality. See text for explanation of symbols.

Why is this loss not the entire parallelogram from X_S to X_P between the two MC functions?

In context of an entire industry, the relevance of the notion of price failure becomes clear. In Figure 3.13, P_S is the socially correct price because it reflects the external cost of producing X, e_X per unit. The competitive price, P_C, in the absence of outside intervention (or "internal" negotiation) includes incomplete information and calls forth too much X. The shaded triangle is the social loss from living with P_c rather than P_S. It is the area from the competitive amount, X_C, back to the socially optimal amount, X_S, for each unit of which MC_{SOC} exceeds MWTP.

Again, why isn't the other half of the parallelogram between X_S and X_C shaded?

A politically relevant complication is worth noting here. It is very unlikely that the people who benefit from the reduction of the external costs will be the same people who pay more for X if some way is found to make the producers pay attention to the externality. And yet another set of people will be those who own the resources used in producing X or who work in the industry. The diagram produced so easily may not look "right" to any of the parties; and the actual "solution" to the problem negotiated through the political process may not look anything like the economically optimal solution. (I should also add that the "analysis" here is only partial in its view of the economy. Another potential source of differences between simple microeconomic conclusions and what actually is accomplished is the taking of a general equilibrium view. See also the discussion of the so-called Theorem of the Second Best in Appendix 3.II.)

A final note from this discussion of externalities. When you look at Figure 3.12 it might occur to you that a straightforward way to "solve" the problem would be to impose a tax on the production of X that was equal to e_X, per unit, the marginal external cost. Then the producers would "see" the socially correct marginal cost function and would choose to produce X_s. This observation leads us into the world of "policy instruments," the subject of chapters 9 and 10.

PUBLIC GOODS

One of the most important ideas in microeconomics for understanding environmental problems as economic phenomena is that of public goods. There are several ways of naming and listing the attributes that define "public" as opposed to "private," but my choice is the following:

• Public goods have the attribute that it is very difficult (often technically impossible or only possible by going to ridiculous extremes) to exclude people from enjoying them. The classic example is air quality. If the air quality is improved in a city or region, each person who uses that air experiences the improvement. Excluding someone would require either expelling them or forcing them to wear some sort of device that would deliver the old air quality to them alone.

• While additional units of the public good have marginal resource costs, adding additional consumers does not. For private goods, on the other hand, the marginal cost of the last unit is the same as the marginal cost of adding a consumer (simplifying by assuming the last consumer wants one unit—the generalization does not destroy the usefulness of the contrast).

It is important to be clear that "public" in this technical economic sense does not have any necessary one-to-one connection with who or what provides the good. That is, governments provide many goods and services that are in this sense "private" though they are publicly provided. Postal service; electricity, as from the TVA and the Corps of Engineers' dams; and, in many countries, railroad service are all examples. The debate about "privatization" of government services is, at its heart, a debate about the justification for public provision of intrinsically private goods.

But truly "public" goods are not efficiently provided privately. This is because the appropriate price signals simply *fail to exist*. To see how and why this happens, we have to look at the implications of the attributes listed above. The most important of these implications is that the social value of the marginal unit of a public good is equal to the sum of the MWTPs for every consumer. This, in turn, means that the aggregate demand function for a public good is the *vertical sum* of the individual demand functions. That is, to find the aggregate MWTP function, we pick quantities provided and add MWTPs for all the consumers, as illustrated in Figure 3.14. The graph also includes the MC of providing additional units of Q. Q^* is the socially optimal provision level (where $MC(Q_i^*) = \Sigma\ MWTP_i(Q^*)$).

But look at the implied "price" of Q^*(equal to the marginal cost of provision at Q^*). At that "price" none of the consumers, A, B, or C, desires Q^*. In fact, B and C want *none* of Q at that "price." So, even though it is possible to define a socially optimal level of provision of Q, it is *not possible* to find a "price" that both

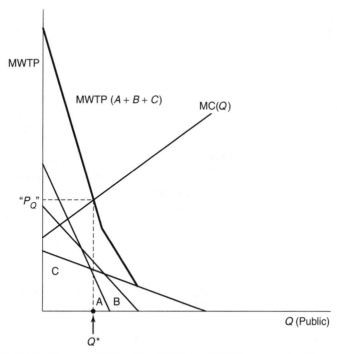

Figure 3.14 Public Goods and Price Signal Failure. MWTP, marginal willingness to pay; P, price; Q*, socially optimal quantity; MC, marginal cost.

equals MC at that provision level *and* "clears the market" in the sense that the amount produced is the amount desired. This is a necessary consequence of the vertical addition—not a trick achieved in this graph alone.

Of course there is another problem with pricing a public good—the difficulty of collecting. If exclusion of additional consumers is really impossible or at least very expensive, whether a market clearing pricing "exists" in theory seems quite beside the point. It is also true that if serving another "customer" does not cost anything, resources devoted to charging that person are wasted.

So public goods cannot be provided at all efficiently by markets. And when public goods (or "bads," such as air pollution) result, in addition, from complex externalities, private solutions are usually not available—and if available are not efficient. The public good aspects of pollution make successful negotiations between polluters and pollutees that much less likely. Government intervention becomes necessary despite the Coase theorem.

Some more qualifications and caveats are, however, necessary. First, there are very few "pure" public goods. National defense is one of the few. Avoiding global climate change might be another, though it is a different "good" at each spot on the globe. Second, many goods and services are mixed, in the sense of having private and public aspects. The prevention of crime (public safety provision) is an example. The public good aspect is the sense of security for citizens (and, one hopes, insecurity for would-be criminals) provided by visible and invisible policing activity. But citizens may take private actions as well—burglar alarms, cellular phones, cans of mace, auto ignition codes are all ways we can protect ourselves and our property without protecting others. (Indeed, it is arguable that these actions displace crime to the homes, persons, and cars of others.) Third, the amount of most public goods, such as public safety and the usual sorts of air pollution, vary over space, so that by choosing where to live, to work, to shop, to recreate, and so on we can choose our own menu of such goods. Fourth, most real goods that have some public aspects are also "congestible." That is, adding new consumers has a cost in terms of imposing inconvenience costs on all the other consumers. This could be true for art, fireworks, waterfront views, and so forth.

And finally, a lot of human ingenuity goes into devising ways to make public goods private so that they can be provided by markets. A funny example occurred to a cartoonist a couple of years ago. He showed an airplane full of people watching a movie, with one forced to wear a blindfold because he had not paid to see it. Within the airplane cabin, the movie is a public good, but exclusion would be technically quite easy, though unquestionably silly.[7] Other examples of ingenious exclusion that involve a lot more money include:

- scrambled TV signals
- patents on inventions (embodied knowledge)
- stadiums that enclose sporting events
- classrooms that enclose lectures

None of this is necessarily bad. The incentives created by privatization probably on balance improve society's welfare in such areas as invention—of drugs, machinery, computer software—even though the knowledge embodied in these items, *once discovered*, is an example of publicness. It is the "once-discovered" modifier that is the hooker here. Changing the set of available public goods through research and development involves complex overlapping incentive structures, and at some point in the process, government "wisdom" and scientific curiosity seem to become insufficiently directed instruments. Whether this is also true of the arts—from painting to theater to movies and television—is a perennial topic for public debate.

NOTES ON OPTIMIZATION AND THE CHOICE OF ENVIRONMENTAL POLICY

You have read in this text (in Chapter 2), and possibly elsewhere, that one or another environmental policy is "inefficient," and therefore, by implication or by explicit statement, undesirable, at least relative to an efficient policy in the same problem setting. Almost always such statements mean that the policy does not maximize benefits minus costs (minimize damages plus costs). This sort of claim sets us up to go over a few last review and extension subjects before diving into the more obviously environmental course material.

EFFICIENCY AND DISTRIBUTION

We have defined social efficiency in Pareto terms. The Pareto "frontier" was the collection of points representing ways of organizing production and distribution such that on this frontier no person or group could be made better off without, in the process, making some person or group worse off. Pareto "moves" were defined as policies or projects that make at least one person or group better off without making any other person or group worse off. This is a very demanding definition of a desirable policy, for reasons discussed below. But it does not include any requirement about which person or group benefits most or least, or how the relative benefits of any two groups stack up.

In the Pareto frontier diagram, movements along the frontier are movements that change distribution, where everything (prices and resulting production and consumption most especially) are assumed to have adjusted to that change. In the normal sort of efficiency analysis done in environmental economics, these adjustments are not—and, in practice, could not be—made. So even if the distributive consequences of particular policies are estimated (in the sense of who enjoys the benefits and who pays the costs), those calculations are done at the prices appropriate to the status quo—the situation generating the prices used in the analysis. These are almost certainly not correct for other distributional situations. But we have insufficient information to know what might be correct in any other situation. As a general, depressing, but not very helpful rule then, efficiency analysis is itself distribution dependent, because it is price dependent. This is a first caveat.

As I noted in passing above, the Pareto criterion is a very demanding one; and it is demanding in two senses. First, policies that would satisfy it are, in practice, rare. It is very difficult to avoid making *any* person or group worse off when a new policy is put in place. In the normal course of things, some people will pay on net while some will benefit on net. The "log-rolling" or vote-trading aspect of the democratic tradition is one way of dealing with this reality: On net (again) over a host of policy decisions, a democratic decision process in effect (and in theory) works toward rewarding everyone at least some of the time. But in environmental economics, and looking at possible policies in isolation, the approach is to *assume* that the Pareto problem (leaving no one worse off) *could* be solved by using (nondistorting) lump-sum taxes and payments. The resulting criterion, called in the jargon the "potential-Pareto" criterion, requires that the *total* of all benefits exceeds the *total* of all costs so that the "winners" *could* be taxed to compensate the "losers." It is much less demanding than the pure Pareto definition both because it does not actually require that everyone ends up no worse off after the proposed policy is put in place and because we do not actually have to know who benefits and who pays the cost in net; we only have to know the *aggregate* benefit and cost resulting from the policy.

Said another way, the second problem with the Pareto criterion is that it is informationally demanding. To apply it, one has to estimate the effects of a proposed policy or project on *every* individual. This is a great deal harder than estimating total effects, though, as we shall see in the damage/benefit chapters (6–8), even the totals offer more than enough challenge. So by settling for the potential Pareto criterion we "solve" the two problems at once.

Not surprisingly, the potential Pareto criterion is the basis of cost-benefit analysis (CBA). This form of analysis is almost always the basis for economists' comments on actual or proposed policies. But given the background above, especially the fact that only aggregate effects are reflected in the criterion, it is hardly surprising, either, that politicians only occasionally pay attention to what CBA indicates is desirable. When they do pay attention it is often because many studies, over years or decades, have pointed out that some policy or set of project decisions is consistently and tremendously *in*efficient—that large amounts of resources are being wasted. This, for example, was the case with western U.S. water development (dam) projects.

OPTIMIZATION IN MICROECONOMICS

The economic person of microeconomic theory is always capable of figuring out the best she or he can achieve in a given situation and how to achieve it. To mimic these assumed abilities, we have to be able to do some optimizing ourselves. In this text, the demands on your memory of calculus will not be enormous, but you should be able to set up and solve the necessary conditions for optimality in simple constrained and unconstrained situations. One or two examples have already come up.

UNCONSTRAINED OPTIMIZATION

The unconstrained situation will be typified for us by the pair of problems:

maximize (benefits − costs of producing benefits)

minimize (damages + costs of avoiding damages)

Let benefits be a function of pollution reduction, R: $B(R)$. Cost of pollution reduction we can write as $CR(R)$. Damages are a function, $D(P)$, of pollution level, P; and the costs of avoiding damages we'll call $CA(P)$. With this notational baggage in hand we can rewrite the above as:

$$\max_{R} [B(R) - CR(R)] \tag{3.5}$$

and

$$\min_{P} [D(P) + CA(P)] \tag{3.6}$$

The "first-order" (necessary) conditions to find the max and min respectively are:
For the max problem:

$$\frac{dB}{dR} - \frac{dCR}{dR} = 0 \text{ defines } R^* \tag{3.7}$$

For the min problem:

$$\frac{dD}{dP} + \frac{dCA}{dP} = 0 \text{ defines } P^* \tag{3.8}$$

To remind you of the graphic versions, I have sketched both problems in Figure 3.15. For simplicity at this point the functions are assumed to have shapes that make for simple optimization. In particular: dB/dR is assumed to be falling as R increases; dD/dP is assumed to be rising as P increases; dCR/dR is assumed to be rising as R rises; and dCA/dP is assumed to be rising as P falls. These diagrams will recur frequently through the course, so you should make sure you understand them. You should also understand the relation between them for a given problem. This is defined as follows:

The benefits of a policy, quality target, or whatever, equal the reduction in damages caused by that choice. The costs of the policy, etc., equal the increase in costs attributable to the policy, etc. Thus, algebraically, let P_0 equal the existing level of pollution. So we have:

$$D(P_0) = \text{current damages}$$

$$CA(P_0) = \text{current costs of avoiding even greater damages}$$

Then for any specific (lower) alternative pollution level, $P_1 < P_0$, we have:

$$\left.\begin{array}{l} B(R) = D(P_0) - D(P_1) \\ CR(R) = CA(P_1) - CA(P_0) \end{array}\right\} \text{ where } R = P_0 - P_1 \tag{3.9}$$

More generally, our two problems become:

$$\min [D(P) + CA(P)] \tag{2$'$}$$

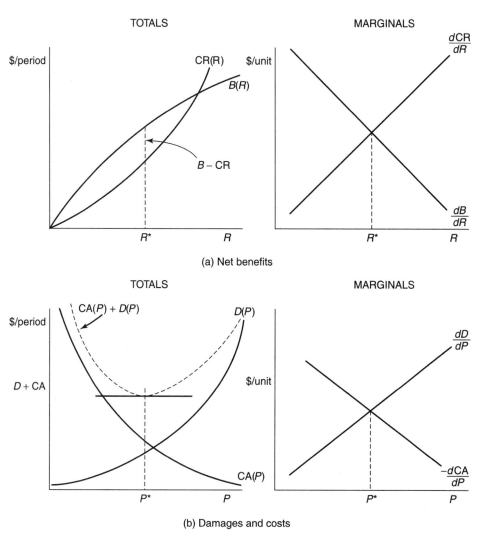

Figure 3.15 Optimization Problems from the Environment. B, benefits; C, cost; R, pollution reduction; D, damages; CA, cost of avoiding; P, pollution.

and

$$\max [D(P_0) - D(P) - (CA(P) - CA(P_0))] =$$
$$\max [B(R) - CR(R)] = \max [D(P_0) + CA(P_0) - (D(P) + CA(P))] \quad (1)'$$

But $D(P_0) + C(P_0)$ is just a constant and does not affect the optimal choice of P. So the two problems are really the same problem in the same setting, once we understand the relationships, because $\min[D(P) + CA(P)]$ is the same as $\max[-(D(P) + CA(P))]$.

> *You should be able to find benefits and related costs from pollution reduction, start-ing with a graph showing damages of pollution and related costs of avoiding them. Can you see how to do it?*

CONSTRAINED OPTIMIZATION

Constrained optimization problems are of the form: max (or min) some function of one or more variables subject to requirements on the values of the variables. The problem that should already be familiar to you is the consumer's utility maximiza-tion exercise subject to her or his income constraint. For a fairly general situation, though involving only private goods, this is:

max $u(x_1, x_2, \ldots, x_N)$ subject to

$$\sum_N (P_i x_i) - M \le 0 \tag{3.10}$$

where the P_i are prices and M is income and $x_i \ge 0$ for all. That is, you either con-sume x_i or you do not. You cannot "deconsume" it.

To make things easy on ourselves we shall almost always confine ourselves to equality constraints. In the consumer problem this means we can write

$$\sum_N (P_i x_i) - M = 0$$

This allows us to use the technique called "Lagrange Multipliers," in which we rewrite the problem as:

$$\max L \equiv \max u\,(x_1, \ldots, x_N) - \lambda \left[\sum_N (P_i x_i) - M \right] \tag{3.11}$$

and λ is the multiplier. The necessary (or first-order) conditions (FOCs) for success in this effort are:

$$\frac{\partial L}{\partial x_1} = \frac{\partial u}{\partial x_1} - \lambda P_1 = 0$$

$$\vdots \qquad \vdots \qquad \vdots \tag{3.12}$$

$$\frac{\partial L}{\partial x_N} = \frac{\partial u}{\partial x_N} - \lambda P_N = 0$$

plus the income constraint, which is

$$\frac{\partial L}{\partial \lambda} = \sum_N (P_i x_i) - M = 0 \tag{3.13}$$

More than one constraint requires more than one multiplier. In totally abstract terms, for example, max $f(x, y, z)$ subject to $g(x, y) = 0$ and $h(y, z) = 0$ would be done as: max $L = \max f(x, y, z) - \lambda_1(g(x, y)) - \lambda_2(h(y, z))$ with FOCs:

$$\frac{\partial L}{\partial x} = \frac{\partial f}{\partial x} - \lambda_1 \left(\frac{\partial g}{\partial x} \right) = 0$$

$$\frac{\partial L}{\partial y} = \frac{\partial f}{\partial y} - \lambda_1 \left(\frac{\partial g}{\partial y} \right) - \lambda_2 \frac{\partial h}{\partial y} = 0$$

$$\frac{\partial L}{\partial z} = \frac{\partial f}{\partial z} - \lambda_2 \left(\frac{\partial h}{\partial z} \right) = 0 \qquad\qquad (3.14)$$

$$\frac{\partial L}{\partial \lambda_1} = g(x,y) = 0$$

$$\frac{\partial L}{\partial \lambda_2} = h(y,z) = 0$$

Notice the difference in notation between $d(B(R))/dR$ and $\partial f(x,y,z)/\partial z$. The first is the *total* first derivative; the second the first partial derivative. Sometimes partial derivatives are written more compactly as:

$$\frac{\partial f}{\partial z} = f_z$$

As you will recall, you can take derivatives of derivatives as well, for example,

$$\frac{d^2 B}{dR^2} = \frac{d(dB/dR)}{dR} \qquad \text{and} \qquad f_{zy} = \frac{\partial(\partial f/\partial z)}{\partial y}$$

The former is the second derivative. The latter are called "cross-partials."

REMINDERS

In this chapter a few notions and techniques basic to understanding environmental economics have been reviewed. Some of these may be familiar to you. You may even find that everything was already covered in your intermediate microeconomics courses. But chances are that at least some concepts will be new. Here is my catalog of what you ought to take with you from the above material as you embark on the rest of the chapters.

- A schedule of marginal willingness to pay (MWTP) for given quantities of a good as another way of interpreting a demand function.
- Marginal cost (MC) as marginal sacrifice.
- The welfare significance of having MC equal to MWTP everywhere in the economy, with prices as the decentralized signaling system that gets us there.

- Surpluses—excesses of MWTP over MC as money measures of the value of having a product or market; and, even more usefully, losses of surplus as measures of the damages from particular policies or market failures.

- Connecting these surplus notions directly to utility via indifference curves.

- Market failures as price system failures, especially:

  a. Failure of prices to contain the socially correct information when there are *externalities*.

  b. Failure of prices to exist that both equate demand and supply and equate the *social* MWTP to marginal cost where public goods are involved.

- The simplest sort of environmental optimization problem—assuming a great deal of knowledge of benefits and cost—maximize the net benefits of a policy by finding the "best" level of pollution reduction.

- The political (distributional) problem with benefit-cost analysis—why it is almost never used by politicians as the basis for policy choice.

- But, why it may still be useful, even if only to rule out egregiously bad choices.

--- APPENDIX 3.1 ---

SOME BASICS

RATIONALITY

Microeconomics deals with the behavior of individual actors on the economic stage and the implications of such individual behavior when a situation involves many actors. At the heart of the subject is the idea of *homo economicus*, or economic (wo)man. This somewhat artificial person is assumed to be selfish or perhaps "familyish"; that is, motivated only by consideration of what happens to himself or herself (or to her or his family). The person is also taken to be rational and able to do quite complex calculations, at least so far as they involve familiar actions or goods and are repeated regularly.

Rationality here has a special meaning, probably best summarized by three propositions:

1. Our person can always decide which of two situations she or he prefers (or that they are equally desirable). These situations can involve "bundles" of goods and amounts of income. So, for example, looking at two simple *vectors*[8] (income and amount of good Q), the person can say which is better or if both are the same in terms of how well off they make her/him. (See figures 3.I.1 and 3.I.2 for more elaboration.)

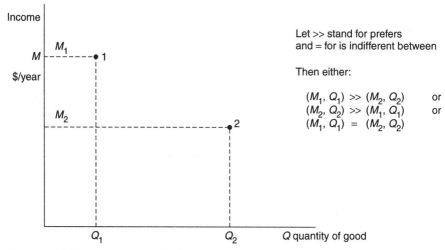

Figure 3.I.1 Simple Consumer Choice

2. If this person is allowed to choose between (M_1, Q_1) and (M_2, Q_2) and chooses (prefers) (M_1, Q_1), the person will not then turn around and choose (M_2, Q_2) as preferred to (M_1, Q_1) when both are again available.

3. Any sequence of judgments between situations such as those in (1) will be *transitive*. Formally, where I use $>>$ to mean "is preferred to,"

$$\text{If } (M_1, Q_1) >> (M_2, Q_2)$$

$$\text{and } (M_2, Q_2) >> (M_3, Q_3)$$

$$\text{then } (M_1, Q_1) >> (M_3, Q_3) \text{ must be true.}$$

These requirements are often captured in consumer choice graphs using "indifference" curves. These curves may be thought of as lines of equal "elevation"

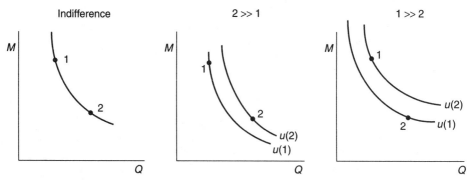

Figure 3.I.2 Indifference Curves and Preference Relations. *M,* income in $/year; *Q,* quantity, *u,* utility.

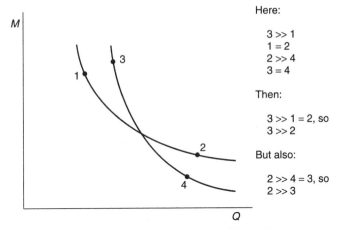

Figure 3.I.3 Crossing Indifference Curves. *M*, income in \$/year; *Q*, quantity.

(utility) over the space of alternative packages or bundles. In this context, rationality just means that the utility "mountain" has a smooth shape, without complex folding. For the simple money/quantity-of-good points, being able to make the judgment says one can decide that point 1 is preferred to point 2, or vice versa; or that points 1 and 2 are equally good. Thus, Figure 3.I.2 is a graphical version of the preference relations attached to 3.I.1. Transitivity requires that the indifference curves never cross each other. If they do cross, notice the logical problem you get into, shown in Figure 3.I.3. (See Box 3.I.1 for more on intransitivity in actual survey responses.)

Apparently Intransitive Preferences in Survey Responses

Intransitivity is not just a figment of the fevered imaginations of economists. People can actually claim to have such preferences in situations where they are asked to make several hypothetical judgments among vectors of attributes. For example, in some research into how to describe forest ecosystems and ask people questions about relative values of different systems, we asked people about three forests, each described by a six-dimensional vector of "attributes" (such as type of forest and how "patchy" each forest was). We asked them to make three preference judgments: Forest 1 vs. Forest 2, 2 vs. 3, and 1 vs. 3. The possible answers to these questions define eight possible paths through a "decision tree." (Figure 3.I.4.) Two of the paths—two of the possible sets of answers—would indicate intransitivity of preferences. In our surveys, 6 people of 132 gave intransitive answers. We took this to be evidence that they were either confused by the amount of information in the six-dimensional vectors or were roughly indifferent among the forests but could not figure out how to indicate that answer.

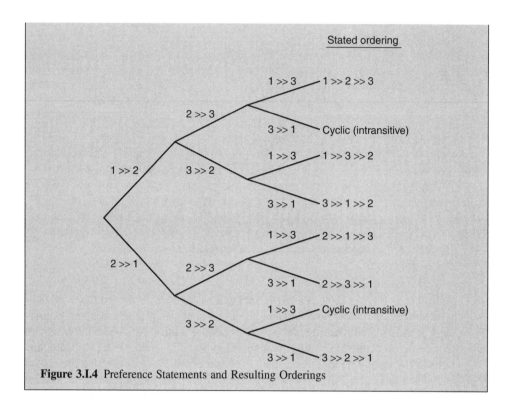

Figure 3.I.4 Preference Statements and Resulting Orderings

DEMAND FUNCTIONS AND WILLINGNESS TO PAY

Central to a great deal of microeconomics is the idea that consumers will trade money for a good or service along a schedule relating price to quantity purchased. This schedule is called a demand function (or curve or relation). You have almost certainly been exposed to the derivation of an ordinary demand function, starting with indifference curves between money (income) and quantities of the good. Varying price varies the "best" consumption decision available to the consumer. And for almost every good, as price falls, the optimal amount purchased (consumed) increases. That derivation won't be repeated here, but something closely related to it came up in the chapter when I described the derivation of "willingness to pay" for a change in prices with ordinary (or "Marshallian") and what are called compensated (or "Hicksian") demand relations.[9]

If you can't see in your mind's eye how a demand curve might be derived or what a "price line" looks like in income-good space, better go back to an earlier textbook now.

In most of micro (dropping the "economics," as is common in the trade) we are looking at demand relations for *private* goods or services. These are the ordinary

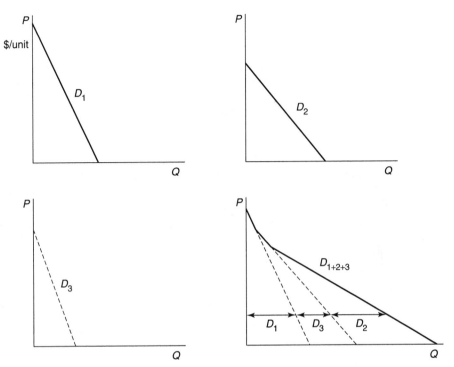

Figure 3.I.5 Horizontal Addition of Demand Functions for Private Goods. *P*, price; *D*, demand; *Q*, quantity.

things of life, from food and clothing to cars and dishwashers. Our interest is usually in how much of the good or service will be bought at a given price. To get the total purchased by a group of people, each of whom has his or her own demand relation, we add those relations "horizontally." That is, for every possible price, we add the quantities demanded by all the people. Figure 3.I.5 shows this graphically for three people. As noted in the chapter, economists have chosen to *talk* about quantity as a function of price, but to *graph* the relation unconventionally, with quantity on the horizontal axis, as though the major interest were in price as a function of quantity.

TIME AND UNCERTAINTY

So far, the discussion has implicitly assumed that events are happening in the present and as though we (or our economic individuals) were certain of the effects or outcomes of decisions. Neither assumption has much to do with reality, and while some interesting results can be derived from this starting point, in many situations too much violence will be done by assuming total timelessness or total certainty (or both). For these situations it is necessary to have some additional tools available— or at least to be aware of some of the *possible* tools.

TIME

Discounting

The least challenging problem involving time is simply that it passes and that, in the economies we are dealing with, this passage brings implicit opportunity costs. Those costs are the result of the "productivity" of the economy, or rather of the productivity of saving and investing in it—perhaps by building a piece of machinery that will be part of another production process in the future. It also seems that individuals tend to prefer present to future gratification. This is usually referred to as "time-preference," though "present preference" might make the idea clearer.

To see how the productivity consideration alone leads to the operation called "discounting," let's look at a very simple pair of alternative investment projects, one to occur in the present period, $t = 0$, and one in the next period, $t = 1$, where postponement provides us with the chance to "invest in the economy." The benefits of each project are B per period for every period after the investment and into the indefinite future. The productivity of the economy is captured by the rate of return $(1 + r) \geq 1$ (r might be 0.05 or 0.20, for example. We assume away $r < 0$.)

Here are the two streams of payoffs. Project 1 involves investing now in the project. Project 2 involves investing for one period "in the economy," which returns $1 + r$ for every unit invested.

	Period 0	*Period 1*	*Period 2*	*. . . T*
Project 1	$-I_0$	B	B	*. . . B*
Project 2	$-I_0$	$-I_0 + I_0(1 + r) = rI_0$	B	*. . . B*

Projects 1 and 2 differ only in period (1), and the choice between them depends on the relative sizes of rI_0 and B; or equivalently the difference between I_0 and B/r. But B/r may also be thought of as the infinite sum: $B/(1 + r) + B/(1 + r)^2 + \ldots + B/(1 + r)^T$ as $T \to \infty$.[10] So the decision whether to do project 1 may be thought of as depending on the relative sizes of I_0 (the cost) and what is called the *discounted sum* of the net benefits, B over the project period, which here has been taken to be infinite. The discounted sum is usually referred to as the *present value* of the net benefits. $(1/(1+r))$ is called the "discount factor" and r the "discount rate.")

Another way of thinking about discounting is as a justifiable way of making comparisons possible between *vectors* that reflect the time patterns of costs and returns from alternative current decisions—not just investments. Thus, graphically, two alternative decisions, X and Y, might imply two very different time paths of net returns (Figure 3.I.6). For some of the time until T, when both projects end, x looks better; for some of the time it looks worse. To decide between the two vectors of net returns $[NR_1(x), \ldots, NR_N(x)]$ and $\{NR_1(y), \ldots, NR_N(y)\}$ we need to transform them each into a scalar (single number). One way would be to add up the net returns from each. But, as we have just seen, taking account of the economy's productivity (return to investment) tells us to use the weighting factor $[1/(1 + r)^t]$ for each period t's returns.

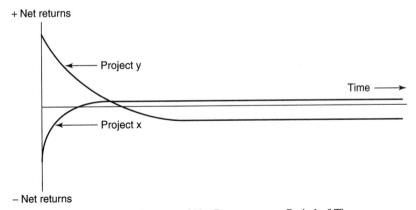

Figure 3.I.6 Two Possible Patterns of Net Returns over a Period of Time

This is all pretty easy, though the formulae for some related concepts can be fairly complicated. But there is one important qualification you ought to at least tuck into a corner of the economics file in your brain. This involves our ability to compare two projects that have different "natural lifetimes." (For example, the time until the reservoir behind a dam silts up might be 150 years. The time until a fossil fuel power plant is worn out and physically needs replacement might be 30 years.) To be able to compare the discounted sums of returns from two projects of different lifetimes in the simplest way, we must assume that the shorter project can be lengthened by reinvestment of its net returns and that the return on that reinvestment is r, the same as the discount rate. Demonstrating this for a simple example will give us a chance to practice manipulating these expressions. So let's take a simple example in which x is a three-period project with net returns:

$$-I_x \qquad NB_{x1} \qquad NB_{x2}$$

and y is a five-period project

$$I_y, NB_{y1}, \ldots, NB_{y4}$$

The present values are:

$$X: \quad -I_x + \frac{NB_{X1}}{1 + r} + \frac{NB_{X2}}{(1 + r)^2} \tag{3.I.1}$$

$$Y: \quad -I_y + \frac{NB_{Y1}}{1 + r} + \frac{NB_{Y2}}{(1 + r)^2} + \frac{NB_{Y3}}{(1 + r)^3} + \frac{NB_{Y4}}{(1 + r)^4} \tag{3.I.2}$$

Now, if we can lengthen X by reinvestment at return r, we can, at least in principle, produce X', which has the same length as Y:

$$-I_X + \left[\frac{NB_{X1}(1 + r)^3}{(1 + r)^4} + \frac{NB_{X2}(1 + r)^2}{(1 + r)^4} \right] \qquad (3.I.1')$$

The term in brackets is now a return in the last period, but you can see by cancellation that the present value calculated this way is exactly the same as for the simpler version of x, *so long as r is the rate of return to reinvestment.* If that return is, for whatever reason, either higher or lower than r, then we have to do the full calculation. (This is part of the problem that Krutilla and his colleagues faced in analyzing the desirability of a hydroelectric dam on the Snake River. I will talk about how they handled it in Chapter 13.)

IGNORANCE OF THE FUTURE

A second connection between time and microeconomics is through uncertainty. Time is a veil, and we cannot see beyond the present. So when our models predict that if we adopt policy Z, result R will follow in some natural system, we are in effect assuming *both* perfect understanding of how the system operates today *and* that nothing will change the "rules" between today and the next period (or the one-hundredth period, or whatever). It is perhaps easiest to see how tenuous such assumptions are when we look at the human "system" and one of the biggest "rule changes" in that system—technological change. Try the thought experiment of projecting forward from, say, 1950 to the end of the twentieth century to try to estimate the human impact on the global environment. Between then and now such massive, and then-unforeseeable, changes have intervened as: those in medicine that have lowered infant death rates and extended life expectancies faster than birth rates could adjust; those in crop genetics that have made it possible to increase basic grain crop yields (at least where irrigation water and fertilizers have been available) guaranteeing that cropping changes imply their own impacts on the environment; those in our ability to obtain fossil fuels and in demand for the resulting energy, usually as electricity; and those in the availability of leisure time and in the technology of transportation that have together made possible a huge growth in the extent of the use of natural systems for recreation. Similarly, standing in the present, we cannot see what 2050 will look like. The "futurists" among us may make educated guesses, but the apparently infinite inventiveness of humanity means that there is practically a zero probability of anyone getting it right. And even if someone did, we couldn't be sure of that in advance and might be as inclined to reject as to accept the eventually correct picture when it was offered as a prediction.

More mundane but just as important for some purposes, we can't know what the natural world will present us with tomorrow or next week or next year. We know something about what *has* happened in the past—temperatures, rainfall, tropical storm tracks, etc.—but these at best define *distributions* of possible events from which nature, in effect, draws for next week or next year. If we are quite clever at extracting the information in past events, we can at least predict what range of events is most likely, what extreme events have probabilities less than or equal to 0.01, and similar helpful, though indefinite statements. But we can never *know* exactly what will happen. And, if the distributions of possible events are changing over time, as many scientists believe is happening in the global climate system, we have even less to go on.

RISK AND UNCERTAINTY

The last subsection used time as a way into the subject of risk and uncertainty, stressing that both the inherent randomness of natural systems and the path of human knowledge *and* our ignorance of such complex systems lie behind our *uncertainty* about future events. When, as is very common, the range of possible future outcomes includes some that are relatively or absolutely bad, there is *risk* present. But see Box 3.I.2 for a discussion of other uses of these words that you may well come across.

Later in the text (chapters 12 and 13) we'll spend some time looking at alternative ways of making decisions under uncertainty, and at some of the problems people seem to have in dealing rationally with uncertainty. For this review section we can be content with the following:

Assume there are N possible outcomes for the event "the state of nature in period t" given decision x: $A(x)_{1t}, \ldots, A(x)_{Nt}$. These outcomes might be levels of water quality in a river, where x was a possible pollution control policy, and the reason for the randomness was caused by possible variations in rainfall (river flow, sunlight, and temperature).

Box 3.I.2

"Risk" and "Uncertainty"—Varying Uses

At one time the only acceptable usage in economics—and still a common usage in several fields, including environmental engineering and economics—gave separate meanings to these words. "Risk" was reserved for situations in which probability information over possible outcomes was available. "Uncertainty" was used for situations in which such information was lacking. This distinction has lost its force for many of us because of the respectability of what are called "subjective probabilities."

These are probabilities based on expert judgment or the intuitive distillation of experience rather than on either physical laws or historical data—the bases of so-called objective probabilities. If one is prepared to grant the usefulness of the "subjective," then no situation is ever "uncertain" in the old sense.

The word "risk" has its own problems. Some writers use risk for bad outcomes. Some use it for analyses in which both expected outcomes and the *variance* of those outcomes are taken into account. Still others use "risk" as synonymous with "cancer" (or sometimes other bad health effects). It is always a good idea to be sure you understand how a new author is using this very elastic word.

Assume we can attach to each state two measures:

- a valuation, $V(A)$ ($V(\ )$ may simply be the money value)
- a probability, $P_1, \ldots, P_N$

where $\sum_{i=1}^{N} P_i = 1$, a basic requirement for probabilities, the meaning of which should be clear.

Then, if we face the choice between two possible decisions (policies) x and y, about the consequences of which we have similar knowledge, a very useful criterion for choice is: Choose the action with the highest *expected value*—the highest probability-weighted sum of possible value outcomes:

Thus (dropping the t), choose x or y according as $E(x) \gtrless E(y)$

$$E(x) = P_1\, V(A(x)_1) + P_2\, V(A(x)_2) + \ldots + P_N\, V(A(x)_N) \qquad (3.I\text{-}3)$$

$$E(y) = P_1\, V(A(y)_1) + P_2\, V(Ay_2)) + \ldots + P_N\, V(A(y)_N) \qquad (3.I\text{-}4)$$

All this can be further complicated by allowing x and y to produce completely different distributions in terms of possible outcomes (number *and* probability as well as values).

This criterion, or rule for decision, makes use of both the valuation and probability information available. (The probabilities could, as noted in Box 3.I.2, be of "subjective" or "objective" origin.)

As we shall see in Chapter 12, however, this is not the only possible criterion. As in the problem posed by different time paths of net benefits for alternative projects or policies, the essence of the challenge is to transform a comparison of two or more vectors into a comparison of two or more single numbers (scalars). This can be done by combining elements of each vector according to some rule, as in the expected value criterion, or by concentrating on a particular element in each vector according to some rule—such as, compare the worst outcomes possible under each choice and pick the project/policy that gives the least-bad worst outcome.

One thing to remember: For *general valuation functions*, $V(A)$, the following holds:

$$E[V(A)] \neq V[E(A)]$$

That is, the expected value of the valuations of the outcomes is not the same as the valuation of the expected value of the (physical) outcomes. This can be illustrated in a very simple example. Let $A(x)$ be the value of the uppermost face on a single die that has been tossed. So $A(x_1) = 1, \ldots, A(x_6) = 6$. Let $V(A) = A^2$. Then:

$$E(V(A)) = \frac{1}{6}(1) + \frac{1}{6}(4) + \ldots + \frac{1}{6}(36) = \frac{91}{6} = 15\frac{1}{6}$$

$$V(E(A)) = \left[\frac{1}{6}(1) + \frac{1}{6}(2) + \ldots + \frac{1}{6}(6)\right]^2 = (3.5)^2 = 12\frac{1}{4}$$

What if V(A) *were linear, for example* V = 2A? *Does this constitute an exception to the above rule?*

APPENDIX 3.II

EXTENSIONS

CORRECTING MARKET FAILURES: IS PARTIAL CORRECTION BETTER THAN NOTHING?

One problem that occurs in various forms in many branches of applied welfare economics concerns what can be said about situations in which more than one form of market failure is present—monopoly and externality, for example. For a variety of reasons, it may be tempting to try to solve one of the problems and to ignore the other. This might be true in the example just mentioned because a different agency of government deals with each of the sources of failure. Unfortunately, a negative general result was established decades ago that tells us we cannot take this half-a-loaf approach. Referred to usually as the "General Theorem of the Second Best," it ought to be called the "general theorem of the *lack of* a second best." Informally, it says that if there are two or more simultaneous sources of market failure, or failure of price to equal social marginal cost, then partial correction (correcting fewer than all the problems) may or may not improve the situation.

A simple example involves combining the monopoly and externality problems. That is, assume a simple economy is burdened with both a monopolist and the external (pollution) costs created by the production activity of that monopolist, as in Figure 3.II.1.

Here, D is the demand (MWTP) function. MR is marginal revenue as seen by the monopolist. MC_P is the monopolist's private marginal cost function. MC_{SOC} is the social marginal cost function, including the marginal external costs created by the monopolist's production. In the absence of any policy intervention, the monopolist will produce at Q_M, where $MC_P = MR$, and create the social cost labeled (a). [Notice that the reference point is the quantity at which $P = MC_{SOC}$, not that at which $P = MC_P$.)

Now assume that an enthusiastic and powerful environmental agency acts to make the monopolist see and react to the MC_{SOC} function, perhaps by introducing a varying tax per unit of X that for each value of X equals the marginal external damage created. (Note the big assumption here: That the agency knows MC_{SOC}.) Now the monopolist equates MR to MC_{SOC}, which might seem like an advance. Except for the evidence of our eyes, because introducing the environmental policy alone has increased the social loss by the area (b). What result is obtained if we assume the partial correction to involve making the polluting monopolist behave like a polluting competitor—producing where $P = MC_P$? It depends on the shape of the marginal damage function, which in turn determines how the triangle (c) compares with (a).

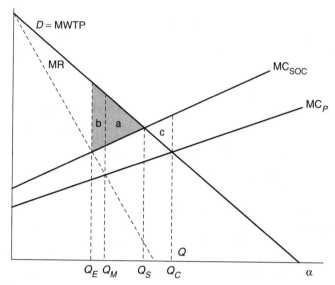

Figure 3.II.1 Two Causes of Market (Price Signal) Failure—Monopoly and Externality. See text for explanation of symbols.

Think about how all this might work out for a public good, the production of which involved the generation of external costs via pollution.

OPTIMIZING WITH INCONVENIENTLY SHAPED FUNCTIONS

Most of the time in this text, the assumption will be made, explicitly or implicitly, that the functions involved in any optimization exercise have "convenient" shapes—shapes that make exercise meaningful and that do not raise additional complications and questions. For example, in the unconstrained $B - CR$ and $D + CA$ problems, we shall almost always assume the shapes used in the graphs above—with $dCR/dR \geq 0$, $d^2CR/dR^2 \geq 0$; and $dCA/dP \leq 0$, $d^2CA/dP^2 \geq 0$; $dB/dR \geq 0$, $d^2B/dR^2 \leq 0$; and $dD/dP \geq 0$, $d^2D/dP^2 \geq 0$.

But we need to be clear that these will be assumptions of convenience. Other shapes are certainly possible and occasionally we shall have to think about what one or another difficult combination means for our conclusions. Suppose, for example, the reduction-of-pollution cost function had the shape sketched in Figure 3.II.2. Now suppose total benefits of removal grew linearly with removal (Figure 3.II.3). Then the FOCs for the optimization $\max(B - C)$ would show two alternative "optima," Figure 3.II.4. But look more carefully at the shapes. At R^*_1, total

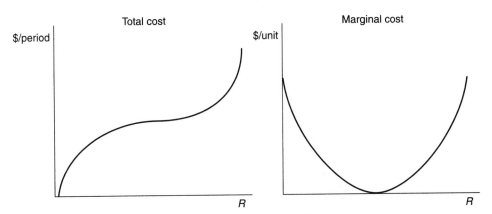

Figure 3.II.2 An "Inconvenient" Cost Function. *R*, pollution reduction.

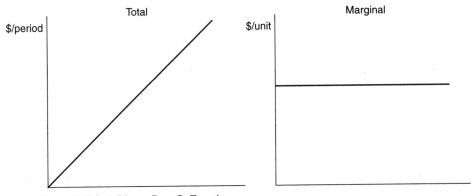

Figure 3.II.3 A Linear Benefit Function

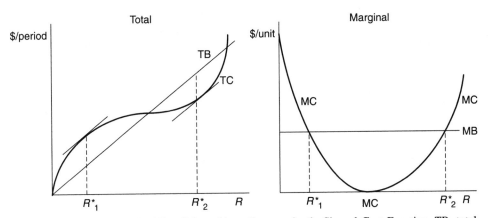

Figure 3.II.4 Marginal Equalities with an Inconveniently Shaped Cost Function. TB, total benefit; TC, total cost; *R*, pollution reduction; MC, marginal cost; MB, marginal benefit.

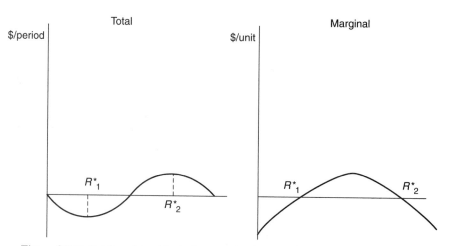

Figure 3.II.5 Net Benefits with the Inconveniently Shaped Cost Function and Linear Benefit Function. R, pollution reduction.

costs are greater than total benefits; the apparent optimum is a sort of "antioptimum." Choosing it would be the largest possible efficiency mistake. Looking at the graph of $B - C$, Figure 3.II.5, may be helpful. Now the misleading nature of R^*_1 is clear. In complex optimization problems, such difficulties are revealed by checking the "second-order conditions" at each apparent optimum. These are conditions on the second derivatives of the functions, including the relations among second and cross partials where multiple variables are concerned. They can be found in almost any intermediate-micro text, or in a differential calculus book.

WHEN AVAILABLE FUTURE DECISIONS ARE CHANGED BY PRESENT DECISIONS

A second complication involving time in a central way might be thought of as the consequence of its irreversibility as this is reflected in the irreversibility of decisions. We shall spend some time later on a sort of pure irreversibility problem in which a decision, taken today, makes one situation apply for all time, while making another impossible for all time. This problem is usually taken to represent the develop-vs.-preserve debate for places—river canyons, forests, and wetlands. A more complex version of this problem is the general *dynamic* decision setting, in which decisions taken today affect what decisions (what options) are available to be made next year or next century.

At the heart of these problems is the "state" of some system, perhaps a piece of machinery or a natural system such as a wetland. The state is represented by a number—the "condition" of the machinery, for example—and it changes over time according to some theoretical or empirical "law." In the machinery example, the condition of the machinery deteriorates because of corrosion, the heat of friction on moving parts, and so forth. The state of the system enters human decisions in two ways: It can be changed at some expense; and its level determines the amount of damages or benefits generated in a period. Thus, again for machinery, its condition can be raised by appropriate maintenance. And its condition determines how likely it is to break down in any period, creating damages for its owner.

In fairly general algebraic terms a dynamic decision problem for a situation in which machinery deteriorates looks like this:

The state of the "system" in period t, S_t, is a function of the state at the beginning of the problem period, S_0, and the time elasped; where the function, here called $h(.)$ embodies the relevant version of the "decay law" for the problem.

$$S_t = h(S_0, t) \text{ or } h(S_t - 1) \quad \text{where } \frac{\partial h}{\partial t} < 0 \quad (3.\text{II}.1)$$

The cost of changing S_t is a function of both the state the system is in and the size of the change made.

$$C_t = f(S_t, \Delta S_t) \quad \text{where } \frac{\partial g}{\partial S_t} < 0 \text{ and } \frac{\partial f}{\partial \Delta S_t} > 0 \quad (3.\text{II}.2)$$

The damages from deterioration of the machinery are larger, the more deterioration has occurred.

$$D_t = g(S^* - S_t) \quad \text{where } \frac{\partial g}{\partial S_t} < 0 \text{ and } S^* \text{ is the "best" possible condition} \quad (3.\text{II}.3)$$

(This says that damages rise as S falls—as condition deteriorates.

To tie this down, we need some requirement on the condition at the end of the time span (the "horizon") over which the problem will be examined. For example, $S_t = \hat{S}$ in period T.

Because of the built-in condition change, (the $h(\ )$ function), and its connection with current decisions via repair costs $f(\ )$, and via damages $g(\ )$, the ordinary optimization methods that look only in the immediate neighborhood for a solution (they are said to be "myopic") don't work. If we made the problem discrete, in the sense that only a finite number of changes in S could be purchased, and if we looked at the problem only once a year, it would be possible to solve it by brute force. For any starting point, S_0, we could define and calculate the net damage plus cost (or net benefit) of every possible path from $t = 0$ to $t = T$. Such problems get very large very fast, however, in the sense that the number of possible paths becomes large. Even with modern computers, solving by brute force can be expensive and time consuming. To make things somewhat faster, "dynamic programming" techniques are available that in effect chop off possible branches of the tree of paths by observing the following:

If, at $t = \hat{t} < T$ we have, for two paths P^1 and P^2, that:

$$S_{p^1}(\hat{t}) = S_{p^2}(\hat{t})$$

the states are the same at $\hat{t}$ for both paths, and that:

$$\sum_0^{\hat{t}} [D_t(P^1) + C_t(P^1)] < \sum_0^{\hat{t}} [D_t(P^2) + C_t(P^2)]$$

the cost and damage total to $\hat{t}$ is less on path 1 than along path 2. (Remember, the example is still the one involving deteriorating machinery.) Then there is no way that decisions taken along the extension of P^2 can lead to a better result than those available along the extension of P^1. (This is because the set of available decisions is the same for both paths at $\hat{t}$.)

Think about how this problem setting might apply when S$_t$ describes a natural system such as a wetland.

NOTES

1. Total WTP for a nonmarginal change might be labeled TWTP, but I will be consistent with common usage in environmental economics and use WTP, distinguishing *marginal* from total by the addition of the letter M, thus: MWTP.
2. Producer surplus is defined as the difference between revenue and variable cost of production. Notice that this is not quite the same thing as profit, which is revenue less variable *and* fixed costs of production.
3. With a queue, the result would be more difficult to analyze. While WTP would presumably be related to willingness to spend time by arriving early to be near the front of the line, income and how it was earned would also be relevant to the decision about queuing.
4. You can convince yourself of this by drawing a total cost function with declining (but positive) marginal cost and drawing in any one of the tangent lines. Compare the slope of this line with the slope of a line from the origin to the point of tangency. This second slope is cost divided by quantity, or average cost.
5. Strictly speaking, this depends on the range of outputs over which marginal cost is declining with increases in Q.
6. A phrase you may run across in your readings is "Pareto relevant externality." This refers to the requirement that after paying the costs of negotiating a solution (the "transaction costs") there should still be enough gains left that each "side" could be at least as well off as before the solution. If the "transaction" would be so difficult and expensive as to fail that test, the externality is "not relevant" to social welfare and is better left alone because the cost of fixing it exceeds the gains from doing so, net of the transaction costs.
7. Not so long ago, access to the sound track for movies on airplanes was rationed—a fee was charged for earphones. This was not quite so silly as the blindfold. Or as silly as it would have been to broadcast the sound to the cabin at large and force nonpayers to wear

earplugs. But apparently it was not worth the hassle, for it is no longer done, at least not on international flights.

8. A vector is a way of summarizing information about multiple dimensions. (1, 5, 7, 4) is a four-dimensional vector. So is (x_1, x_2, x_3, x_4). x_1 by itself we call a *scalar*.

9. Hicksian after Sir John Hicks, who introduced the concept. Along these demand functions the consumer is assumed to be "compensated" so that utility is held constant as price and quantity change. This "compensation" may take the form of a tax as when price falls and the consumer would otherwise be better off. Marshallian after Alfred Marshall, who codified demand theory. No compensation is assumed in the Marshallian version, and the demand functions are often called "ordinary" in the sense that this is the way the world ordinarily works.

10. The formula for this sum is: $\dfrac{B/(1+r)}{1 - 1/(1+r)} = \dfrac{B/(1+r)}{r/(1+r)} = \dfrac{B}{r}$.

REFERENCES

Bator, Francis. 1957. "The simple analytics of welfare maximization." *American Economic Review* 47(1):22–59.

Coase, Ronald. 1960. "The problem of social cost." *Journal of Law and Economics* 3 (Oct.):1–44.

4

An Introduction to the "Environmental" Part of Environmental Economics

The microeconomic theory of consumer and producer behavior is of quite general applicability because it is confined to the implications of quite general assumptions about how humans behave (e.g., that they are rational and self-interested). These implications can carry us a long way in developing an ability to predict what will happen when a particular policy is tried and even in judging among particular policies. But when we want to get highly specific in what we are studying it is usually important to obtain some background knowledge about the physical and institutional realities that impinge on the field to which we are going to apply economics. Thus, to do useful work in health economics it helps to understand something about how health care is organized, for example, about who makes the decisions about care when faced with sickness; who pays the bill for that care, what incentives individuals have for "taking care" of themselves, and so forth.

In studying the economics of the environment it is important to understand something about the environment itself, for it turns out that the way the environment interacts with human actions is relevant to the conclusions of economics about the characteristics and relative desirability of different possible policies. An example that I find telling in this regard comes from the early instrument-choice literature. In that literature, the assumption was usually made, implicitly if not always explicitly, that what matters for ambient environmental quality (AEQ) is the *sum* of discharges. To pin this down, consider a very simple model with two dischargers. Define the following:

P_{01}, P_{02} = Raw pollution loads before any effort at reduction (for example, pounds per day)

R_1, R_2 = Amount of reduction achieved by the sources (also pounds per day)

$D_1 = P_{01} - R_1; D_2 = P_{02} - R_2$ = discharges by the two sources (same units)

$C_1(R_1), C_2(R_2)$ = costs of reduction

α = a "transfer coefficient" that represents the events occurring in the natural world between the point of discharge and where ambient quality will be measured

Now, if only the sum of discharges matters and if the policy is to set an ambient quality standard (for convenience assumed to be defined and monitored at one point), the efficiency problem is:

$$\text{minimize } R_1, R_2 \quad C_1(R_1) + C_2(R_2)$$

subject to

$$\hat{\text{A}}\hat{\text{E}}\text{Q} = \alpha(\text{D}_1 + \text{D}_2) = \alpha(P_{01} - R_1 + P_{02} - R_2)$$

or, using the Lagrange multiplier approach to constrained optimization (Chapter 3),

$$\min L = C_1 + C_2 - \lambda(\alpha(P_{01} - R_1 + P_{02} - R_2) - \hat{\text{A}}\hat{\text{E}}\text{Q}) \tag{4.1}$$

for which the FOCs are:

$$\left. \begin{array}{l} \dfrac{\partial L}{\partial R_1} = C'_1 + \lambda\alpha = 0 \\[2ex] \dfrac{\partial L}{\partial R_2} = C'_2 + \lambda\alpha = 0 \end{array} \right\} \text{ or } C'_1 = C'_2 \tag{4.2}$$

$$\frac{\partial L}{\partial \lambda} = \alpha(P_{01} - R_1 + P_{02} - R_2) - \hat{\text{A}}\hat{\text{E}}\text{Q} = 0$$

Thus, the least-cost solution is to equalize the marginal costs of reduction at the two sources, so if we wanted to use an emission charge as policy instrument here, it would be the same for each source. This, in turn, suggests that it might be found by trial and error. This was the path trod by early enthusiasts for charges.

But the view of the natural world adopted in that problem is what economists would, in other contexts, call a "special case." For common, garden variety, local pollution problems it applies only in rather special circumstances. These circumstances create what is informally called a "mixing bowl." The classic example is what can happen in a valley if an atmospheric "inversion" traps discharges in the valley.[1] This is shown schematically in Figure 4.1. This is also a roughly appropriate model for the global problem of "greenhouse" gas accumulation (the "climate change" problem).[2] But it is not, in general, appropriate for the local or regional pollution problem that the early writers thought they were addressing. In that setting, it is more useful to think of a plume (whether in water or air) with shape and size determined by prevailing current or wind along with the roughness of the surface (streambed or ground) and other factors. Schematically, seen from above in Figure 4.2, teardrop-shaped lines of equal pollution concentration are associated with each source. If there is no chemical interaction between the plumes, the total pollutant concentration at a point is the sum of that attributable to each source. The

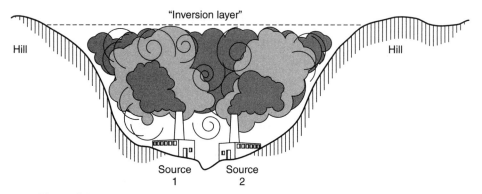

Figure 4.1 An Inversion Mixing Bowl

levels are labeled 50, 100, and 150 for illustrative purposes. Now the first thing we see is that it matters where the measurement point is located. Look at A, B, and C. The first two are more strongly influenced by source 1, the third by source 2. By interpolating by eye we can approximate the contributions from each source at each point and the resulting total concentrations:

	From 1	*From 2*	*Total*
A	110	negligible	110
B	120	75	195
C	60	160	220

While, in such a simple problem setting one could imagine finding a location that made the influences equal, this would not be possible with many sources. And, yet more generically, taking account of changes in wind direction ("prevailing," after all, only means most common) the plumes become more complex patterns. They look more like flower petals around the source, so that relative influence of sources is time varying for any choice of measurement location. But to make the point I am

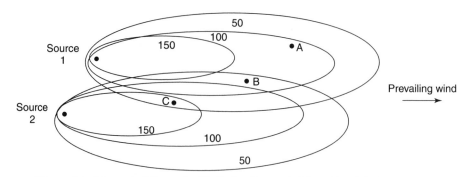

Figure 4.2 Schematic "Plumes" of Pollution Downwind from Two Dischargers

trying to make here, the simple plume setting will do. In that setting, the simplest appropriate "model" of the natural world would be:

$$\text{AEQ at whichever monitoring point is chosen} = \alpha_1(P_{01} - R_1) + \alpha_2(P_{02} - R_2)$$

where α_1, α_2 are *source-specific* transfer coefficients. So the efficiency problem becomes:

$$\min_{R_1, R_2} L = C_1 + C_2 - \lambda(\alpha_1(P_{01} - R_1) + \alpha_2(P_{02} - R_2) - A\hat{E}Q) \qquad (4.3)$$

and the FOCs are:

$$\left.\begin{array}{l} C'_1 + \lambda\alpha_1 = 0 \\ C'_2 + \lambda\alpha_2 = 0 \end{array}\right\} \text{ and } C'_1 \neq C'_2 \qquad (4.4)$$

$$\alpha_1(P_{01} - R_1) + \alpha_2(P_{02} - R_2) - A\hat{E}Q = 0$$

I shall come back to this problem setting in the first chapter on policy instruments (Chapter 9) and at that point look at further complications. But for now it is enough to see that the almost trivial-seeming change in the way the natural world is viewed has changed the case for a policy prescription. When equalizing marginal costs of discharge reduction is not the necessary condition for static efficiency, then a *single* emission charge (or a single permit market price) is not the efficient policy approach. And getting to an efficient *set* of source-specific charges via trial and error no longer looks so straightforward, even in principle. This change of *economic* conclusions follows from our new understanding of the natural world.

FUNCTIONS OF THE ENVIRONMENT RELEVANT TO ENVIRONMENTAL ECONOMICS

The title of this section was chosen to emphasize the narrow goals of this chapter. This is not "all you ever wanted to know about nature without even realizing it." Specifically, I am not going to try to spell out the "life-support" services of nature (though these will be referred to in the first chapter on benefit and damage estimation, Chapter 6). Nor is this an excuse to bring a bit of the economics of renewable or nonrenewable resources into the course. Rather, I am going to try to give you an overview of the relation between human-generated pollution discharges and human-experienced environmental quality, looking at this relation as the result of the actions and reactions of the natural world. Further along, I will try to give you a feeling for how these actions and reactions are represented in mathematical "models"—simplified versions of environmental quality management problems and settings.

First, a brief description of what the environment does to and because of pollution.

1. It *transports* material or energy, as with particulates or gases in the discharge plumes mentioned above, or sediment in a river. This is a matter of the pollutant(s) being caught up in the flow, whether that is a flow of air (wind), of a stream of water (current), or of a sheet of water as it flows across the ground during a rainstorm. This process is usually called "advection."

2. It *dilutes* or *"diffuses"* the material or energy. This can be thought of as the result of the random molecular movements of material pollution or of molecules of the air or water heated by waste energy. This is the action that would spread a drop of a colored (and water-soluble) liquid throughout a glass of water in time, without anyone stirring the water. Diffusion is a major reason for the plume shape, because it carries the energy or material pollutant at right angles to the advection path.

3. It *transforms* pollutants in at least two ways:

a. Chemical transformations. For example, SO_2, from the burning of a sulfur-containing fossil fuel such as coal, becomes SO_4^{-2}, the sulfate ion, while being transported in the atmosphere. The sulfate ion is at the heart of the acid precipitation problem. (A similar reaction occurs with oxides of nitrogen and leads in the same direction.)

b. Biological (or biochemical) reactions. Thus the organic material in human and animal waste is attacked by bacteria in water courses. These bacteria feast on the organics but use up dissolved oxygen (O_2) in the process, producing environmentally stable compounds but also producing stress for the other denizens of the water body, who now have less oxygen to breathe.

4. It *stores* elements and compounds in various ways for various lengths of time. Thus, for example, plants, from simple algae in lakes and streams through grasses, crops, and flowers, to trees, store carbon. Algae may only live for a day, so the storage is quite temporary. But trees may live for hundreds of years until they die and decay begins. More exotic compounds may also be stored in plants and animals. For example, man-made pesticides may be stored in the fatty tissues of various animals. Heavy metals, such as mercury or chromium, may be taken up from soil or water by certain plants and "sequestered" for the life of the organism.

5. The above four actions suggest a fifth—the response of the ecological system overall. Thus, a high organic loading on a stream can make for healthy microbes and some small plants and animals, but at the same time can reduce or eliminate populations of some species of plants, insects, and fishes that people care directly about. Toxic chemicals can kill directly, or like the DDT spraying mentioned in Chapter 2, can interfere with some specific life function, such as reproduction, not killing individuals but preventing successful propagation of one or more species. The system can also perform an accumulating function, as small concentrations of a toxic in some foundation species of the food web become much higher concentrations in species that feed on the foundation directly or through several "layers" of species.

It is important to recognize and remember that the performance of all these functions involves space and time; and that both space *and* time can separate the effect noticed by humans from the stress introduced by humans. Below we'll look at a very simple water-quality model that will make this explicit by showing how the flow of a river carries the oxygen-using effect of organic pollution downstream from the discharge point. This phenomenon illustrates why economists can benefit from understanding environmental phenomena when pursuing their own deductive modeling exercises.

MODELS OF THE NATURAL WORLD

Bringing the natural world into economics can mean something as simple as tweaking an abstract model, as illustrated in the policy instruments example. For other purposes, it may seem necessary to marry an economic and an ecological model—for example, if we wanted to trace out the complex interactions among several different water pollutants, such as organics, fertilizers, and toxics. Another example, less abstract, is the formation of ground-level ozone. This happens when unburned, reactive hydrocarbons such as gasoline and paint fumes react in the presence of nitrogen oxides and sunlight. The relation between the hydrocarbons and the nitrogen compounds is important in understanding whether particular efforts to reduce ozone concentrations, for example by mandating reductions in gasoline fume emissions from autos and gas stations, is likely to succeed in particular regions.

There are many dimensions along which to characterize models of the natural world—for example: how time is dealt with; whether the randomness of the natural phenomena is reflected; how space is included; and whether the modeling proceeds from "first principles" (of physics, chemistry, or ecology or all of these) or is based on empirical data. For our purposes, it will be enough to look at some variations on two themes:

- models that look at the *plumes* used in the illustration at the beginning of the chapter and, in effect, use time and space in continuous form; and

- models based on discrete but connected *compartments* into which the air or water is divided and within which more or less complex chemistry and ecology may be modeled.

A SIMPLE "PLUME"

Let's look first at a simple example of a plume-type model, called a "Streeter-Phelps DOD/DO" model. This is especially simple because it does not involve diffusion, as in a real plume, but only looks at reactions along a line down the middle of a river. It traces the reaction of a stream to the introduction of biochemical oxygen-demanding organics (BOD) as microbes stabilize the organics and in the process take oxygen out of solution in the water.

The rate at which this reaction goes on is controlled largely by water temperature. At 68°F (20°C) roughly 39 percent of the BOD present is oxidized per day.

Offsetting this effect to some extent is reaeration, a process by which atmospheric oxygen is dissolved into the water, generally through mechanisms that produce surface roughness (rapids, waterfalls, waves, for example).

A natural stream without pollution or problems with algae or decaying bottom deposits will have dissolved oxygen equal to what is known as the saturation value. This is about 9 parts per million (ppm) at 20°C. The introduction of BOD, as from the outfall of a municipal wastewater treatment plant, leads to a dissolved oxygen deficit (DOD, the reduction in dissolved oxygen below saturation level at the ambient water temperature) downstream from the point of introduction. The amount of the deficit changes over time (and distance) as the balance between BOD decay and reaeration changes.

The expression for DOD as a function of distance (R) downstream may be written as:

$$\text{DOD}(R) = \frac{k_1}{k_2 - k_1} [\text{BOD}_0(e^{-k_1 R/V} - e^{-k_2 R/V})] \qquad (4.5)$$

where k_1 = the BOD decay rate coefficient
        k_2 = the reaeration coefficient
        BOD_0 = the pollution load (expressed relative to the stream flow)
        V = the stream velocity (in the same distance units as R)

Graphically, the two expressions in the parentheses look roughly like Figure 4.3. The difference between the two expressions leads to the oxygen sag curve, as in Figure 4.4. To put some numbers into this algebra, consider a moderately large river with water temperature at about 20°C and fairly swift flow. Under these assumptions, we might have:

$$k_1 = 0.39$$

$$k_2 = 1.00$$

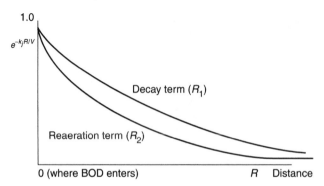

Figure 4.3 Decay and Reaeration as Functions of Distance. See text for explanation.

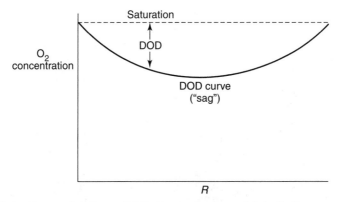

Figure 4.4 An Oxygen Sag Curve. DOD, dissolved oxygen deficit; R, distance.

so that:

$$\frac{k_1}{k_2 - k_1} = \frac{0.39}{0.61} = 0.639$$

And we'll take V to be 50 km/day (about 1.25 miles/hour), so that

$$\frac{k_1}{V} = \frac{0.39}{50} = 0.0078$$

$$\frac{k_2}{V} = \frac{1}{50} = 0.0200$$

Then the DOD equation becomes:

$$\text{DOD}(R) = 0.639(\text{BOD}_0)(e^{-.008R} - e^{-.02R}) \qquad (4.6)$$

Let's define $z(R) = 0.639(e^{-.008R} - e^{-.02R})$. Then for various values of R we get the values of $z(R)$ reported in the fourth column of Table 4.1. These values are the conceptual equivalents of the "transfer coefficients" used in the opening example. They give the effect on concentration of DO at a particular downstream point of the introduction of BOD at a concentration of 1 mg/l.

To obtain a transfer coefficient more obviously cut from the same cloth as the $\alpha(R)$ used above, it is only necessary to transform the standard into DOD terms and to correct the units of $z(R)$ so it can be multiplied by discharge rate in pounds (or 1,000 lb). To do the first, we observe that if the applicable standard is DO $\geq$ $\hat{S}$, and saturation DO is, say, S_O, then it must be true that $S_O - \text{DOD} > \hat{S}$ or DOD $<$ $S_O - \hat{S}$.

To do the second, we can just divide the $z(R)$ in Table 4.1 by 190 (to create an $\alpha(R)$ to be used with BOD in 1,000 lb/day units). So let's say we have saturation

TABLE 4.1 Illustrating the Simple BOD/DO[a] Model with Some Numbers

R(km)	$e^{-.008R}$	$e^{-.02R}$	z(R) (mg/l per mg/l)	DOD(R)(mg/l)
0	1.00	1.00	0	0
1	0.992	0.980	0.008	0.017
5	0.961	0.905	0.036	0.076
10	0.923	0.819	0.066	0.139
20	0.852	0.670	0.116	0.244
30	0.787	0.549	0.152	0.319
40	0.726	0.449	0.177	0.372
50	0.670	0.368	0.193	0.405
75	0.549	0.223	0.208	0.437
100	0.449	0.135	0.201	0.422
200	0.202	0.018	0.118	0.248
300	0.091	0.002	0.089	0.187

[a]BOD, biochemical oxygen-demanding organics; DO, oxygen deficit.

equal to 10 mg/l DO and a minimum standard of 6 mg/l. Our constraint would be DOD < 4 mg/l, and our $\alpha(R)$ would be z(R)/190. So, for example, at 75 km downstream, $\alpha(75)$ would be 1.09×10^{-3}.

To get a better feeling for what this means, consider a river the size of the Cumberland in Tennessee—roughly 14,500 million gallons per day average rate of flow at its confluence with the Ohio—not too much smaller at Nashville, about 70 percent or 10.3 million gallons per day. This is about 39 billion liters per day. A population-equivalent load of BOD—the amount of BOD generated by an average person—may be taken to be about 0.25 lb (about 113.5 g). If Nashville holds about 750,000 people and we ignore industry, the BOD load imposed on the Cumberland by Nashville would be about 190,000 lbs (86.6×10^9 mg) per day. For a river as big as the Cumberland, this translates into a BOD_0 term of 2.1 mg/l. Using this value and the z(R), we see that the city has a very small effect (less than 0.5 mg/l reduction) on dissolved oxygen downstream at average flow rates and under the other simplifying assumptions *and* ignoring all other cities and industries.

If metro Nashville ever grew to hold as many as 10 million people (again ignoring industry), the corresponding BOD_0 term would be about 28 mg/l at average flows, and at the low point of the sag, the DOD would be 5.6 ppm, which is to say that the actual stream oxygen content 50 miles (80 km) downstream would be less than half of saturation and probably the river there would not be able to support gamefish such as bass.

Key things to understand here include:

1. The environmental effects of a discharge vary with distance from the discharge point.

2. If there were many dischargers at many points along the river, their effects, *in this simple model*, would be additive, that is, at any point we would add the DOD

results for all upstream sources to get total DOD at that point, just as we added plumes above.

3. By suitable translations of units we can derive from such a model α coefficients more closely identifiable with those in the simple example—taking pounds of BOD per unit time and translating into "steady-state" DO concentration. (The concentrations that would be found if both discharge and stream conditions had not changed for a long time.)

Air quality problems, such as those created by emissions of particulates or gases, may also be modeled using "plume"-type continuous models. The simplest of these assumes a continuous wind, in terms of direction and force, and models advection downwind of the emissions from a stack, as well as diffusion of the pollutants in both the horizontal and vertical directions at right angles to the wind. A simple sketch of a plume is shown as Figure 4.5.[3]

Using the distance from the plume center line (the wind direction line from the source) the equation can be used to predict an average concentration from a continuously emitting stack, with a constant wind (steady-state conditions).

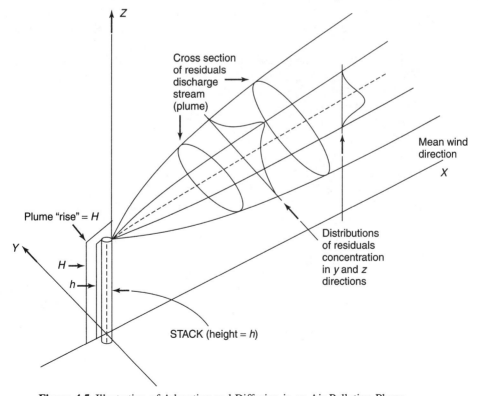

Figure 4.5 Illustration of Advection and Diffusion in an Air Pollution Plume

To capture more complex situations, the "plumes" from individual sources can be calculated for the whole circle of possible wind directions, taking account of the percentage of the time the wind is predicted to blow from each direction. And for several (or many) sources the plumes can be superimposed to produce predicted average concentrations for one wind direction or the average of averages over all possible directions. When these plumes are assumed to be noninteracting (additive), it is simple to back out the contribution of any specific discharging stack to the pollutant concentration at a particular point. For any specific set of assumptions about winds and other meteorological conditions, this kind of steady-state calculation can also, then, produce the as, the "transfer coefficients" used in the illustrative model at the beginning of the chapter.

COMPARTMENT MODELS

Compartment models can be used to break up complex spatial situations into discrete units. At one extreme, the mixing-bowl model of a segment of a steep-sided valley in atmospheric inversion conditions is a single-compartment model. The action goes on within the compartment, and the important quantities are the pollutant inputs and the "losses" from the compartment from its top. Most valleys are not perfectly confined bowls, so the analogy is not perfect, and some losses occur along the valley through the "passes" at either end of the region of special interest, as well as out the top.

It doesn't take much imagination to see the similarity of the steep-sided valley full of air (and pollution) to the steep-sided riverbed full of water and pollution. What changes from the isolated mixing bowl is the flow: water flows in the downstream direction, carrying material and energy along (advection). There will also be interaction with the atmosphere at the surface of the river—the gaining of additional dissolved oxygen and of new pollution *settling out of the air*; and interaction with the bed and banks—polluted or clean groundwater joining the river flow, material in the bed becoming suspended by turbulence or settling out where turbulence is low.

A "one-dimensional" river model would be based on compartments at least roughly similar to the one sketched below in Figure 4.6. Most compartment models make use of a couple of simplifying assumptions that amount to: (1) requiring the inputs and outputs, *in total*, to be in balance over the chosen time period, and (2) requiring that perfect mixing occurs within the compartment—there are no subcompartment plumes to complicate calculations. I will come back to time and changes in conditions over time in a few pages, but for now just notice that over short periods of time both or either the amount of water and the amount of other material or energy in the compartment can be changing. For example, in the early stages of a flood, water inflows are greater than outflows and "the compartment" itself is swelling.

Building a river quality compartment model, then, requires that we understand and have measurements for:

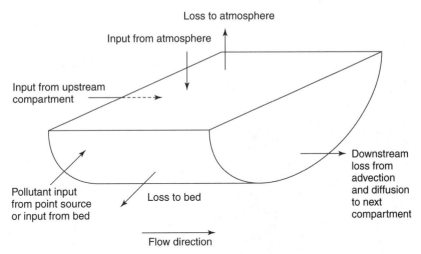

Figure 4.6 A River Compartment

- All the inputs to each compartment, including those from upstream, from atmosphere, from the riverbed, and from any wastewater discharges
- All the outputs or losses, including those to the next compartment downstream, to the atmosphere, and to the bed
- The process(es) going on within the compartment (that are of interest for the problem being addressed)

The last of these knowledge requirements brings us face to face with aquatic chemistry and biology—or more generally, with stream ecology. In principle, we would like to have an ecological model of the life, transformation, and death processes within each compartment. A sketch that shows the organisms and compounds this might involve is included as Figure 4.7.

If such a model were based on an accurate understanding we could predict how changes in pollution loads would affect, for example, the population of algae or of bass, and the concentration of dissolved oxygen. This kind of model would involve numerous differential equations that showed how the populations and chemical concentrations varied and interacted. But, if we were willing to settle for knowledge of dissolved oxygen alone as a summary indicator of the condition of the water, we could get by with a single equation model for each compartment that would, in effect, be a discrete piece of the Streeter–Phelps continuous model discussed earlier. For a fundamental complication implied by the use of more realistic models, see Box 4.1.

There are further complications that may be encountered in specific applications. For example, in waters influenced by ocean tides, the flow of water is not always in the same direction, and while, on net, a river will send its water and some

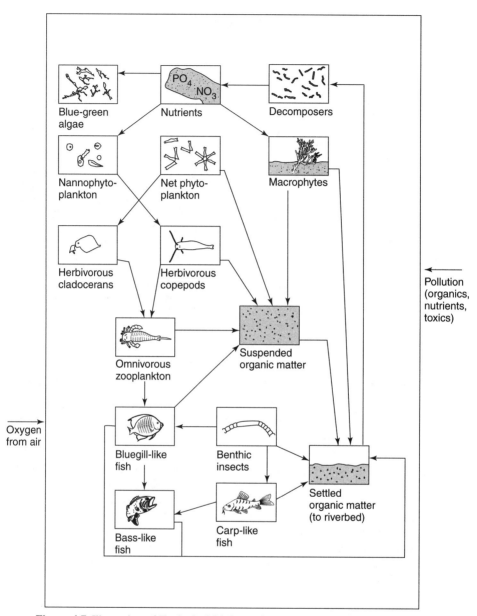

Figure 4.7 Illustration of Ecological Linkages in a Water Body (*Source:* Park, Richard A., Don Scavia, and Nicholas L. Clesceri, 1975. "CLEANER: The Lake George Model," in Clifford S. Russell, ed., *Ecological Modeling in a Resource Management Framework.* Washington, D.C.: Resources for the Future.)

part of its pollutant load to the sea, understanding of some environmental quality problems may necessitate modeling the shifting tidal currents. Another problem can arise if ecological processes involve different mixing zone sizes than seem to work

---

Box 4.1

A Complication—Water Quality and the Interaction of Sources of Pollution

In the Streeter–Phelps model the effect of each source on DO in the river is independent of what is happening at every other source. More modern and sophisticated—more ecologically correct—models, however, have built in dependencies among the sources. The effect of these is to make the impact of any particular source a function of the quality of the water at the point of the source's discharge. Since this quality is a complex function of the discharges of all upstream sources, the effect of a particular discharge is a function of the discharges upstream from it. (You can think of the mechanism causing this as one that makes the constants (the ks) in the Streeter–Phelps model into functions of existing water quality.)

The importance of this complication for economics lies in its implication for the knowledge needed to be able to estimate the benefits of reducing the discharges from any single source of pollution. I will come back to this in Chapter 5.

logically for the water flows and simple chemistry. This might happen if we are interested in fish that move over long distances compared with the size of the physical mixing zones, as might be the case again in tidal waters. (The more general problem of space as an argument in the functions that describe ecological processes will come up again below.)

The third problem to be mentioned, and one that leads into air quality models, is the possibility that two- or even three-dimensional models may be required to capture a problem. An example might be a situation, common in lakes, in which water tends to stratify—to not mix vertically. Then we need to introduce at least two compartments, bottom and top, along with the horizontal divisions. A sketch of such a situation is shown as Figure 4.8.

Air pollution modeling can also use the compartment approach, with the basic equations again based on the notion of conservation of mass (what goes into a box must be balanced by what goes out—unless our interest is in the dynamics of some situation in which pollution levels are changing). By comparison with the water-

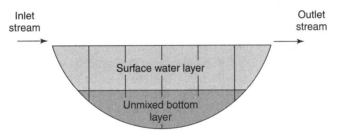

Figure 4.8 Cross Section of a Lake with Water Layers

modeling case, the spatial context is inherently more difficult because there are no confining banks and no unidirectional flow. Each compartment in a three-dimensional "stack" must, in general, be connected mathematically to every one of the six compartments with which it shares a face. But within each compartment, perfect mixing of pollutants is still assumed, so that the concentrations calculated are taken to be uniform throughout the compartment.

What goes on in the compartment may simply be dilution of the incoming load of pollution. There may be losses upward (as when chlorofluorocarbons depart for the stratosphere) and downward through settling out (or "raining out" when pollutants are gathered up on or dissolved in rain or snow). Chemical reactions may also be part of the model of each compartment, as in the ozone-formation process mentioned earlier. Long-distance atmospheric models can mimic the transformation of sulfur dioxide (SO_2) and nitrogen oxides (NO_x) into acid-forming ions—sulfate and nitrate. But it would be a very unusual atmospheric model that would have within it an ecological model analogous to those constructed for bodies of water.

MORE ABOUT SPACE, TIME, AND RANDOMNESS

Most of the discussion to this point in the chapter has been about "averages" and the steady state, as background for understanding, at least in a rough way, the derivation of the transfer coefficients introduced above and used elsewhere in the text. Before moving on, though, it will be worthwhile to spend at least a little more time on the complications involving space, time, and random variation in the environment.

SPACE

In the models discussed so far, space plays a role roughly analogous to that played by time in the simple benefit/cost exercises involving projected future results and requiring discounting. That is, space has to be taken into account; and when sources are located differently with respect to specific points of interest, this spatial differentiation is what creates the need for individually tailored charges on emissions. A challenge for model builders is to pick the most useful set of compartments for breaking up the space, balancing the added computational difficulty and cost implied by more, smaller compartments against the gain in resolution. ("Resolution" in this context may be thought of as increased probability of finding a peak pollutant concentration somewhere in a region. Remember that within each compartment, perfect mixing is assumed so potential intra compartment peaks get averaged out.) But only the connections among the compartments and the activity within each compartment have to be modeled. The number of compartments or the total extent of the system being modeled plays no causal role in itself.

For most water and air quality problem settings this view of the total extent of the system is a sufficiently good approximation. It seems to be less satisfactory, in general, where the concern is with land-based ecological systems. There, the *extent* of a habitat type, such as forest or prairie or desert, will in part determine what the ecological system looks like and how it functions. That is, space becomes a causal variable and not just a part of the background framework. Two examples may make this clearer. First, some species of birds and other animals prefer "edge" habitats, where forest borders grassland, whereas other species prefer interior habitats. Thus, if the area of landscape covered with forest is small, so that the edges are important and the interior space is small or nonexistent, the species mix will be different than if a larger area were forested, creating a large interior. Second, most species require minimum ranges in which to find food. The larger predators usually require the most space per individual or family. So a particular piece of habitat, with given vegetation, water, and insect life, will support a different set of animals if it is large than if it is small. Said another way, if you think about using a compartment approach to modeling a land-based ecological system, the number of compartments of a given size will matter in more than just the computational and resolution senses.

This problem of extent as a causal variable is logically separate from, but related to, the choice of system boundaries—how much has to be included in the model to make it useful in the problem setting of interest. As an example, think about trying to build a model that would, with reasonable accuracy, predict changes in spawning salmon runs into a river as a result of cleaning up pollution in the tidal portion of the river. (Assume, therefore, that we know how to model the effect of a pollution "block" in the tidal river on spawning runs—that is, what fraction of returning fish are discouraged at different levels of pollution encountered on entering the river.) If our interest were in the effect of the cleanup only and not in good prediction, we might get a reasonable idea by assuming that a certain number of adult salmon return from the sea to the river mouth each year (or each month of the spawning season). The differences between before and after cleanup in the number of adult salmon successfully spawning could be a useful indicator of the effectiveness of pollution control. But if we want to know how many fish are likely actually to be in the river in a future month, we may have to widen the model to include some representation of the ocean home of the salmon prior to spawning so that we get a better fix on returns to the mouth of the river.

TIME

Again, this subsection will just touch on some of the complications that crop up when we leave behind the time*less* steady state of the earlier discussions, either because we must or because we want to investigate exactly those complications. But first it needs to be said that "steady state" does not have to be identified with mean conditions. For example, steady-state water quality models might and often do use for their steady flows levels that are in the lower tail of the distribution, such as the "ten-year/seven-day low flow," (the daily flow, averaged over a week of daily flows, that, on the basis of historical data, is expected to be observed only once in ten years). Because of the effect of flow on pollution—moving it faster, diluting it more, and increasing the reaeration rate—if desired ambient conditions are predicted to be

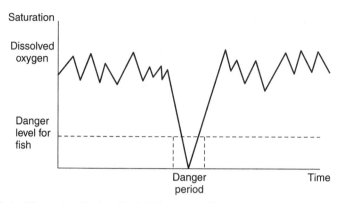

Figure 4.9 An Illustrative Oxygen Deficit Trace over Time

achieved at the low "design" flow, they will be met at higher flows as well. Lower flows, which are of course possible, may lead to failure to meet the desired conditions. Similar approaches can be taken in an air quality model, with wind speed and direction, and other meteorological parameters open to choice in defining the steady state to be explored.

Outside the world of the steady state, and therefore a bit closer to reality, conditions change as time passes. In watercourses, flows, temperatures, and sunlight inputs change and produce constantly varying levels of activity by the elements of the ecosystem. One approach to modeling that recognizes this reality is to run the model over many time periods, with variations between periods in the background conditions. This could produce a "trace" of ambient quality conditions over the same time frame. This trace could, in turn, be used to predict how often certain desirable conditions would be attained (or not attained) over some long period; and how bad conditions might become under particular combinations of the changing background inputs. As a simple example, look at the hypothetical dissolved oxygen trace in Figure 4.9.

RANDOMNESS

The chapters on randomness, probabilities, risk, and related problems come later in the text. For now it is important to keep in mind—at least in the back of your mind—that actual rainfall, wind speed, temperatures, cloud cover, and so forth are "random events." One way of seeing what this means is to think about 100 years of daily conditions (36,500 days) as that many drawings from a giant bowl that contains millions of descriptions of *possible* days. Another 100 years—another 36,500 drawings—would look different from the first one, both in the sequence of conditions from one day to the next and in the extremes attained. This means that the most realistic output from a natural world model would use the language of probability rather than of implied certainty. For example, it might say that with a particular set of pollution discharge limitations in place, the probability of achieving desired ambient quality standards would be p; or that the probability of failing by more than y parts per million to meet an ambient dissolved oxygen standard is q.

Question to think about: What is the difference for policy purposes between knowing that a certain set of assumed steady-state background inputs produce dangerously low DO (for given discharges of pollution), and knowing that with use of, say, 100 years of recorded background in a time-varying model, dangerously low DO is observed on t *different occasions or* z *percent of the time?*

IGNORANCE

But what about a situation in which we have neither long data records nor relevant laboratory results to fall back on? That is, what about situations in which we not only don't know the future sequences of rainfall, temperatures, and other background inputs but in which we don't really understand the system itself very well? Examples of environmental problems in which the ability to build predictive natural system models seems substantially less well developed than for the standard local air and water pollution settings include:

- how global climate change will look at the level of the region, such as the southeastern United States, or the north of Scandinavia
- how climate change (change in background conditions) will affect ecological systems
- how tropical rainforests will, in the long run, respond to current extensive logging
- what will happen if a new species of plant or animal is introduced accidentally or on purpose into an ecosystem in which it has never lived
- what will be the long-term chronic effects of low but persistent levels of particular man-made exotic chemicals in the natural environment

One possibility for at least getting a feel for the range of possible outcomes is to build a model with the best basic structure available (based on the best available knowledge) and explore its responses under a wide range of imposed changes to that structure. That is, the basic structure could be changed both in terms of the functional forms used and of the values of the key parameters in the functions. (The k constants in the BOD/DO model earlier in this chapter are parameters in this sense.) It may be, unfortunately, that even for a fairly small range of possible forms and values, the range of predicted outcomes is so large as to leave us none the wiser. It is also possible that none of the modifications explored actually captures what is later found to be the "true" situation. This is the essence of ignorance. Facing this kind of extreme uncertainty about the natural world, it may seem only reasonable to try to avoid *any* serious interference, such as the extensive logging referred to above. Later in the text (Chapter 13) I will come back to some decision approaches designed specifically for this type of situation. But for now, just notice that this general approach is often not an easy sell politically. Knowledge of the benefits that will be foregone by playing it safe will often be quite readily available, and those who stand to benefit will be visible and outspoken, while the potential damage will be speculative and will often lie in the fairly distant future. This, then, is an argument for improving our understanding of the natural world through research, probably research informed to some extent by the results of sensitivity analysis to identify the key elements of ignorance.

CONCLUDING COMMENTS AND REMINDERS

The major point of this chapter was to give you some background for and understanding of the why and how of including models of the natural world in economic analysis of environmental problems. Most of the attention has been given to pollution control problems and models because these are the most highly developed and most frequently encountered, but the basic ideas are quite transferable to more exotic situations—if the models are available. The trick is to find the analog of discharge, the element of human interference with, or "insult" of, the natural world.

For the chapters that follow, the reader will find it useful to remember two versions of the models discussed here. The first is the simple transfer coefficient, referred to as $\alpha(R)$ in this chapter, but sometimes written elsewhere as α, suppressing the implied distance argument while still maintaining the idea that distance (location) matters. The other version of the natural world models you will encounter, and this in the very next chapter, is a very general one. In it, the dissolved oxygen at a particular location, for example, is written as a function of upstream ambient water quality in several dimensions, and the discharges of several pollutants, in addition to BOD, to the reach being modeled. In effect, the functions that are written in general form stand for ecological models of the kind described in words and schematics in this chapter.

Another way of summarizing the lesson of the chapter is to say that an understanding of the natural world, in its role of absorbing, transforming, and moving around the effects of human "insults," is especially important in two facets of environmental economics. The first you will come to is benefit or damage estimation. Thus, humans may be said to value the environment as we find it—which is to say its *ambient quality*. But our policy interest usually involves making rules for or imposing charges on the "insults," such as pollution discharges. So we need to be able to see how the value attached to environmental goods and services will vary with what we do about those discharges. Natural world models do the translating. The second facet is one you met at the beginning of this chapter—the analysis of the properties of alternative instruments of environmental policy. You have already learned what a big difference a seemingly small change in a natural world model can make for assertions about these properties.

NOTES

1. The word "inversion" refers to the change in the pattern of temperature change with height, from the normal—the air cools as we go up—to the "inverted"—at least for some vertical distance, the air warms as we go up. The valley sides stop horizontal motion, the inversion stops vertical mixing. The result is mixing only inside the "bowl," and location of the sources doesn't matter.
2. There is apparently not perfect mixing between the northern and southern hemispheres; hence the hedge "roughly."
3. There is actually a plume in the river below each point discharge, but for many purposes—especially analysis of regional pollution problems—these are assumed away by assuming "perfect mixing" of the pollutant (almost) immediately below the discharge pipe. This "works" because the river is confined so that the random diffusion process cannot go on forever at right angles to the flow. Fairly quickly the concentrations are determined entirely by advection, dilution, and the biochemical reactions.

Cost-Benefit Analysis and the Management of the Environment

Back in Chapter 3, as part of the review of optimization as well as a way into a central question for environmental economics, there was some discussion of the related problems, which when solved define an optimal "policy." That is, they provide an optimal level of discharges of pollution, or of reduction of discharges from the pre-policy level. The problems were stated as:

$$\min_{(P)} (D(P) + CA(P)) \quad \text{and} \quad \max_{(R)} (B(R) - CR(R)) \tag{5.1}$$

where $D(P)$ stood for the damages of pollution, P, and $CA(P)$ for the costs incurred at that pollution level by the discharger(s); while $B(R)$ stood for the benefits of pollution reduction, R (the damages avoided), and $CR(R)$ for the costs of achieving R by reducing the amount actually discharged below the original status quo, which was called P_0. So $P_0 - R = P$ (later to be referred to as D, for discharge.) Let me now drop the R in $CR(R)$ and just use $C(R)$ for cost of discharge reduction.

In this chapter the very simple framework is expanded in several ways. First, I want to build on the lessons of Chapter 4 by emphasizing that benefits accrue (or damages are incurred) for the most part because of human exposure to ambient environmental quality conditions throughout localities, regions, or nations depending on how ambitious the problem solvers are in defining the problems. Second, anticipating the lessons of chapters 6 through 8, on the mechanics of benefit and damage estimation, I emphasize that the same general environmental quality phenomenon, such as a change in the level of ambient water quality, broadly defined, causes benefits (or damages, if quality is made worse) that accrue via several "routes." Said another way, there are almost always several dimensions to the effect of environmental quality on human well-being. For example, ambient water quality can affect health, the aesthetics of daily life, recreation, and broader concerns about the maintenance of aquatic ecological systems. All of these effects can give rise to benefits or damages.

Taking account just of these two sources of complication gives rise to a notationally unfriendly version of Equation (5.1) for water quality optimization in a (still-small) region, with some spatial differentiation, a few dimensions of water quality, and a few routes to benefits. It is possible, though I would say only just possible, to imagine pulling together the information necessary for actually building such a model for a real region. (As we shall see, especially in chapters 7 and 8, the state of the art in benefit estimation would be the weakest link in the necessary chain of tasks to accomplish this.)

But the simple regional version of the model is far from the most difficult challenge that the cost-benefit framework can give rise to, and the complications that might reasonably be added involve: looking across several (or many) regions, as would conceptually be necessary if a national optimum were sought; taking into account dynamic elements of the problem such as those introduced by bioaccumulation of some toxic compound; reflecting uncertainty, whether due to natural world randomness, our ignorance of ecosystem functioning, the possibility of exogenous economic change, or all of the above; or including the impact of embedding the environmental problem in the general economic system instead of separating it out as is done implicitly in the simple model.

Next, having gotten the flavor of how complicated the analysis might be made, we can look at how it might be simplified. These simplifications in practice take two major forms. In one, the open-ended optimization requirement is relaxed, and the question addressed becomes which of a few defined alternatives is the best, rather than what is the best of all possible alternatives. (An even greater simplification is to look only at one predefined alternative and ask whether it passes a cost-benefit test—whether the benefits it produces exceed the costs required to produce them.) The second form of simplification is one that works around the weak link—benefit or damage estimation—by asking a different question: What is the cheapest way of achieving at least a particular specified level of ambient environmental quality throughout a region (or a nation).

Before going on to pursue this agenda, let me be explicit about two matters left implicit in the above brief description. First, avoiding optimization of net benefits (not trying to maximize $B(R) - C(R)$) does not imply anything about what complications are dealt with. Thus, for example, testing a particular prespecified policy alternative for nonzero net benefits could be done with uncertainty taken explicitly into account. Or the costs of achieving some specified level of ambient environmental quality could be minimized in a dynamic setting involving bioaccumulation and the choice of a time-path of discharge reduction.

Second, it may have occurred to you to wonder where these "prespecified" policies or ambient quality standards come from. As a practical matter there are two major sources, but usually they are both involved. The sources are:

• the political and subsequent regulatory process, and

• technical and scientific analysis

An example of the first would be a law specifying a national ambient air quality standard (the minimum air quality acceptable nationally). An example of the second would be an engineering study of options for building sewers and wastewater treatment plants that produced two or three alternative plans that were deemed technically best. An example of the combination would be the Clean Air Act in the

United States. This defines the National Ambient Air Quality Standards (NAAQS) in words. (Recall that the "primary standards" are supposed to protect the health of the most vulnerable part of the population.) The translation of these words into actual ambient quality standards involving defined concentrations and corresponding time periods for which readings are to be averaged (e.g., hourly readings averaged over twenty-four hours or over a month) was a technical exercise based on examination of the accumulated evidence of the health effects of air pollution components.

With the above chapter map in mind, let me now turn to creating the more complete and complicated, but still quite simple, model for maximizing the net benefits of ambient quality.

GOING BEYOND THE SIMPLEST OPTIMIZING PROBLEM

The list of simplifications behind the single-dimension, timeless, and certain $B(R) - C(R)$ is, as just suggested, a long one. The real situations faced by governments in devising and analyzing environmental policies or designing projects have the following characteristics:

• There are generally many sources of pollution; they have different cost-of-reduction functions, in that $C_j(R_j)$ is not the same as $C_i(R_i)$ even if $R_i = R_j$ and they are located in different places.

• Pollution is itself not a single dimension thing as is implied by a single R. Sources discharge hundreds of compounds: Some are specific, such as SO_2 to air (sulfur dioxide gas). Some are measured by their effects. (BOD_5 measures a quantity of organic material that is oxidized in a water course over five days and that may include many different specific compounds such as carbohydrates, proteins, and fatty acids.) And some are combinations of specific compounds that are difficult and, for policy purposes not worth it, to sort out. (Reactive hydrocarbon (RHC) measures such "lumps" of pollutants as the gasoline compounds that boil off the surface of the gas in your car's fuel tank on a hot day.)

• It (almost) goes without saying that reduction is just as multidimensional as pollution itself.

• Similarly, but in an even more complex way, benefits are multidimensional in the sense that they are "generated" at many places and by many different elements of the pollution reduction effort. Without trying to be either inclusive or highly technical let's just look at the three pollutant examples used above.

a. SO_2 as a local phenomenon was one of the major targets of the first version of the Clean Air Act and is a much smaller problem now than in the mid-twentieth century. This gas, especially in combination with small particulates in the air, can cause both acute and chronic (short- and long-term) problems for the human respiratory system. At very high, short-term concentrations, as in the "inversions" described in Chapter 4, it can lead to death for some of the most sensitive populations, such as the old, the already ill, and those with serious asthma. So the benefit of reducing SO_2 that is experienced locally, because it is emitted from short stacks, is mainly seen in the form of better health experienced by people living within, say, 20 miles of the plant. The distribution of damages—hence benefits—depends on wind patterns.

But SO_2 from a very tall stack, ordinarily a stack at a large coal-fired electricity-generating plant, stays up in the air long enough for two other things to happen. First, chemical reactions can occur that convert SO_2 to the sulfite and sulfate ions. These can, in turn, combine with water to form acids, sulfuric acid in the case of sulfate. These acids can then be deposited on the ground via rain, snow, and "dry deposition" in which acid droplets adhere to particles that are heavy enough to fall. The other phenomenon of importance is that the sulfur oxides can stay aloft for a long time and hence cover a long distance. The effect of these dual events are that damages can happen far from emissions (and thus be hard to trace to the emitter) and involve other parts of life than health. For example, midwestern and midsouthern power plants, burning fairly high-sulfur eastern coal, are generally thought responsible for the "acid rain" problem in the Northeast. This has been characterized as leading to acidification of streams, ponds, and lakes, with accompanying destruction of aquatic ecosystems. This, in turn, damages recreation and has harder to evaluate effects, such as the deaths of unique local aquatic plants and animals. It is also thought that acid rain harms forests, weakening the trees and making them easier targets for pests and diseases, by leaching nutrients from the forest soils. So the benefits of SO_2 removal from these tall stacks accrue largely to people hundreds of miles away and via several routes, of which a major one is probably recreation.

b. BOD, in contrast, is generally more confined and more local in its effects. It is confined to the system of water courses into which it is discharged and by its natural conversion to more stable compounds through the actions of the microbes in those water courses. In the process of stabilization, oxygen is taken out of solution in the water and tied up in the new compounds. Damages accrue to those who have an interest in the water where it is affected by the loss of oxygen. This interest can involve recreational fishing—the lower oxygen affects which species of fish can live in the water, with lower oxygen generally meaning less recreationally desirable fish. If the effect on oxygen is severe enough the stream ecosystem can "go anaerobic" (lose all its dissolved oxygen), which means that different microbes do the work, versions that can live without oxygen. The stable compounds that are produced will include some particularly vile smelling ones such as H_2S, hydrogen sulfide (the rotten egg smell). This change destroys what we think of as the normal aquatic ecosystem, so there are *no* fish, no mayflies, no reptiles.

Thus the routes to benefits of BOD cleanup will depend on stream uses, actual or potential, and on how important the pollution load is relative to the stream. If the cleanup makes a formerly anaerobic stream aerobic, there will be benefits from the end of disgusting smells for those who live, work, or travel along the river where it lacks oxygen. At the other extreme, a cleanup that bumps oxygen up high enough might allow repopulation of a stream segment by trout that would be valued by anglers. Of course, all this is complicated by interactions among the many dimensions of water quality that affect its suitability for various human uses. See Box 5.1 on the "water quality ladder" for an example of an effort to capture these interactions in a single dimension.

c. The reactive hydrocarbons boiling off your car's gasoline on a warm day (or coming out of your tailpipe if your car is inefficient), evaporating as oil-based paint

---

Box 5.1

The Water Quality Ladder

In the early 1980s, researchers at Resources for the Future developed a "water quality ladder" that describes water quality primarily in terms of the uses for which the water is suitable, and secondarily, in terms of a few obvious water quality conditions (clearness, odor, debris, etc.). The use-based levels were located by indexing a set of five objective scientific water quality parameters, using a variant of the National Sanitation Foundation's Water Quality Index (Booth, Carubia, and Lutz, 1976; McClelland, 1974) along with informed judgment.

A number of sources were consulted to find the minimally acceptable concentration levels of five measurable quality characteristics associated with five potential uses of natural water courses. These characteristics were: fecal coliforms (organisms/100 ml), dissolved oxygen (mg/1), maximum BOD-5 (mg/l), turbidity (JTU), and pH. The five quality measures were the only ones for which numerical values could be obtained across all use classifications, a requirement dictated by the index approach. Particular attention was given to state water quality standards because they reported specific critical water quality classifications. The consensus results for each quality level are summarized in Table 5.1.

TABLE 5.1 Consensus Water Quality Characteristics of Five Water Quality Classes

Water Quality Classification	*Measurable Water Quality Characteristics*				
	Fecal Coliforms (0/100 ml)	Dissolved Oxygen (mg/1)[a]	5-day BOD (mg/1)	Turbidity (JTU)	pH
Acceptable for drinking w/o treatment	0	7.0 (90)	0	5	7.25
Acceptable for swimming	200	6.5 (83)	1.5	10	7.25
Acceptable for game fishing	1000	5.0 (64)	3.0	50	7.25
Acceptable for rough fishing	1000	4.0 (51)	3.0	50	7.25
Acceptable for boating	2000	3.5 (45)	4.0	100	4.25

[a] Percent saturation at 85°F in parentheses.

In order to associate each of the five possible sets of scientific measures with a single-valued ordinate on the quality ladder an index was created. The resulting ladder appears in Figure 5.1. It has been used in several studies of water quality benefits.

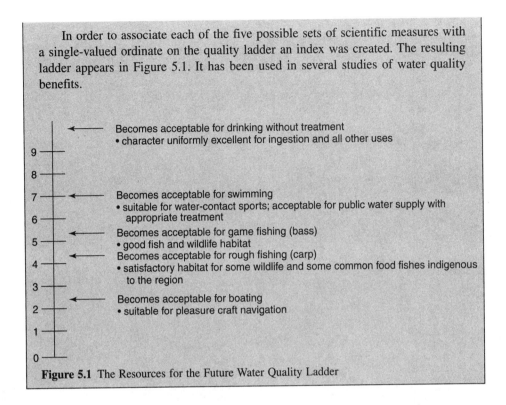

Figure 5.1 The Resources for the Future Water Quality Ladder

dries, or emitted from a dry-cleaning plant, cause damages by getting involved in complex chemical reactions in the atmosphere (hence their name). These reactions are driven by the energy in sunlight and lead eventually to the production of ozone, O_3, at ground level, where it causes damage.[1] The problem is that ozone is a very strong oxidizer. It attacks many compounds such as the artificial rubber in tires, and (evidence seems to show) susceptible parts of the human body, especially the lungs. Damages accrue to people who live in the smog, which tends to be mainly an urban phenomenon, and these damages can take several forms, including shorter lifetimes for products such as tires, and long-term reduction in lung function. The cloud of smog formed over a city on a sunny day can also drift over farms and forests during subsequent hours and create damages to plants and trees. All these routes and all these places are then involved, receiving benefits when there is action to reduce emissions of reactive hydrocarbons.

The difficulties inherent in trying to estimate such diverse and geographically dispersed damages (benefits) will be dealt with in more depth in chapters 6 through 8. For now, just remember that benefits (or damages) are sensitive to place and to type of pollution.

A MORE FORMAL AND COMPLEX MODEL
OF THE OPTIMIZING PROBLEM

Figure 5.2 is a schematic of a richer version of the problem in Eq. 5.1. But to give you a feeling for how quickly things get really complicated, this section goes over the creation of a regional water quality optimization model. The presentation is still abstract, however, in the sense that there are no completely specified functions, only their algebraic representations.

To keep things simple, I confine the problem to a single river basin. In order to undertake such a choice problem it is necessary to have identified all the "discharges" that affect water quality, including, possibly, some natural, uncontrollable ones such as suspended silt from undercut riverbanks. We have to know the cost-of-reduction functions for all the controllable sources and all the specific pollutants that they discharge. For the river itself, we have to know background information such as flow

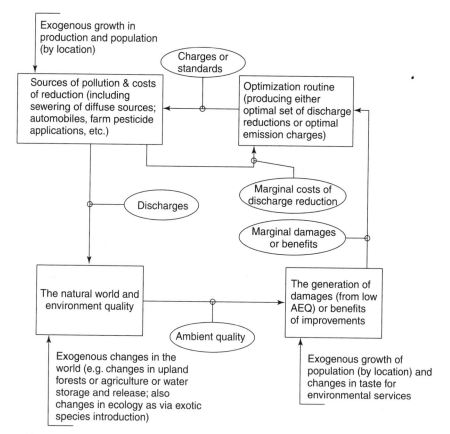

Figure 5.2 A Schematic of a Regional Environmental Quality Model. AEQ, ambient environmental quality.

(volume and speed), temperature, and how "rough" the surface is (one of the determinants of how fast oxygen from the air is redissolved in the water). Then we need a model of the river's ecology that predicts as "outputs" elements of that ecology relevant to estimating the benefits of alternative policies that reduce discharges. Common choices for such elements are dissolved oxygen (as a general indicator of "health"), algal densities, turbidity (or how far you can see into the water before its particulate load blocks the light), coliform bacteria, and "fish." (The quotation marks here are meant to emphasize that the modeled fish may not be as specific as we would like. That is, looking back at the water quality ladder box, we can see that a distinction of recreational importance seems to be between "rough" fish and "game" fish. The former might include carp, catfish, and suckers. The latter label applies to trout, bass, panfish of various types, pike, perch, and pickerel.)

Then, playing off the ambient water quality predictions of the ecological model as well as the characteristics of the relevant human population, we need benefit functions—the willingness to pay of that population (or, often, a representative person in the population) for improvements in the condition of the water in the river system, in terms of the ecological elements, at various places.[2]

All these parts of an optimizing model can be written formally in quite general notation, with n discharges of m pollutants; measures of ambient water quality predicted at q locations[3]; and k benefits "routes" covered at the q locations. This can be "economical" in the sense of saying a lot while using only a little paper and ink, but it lacks something as a way of communicating with those not in the trade. So I propose to be less general and more informal by describing a hypothetical, small, and quite uncomplicated basin, with only a few polluters, reaches, measures of ambient water quality, and "routes" by which the benefits of improvement in those quality measures accrue to the relevant population. (That last notion will be left undefined, though.) It will be assumed that the willingness to pay (WTP) of that population is for changes in quality in the reaches.

Rather than trying to include uncertainty and dynamics in all their complex glory, the first may be handled, as it often is, by using a low flow that is quite unlikely, thus assuring that the predicted quality or better will apply much of the time. (Notice, though, that this remaining element of uncertainty will, in general, be relevant to the WTP for the predicted quality. That WTP can be presumed to be greater for the same in-stream conditions if those conditions will be equaled or bettered 98 percent of the time than if they are equaled or bettered only 90 percent of the time.) The problem setting will treat time in a simple way and even that will be left out of the algebra and confined to later discussion in the text. Specifically, I will assume that the passage of time brings changes in such underlying influences as the number of people involved and their average incomes; and that, as discussed in Chapter 3, discounting of future costs and benefits is in principle necessary.

I will confine the "basin" to six reaches of a river, a reach upstream of all the pollution, which will define the "natural" water quality but is irrelevant to the optimization, and five downstream reaches each receiving pollution from one discharger. Five types of discharge will be allowed for: organic material measured by its oxy-

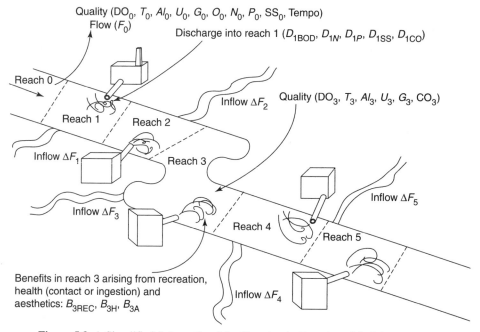

Figure 5.3 A Simplified Schematic of the Situation in Equations 5.2, 5.3, and 5.4

gen uptake (BOD), nitrogen (N), phosphorus (P), suspended solids (SS), and coliform bacteria (CO). The ecological model of each reach will accept those pollutants as inputs, along with background information, such as flow, temperature, and the quality of the water entering the reach from upstream. These models will predict six measures of ambient water quality (AWQ): dissolved oxygen (DO), turbidity (T), algal densities (Al), the "concentrations" of two sorts of fish, type U (rough) and type G (game), and the concentrations of fecal coliform bacteria (CO).

User benefits will be associated with three "routes": recreation (REC), health (H), and aesthetics (A), and there will be a separate user benefit per year for each reach and each route. These will be assumed to have been estimated on a per-user basis, and the number of "users" by type and reach (P_{ij} for the ith reach, the jth route to benefits) will also be assumed known.[4] Nonuser benefits (NU) per "interested" person will depend on *all* the quality measures in *all* the reaches. This population of interested people will in general include some (but probably not all) of the users, plus others. Again, I postpone a discussion of the underlying problem of determining the size of this population (the "extent" of the nonuser "market") to later chapters. Figure 5.3 provides a schematic of the situation.

Even with all this simplification, there will be a formidable amount of notation, and I will try to keep it as intuitively meaningful as possible to avoid the dreaded notation overload syndrome (NOS).

So, this elaboration of max $(B(R) - C(R))$ can be written as follows:

$\underset{\text{[over discharges]}}{\text{Max}}$ $[[P_{1R} B_{1REC} (DO_1, T_1, Al_1, U_1, G_1, CO_1, Y_{P1R})$

$+ P_{1H} B_{1H} (Al_1, CO_1, Y_{PIH}) + P_{1A} B_{1A} (DO_1, T_1, Al_1, Y_{P1A})$

$+ P_{2R} B_{2REC} (DO_2, T_2, Al_2, U_2, G_2, CO_2\ Y_{P2R}) + \ldots$ (5.2)

$+ P_{5A} B_{5A} (DO_5, T_5, Al_5, Y_{P5A}) + P_{NU}\ B_{NU} (DO_1 \ldots CO_5, Y_{PNU})]$

$- [C_1(R_{1BOD}, R_{1N}, R_{1P}, R_{1SS}, R_{1CO}) + C_2(R_{2BOD}, R_{2N}, R_{2P}, R_{2SS}, R_{2CO})$

$+ \ldots + C_5(R_{5BOD}, R_{5N}, R_{5P}, R_{5SS}, R_{5CO})]]$

subject to the constraints that relate discharges to original pollutant raw loads minus reductions and to ambient quality conditions and, of course, that require all discharges to be nonnegative.

The per capita benefit functions are intended to be fairly easily understood, with subscripts for each reach and "route" (REC = recreation; H = health; A = aesthetics; and NU = non use, the last of which applies to the entire river). The arguments of the use-benefit functions are the relevant quality characteristics of the relevant reach, O, T, Al, and so forth. The income arguments (Y_{Pik}) are, ideally, the incomes for the relevant populations (at place i, for use k). In these functions, again for simplicity, the "before" levels of quality are not included, but recall that *benefits* are a function of improvements in quality from some base. The Ps are the relevant populations by reach and benefit route.

COSTS OF DISCHARGE REDUCTION

The costs of discharge reduction—or, more generally, of reductions in negative environmental impacts—seem intuitively fairly straightforward to estimate, certainly compared with the monetized damages caused by those discharges or other actions. After all, the firms, farms, and households that accomplish the reductions must do so by taking quite specific actions, such as installing and operating a wastewater treatment plant just upstream of the point of discharge to a water course. The costs of these actions ought to be discoverable through engineering studies and vendor price lists. Accumulating enough such data ought to allow the statistical estimation of average or representative cost functions that could in principle be applied ex ante in benefit-cost calculations of the type discussed here.

Indeed, Arthur Fraas and Vincent Munley (1984) published estimates of wastewater treatment cost functions for the United States, using data in 1976 dollars. Manipulating their results to make the removal efficiency term explicit, suppress regional variation, eliminate the capacity utilization term from the capital cost function, and update to 1997 dollars, these functions are:

Construction (capital) cost $= 198{,}050\, Q^{0.89}\, I^{0.08}\, (1-E)^{-0.16}$

Annual operating and maintenance (variable) cost
$$= 73{,}620\, Q^{0.79}\, I^{0.17}\, (1-E)^{-0.07}\, U^{-0.46}$$

where Q = volume of wastewater per day (millions of gallons)
I = concentration of BOD in water entering the plant (mg/l)
E = removal efficiency (decimal)[5]
U = capacity utilization (decimal)

You can see that both functions exhibit economies of scale in flow (marginal and average costs fall as flow increases); and that influent concentration also is subject to a similar effect—that is, doubling influent concentration, holding other variables constant, does not double either cost. Thus:

$$\frac{(400)^{0.08}}{(200)^{0.08}} = (2)^{0.08} = 1.06$$

The effect of increasing efficiency of removal may not be quite so easy to see, so here are some numbers:

When E =	$(1-E)^{-0.16}$ =
0.2	1.04
0.4	1.08
0.6	1.16
0.8	1.29
0.9	1.44
0.95	1.61
0.99	2.09

So the effect of increasing efficiency is modest, though nonlinear, until E gets close to 1 (100% removal), at which point the term grows very fast. This is a common observation for such removal processes, not just those involving BOD in water but also particulates and SO^2 in stack gases, and so forth.

To produce graphs that cover a range of volumes and of efficiencies, we can make assumptions about I and U. For example, let's let $I = 200$ mg/l, roughly the mean incoming concentration in the Fraas/Munley data; and let $U = 0.75$ (75% of capacity being used). In figures 5.4 and 5.5 you will find respectively capital and annual operating and maintenance costs for 80 and 98 percent removal efficiencies.

The cost functions for pollution removal by the sources in the example, however, are shown as entirely nonseparable. That is, mathematically, the marginal cost of, say, BOD removal at source 1, $\partial C_1(.)/\partial R_{1BOD}$, depends in general on the level

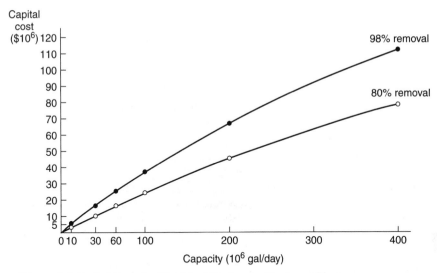

Figure 5.4 Capital Costs for Municipal Wastewater Treatment Plants

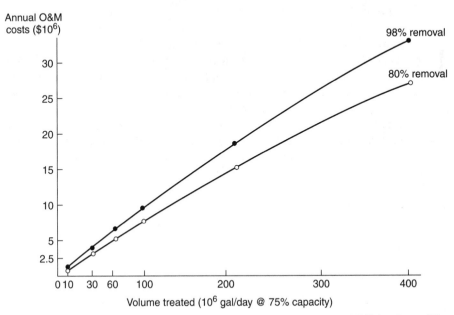

Figure 5.5 Annual Operating and Maintenance Costs for Two Removal Efficiencies and Varying Volumes Treated

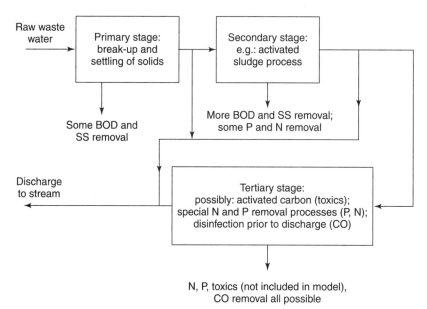

Figure 5.6 Wastewater Treatment Stages in Schematic. BOD, oxygen-demanding organics; SS, suspended solids; P, phosphorus; N, nitrogen; CO, coliform bacteria.

of removal of all the other pollutants by that source. The relationships inherent in the actual cost functions may very well create nonconvexities in the space of feasible solutions and thus lead to practical difficulties with optimization. (See Appendix 3.II.) The actual situation as defined by engineering reality is likely to be even more complex and harder to deal with because treatment technology has evolved to be used in stages, with joint removal of a subset of pollutants at each stage. Thus, in rough schematic the choices are as in Figure 5.6. The model's choices involve whether and how much treatment to do at each stage, but to do any of the secondary stage, some amount of primary-stage capacity must be in place, and so forth. Further, within each process at each stage there is generally joint removal of more than one pollutant. This implies that "the" marginal cost of BOD removal, for example, is not well defined even though the conceptual model uses cost functions that imply a well-defined partial derivative.

NATURAL WORLD LINKAGE

The link between the pollutant reductions and the benefits is the model of ambient water quality, along with some auxiliary relationships. The latter, as noted above, include the identities $D_{ij} = P_{0ij} - R_{ij}$, for each source i and pollutant j; with discharge, D; reduction, R; base or "raw load" P_0; and the river flow identities:

Given flows from the tributaries not being modeled (F_0)

Given inflows to each reach I_q

Given outflows from each reach L_q (5.3)

And, therefore, the net change in flow in the reach: $\Delta F_q = I_q - L_q$

For each reach going downstream the flow is: $F_q = F_{q-1} + \Delta F_q \ (q = 1, \ldots, Q)$

So the flow is measured at the downstream end of the reach. The next reach down receives that flow and, in the reach, net inflows are added to get the flow at the bottom of that reach, and so on.

The river water quality model itself may be very complicated, as discussed in Chapter 4, but the essence can be conveyed by the following.

Given DO_0, N_0, P_0, SS_0, CO_0 in the upstream reach (as well as F_0 and all the net inflows, as above):

$$DO_1 = F_{DO}(DO_0, N_0, P_0, SS_0; F_0, \Delta F_1; D_{1BOD}, D_{1N}, D_{1P}, D_{1ss})$$

$$T_1 = F_T (DO_0, N_0, P_0, SS_0; F_0, \Delta F_1; D_{1BOD}, D_{1N,} D_{1P}, D_{1ss})$$

$$Al_1 = F_{Al} (DO_0, N_0, P_0, SS_0; F_0, \Delta F_1; D_{1BOD}, D_{1N}, D_{1P}, D_{1ss})$$

$$U_1 = F_U (DO_1, Al_1, T_1; Temp_1)$$

$$G_1 = F_G(DO_1, Al_1, T_1; Temp_1) \qquad (5.4)$$

$$CO_1 = F_{CO} (CO_0, D_{1CO}; Temp_1)$$

$$DO_2 = F_{DO}(DO_1, T_1, Al_1, BOD_1, N_1, P_1, U_1, G_1, F_1, \Delta F_2; D_{2BOD}, D_{2N}, D_{2P}, D_{2ss})$$
$$\vdots$$
$$CO_2 = F_{CO} (CO_1, D_{2CO}; Temp_2)$$

and so on, through five equations for each of the five reaches to be modeled (that are influenced by the discharges whose control levels are the decision variables). That is, for each stream characteristic (output of the water quality model) in each reach there is a prediction equation, which, coliforms excepted, depends on all the discharges into the reach and the inputs of at least some of the characteristics and pollutants from the reach above. Coliforms are dealt with separately, as though they do not participate in the ecological relationships that transform the other discharges into stream characteristics. (This seems to be consistent with the way available, off-the-shelf, stream quality models deal with them.) The bacterial concentrations decay as the bacteria die off in the open water, exposed as they are to sunlight, unfamiliar chemicals, and other organisms that eat them.

While this is not intended to be a manual on how to build and use aquatic ecological models, a few additional notes are in order. First, in current reality, models with even this degree of complexity are not usually available for specific basins, let alone in general form easily tailored to represent any basin of interest. What is most often modeled is just the BOD/DO connection, with dissolved oxygen, then, standing for water quality in a broader sense. This, in turn, implies that the benefits of water quality improvement cannot be dealt with in an entirely satisfactory way, since dissolved oxygen is only one of the characteristics that influence people's enjoyment of natural water bodies—though it is key, at low levels, to the level of smell—and does not even figure in the health benefit, unless it is taken to be a surrogate for pathogens. For an effort to make the most out of a limited amount of information, including dissolved oxygen, return to the description of the RFF Water Quality Ladder above.

A second note is that the functions above have some intrareach simultaneity reflected in them. Thus, the DO in a reach will be influenced by the level of algal growth (and death). This will have its greatest effect in widening the daily swings in DO. Growing algae will add to the oxygen content; dead, decaying algae will use up DO. But sufficiently dense algae can produce shade that shuts down other sundriven processes in the water column.

Lacking in the overall formulation is any explicit notice of time. But, since long-lived investments, producing multiperiod returns, are involved, time cannot be ignored. Bringing it in, even in the simplest sense of time passing and populations and incomes changing, requires, first, distinguishing between investment and operating costs; second, repeating the net benefit expressions for each year over the "horizon" (the period agreed on as relevant to the decision)[6]; and, third, doing the necessary discounting and summing over the horizon. Without going back and redoing the complicated model in Eqs. 5.2 through 5.4, it will be possible to indicate what is involved in a simpler way. Thus:

1. The cost part of the problem would include an initial investment term at each source related to each stage of pollutant reduction. This would be the cost of a certain amount[7] of capacity and would imply a particular variable cost function. Then the variable costs of reduction for each period would be included, discounted as appropriate for the period.

2. The per capita benefit functions would be different for each year at least because of the dependence on income. An additional, and much harder, challenge, relevant to the developing country context discussed in Chapter 15, would be to reflect increasing leisure time and changing tastes. As a general matter, all these changes would probably increase the recreation and aesthetic benefits attached to a specific water quality. How they would affect health benefits is not so clear.

3. Populations could be growing at different rates, so that total benefits for any route and reach in any year t would differ from those in the first year both because of changes in the per capita valuation and in the population that cares. (Again, of course, the annual benefit numbers would be discounted to the present using the agreed-on interest rate. Or, possibly, a range of rates would be used to explore the sensitivity of the result to this choice.)

Notice that a fuller elaboration of the problem could have the cost side changing as well to reflect increasing production and therefore increasing raw pollution loads, so that achieving the same discharge in year t would cost more than in year 0. (As note 6 pointed out, though, this combined with the possibility of choosing different capacity levels in the first period creates a more difficult problem.)

In addition, the environment itself—the aquatic ecosystem in this example—could introduce a dynamic element to the problem. In Chapter 4 and in the example the assumption has been that the steady-state condition is the relevant concept and that, if discharges are changed, the transition to a new steady state is not prevented by irreversible changes in the ecosystem. But this may not be true. Rather, it may be that present actions imply not only the present condition of the system but also the future possibilities—at least the possibilities over some fairly long period. An example could be the accumulation of nutrients (nitrogen and phosphorus compounds that encourage aquatic plant growth). Once these are discharged into a lake, for example, it may take a very long time for them to be flushed out again, because they are not simply dissolved or suspended in the water but are caught in the cycle of plant growth and death with subsequent decay. The nutrients may tend to settle out on the bottom with decaying plant material but may then be reintroduced into the water column by events such as storms or dredging. If the problem to be analyzed involved such a long-term cycle, the benefits of cutting current discharges would not be adequately captured by responses to current water quality.

Assuming even the simple version of such a model can be successfully put together—no small assumption—and solved, the output available for informing decisions on water quality management has two major parts:

1. A set of (economically) optimal ambient water quality characteristics, by characteristic and reach. (These may be changing over time, so long as the model's construction allows for such changing decisions in a consistent way. That is, roughly speaking, if only adjustments along variable cost-of-discharge-reduction functions is required.)

2. A set of optimal discharges of each pollutant from each source (in each period, if there is variation over time) that corresponds to the optimal quality levels. These can be thought of as optimal discharge standards. Associated with each discharge is its "dual" or shadow marginal cost, which could be the basis for an optimal emission charge that should inspire the sources to achieve the desired discharge level. (Because of the possible interactions among the pollutants in the processes of treatment, these shadow marginal costs are not simple derivatives of the functions in the basic equation but rather "fall out of" the large programming problem.) On charges and standards, see chapters 9 and 10.

FURTHER COMPLICATIONS

Two other possible complications are worth noting. The first is the fuller treatment of uncertainty. So far, all that has been acknowledged in this regard is that future water flows (background conditions for ecosystem functioning) are unknown. This has been assumed to be handled by using in the model calculations a flow in the lower tail of the (historically known) distribution of possible flows. But the fact is that no part of the model is free from uncertainty, not the rest of the ecosystem's functioning, not benefits as functions of ecosystem conditions, not even the costs of taking actions to reduce discharges. A really adequate effort to come to grips with this ubiquitous uncertainty requires, first, that the sources of uncertainty be made explicit. Thus, the parameters (perhaps only a subset judged most likely to be problematic) of the ecosystem model and of the benefit and cost functions are taken to be the result of "draws" from distributions. For example, a parameter might be 0.5 in the basic model. But in the uncertainty analysis it might be recognized that any value from 0.25 to 0.75 is equally likely. Such a process would be repeated for every parameter. Then the model would be solved many times, for many different combinations of possible parameter values. (Each parameter value in a particular run may be thought of as the result of running some sort of random process to choose from the distribution defined for that parameter. As a very simple example, think back to the single die used in the expected value discussion in Chapter 3. When the die is tossed, any value from 1 to 6 is equally likely. If a parameter in the model were seen as taking on any of 6 values *with equal* probability, we could use the die to choose a value for each model run by assigning the numbers 1, 2, . . . , 6 to each of the possible values.)[8]

The results of the many runs would themselves be distributions of net benefits. Such a distribution might well include negative numbers. The next question, then, is how to deal with the information now available. One answer that might occur to you after the brief discussion of uncertainty in Chapter 3 is to try to use the expected value of the project or policy's net returns.[9] Figure 5.7 illustrates the results of such an effort for a real water quality improvement project. It shows that the mean net present value of the project's benefits is 4.6 million (in local currency units). So that on the basis of a point estimate, the project is a go. But it also shows that there is a large chance that the project will turn out to have a negative net present value. (The area under the probability density to the left of zero is over 70 percent of the total area.) A risk-averse decision maker might well pause before committing to go ahead.

There are other ways to look at such a problem, but I have not established the background for discussing them. I will return to a couple of them in Chapter 12 after additional discussion of decision making under uncertainty.

The second possible complication is the embedding of the regional model either in a set of such models covering a complete country, or in a model of the full economy, or both. Embedding the problem in the full economy means constructing the links among the dischargers' costs and the consumers' spending, work, and leisure decisions and the rest of the economic activity going on. The approach used above ignores these links. It is called a "partial equilibrium" model as a result. Building the links and the complete economic model that includes them creates a "general equilibrium" model. Such a model, for example, would show how the industrial

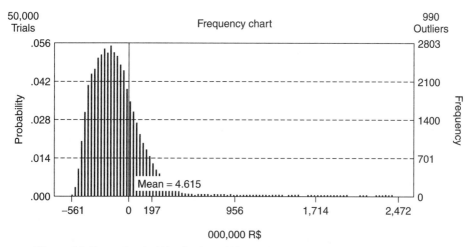

Figure 5.7 Example of a Distribution of Net Project Present Values over Many Samples of Possible Values of Key Parameters

and farm sectors adjusted *overall* to the necessity to invest in and operate pollution control equipment at existing plants or farms.

A second way of broadening the single regional model's compass would be to include other regions. For example, one might try to model all the river basins in some subnational political unit that has responsibility for water quality management within its boundaries. Or, if you were really ambitious, you might try to model those basins for an entire nation. I emphasize that I am talking here about building basin models that interact—otherwise there would be no new information gained at the level of the single basin. That is, if you built ten basin models to cover a U.S. state, for example, and each model was unconnected to any other, the answer you got by running any one of the models, say for basin A, looking for the optimal water quality would be unaffected by the existence of the other models. You would be none the wiser about basin A for having modeled basin B, C, and so on. But what links might there be that it would be useful to include? A fairly obvious one would be through the demand for water-based recreation. Thus, think about two adjacent river basins, both with mediocre river quality, which means that both offer limited opportunities for the kinds of recreation that require high water quality, such as swimming or trout fishing. Now imagine improving the water quality in one, but only one, of the basins. If the distances involved are not too great, you might well expect to see some of the benefits accruing to people living in the other basin. These would be added to the benefits enjoyed by those living in the improved basin. So, if the question being asked were, what is the optimal quality for this river, seen in isolation, the answer, call it Q_1, might be higher than the quality found optimal if both basins were dealt with at the same time, so that the would-be swimmers or anglers of the second basin would respond to their own basin's quality improvement in the context of the jointly improving conditions. That is, the quality improvement in the second basin would *compete* with the improvement in the first basin.

There could be other links included as well, such as possible interbasin transfers of water, or even of wastewater, though both of these are usually very contentious as political issues. Interbasin transfers of wastewater were part of the system devised in Germany in the early part of the twentieth century for managing the water quality problems of the heavily industrialized and densely populated Ruhr area. Interbasin transfers on the water-supply side are more common. For example, both Boston and New York City depend on them.

DOING LESS THAN BASIN-WIDE
NET BENEFIT MAXIMIZATION

Having now lingered over cost-benefit optimization in the environmental context, it seems worthwhile to return the discussion to a somewhat more practical level via the following assertion (to be explored more carefully in chapters 6–8): The major obstacle to building such an optimization model, whether for water quality, air quality, or both together, is that environmental economists cannot now estimate the benefit *functions* that are at the heart of such a model. (Recall that these benefit functions are marginal willingness to pay [MWTP] functions.) This is a matter both of methodology and of data, as we shall see. Accepting the assertion for now suggests two ways of reducing the demands on our abilities while still generating useful information:

- Backing away from the *optimization* part of the analysis by defining a few relevant feasible projects or policies and using cost-benefit analysis to identify the best of these
- Retaining the optimization requirement but settling for *minimizing* the costs of meeting a set of ambient quality goals

Thus, in the first of these simplifications, there is no longer a requirement that we have benefit *functions* covering all feasible levels of the relevant ambient quality measures. For each predefined alternative, it is necessary to estimate the benefits only of the ambient quality levels predicted to be attained. This is substantially easier, though it is still close to the edge of existing technical abilities. The second choice, stepping back from benefit estimation altogether, reduces the analytic load enormously. But, of course, it also does away with any economic efficiency claims for the resulting project or policy.

AMBIENT-QUALITY-CONSTRAINED COST MINIMIZATION

It is worth pausing for a moment to consider a little more fully the background to and implications of leaving behind the requirement that net benefits be maximized. Cost-effectiveness analysis, aimed at finding the least-cost way of meeting ambient water quality standards imposed on the water courses of interest, is an application of constrained optimization. As already noted, the standards to be imposed may be chosen by a national legislature, or the environmental agency may be directed to develop them. The bases for such standards might include safety, health, or aesthetic or ecological considerations. For example, turbidity might be constrained from above to guarantee visibility for the safety of swimmers. Similarly for fecal coliform bacteria and swimmers' health. Dissolved oxygen (DO) could be constrained from below to protect fish of interest to commercial fishermen or recreational anglers. Or a more general "health of the ecosystem" justification might result in a similar DO constraint.

Constraints on the presence of oil and grease would protect against surface "sheens," while constraints on floating sewage solids and DO at very low levels could also be justified on the grounds of minimal aesthetic protection. Constraints on algal bloom densities could be related directly to other requirements such as those on DO or turbidity, or could be aimed at protecting against toxic threats such as those from certain blue-green algae or coastal "red tides." (See Box 5.2.)

Wherever the ambient water quality standards come from, they can be treated as constraints in a more or less complicated and sophisticated watershed cost-effectiveness model, as shown schematically in Figure 5.8, which may be contrasted with Figure 5.2. "More or less complicated" means the model can, in principle, embody dynamic and risk elements, and can allow for different possible locations of contemplated but not-yet-built treatment plants. It should reflect all the chosen AWQ standards and contain natural world models that relate all the known (or understood) pollutant discharges to these standards via aquatic ecological models. What has been abandoned from the first approach is the benefit function part of the model. There is no balancing here. Rather, each element of the standard is of the same absolute importance. The interest of the designers of water quality improvement investments is only in the cost side. So long as all the standards are met (constraints satisfied), all that matters is minimizing the costs of this achievement.

Such a model is very likely to involve multiple constraints, both in the sense of multiple places and multiple dimensions of ambient quality. The actual ambient quality levels at each place are not fully independent of each other because of the structure of the natural world. It is therefore inevitable that only some subset of the constraints will be binding at the optimum, with different subsets binding at different feasible solutions. Comparing across the feasible set purely on the basis of cost involves, then, a rather strong assumption—that it is irrelevant which constraints (AWQ constituents, locations) are more than satisfied and by how much. If this creates discomfort, it is possible to examine the sensitivity of the choice to other knowledge by introducing "credits" for doing better than the standard. These can be specific to quality elements and locations, but this is an inherently arbitrary exercise, and in a large, complex watershed model, can at best only tell you that there was or was not "much" sensitivity.

A few other observations about cost-effectiveness analysis and its "legitimacy" seem to be in order:

BOX 5.2

State Water Quality Standards—An Example

In December 1997, the Tennessee Department of Environment and Conservation issued recommended final revisions to water quality standards. In a roughly fifty-page document, about thirty pages were devoted to a list of every covered section of every covered water body with the "Use Classifications" for each such section indicated. Table 5.2 is a sample part of a page covering sections of the lower Cumberland River and tributaries.

TABLE 5.2 Sample Page from State Water Quality Standards

Stream	Description	Domestic Water Supply	Indus. Water Supply	Fish and Aquatic Life	Recreation	Irrigation	Livestock Watering and Wildlife	Navigation	Trout Stream
Cumberland River	Mile 74.6 (KY-TN line) to 118.3 (Cummings Cr.)	X		X	X	X	X	X	
Saline Creek	Mile 0.0 to Hwy 120			X	X	X	X		
Saline Creek	Hwy 120 to Ft. Campbell Bdy		X	X	X	X	X		X
Saline Creek	Ft. Campbell Bdy to Origin		X	X	X	X	X		
Bear Creek	Mfile 0.0 to Origin			X	X	X	X		
Long Creek	Hwy 49 to Origin			X	X	X	X		X
Elk Creek	Mile 0.0 to Origin			X	X	X	X		
Wells Creek	Mile 0.0 to 5.2			X	X	X	X		
Wells Creek	Mile 5.2 to 7.2			X	X	X	X		
Wells Creek	Mile 7.2 to origin			X	X	X	X		
Yellow Creek	Mile 3.4 to Ruskin Cave			X	X	X	X		X
Cumberland River	Mile 118.3 to 125.3 (Red River)	X	X	X	X	X	X	X	
Cumberland River	Mile 125.3 to 175.7 (Richl. Cr.)	X	X	X	X	X	X	X	
Red River	Mile 0.0 to 2.0		X	X	X	X	X	X	
Red River	Mile 2.0 to 15.0	X	X	X	X	X	X	X	
Red River	Mile 15.0 to 51.2 (KY-TN line)	X	X	X	X	X	X		
So. Fork Red River	Mile 20.4 (KY-TN line) to 22.2			X	X	X	X		
So. Fork Red River	Mile 22.2 to 23.2			X	X	X	X		
So. Fork Red River	Mile 23.2 to Origin			X	X	X	X		

Big West Fork	Mile 0.0 to 14.6 (Ky-TN line)		X	X	X	X	X
Little West Fork	Mile 0.0 to 10.4		X	X	X	X	
Sulphur Fork	Mile 0.0 to 26.6	X	X	X	X	X	
Sulphur Fork	Mile 26.6 to 28.6		X	X	X	X	
Sulphur Fork	Mile 28.6 to Origin	X	X	X	X	X	
Carr Creek	Mile 0.0 to 9.7			X	X	X	
Carr Creek	Mile 9.7 to 11.2			X	X	X	
Carr Creek	Mile 11.2 to Origin			X	X	X	

The "use classifications" are, in turn, keyed to pages of "Criteria for Water Uses," of which part of those for "Fish and Aquatic Life," are reproduced below:

a. Dissolved Oxygen. The dissolved oxygen shall be a minimum of 5.0 mg/l except in limited sections of streams where it can be clearly demonstrated that (1) the existing quality of the water due to irretrievable man-induced conditions cannot be restored to the desired minimum of 5.0 mg/l. . . .

b. pH. The pH value shall lie within the range of 6.5 to 9.0 and shall not fluctuate more than 1.0 unit in this range over a period of 24 hours.

c. Solids, floating materials and deposits. There shall be no distinctly visible solids, scum, foam, oily slick, or the formation of slimes, bottom deposits or sludge banks of such size or character that may be detrimental to fish and aquatic life. . . .

e. Temperature. The maximum water temperature change shall not exceed 3°C relative to an upstream control point. The temperature of the water shall not exceed 30.5°C and the maximum rate of change shall not exceed 2°C per hour. The temperature of recognized trout waters shall not exceed 20°C. . . .

f. Taste and odor. The waters shall not contain substances that will impart unpalatable flavor to fish or result in noticeable offensive odors in the vicinity of the water or otherwise interfere with fish or aquatic life.

(continued)

BOX 5.2

State Water Quality Standards—An Example (cont'd)

g. Toxic substances. The waters shall not contain substances or a combination of substances including disease-causing agents which, by way of either direct exposure or indirect exposure through food chains, may cause death, disease, behavioral abnormalities, cancer, genetic mutations, physiological malfunctions (including malfunctions in reproduction), physical deformations, or restrict or impair growth in fish or aquatic life or their offspring. . . . (see Table 5.3.) Thus, the document creates a full set of statewide ambient standards on which, for every individual criterion, the strictest requirement (the most demanding use classification) governs.

TABLE 5.3 Example of Toxic Substance Criteria

Compound	Criterion Maximum Concentration µg/l (CMC)	Criterion Continuous Concentration µg/l (CCC)
Arsenic (III)	360	190
Cadmium	1.8/3.9/8.6	0.7/1.1/2.0
Chromium	—	100
Chromium VI	16	11

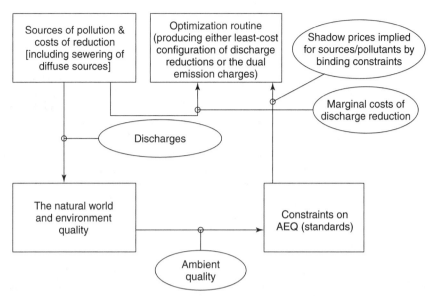

Figure 5.8 Schematic of a Regional or Watershed Cost-Effectiveness Model. AEQ, ambient environmental quality.

1. The cost-effective meeting of politically chosen standards has no built-in economic "legitimacy," though it may be highly practical and internally logically consistent. It is always possible for economists or others to question the "efficiency" of the standards. For example, the executive orders of successive U.S. presidents have had the effect of requiring The Environmental Protection Agency to examine the efficiency justification for the National Ambient Air Quality Standards (NAAQS), even though the legislation establishing these standards requires that they be based on protecting health (the primary standards) or "welfare" (the secondary standards) without regard to cost.

2. If the interested agency or legislature is prepared to adopt a unidimensional (scalar) definition of "effectiveness," and if the scale of the problem is held constant by the definition of the watershed or region, it is possible to look at the problem as one of maximizing the ratio of effectiveness to cost.[10] (This is not possible if the goal being sought is multidimensional, as described above. Then there is no single ratio to maximize.) What would be a scalar effectiveness measure? Possibilities include the minimum DO found in any stream segment in the watershed; the value of some index defined by combining DO and suspended solids predictions; or a summary ecological prediction such as habitat quality units.

3. Only in very simple problem settings would it be possible to impose the requirement that every solution creates *exactly the same* level of effectiveness. But where that is possible, least-cost analysis (LCA) is the name of the game,[11] and the ambiguity introduced by varying levels and locations of "slackness" disappears. (To be clear, the difference between this and the vector-constrained problem is that there is no "slackness" with the single effectiveness measure and imposition of a single required level of that measure.)

4. It is possible to extend this method of cost minimization by requiring that the project or policy that is identified in this way also pass a benefit-cost test. That is, after finding the cost-minimizing way of meeting a given set of ambient quality standards, benefits of that solution can be estimated and compared with the costs. If the costs exceed the benefits the alternative is rejected. (Notice that this rejection amounts to rejection of the ambient quality standards.) This is a common approach in applications for loans for environmental quality improvement projects made to such international lending agencies as the Inter-American Development Bank.

MULTIOBJECTIVE ANALYSIS: A SLIGHTLY DIFFERENT USE OF OPTIMIZATION

Finally, it is worth mentioning one other related thread of the project (or plan) evaluation literature. This is multiobjective, or multicriteria, decision analysis, which involves a priori rejection of the notion that all project effects can meaningfully be transformed into terms of a single number—money almost always. An example of such an effect might be the distributional consequences of a project, where the fractions of costs and benefits going to particular neighborhoods or income classes are estimated. But these fractions do not translate to dollars equivalent in meaning to the efficiency benefits. The multicriteria methods, and there are many, involve supplying new, all-encompassing scales on which all the criteria *can* be measured in the same units. This might be achieved, for example, by asking the somewhat mythical "decision maker" for his or her relative weights for results along the several dimensions. Or hypothetical weights could be used to explore the sensitivity of decision to this choice. These methods may be seen as attempts to *mimic* part or all of the political choice process when alternative weights are used for outcomes that include criteria other than aggregate efficiency. Another way to proceed is to use optimization to find the "shadow prices" of, say, distributional effects, in terms of net efficiency benefits forgone at the margin. This technique might be seen as an attempt to more usefully *inform* the political process.

CONCLUSION

The purpose of this chapter has been, first, to give you some appreciation for just how simple the max $(B(R) - C(R))$ version of the environmental decision problem really is. In the process, the ideas presented in isolation in Chapter 4 have been woven into an economic model so you can see how ambient quality predictions feed benefit functions. The fact that these *functions* (not just point estimates) are required for optimization has been stressed, and the likelihood that this constitutes a serious barrier to full-blown optimization has been noted. Even when our efforts stop short of attempting to estimate benefit functions, the discussion in the chapter should remind us of several complications. First, benefits accrue because of particular combinations of natural situations, environmental quality, and human interaction with those conditions. These interactions may be more or less unavoidable, as is true for people living in many urban areas with air quality problems such as smog. Or they may result from choices made on the basis of tastes, learning, leisure, and disposable income, as in trout fishing. But, in general, place matters, in combination with what I have called the benefit route or type. In the next three chapters we shall take a much closer look at benefit estimation, to see what is involved and to try to understand why it so difficult and controversial.

NOTES

1. Stratospheric ozone *prevents* damage on the earth's surface by blocking ultraviolet radiation from the sun. Some call this "good ozone," as distinguished from the "bad" variety in urban smog. But it's all the same compound just differently located, with no way to add to the stratospheric concentration while getting rid of that at ground level.
2. Identifying "the relevant population" is a good deal harder to do than to write and will be discussed more fully in chapters 7 and 8. But for now, just note that there can be two bases for an answer. One is: Who cares about the water quality? The people who care may live either in or out of the basin and they may or may not care because they actually use the river. A second is: Whom is the government unit contemplating the quality improvement willing to count? The answer to this will generally be based on citizenship, not on caring. If basin and government units don't coincide, the citizenship requirement can be very awkward.
3. These locations are usually identified as "reaches" as noted in Chapter 4, and "perfect mixing" is usually assumed, so that water quality is assumed everywhere the same in a reach.
4. The major difficulties associated with allowing for the effects of other "competing" rivers and the shifting of use patterns in response to changes in quality will be ignored here.
5. Removal does not mean that anything disappears. It only means that the undesirable substances are either transformed to something less problematic for the environment or are transferred into a different, more easily dealt with waste stream. In wastewater treatment, the BOD organics are settled out and become "sludge," which can be burned, buried, or composted.
6. This "agreement" is usually based on some notion of the "useful life" of the facilities involved in the discharge reductions (municipal wastewater treatment plants and industrial facilities designed to deal with particular problems such as oily water or acids, or complex organic chemicals). A big simplification is usually included here, as well. It is that the facilities continue to operate as designed and built until after the horizon, when they may (or may not) just fall apart. It would be possible to build in exogenously determined declining efficiency (the cost for the same level of removal could rise over time) but this raises the possibility of intervention to raise efficiency through rehabilitation (a sort of partial investment in a new plant). And this gets perilously close to a true dynamic problem because of the choice of rehab timing and the logical link between how bad things have gotten and the cost of the rehab. (See Appendix 3.II)

7. This is also quite a bit easier to say than to accomplish, both in the sense of determining the actual cost functions and relations between fixed and variable costs, and in the sense of solving the resulting programming problem, where the choice of capacity and type of treatment is not continuous but rather involves picking one from a menu of choices. In actual examples it is often convenient to approximate the correct formulation by making the cost function into total cost, with capital charges being applied on top of variable costs in each year. If, as noted as a possibility below, raw pollution loads are also changing, however, this quick and dirty way out no longer will work. It will be necessary to solve a dynamic programming problem.

8. Computers usually have software that allows them to generate random numbers under rules that mimic different distributions, such as the equally likely one of the die or the "bell-shaped curve" of the normal distribution.

9. This could be done by what might be called brute force—simply adding up all the net benefit numbers obtained from the runs and dividing by the number of runs. This would be the observed mean and an estimate of the mean of net benefits. An alternative would be to try to "fit" the distribution of returns to a function describing a probability process—for example the "normal," bell-shaped curve—and then to take the expected value of that function.

10. Holding scale constant protects against a solution that chooses only small, highly effective actions (projects) while leaving much of the region alone because it is harder to deal with. This is a general problem with ordering choice on the basis of ratios.

11. Some writers use "least-cost analysis" as a synonym for cost-effectiveness analysis. The terminology difference is maintained here only to highlight the difference between guaranteeing that every option has the *same* physical result (LCA) and allowing for "slack" so that all the alternatives are different though none is worse than the constraint requires (cost-effectiveness analysis or CEA).

REFERENCES

Booth, William E., Paul C. Carubia, and Francis C. Lutz. 1976. *A Methodology for Comparative Evaluation of Water Quality Indices*. Washington, D.C.: Council on Environmental Quality, NIIS, PB, pp. 251–572.

Fraas, Arthur G., and Vincent G. Munley. 1984. "Municipal wastewater treatment cost." *Journal of Environmental Economics and Management* 11(1):28–38.

McClelland, Nina I. 1974. *Water Quality Index Application in the Kansas River Basin*. Washington, D.C.: U.S. EPA EPA-907/9-74-001.

DAMAGE AND BENEFIT ESTIMATION
Background and Introduction

Economists have been accused of "knowing the price of everything but the value of nothing." At the heart of this criticism is the notion that value and price are quite separate ideas. In the context of the environment this notion might be restated to say something like: We admit that shirts, haircuts, pizzas, and cars have prices, but the environment has value; putting a price on part or all of the environment would tend to destroy that value by seeming to make the environment just another thing or service we can buy. In this usage the word "value" refers to fundamental principles or ideas that we believe in and even act on. Freedom is such a value. So, for many, is religion; and for others, patriotism. Most people, confronted with a question such as, How much (in dollars) is freedom worth to you?, would find the question offensive. And that is the reaction of many people to the idea of asking similar questions about the environment, or about some closely related matters such as human health.

Yet here we are setting off on three chapters that discuss techniques for putting dollar *values* on environmental conditions—"pricing" parts of the environment. So it is worth taking a little time at the beginning to try to put this effort in context— both the practical context of policymaking and a broader context that touches on the problem of "pricing" a "value."

PRACTICAL ARGUMENTS

First, the practical. And to be intensely practical, we observe that, beginning in 1981, with then-new President Reagan and continuing into the Clinton terms, efforts to identify, quantify, and compare costs and benefits have been required of U.S. executive agencies as part of the background to major regulatory decisions. In the environment, that means, for example, that when EPA recommends National Ambient Air Quality Standard (NAAQS) changes it must accompany these with an analysis of the costs to society of meeting the standards and of the benefits of having them met, as the latter accrue via changes in human health, rates of deterioration of materials, effects on agricultural and forest production—whatever relevant results can be identified. This analysis must be done *even though* the NAAQS decision (and many others in the environment) cannot, by law, be made on the basis of such analysis but rather must usually be based on the protection of human health without reference to cost.[1] (See Chapter 2.)

So, practically speaking, presidents have thought it worthwhile to have benefits in money terms estimated for environmental policies (and for many others as well) perhaps as a rough check on where the requirements of the laws are leading us in "efficiency" terms. (The presidents have varied in the degree to which they have required a formal cost-benefit analysis and the "hardness" of the monetization requirement.) In addition, laws such as the Resource Conservation and Recovery Act of 1976, and CERCLA (Superfund) of 1980, recognize that certain actions (accidental or deliberate) of firms, farms, and individuals create damages to the environment (destroy environmental goods and services). These laws make it possible for environmental "trustees," such as state environmental agencies, and the National Oceanic and Atmospheric Agency (NOAA) to try to recover in court the money value of the "natural resource damages" caused by actions such as the spilling of oil from a barge. Since we are now talking about real money, it is hardly surprising that a good deal of effort has gone into the codification of methods for calculating such damages.

But by far the biggest and best publicized case of natural resource damages in recent U.S. history was the grounding of the Exxon Valdez in Prince William Sound, near Anchorage, Alaska. (See Box 6.1.) The "valuing" of the damages from this single incident, involving many highly skilled academic consultants on each side, undoubtedly did more to advance the state of the art of environmental valuation than any other single event before or since. Perhaps the only other influence of comparable importance was the decision, taken in the 1970s by Alan Carlin, a U.S. EPA employee, to pursue the problem of benefit estimation through a small program of grants and cooperative agreements that he controlled. In a very real sense, his interest (and bureaucratic skill) prepared the way for the CBA and damage-assessment requirements, though as we shall discover below, there remain many questions and challenges.

Finally, a more general but still tactical and practical observation. Whether or not there is an executive order in place requiring that cost-benefit analysis be done—that benefits be estimated in money terms—discussions of public policies dealing with the environment will be one-sided and, in that sense biased, if the only money figures on the table are the policies' costs. It is all very well to argue that, given a political choice of goals, all that *is* of interest is the cost of meeting those goals; and that economists can be most helpful by working on least-cost ways of meeting goals. But all too often the process by which the goals are chosen involves only assertions about physical effects and the costs of producing them. This may keep the arguments "pure" and treat the environment as a fundamental "value," but it leaves the path open to ridicule: "x hundred million dollars for a few owls? Get serious"; or "It would be cheaper to save that same number of human lives by making everyone wear seat belts when in their cars" (so let's not clean up that hazardous waste

---

Box 6.1

The Grounding of the Exxon Valdez

At about midnight on the night of 23/24 March, 1989, the Exxon Valdez, carrying over 50 million gallons of North Slope crude oil, ran aground on a reef in Prince William Sound. Tanks were ruptured and in a few hours over 20 percent of the cargo had been spilled—11 million gallons. This oil spread rapidly with wind and current and by August of that year had covered 10,000 square miles of water, contaminated over 1,000 miles of shoreline (about half the Sound's total), and killed thousands of fish and mammals, the latter including the especially photogenic seals and otters of the region.

The Sound itself is remote but accessible by boat and plane from Anchorage, Alaska's largest concentration of population. It is about the size of Chesapeake Bay, on the East Coast of the lower forty-eight states. But it is almost a wilderness, into which empty both rivers and some of the world's largest glaciers outside Greenland and Antarctica. It is popular with the Alaska coastal cruising vessels, which bring in a large number of viewers each year.

No one is quite sure what effects from the spill will endure and for how long; but its immediate effects were quite dramatically awful, with oil-soaked birds, otters, and beaches in great numbers. And, at the time, there were many predictions of very long-term damages to the underwater life of the Sound.

---

site); or "If we can farm salmon in saltwater cages, why all the fuss about making sure that wild salmon are able to travel up (and down) the rivers of the Northwest?"

I would maintain that it is better *for the environment* to be brought down off the pedestal created by the claim that nothing to do with it should be *valued* in money terms. Better to argue, as the dueling experts did in the Exxon Valdez case about valuation methods; to see on the table ranges of benefit or damage (valuation) estimates. Not that these will necessarily drive any policy decisions, for there will still be powerful symbolic and distributional forces at work. But one easy road to rhetorical victory will be closed. And, it is important to understand that, properly done, benefit or damage estimation is not biased against cleanup or preservation. Such biases *can be* created by technical choices made. But they can also be discovered and exposed. (Of course, the same goes for attempts to "help" the environment by building in bias in its favor.)

Tactical arguments are all very well, and might even persuade you that holding your nose and diving into benefit estimation is necessary. But I'd like to try to give some reasons for thinking more positively—at least less negatively—about the enterprise.

ETHICAL OBJECTIONS AND COUNTER CONSIDERATIONS

VALUING THE ENVIRONMENT?

First, we are not talking about valuing "the environment" in implied contrast to zero environment or death for us all. We are talking, instead, about situations in which we have to choose among alternative environmental states that are all stable for quite long periods and all of which permit us to continue to survive at something very close to current living standards. (In the case of damage estimation, some one's action has, in effect, chosen a new state of the environment for us and the task is to estimate how much less desirable that new state is than the status quo that preceded it: the damages.) That is, we are going to be valuing, almost always, quite small changes in the status of the environment, at least as seen in the big picture, both spatially and over time. Said one more way, the policy decisions to be informed will almost never involve conscious tinkering with the "life support" function of the natural environment—the cycling of carbon, oxygen, and nitrogen; the reintroduction of fresh water into the system via evaporation and precipitation; the cycle of growth and death of plants and animals at all scales, both of the individual organisms and of their range in the world.

As with just about every statement in this field, however, a couple of qualifications are in order. First, some potential environmental effects of human actions strike at least some observers and advocates as so important that we really *ought* to be thinking as though human life was threatened via stress on ecological systems.[2] A good part of the policy argument about global climate change—once we get by the disagreement over whether this concern has any real meaning—is over the assertion that such change will, in fact, be catastrophically damaging to human society. Second, the currently fashionable word "sustainable," and the real concern it labels, is a more general version of the notion that survival may in fact be at stake in our interactions with the environment. To the extent this is true, the techniques to be described below, and the arguments to be made on their behalf in the rest of this introduction, have to be examined very closely to make sure that extreme possibilities really are reflected in them.[3] Third, the more extreme the possible future situations the more uncomfortable we may very well be with money damages. Even market prices and people's subjective judgments about "value" will be changed by large changes in ecosystem values. And since all valuation methods start either from indirect information from markets or direct statements from people about the values they attach to environmental changes, there is no longer any unshifting ground on which to stand in doing damage estimation. Finally, though, it should be said that there seems to be a tendency on the part of some advocates for the environment to equate ignorance of future effects with "huge" or "incalculable." This becomes just another way of putting the environment back on its pedestal, now because it is too important to life rather than because it is "special" in the same sense as freedom or patriotism. We should be skeptical of this rhetorical device, too.

Isn't Something Being Left Out?

Related to the problem of ignorance raised just above is the notion that there is (must be) something "left out" of damage and benefit estimation. This "something" is not the life-support function already discussed, but rather something reflecting what is seen as the *intrinsic importance* of natural systems and the organisms that make them up. Here "intrinsic" means independent of human values. Economists tend to find this puzzling, focusing as we do on human society. And trying to assess the philosophical basis for the claim of a "value" that has nothing to do with humans would carry me quickly out of my depth and the text away from its goals. But let me suggest that one source of this discomfort may be traced to the fact that much of our knowledge of environmental problems and their solutions comes from stories and pictures, especially pictures, that show us the effects of human actions on identifiable individual animals (even plants, especially if these are large and old). It is troubling to think that, if we do a benefit calculation and fail to persuade the political world to protect those plants or animals, we have somehow become accomplices in harming them. The problem here seems to me close to one that is central to health-care policy problems. Thus, when a particular person is seriously ill, no one (or almost no one/almost nowhere) argues about the costs and benefits of treatment. (Similarly, no expense is spared to save seagulls, otters, and other identifiable individual animals caught by an oil spill.) But that does not rule out public discussion and policymaking on the a priori (or ex ante/before) basis, when sickness is a statistical risk, of the "value" of certain life-saving screening, inoculation, and chronic treatment regimes in health care. For example, we decide which of these will be offered free to certain populations, which will be covered under health maintenance organizations' rules in U.S. work places, and so on. When we try to live with a priori rules for treatments, however, we run into the identifiable individual problem—a particular woman has breast cancer and wants bone-marrow treatment that is not "covered" by her insurance. Her case becomes news, probably results in a lawsuit in the United States, and the "rule" almost never can be maintained.

So—we can have these conversations and do the calculations for nature in general, even for specific types or locations of systems. But we are *not* able to maintain the position that an identifiable otter should be sacrificed on the altar of industrial expansion. This is why pictures of people "saving" a particular tree from the chain saw are so effective as images.

Current or Future Generations' "Values"?

It is also argued quite vigorously that it is wrong to base values on the current generation's preferences. Because: (a) we won't be the ones who benefit or are damaged, and (b) our preferences have, in any case, been manipulated by advertising and are no longer "pure" or "valid." This tends to get mixed up with the problem of "discounting" as well. Again, we are getting close to some very deep issues. But let me observe that we have no firm and comprehensive knowledge of future generations' preferences. We can guess some general things, of course, for example, that they will share our preference for being alive over being dead; that at least some significant fraction will "value" the natural world highly; that they will also like their creature comforts (being warm, eating well, listening to music). Altogether, we can guess that they will be much like us, and we can hardly do better than to adopt a kind of Kantian imperative or golden rule. Thought of another way, we should *not foreclose options for future generations casually*. A major problem, however, will always be to convince each other that project *j* forecloses more options than it opens, or vice versa.

About manipulation. Again we have an unsettleable dispute. Who gets to decide what constitutes purity/validity and what is manipulation/invalidity? Is, for example, the desire to use resources up in traveling to experience other climates and cultures a *valid* preference (or "taste" as economists often say)? What about the taste for larger rather than smaller living spaces, for meat in combination with grains and vegetables, rather than the latter alone? Note also that what we might call "counter manipulation" is possible, and indeed prevalent; if we characterize commercial advertising as "manipulation." Thus, we are persuading ourselves (we are being persuaded by some among us) that it is not socially acceptable to buy furniture made from wild tropical hardwoods—that a forestry certification process should be used and consulted to make sure that a chair or table comes from a "sustainable" harvest regime. (See Chapter 10 for more discussion of information as an instrument of public policy.)

Having now spent rather a long time on acknowledging the existence of deep ethical objections to "valuation of the environment," and having tried to encourage you to think that matters here are not simple, not black versus white, it is time to take on a few of the misunderstandings about economics itself that help to energize those who object to benefit and damage estimation and monetization.

SOME IMPORTANT MISUNDERSTANDINGS ABOUT ECONOMICS

THE MARKET BIAS

It is often maintained by critics of valuation efforts that economists, obsessed as they are by markets, simply ignore all "values" not captured by market prices. In the environmental context, this means ignoring everything but:

1. Resource commodities, such as lumber, fish caught commercially, and electricity made using the energy in falling water
2. A few privatized services, where this privatization has been accomplished. Examples are the rights to fish and hunt, especially in Europe, but more and more in the United States.

Comments

In fact, nothing could be further from the truth. Most applied fields of microeconomics are dominated by questions about market *failures* and how to deal with them. Environmental economics in particular is perhaps 60 to 70 percent "about" valuing *nonmarketed* environmental goods and services.

THE BIAS AGAINST THE FUTURE

Another line of criticism is that economics is "biased" against the future because:

1. As already noted, it uses current-generation values (preferences) in its calculations;
2. It condones, indeed requires, discounting of future flows of costs and benefits (even if these have *not* been monetized.

Comments

As has already been discussed (Appendix 3.I), discounting can be shown to be required for consistent decision making when the economy in general is "productive." That is, if investment of resources today (in technology, agriculture, knowledge, whatever) will produce more resources tomorrow than were invested, then *not* discounting future returns or costs will lead to bad decisions. If the foreseen ecological damage is, in fact, so severe that future productivity in this sense *cannot* be assumed, then discounting will not be justified.

It is also worth noting that discounting works two ways. If the contemplated possible damage is merely large (and distant in time) and not destructive of the entire system, it is possible in a productive economy to invest a small amount today and thus create a large fund in the future that could be used to repair or compensate for the damage.

I have already talked a bit about the use of current preferences—as a matter of necessity. Here one additional point might be made. Part of the preference set of present generations is saving for the future—for retirement and for the welfare of children and of children's children. Current generations are not totally selfish in the temporal sense, though some may think that collectively we could be more generous with the future.

THE PROBLEM OF IGNORANCE

Since neither economics nor ecology are as yet all that good either at prediction or the valuation of the predicted situation, aren't we asking for big trouble by basing decisions in any way on the result of their combined efforts at damage or benefit estimation?

Comments

First, it may sound too flippant, but is none the less relevant: We cannot avoid ignorance about the future, though as understanding of natural systems and their reactions to human-caused disruptions improves, we may narrow the range of uncertainty. We can make analytical efforts today to capture the current range of uncertainty and allow for it in decision making.

Second, if there is a bias in current economic methods it is likely to be toward *over*estimating future benefits or damages. (See Chapter 8 on "direct" valuation methods.)

In any event, there is a range of situations for which valuation may be desired. The techniques are better for some parts of this range than for others. The implication ought to be to become more wary as you move from the former to latter regions. Examples from this range in increasing difficulty are:

1. Preserving or managing a familiar, local place—park, wetland, beach, forest
2. Setting a policy for managing all such places in a region or for separating such places into groups to be managed differently
3. Setting a general goal, such as ambient environmental quality (degree of pollution we experience in everyday life) or no net-loss of wetlands, or no net increase in world CO_2

An Observation
Another dimension of importance is the spatial extent of the goal, which implies something about diversity of beneficiaries.

4. Evaluating a complex law with several interlocking parts—several interrelated goals, for example, air pollution control, where there may be air quality standards as well as rules about different treatment of old and new technology, and "blind spots" (e.g., the early U.S. Clean Air Act concentrated wholly on local SO_2, and particulates, etc. The building of tall stacks was actually encouraged. These made the acid rain problem greater.)

SOME POSSIBLE BASES FOR VALUING ENVIRONMENTAL GOODS AND SERVICES

The reason we have to talk about this subject at all is that many environmental goods and services—indeed, most of the ones that people worry about when they discuss "environmental quality"—are not traded in markets. So we can forget about there being an easy method based on market prices—*except* where a few commodities are concerned: timber, electricity from falling water, fish when harvested commercially[4]; or where specialized rights have been established as they have for recreational hunting and fishing in the United Kingdom, Sweden, and Norway, for example. This is not to say that markets hold no potentially useful information, however. One of the two major categories of benefit estimation technique makes use of such information indirectly—by filtering it through techniques that tease out the implications for the values of related environmental goods or services.

Another possible route to inferences about benefits that may already have occurred to readers is via the costs of politically chosen levels of quality or programs that preserve features of the environment. The idea here boils down to this: If a policy or program has been chosen by the political system (legislature plus regulatory agency, in some combination), then we ought to be able to infer that the benefits outweigh the costs. And since we can estimate the costs much more straightforwardly than the benefits, we can find at least a "lower bound" for benefits quite easily.

The problem with this attractive idea lies in the basis for the inference that benefits exceed costs. There is no such guarantee in democratic politics, where the distribution of benefits and costs and the symbolism of programs weigh at least as heavily as totals in the decision process. Three simple examples illustrating this concept are set out in Box 6.2. The bottom line is that no inferences can be drawn about the aggregate benefits of a policy, program, or project and their relation to its total cost, just because it has been undertaken in a democratic society.

A related but distinct suggestion, regularly made when difficult estimation/monetization problems are faced—as they are, for example, where health effects, even death, are part of the results of a policy—is to look to court decisions in cases

---

Box 6.2

Distribution vs. Efficiency When Outcomes Are Determined by a Majority of Yes/No Votes and Voters Are Rational

Consider two simple examples that show there is no necessary connection between success in a vote and aggregate efficiency (benefits exceeding costs). Tables 6.1 through 6.3 show the benefits accruing to and the costs incurred by the three voter citizens in a tiny "nation." It is assumed that each citizen votes in accordance with his/her projected net benefits. Policy 1 succeeds in a vote because two of the three voters are benefited by it. But it fails the $B - C > 0$ test (efficiency test) because the third voter really does very badly out of the policy (see Table 6.1). Policy 2 fails

TABLE 6.1 A Project That Fails the Benefit-Cost Test but Passes in a Vote

	Voters			
	A	**B**	**C**	**A+B+C**
Policy (1)				
Benefits	6	8	2	16
Costs	5	4	10	19
Net benefits	1	4	−8	−3
Votes	Yes	Yes	No	2 yes/1 no

TABLE 6.2 A Project That Passes the Benefit-Cost Test but Fails in a Vote

	Voters			
	D	**E**	**F**	**D+E+F**
Policy (2)				
Benefits	5	5	5	15
Costs	7	1	6	14
Net benefits	−2	4	−1	1
Votes	No	Yes	No	1 yes/2 no

a vote but passes the efficiency test (see Table 6.2). In this case the positive net benefit of the "winner" is sufficient to offset the negatives suffered by the other voters when the aggregates are looked at but not when only votes count.

Just to round out this thought, consider a pair of projects, neither of which can pass a majority vote and both of which are inefficient. It is still possible that by swapping votes ("log rolling") *both* policies could pass a vote (see Table 6.3). So, in effect, H agrees to vote for #3 and J to vote for #4 as a trade that buys #4 for H and #3 for J. This is a schematic of how many water projects, each individually and all collectively inefficient, could have come to be built in the western United States.

TABLE 6.3 An Example of Log-rolling to Get Two Inefficient Projects Passed in a Vote

	Voters			
	H	**I**	**J**	**H+I+J**
Policy (3)				
Benefits	1	2	10	13
Costs	5	5	5	15
Net benefits	−4	−3	5	−2
Votes on 3 alone	No	No	Yes	1 yes/2 no
Policy (4)				
Benefits	11	2	3	16
Costs	6	6	6	18
Net benefits	5	−4	−3	−2
Votes on 4 alone	Yes	No	No	1 yes/2 no
(3) & (4) Together				
Benefits	12	4	13	29
Costs	11	11	11	33
Net benefits	1	−7	2	−4
Votes	Yes	No	Yes	2 yes/1 no

where money damages and compensation are assessed. Again, the basic justification is roughly that the courts reflect and focus social concerns, whether the amounts involved are determined by judges or juries. But there seem to be two difficulties here for the would-be benefit estimator. First, and most telling, court cases are always decided after the fact of the damage or injury and usually involve identifiable individuals or small groups as injured parties. As already discussed, society's attitudes toward specific individuals are usually dramatically different from its attitudes toward "statistical" individuals—the additional unidentified people out of one million who *might* on average suffer a disease in any year because some action has been taken (or not taken). A second difficulty, of growing importance I would guess, is that judges and juries are often given information about what experts (including environmental economists where appropriate) believe the damages are worth and why. To the extent it is true, the process of using court awards to value damages becomes a tail-chasing exercise—all we find out is what we already knew, and that filtered through the emotional and procedural machinery of a trial.

THE HEART OF THE ECONOMIC APPROACH

Economists generally accept the proposition that people are willing to trade money for changes in environmental quality—to pay something for more of a desired change; to accept compensation for suffering an undesired change. So, in principle, for every affected individual and every quality change there is assumed to be a discoverable schedule of marginal willingness to pay (MWTP) for a "good" or marginal willingness to accept (MWTA) for a "bad." For a group of people who constitute the relevant decision group for an environmental quality change, there will be an aggregate schedule. Since environmental goods and services are almost always public—in the technical, economic sense we discussed in Chapter 3—the aggregate schedule usually represents the *vertical sum* of the individual functions. (That is, for any given quantity of the good or service, the marginal willingness to pay of all the consumers of the good are added to get a social or aggregate MWTP schedule.) The trick is to find either the individual schedules or the aggregate schedule itself in the absence of directly relevant market data.

As with nearly every proposition in the benefit estimation area, several qualifiers and warning flags are in order after just that simple introductory paragraph. First, while people may in principle be willing to pay for environmental quality, they may never have thought about the proposition in any particular case. The less familiar and more subtle the environmental change, the less likely randomly chosen individuals are to have any sort of WTP notion in their heads. We shall return to this qualification in Chapter 8 when we talk about techniques for asking people about their WTP directly. A second set of difficulties is concealed beneath the seemingly innocent phrase "the relevant decision group." For almost any significant environmental quality policy question—be it about damages from an oil spill, benefit from an ambient quality standard, or the counterbalancing effects from changing the management rules for a publicly owned forest—this relevant group will be hard to identify in advance. Where there are users, they of course will count and will, again in principle, be possible to identify. Those who care but do not use will, however, be difficult to find. (Actually, the problem may be one of *limiting* the asserted group of caring nonusers.) And yet they may be willing to pay in aggregate a substantial amount to maintain, preserve, change, or whatever the resource or place they care about. This question of "the extent of the market" (though there is no market in the usual sense) often will have to be discovered as the benefit or damage estimation procedure rolls along, or even after it is complete, when the data can be analyzed. This point will also come up again in later discussions. Finally, we have to recognize that willingness to pay and willingness to accept compensation are only as symmetric as they sound when we are talking theory. In practice, it has proved extremely difficult to obtain persuasive estimates of WTA in situations when this is the correct concept (for example, when a de facto property "right" to a particular environmental situation is to be violated, as when a new airport will be built and the runway glide paths will pass over or near existing houses).

But for now, let us go on with some basics to clear the way for discussions of actual techniques when the qualifications will reappear in less abstract form. And the most basic of the basics is the diagram in Figure 6.1 in which WTP and WTA are defined for a given individual, with a given income, facing a given, unpriced, quality change (but with alternative starting points). (This was seen already in Chapter 3.)

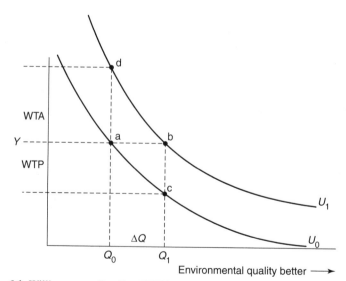

Figure 6.1 Willingness to Pay For (WTP) and to Accept (WTA) Changes in the Quantity of an Unpriced Good

	Utility	Income	Quality
a:	U_0	Y	Q_0
b:	U_1	Y	Q_1
c:	U_0	$Y - \text{WTP}$	Q_1
d:	U_1	$Y + \text{WTA}$	Q_0

Here, Y is given income; ΔQ, the quality change; and U_0 and U_1, indifference curves (equal utility schedules) for combinations of money income and environmental quality. Points (a) and (c) are both on U_0. The differences between them are offsetting changes in Q (improvement of ΔQ) and income (payment of WTP). Analogously for (b) and (d). If the individual starts at (b) and is to suffer a loss of quality, ΔQ, compensation of WTA will keep the person on the same indifference curve. Because of the shapes of the indifference curves (the usual shape from microtheory's foundations) WTA > WTP will be true.[5]

Notice that there is no price for quality here. The price is zero because Q is a public good. So there are no tangencies. The consumer does not pick a consumption level for Q, to maximize utility for given prices and subject to an income constraint. Rather, the combination of given (by the political system, or some other machinery) Q_0 and given income implies a level of utility. (The rest of the maximization exercise involving private goods can be thought of as going on in the background. This becomes relevant to damage and benefit estimation because it is the basis for the *indirect* methods to be described below.) For now we can think of the fundamental definitional graph as the basis for asking the consumer WTP or WTA questions of the form:

- How great a reduction in income could you accept and remain as well off as you are now if current environmental conditions were improved by ΔQ (with, of course, great care being taken to describe the relevant features of the "current conditions" and the contemplated improvement)? or

- By how much would your income have to be increased (how much compensation would you require) to stay as well off as you are now if current environmental conditions were made less attractive (desirable, healthy, . . .) by the amount ΔQ?

It is worth noting, however, that even if we get useful answers to such questions (and there is substantial dispute on this point, which will be taken up in Chapter 8) we still have not connected ourselves back to the MWTP basis for valuation. We do not, in other words, have an estimate of the MWTP function for the environmental good in question. To see what we do have in terms of the MWTP diagram, consider Figure 6.2. We have the area (total WTP) under the MWTP function between Q_0 and Q_1. That area could reflect a steep or relatively flat MWTP schedule. (Three alternatives are sketched in the diagram. These are all linear, but there is no reason to require or assume linearity.) Among other things, this means we have no basis for extrapolation outside the range attached to the question. This will be a problem in

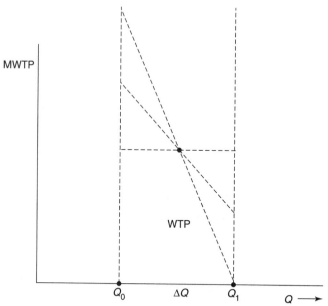

Figure 6.2 Contrasting Marginal Willingness to Pay (MWTP) Functions Consistent with a Given Total Willingness to Pay (WTP) Estimate

practice with most of the techniques for benefit estimation. We will be observing the effect of asking about one or a few quality changes, and while we may be able to assume a functional form that implies something about levels or changes not observed or not asked about, we will not be able to put very much weight on those implications for most purposes. (See Box 6.3 for a reminder of the connection between damages and benefits.)

BENEFIT "ROUTES": A BRIEF REVIEW

In Chapter 5, the discussion of benefit-cost analysis of environmental policies and projects stressed that one of the complicating features of these problem settings is that the benefits of prospective or actual environmental change accrue to society in different places and via different routes. Recreation, health, aesthetics, and effects on materials were all mentioned as examples of such routes.

The description of the "water quality ladder" in Chapter 5 elaborated on the connection between ambient water quality and recreation as the basis for benefits. That is, as water quality improves, more highly valued varieties of recreation become possible (and none is ruled out), and a day spent doing any one (or several) activity(ies) is valued more highly. For example, if the water were dirty enough you wouldn't even want to float on it in a boat. At some cleanup level you could imagine boating on it. At higher levels of quality, fishing becomes possible (in the senses

---

Box 6.3

Damages and Benefits
(A Reminder)

The WTA notion just defined applies to a situation in which a future reduction in environmental quality is contemplated, and in such a situation it measures the (money) damages to be created by the reduction. But much environmental policy, and thus much environmental benefit-cost analysis, involves changing things by making the situation better. In those cases, benefits are often best thought of (and measured) as damages avoided. Thus think of a situation in which pollution, P, causes damage, $D(P)$ (in $ per year). If we knew $D(P)$ (with $dD/dP > 0$), the damage function, and if the existing pollution level is $P_0 > P_1$, then a useful and natural definition of the benefits of a policy to reduce P from P_0 to P_1 (ΔP) would be:

$$B(\Delta P) = D(P_0) - D(P_1)$$

Graphically for a hypothetical $D(P)$, the relation is as shown in Figure 6.3. This observation does not solve any of the tough problems, because obtaining D(P) will be just as hard as going directly to a MWTP function for reductions in P. But sometimes we will have data relevant to damages. And, in any case, it is useful to be clear about the conceptual relations here.

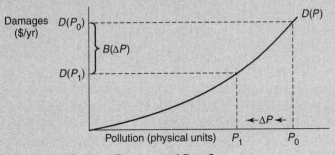

Figure 6.3 The Relation Between Damages and Benefits

that there are fish to catch and that you can stand the closer water contact implied by fishing).

The health route to benefits involves reducing the harmful effects of ambient environmental quality on human health status—reducing incidents of diseases traceable to water contact, reducing the number and severity of respiratory problems traceable (at least statistically) to pollutants in the air, those sorts of things.

Aesthetics is a broad label for changes in how the environment looks and smells to us. A river covered with an oil sheen or with, as they say, ugly floating solids, is much less valuable as a prospect than one not so burdened. Looking at a "brown cloud" of urban gaseous pollutants to the west of Denver is a lot less fun than looking at the front range of the Rockies.

Materials being used by people can be damaged by pollution and thus have shorter lives—require more frequent replacement. For example, acid rain damages rain gutters on houses; ozone damages tires; salt in ambient water can damage equipment when the water is withdrawn for treatment and use in industry or municipalities; and soot-fall leads at least to more frequent need to clean up surfaces and may also shorten the lives of surface finishes such as house and auto paint.

Such routes, where the environment is more or less useful to humans, are generally referred to by the label "use values," or even "direct use values." Another category of use value is recognized in situations when the policy or action is aimed at some environmental condition that has both direct and more roundabout effects. For example, a policy or project might be aimed at protecting a coral reef from destructive pollution. The reef has direct use value to those who snorkel or dive on it or who fish around it. But it also might protect a beach from the sea, and the beach itself is more useful when it is protected than if it were to be exposed to more wave action. The additional use value of the beach could be seen as an indirect use value of protecting the reef.

As noted in Chapter 5, *non*users of some part of the environment may also receive benefits from its preservation or enhancement. These benefits may accrue because the people value the *knowledge* that part of the environment is in better shape. An example might be that people in Europe and North America value the knowledge that the great animal herds of East Africa are being better protected from poachers, or that parts of the Indonesian and Malaysian rain forests are being spared from the chain saw, even though they have no intention of ever going to visit either one and have no very clear idea that either will be indirectly useful to them.[6] This knowledge-based benefit is sometimes called an "existence" benefit. It can also apply to less exotic objects. For example, you could value the knowledge that the United States is protecting features of its environment, such as wilderness, because you think that is how a responsible nation should behave.

A distinction is usually drawn between this "pure" existence value and something called "bequest" value, where the motivation is a concern for future generations, not the current one. Notice that this route to value depends entirely on some poorly defined mix of concern for one's descendants and everyone else's descendants and therefore is, to some extent, altruistic. This gives a name and a bit more substance to the point made above, that the current generation may be more selfish than you would like, but is recognized as not entirely selfish, even by economists.

The last route to benefits, with its concern for the future—which is always uncertain—suggests the possibility that people might be willing to pay for resolution of that uncertainty. Roughly speaking, this idea gave birth to the notion of "option value" as another route to benefits. There is now a general consensus in the economics literature that option values are not a separate form of value but represent a difference between ex ante and ex post valuation. If an individual is uncertain about the future value of a wetland but believes it may be high or that current exploitation and conversion may be irreversible, then there may be *quasi-option* value derived from delaying the development activities. Quasi-option value is simply the expected value of the information derived from delaying exploitation and conversion of the wetland today. Again, there is consensus that quasi-option value is not a separate component of benefit but involves the analyst properly accounting for the implications of gaining additional information. "I think it is time to expunge option value from the list of possible benefits associated with environmental protection" (as Freeman put it in the latest revision of his classic book on benefit estimation, *The Measurement of Environmental and Resource Values: Theory and Methods*, 1993, p. 264).

The sum of all the "values" predicted to be produced by an environmental policy or project is often referred to as "total economic value."

The next two chapters will deal with the two major methods of obtaining benefit (or damage) estimates:

- *Indirect*, in Chapter 7, in which market reactions traceable to changes in environmental quality are exploited for the information they contain about willingness to pay for those changes. That is, the environmental changes may leave "footprints" in markets from which we can infer something about WTP for the change.

- *Direct*, in Chapter 8, in which hypothetical questions of the type set out above are constructed and asked directly of a sample of relevant "consumers" of the environmental good in question.

Not surprisingly, we shall find that each approach has strengths and weaknesses so that there is no obviously best way to proceed, though the flexibility and inclusiveness of the direct methods seem to me to make them the more promising as a place to put methodological investment.

CONCLUSION AND REMINDERS

This chapter has been aimed at persuading you that estimating money values for aspects of the environment is both practically useful and defensible in principle. I have stressed under the practical label that such valuation is, in fact, required in the United States by executive order, even when the information cannot, by statute, be used as the basis for decision. I have also noted that when we do not try to value benefits or damages in money terms we leave a large hole in the policy argument, a hole that invites rhetorical exploitation. In the matter of principle, I have tried to argue that we are not up to the devil's work when we do damage and benefit estimation: our ignorance does not imply a bias "against" the environment; we are not committing ourselves to ignore specific individual problems as and when they occur; while we are stuck with our own preferences for practical reasons, our methods are

TABLE 6.4 A Preliminary Look at Choice of Method

	Reactions to Environment	
	Cause Transactions or Actions That Can Be Priced	**Do Not Involve Actions or Transactions but Only Changes in Mental States**
Benefits arise from use	Indirect methods exploit the transactions (e.g., travel to fish; buy a different house; repair house gutters more often)	Direct methods might be used but this may be a very small category (e.g., backyard bird watching; looking at a view while on a trip for another purpose)
Benefits arise from knowledge and concern, not use	Indirect methods might conceivably be used, but many problems make success improbable (e.g., using contributions to environmental groups)	Direct methods can, in principle, be used (e.g., knowledge that rain forests are being preserved in another country)

not egregiously biased against the future, both because we care about our descendants and because discounting arises from the productivity of investment, not from a silly bias.

Further, the chapter included discussion of some possible bases for inferring environmental values and rejected the idea that political votes or judicial decisions can be used this way. Instead, we have to go back to the notion of individual WTP or WTA and to look for ways to discover these values. A fairly brief discussion of where we can look, and what difficulties we can expect, closed the chapter proper. Table 6.4 puts these ideas in a framework contrasting, first, situations in which markets are involved, via either clear or implied transactions, with situations in which markets are lacking more or less entirely; and, second, the use versus nonuse dichotomy. Perhaps the overarching thing to take away from the table is that where there are transactions, even implied ones, it is usually possible to devise ways to use the information they contain. The resulting "indirect" methods are discussed next, in Chapter 7. Where no transactions occur, other methods must be used. These are the "direct" methods, the subject of Chapter 8.

NOTES

1. This applies to the "primary" NAAQS. "Secondary" standards may be tougher and have a broader basis, but that basis still does not involve balancing costs and monetized benefits.
2. I note in passing that a group of ecologists and economists gathered in June 1996 to attempt to answer the question: What is the value of the world ecosystem? At least one of the participants has said that she saw the exercise as a "warning shot" across the bow of industrial society; a statement of what we might be in a position to destroy if we do not take care because our disruptive power is now so massive.

3. There also may be discomfort with taking expected values and with discounting the future when possible outcomes are extreme. See Chapter 13 for a description of some alternatives developed by economists to help us think about decisions in such situations.

4. As it happens these commodity values are frequently what is *given up* in return for enhanced quality in a broader sense, as when a forest is "preserved" from logging for recreation or to protect one or more plant or wildlife species; or when a dam is not built so that a salmon spawning run can continue unimpeded.

5. This is a simplified version of the presentation to be found, for example, in Myrick Freeman's *The Measurement of Environmental and Resource Values: Theory and Methods* (1993), where the complex edifice, traceable back to the English economist Sir John Hicks, is set out in a much more complete way.

6. As this statement implies, you could also value the rain forest, for example, because you thought it might someday reveal useful drugs from some of its exotic species, or because it plays a role in tying up carbon that might otherwise become part of the increasing CO_2 concentrations in the earth's atmosphere. We might call these valuation bases uncertain use values. Ways of dealing with this difficult problem are discussed in Chapter 13.

REFERENCES

Freeman, A. Myrick. 1993. *The Measurement of Environmental and Resource Values: Theory and Methods*. Washington, D.C.: Resources for the Future.

7

INDIRECT BENEFIT ESTIMATION

There is a substantial amount of ingenuity involved in, first, identifying the places in which indirect effects of environmental quality changes might be found in market data; second, in providing the theoretical underpinnings for interpreting these effects in the benefit estimation context; and third, in doing the actual measurement, which almost always requires very large quantities of data (often not quite the "right" data) and poses tricky econometric problems. This chapter will describe four types of methods and point out the conceptual relations among them. Along the way, some of their problems and shortcomings will be described. But it is important to make clear up front that the great collective advantage, especially in the eyes of economists, of these methods is that they are based on interpreting the actual decisions made by consumers. Said slightly differently, they are based on *revealed preferences*. The "direct" methods are, in these terms, based on *stated preferences* and hypothetical decisions. (But see Box 7.1 for an elaboration of this two-way distinction.) Because the indirect methods had this basic credential they tended to get by far the greater share of the methodological investment, at least until the mid to late 1980s. This produced fairly well-developed sets of general rules and procedures for their application, though many important choices at the nitty-gritty level are still matters of craft or art rather than of following scientifically determined steps. Even so, if it were true that to every benefit question there were an indirect-method answer, the world of environmental economics would be a lot more straightforward but probably less interesting.

DEMAND SHIFTS: COMPLEMENTARITY

The intuition behind this subset of methods is roughly as follows: Improvements in environmental quality can make marketed goods to which the environment is complementary more attractive. Examples that might occur even to someone only casually interested in the environment are: boats and fishing equipment as related to water quality; houses with views as related to the aspects of air quality that affect visibility; hiking and camping equipment as related to the availability of public forests and wilderness.

Box 7.1

A Slightly More Elaborate Typology of Benefit Estimation Methods

The body of the text divides these methods into direct and indirect, on the basis of the distinction between indirectly inferring values from related market data and directly asking for the values from those presumed to hold them. If we also take account of a separate distinction between observed behavior and hypothetical responses to hypothetical questions, we come up with the four-way distinction among methods shown in the Table 7.1. The major reason for this elaboration is the growing interest of environmental economists in the comparison methods of the lower right-hand box. These involve asking survey respondents to do such tasks as rank a number of vectors of characteristics of a situation but do not involve straightforward questions asking some version of, "What is your willingness to pay (WTP) for the described situation?" They have been used by marketing researchers and transportation economists for some time. The distinction between those survey methods and the ones in the upper right-hand box (usually labeled the "Contingent Valuation Method" or "CVM") is that the latter ask directly for a statement of WTP, while in the former WTP must be inferred from the information in the vectors and the ranks or preference statements supplied. I will return to all this in Chapter 8.

TABLE 7.1 Distinctions Among Benefit Estimation Methods

	Based on	
	Observed Behavior	**Hypothetical Responses**
Direct information on willingness to pay	Market values of environmental commodities (not discussed further)	"Traditional" contingent valuation methods (Chapter 8)
Willingness to pay must be inferred from indirect data	Methods of using data from related markets (Chapter 7)	Applications of comparison methods (often called "conjoint analysis" collectively) (Chapter 8)

Three methods for exploiting such relationships are:

- weak complementarity (see Box 7.2.)
- hedonics
- hedonic travel cost (this will be discussed in the travel cost section)

They are distinguished by the market settings in which they are used.

Box 7.2

Complementarity

A market good, X, and some measure of environmental quality, Q, are complementary if the demand for X, where the amount demanded is X, is given by

$$X = X(P, Q, M)$$

(with P a price vector and M, income) such that $\partial X/\partial Q > 0$, and higher Q means improved quality.

"Weak" complementarity involves two additional conditions. First, there must be a price such that demand for X can be driven to zero and yet utility can still be maintained at the status quo–level, U_0. If we use X_c to stand for compensated demand quantities, then this condition requires that

$$X_C(P_X^*, Q, U_0) = 0$$

for some P_X^* that is sufficiently high. (I focus on the P_X element of P. Other prices are assumed not to change.)

The other condition is that when $P_X \geq P_X^*$, the MWTP for changes in Q is zero. That is, when X is not being consumed, changes in quality, Q, do not matter. These conditions allow the method of using compensated demand curves sketched in the text to produce the full benefit of a change in Q.

"WEAK COMPLEMENTARITY"

The first, weak complementarity, was probably the first theoretically fully developed method for getting at environmental benefits. (It is usually associated with Karl-Göran Mäler, whose pathbreaking 1974 book *Environmental Economics* established many fundamental results in theory.) The idea is that an improvement in environmental quality shifts the *compensated* demand function for the weakly complementary good up, increasing the surplus associated with the existence of that good. This is shown graphically in Figure 7.1, where Q_0 is the quality before the improvement and Q_1 the quality after it. This method has been generalized to more than one weakly complementary good—as with water quality and several forms of water-based recreation.

It is also worth noting that the same analysis can be done with ordinary demand functions, but the result in general will not equal the correct, benchmark value based on the compensated demand functions. Graphically, for linear demand functions and a fixed market price, p_0, see Figure 7.2. The compensated demand functions, $X_{C'}(\ )$, is steeper and does not shift as far right when Q improves, because the purpose of compensation is to reduce income to hold utility constant at the base level U_0, corresponding to p_0, X_0, and M_0. The change in consumer surplus (the area between

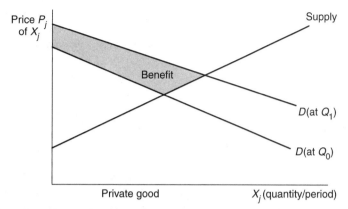

Figure 7.1 Effect of an Improvement in Environmental Quality on the Demand for a Complementary Good. *D*, demand; *Q*, quality.

the ordinary demand curves) is $a + b + c$. The benchmark measure of the value of the change is $b + d$. The difference is $a + c - d$, and its size and sign depend on the details of the situation. So use of ordinary demand relations introduces error, but how much and what direction will depend on the specific case.

I shall return later to the general problem of finding all (and only all) the benefits of a change in environmental quality via indirect methods such as the one just described. But at this point it may occur to some readers that if consumption of X (or of several Xs) increases due to an improvement in Q, that must mean something for expenditures—and hence surpluses—for other goods and services. Why don't the calculations of the net change show a wash—a zero net addition to total surplus

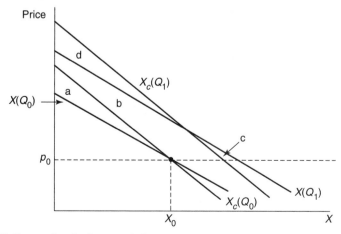

Figure 7.2 Contrasting Ordinary and Compensated Demand Functions in the Situation of Environmentally Induced Shifts. See text for explanation of symbols.

across all goods and services? In fact, computable general equilibrium models have been and are being used to measure the net benefits of policies, at least in the research sense. These models trace not only the full set of adjustments on the demand side but on the supply or cost side as well (at least insofar as their inevitably simple structure permits). For our purposes, however, the intuition behind the partial equilibrium methods is that while the main adjustments to a nonmarginal ΔQ, such as those in demand for complementary goods, will be nonmarginal, the secondary adjustments following from those demand shift effects will be spread across all other goods and services and thus can be ignored as a first approximation.

Hedonic Price Analysis

The second major indirect benefit or damage estimation method based on demand shifts is called, in the jargon shorthand of the profession, "hedonics." This label, while not especially helpful for either memory or understanding, comes from a considerably older thread in the national accounting literature in which prices of marketed goods (or services) are analyzed to disentangle the effects of changes in the many separate characteristics that together define particular variants of each good or service. The purpose for which this analysis was first proposed was to provide a basis for adjusting the national accounts for changes in the *quality* of a good or service between two periods when the name (and usually the fundamental purpose served) did not change.

Thus, between 1950, say, and 1990 the characteristic of the good called the automobile changed dramatically. Comfort, acceleration, gasoline consumption per mile, sound system, interior noise level, and exhaust system are just a few of the areas in which an "average" car in 1990 would differ from one in 1950. The price of the former would presumably also differ from that of the latter, *after* correcting for intervening inflation. This difference would at least in part be accounted for by the difference in quality—in characteristics. Any price difference remaining after factoring out quality changes would represent a real change in the relative price of the "same" car at the two times and could be used as part of a calculation of the real value of consumption in either period.

The technique requires a great deal of information. In the car example, it is necessary to have price and quality (characteristics) data for many different combinations of the characteristics. With those data, an equation can be estimated of the form:

$$P_i = f(z_{1i}, z_{2i}, \ldots, z_{Ni}) \tag{7.1}$$

where P_i is the price of the ith variant of good or service, x, in question, and $\{z_{1i}, \ldots, z_{Ni}\}$ is the vector of the N characteristics that are supposed to determine the price of x. So, if there are dozens of characteristics there would have to be hundreds of observations on price-quality combinations to allow for econometric inference of the equation coefficients. This equation allows you to "predict" the price of a car with any mix of the z characteristics—those of 1950 or of 1990, or of a date in between.

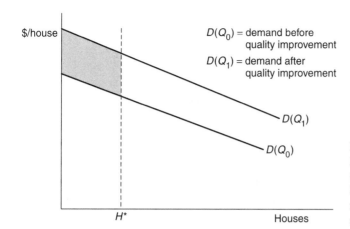

Figure 7.3 A Shift in the Marginal Willingness to Pay (WTP) for a Given Housing Stock Due to an Environmental Improvement. H^*, size of housing market.

In 1974, Sherwin Rosen suggested that this technique could be extended to include among the characteristics those relevant to environmental quality (Rosen, 1974). For example, we might well expect to find that, everything else equal, the price of a house will vary with changes in the air quality that surrounds the house. More specifically, we expect that relevant environmental quality improvements will shift demand up just as in the section on weak complementarity, for that is what is at stake here.[1] But, in the case of housing, the shift does not cause people to buy more houses. Each family (generally) will continue to own (or rent) one house. But they will be willing to pay more for that house. One can visualize this part of the argument as in Figure 7.3, analogous to that presented for complementarity more generally. Here H^* is the size of the housing market in the short run. The shaded area is an increase in net total WTP for the housing stock.[2]

But to understand the hedonic method, it is necessary to dig beneath the surface of this conceptual similarity to the complementarity method. So let us return to the "hedonic price equation":

$$P_H = f(z_1, \ldots, z_N) \tag{7.2}$$

where P_H is now the price of a house with characteristics $\{z\}$. The notion originally suggested by Rosen was appealingly simple. As a first step in understanding it, consider what the graph of P_H might look like if we could hold constant all the z_i but the one $z_j \equiv Q$, for quality, of interest. This quality measure might, for housing, be visibility, odor, particulates, or smog, for example—whatever makes it more or less pleasant to live in (be in the yard of, look out from) a house. Now recall that $f(\cdot)$ is assumed to have been estimated from extensive housing market data that must, of course, include data on the $z_j \equiv Q$ for each house in the sample. Intuitively, we might expect this slice through the N dimensional surface of $f(\cdot)$ to have a form such that price rises with improvements in environmental quality, while the marginal price effect declines as quality improves (see Figure 7.4).[3] Note that it is likely that there will be a lower bound on observed levels of Q. That is, the environmental quality

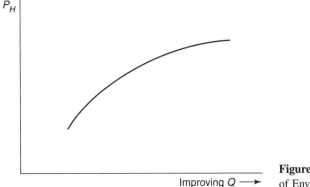

P_H

Improving $Q \longrightarrow$

Figure 7.4 House Price as a Function of Environmental Quality Only

actually experienced around houses will not usually be terrible. So the obtainable function $P_H(Q)$ will be undetermined for very bad quality levels.

The slope of this sketched slice through the price surface is positive but declining. (This was based here on assumption, but is likely to be the case in actual data.) The suggestion from Rosen was to calculate the values of $\partial P_H/\partial Q$ for every house in the sample, using the derivative of the estimated P_H function, and then to estimate the function:

$$\frac{\partial P_H}{\partial Q} = g(z_1, \ldots, Q) \tag{7.3}$$

Under certain assumptions about the housing market, Rosen argued that this function would be the demand function (the MWTP function) for Q as quality is enjoyed via its interaction with housing. For some "average" house (an "average" bundle of all the nonenvironmental characteristics) one could blow up this function by the size of the market to get a total MWTP function. This is illustrated in Figure 7.5, where the area under the function could be evaluated, for example, for a contemplated improvement from Q_0 to Q_1.

Unfortunately, some of these assumptions are problematic. For one thing, the market is assumed to be in equilibrium. Taking the example of a housing market, this assumption requires full information, no moving or transactions costs, and instantaneous price adjustments to changes in supply and demand. Although no existing housing market can be expected to meet these stringent requirements, a reasonably well-functioning market will not, in general, be unduly burdened by its imperfections.[4] However, where the market is relatively inactive, controlled, or distorted, the application of hedonic analysis becomes much more problematic. Second, market actors must be aware of and appreciate the effects of the environmental change to be valued. If there is little information on environmental risks or the risks are not fully appreciated by individual actors in the market, hedonic analysis will not generate a valid estimate of the WTP to avoid these risks. A third problematic assumption is that a sufficiently wide variety of the good is available to approximate a continuous spectrum of choices, over characteristics, allowing consumers to

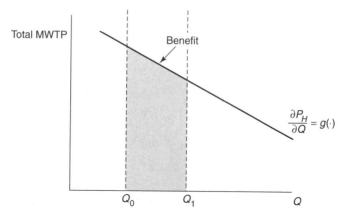

Figure 7.5 A Marginal Willingness to Pay (MWTP) Function for Environmental Quality, Given a Set of Other House Characteristics. P_H, price; Q, quality.

choose their optimum bundles without being constrained by the unavailability of some bundle. That is, they are not forced into corner solutions in which they cannot actually buy the combination of characteristics they want.

Subsequent writers argued convincingly that, independent of the realism of the key assumptions, Rosen's suggestion would not, in fact, work using data from only one housing market. To see why not, think about the information one market would supply for the estimation process. In the space of interest, $\partial P_H/\partial Q$ versus Q, the technique produces "observations" that must fall along the so-called marginal-price curve, because that is how they are constructed. But each point is the result of one family's decision on buying a house. And there is no requirement that that family's MWTP function coincides with the marginal price function. For example, for families of different income but otherwise similar characteristics, and tastes in Q, the situation could be as shown in Figure 7.6 where only the (Q_i, mP_i) pairs are observed. The suggested technique cannot give us the MWTP functions, only the mar-

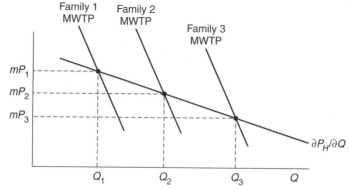

Figure 7.6 Possible Contrast Between Family Marginal Willingness to Pay (MWTP) Functions and the Marginal Price (mP) for the Market. P_H, price of house; Q, quality.

ginal price function, even if all the families differ only in income, and rising income just shifts the MWTP function to the right. Said another way, we have only one observation on each MWTP function (each income level). We have no idea from these observations what the slope is, or the shape more generally for that matter. (See Box 7.3.)

BOX 7.3

Identification

Even in the analysis of market data on price and quantity to try to obtain demand functions, the problem known as "identification" is a serious one. This is because the observations we have are in general the equilibrium results of underlying shifts in the supply and demand functions. We see only the price/quantity pairs at the intersections—not the rest of the functions. Thus we might have, for the same market in three periods, three equilibrium points as shown below by the heavy dots. (See Figure 7.7.) If this were all we knew, an attempt to estimate a function connecting P_X and X might produce the dashed line, which corresponds to neither demand nor supply. To recover demand functions we need to be able to hold the demand shifts constant, in effect, and to observe the effect of shifting supply conditions.

Thus, ideally, we would like to be able to produce the situation represented in Figure 7.8 (generalized and expanded, of course, in number of observations). The imposition of conditions and acquisition of information that make this possible is what dealing with "the identification problem" is all about.

To make the ideas a bit less abstract, though, think about the demand for some weather-sensitive crop such as fresh berries or tomatoes in the summer. The supply curve for strawberries shifts with temperature, sunlight, rainfall, etc., while a family's demand is a function of family income and background. For a given set of families, the aggregate demand function (the *horizontal* sum, since this is a private good) is not weather dependent and can, in fact, be assumed fixed for the season. Thus, we might have something close to the situation graphed above, where the individual supply functions go with days or weeks during the season.

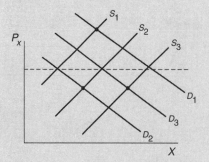

Figure 7.7 A Simple Identification Problem

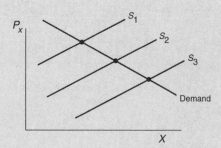

Figure 7.8 Ideal Information for Estimating a Demand Function

If we could obtain marginal price functions for several different markets, and if we continue to think about the families as similar except in income terms—for which total house price serves as a proxy measure—the information available, at least in principle, is expanded, as suggested by Figure 7.9. We would now have several observations of the quality purchase decisions of households at each income level, and from these we could infer the generic shape of the MWTP function as a function of the quality variable. Based on the function for the family of median income, for example, we could obtain an aggregate MWTP for any of the markets and would then be in a position to calculate the benefit from a projected (proposed) change in Q as graphed in Figure 7.9.

Although the problems with assumptions and identification are certainly not all of the practical and technical problems associated with hedonic analysis, they seem to me quite sufficient to give us pause about relying on the method. Further, however, hedonic models can at best provide only a partial measure of the value of a change in environmental quality, because they capture only one aspect of the effect of such a change. That is, hedonic property models only measure WTP for the attributes of quality that are "captured" by choice of residence, while ignoring willingness to pay for improvements in environmental quality as experienced at other points in the urban area, for example, on commuting routes and work places, shopping areas, and recreational areas. Nonetheless, the partial derivative of a first-stage hedonic price function can be used to produce an approximate benefit number for a small change in environmental quality.

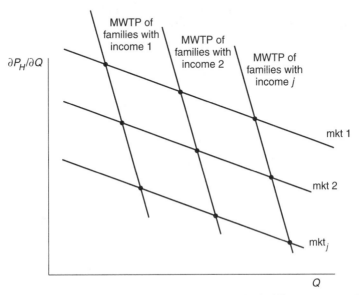

Figure 7.9 Data from Several Markets. MWTP, marginal willingness to pay; P_H, price of house; Q, quality.

However, it has been pointed out by others that even a "correct" application of first-stage estimation can generate estimates that are two to three times as large as the "true" benefits. As a result, even the reduced effort needed to generate first-stage estimates seems unlikely to be merited, given the quality of the results.

COST SHIFTS: AVERTING, REPLACING, OR CURING EXPENDITURE

Again, the idea behind this method is not hard to grasp. It is simply the observation that in some situations, market footprints of environmental quality result because poor environmental quality makes life harder or more expensive, or both, so that a quality improvement can be seen as shifting the marginal cost of maintaining a desired "quality of family life." Some examples might be:

• In the days before laundry driers became ubiquitous, they might have been purchased more frequently by families living in areas of high ambient particulate concentrations in the air. These families would be "averting" the problem of dirty laundry from outside drying.

• Families that live in areas of high ambient ozone concentrations, which is to say most major U.S. cities, have to spend more on replacing tires over any period of time, for given levels of tire use, because ozone speeds up the deterioration of the material making up the tire walls.

• Air pollution generally (fine particulates, sulfur dioxide, oxides of nitrogen and ozone) has a deleterious effect on human health, particularly for people with chronic respiratory conditions such as asthma or who smoke. An improvement in air quality will in general spare these people some episodes of sickness and thus save them money spent on doctors, medicines, even days in the hospital.

Conceptually, what we are talking about here is captured in a general way by Figure 7.10. The marginal costs of maintaining "quality of life" in general reflect both purchased goods (tires, medicines, driers) and the time of household members (as when houses have to be painted more often because of soot in the air).[5] When the costs fall because of an improvement in environmental quality, the cost savings are an indication of the value of the improvement.

As you might reasonably expect by now, none of this is as easy as it sounds when only the intuition is presented. To begin at the simple end, in principle, the material damages from various levels of pollution can be determined by experiments or extensive observation, and replacement rules can be determined by observation or formulated to produce the cheapest results over some time horizon. (The MWTP function can be made vertical in effect.) This approach might be applied to truck and auto tires affected by ozone; copper gutters and roof flashing attacked by acid precipitation; and finishes on houses and commercial buildings potentially harmed

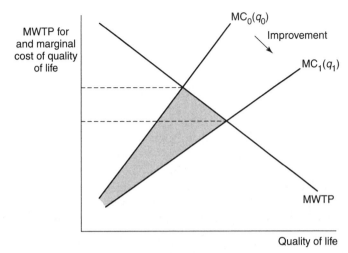

Figure 7.10 Lowering the Cost of Maintaining "Quality of Life." MWTP, marginal willingness to pay; MC, marginal cost; Q, quality.

by a variety of air pollutants. But there are an infinite number of possible combinations of materials, pollutants, and local climate, which plays a role through precipitation and sunlight, the presence of sea or road salt, and other factors that complicate application to specific problems or to many different places simultaneously. So identifying and estimating the material damages incurred even at one place and under one set of ambient quality conditions could be quite a large job.

The problems with material damages pale, however, by comparison with determining the costs of maintaining health. This is most obviously and importantly true because it will be difficult, if not necessarily impossible, to attribute ill health to pollution. For most conditions and situations, air pollution aggravates effects, or makes people more susceptible to infectious agents by irritating the respiratory tract. Economists have a long record of attempting to use the statistical tools of epidemiology to pick these effects out of the background data on sickness. An example is described in Box 7.4.

Again there are difficulties caused by the huge number of possible combinations of pollutants and local conditions, which may, for these purposes, reasonably be said to include pollen and mold spore counts. And, of course, the characteristics of specific populations matter. Age is an obvious thing to worry about. So is income, as a proxy for other habits and for effort at prevention of disease. But even where communities are homogeneous in age and income, genetic background may become important if there are differences in susceptibility to particular effects. Smoking is hugely important and must be included as part of the set of explanatory variables. (The study described in Box 7.4 made smoking a jointly determined variable, along with sick days.)

Air Pollution and Health—Understanding the Relationship

In the 1980s John Mullahy and Paul Portney examined the relation among air pollution, cigarette smoking, and respiratory disease (and its effects in terms of days of sickness). While the papers reporting on their study are couched in heavily economic terms, the study may be seen as epidemiology with an economic twist. That twist is to see more of the causal elements—in particular the smoking behavior—as being determined inside the model (being "endogenous").

Their data on sickness and smoking came from the 1979 National Health Interview Survey, from which they drew a subsample of about 2,400 individuals for whom smoking data were available. Other "explanatory" data on the individuals included their age, gender, and the presence or absence of a chronic health problem. The "sickness" information for each person was the number of days (from 0 to 14) in the two weeks before the interview that the individual reported being restricted in activities by a respiratory condition, with an indication also available of the identity of the "condition" (such as a cold or an asthma attack).

The pollution data were for ozone and (airborne) sulfates, based on data collected at ambient air quality monitoring stations during the same two-week period referred to in the responses to the sickness question. Each individual was matched with the monitoring station nearest the geographic center of the census tract in which that individual lived. The measures actually used were averages across the fourteen days, but for ozone it was an average of highest daily hourly readings, while for sulfate it was a simple average of all the readings.

Each person was also matched to a weather station so that the set of independent explanatory variables included the fourteen-day averages of daily maximum temperatures and of daily rainfall to which each person could reasonably be claimed to have been exposed.

Their statistical results show that smoking is positively and very significantly related to respiratory illness when the former is treated as part of the simultaneously determined set of variables. Ozone concentrations are also positively and significantly explanatory of respiratory sickness (though the effect exhibits what we might call declining marginal causation). That is: $\partial(\text{sick days})/\partial(\text{ozone})$ is positive but declining as ozone increases, as represented in Figure 7.11.

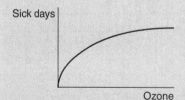

Figure 7.11 Sick Days as Function of Ozone Levels

Interestingly, after account is taken of the effects of smoking, ozone, temperature (the lower the temperature the higher the number of sick days), age (a similar relation to ozone), and gender (males were less likely to report sick days due to respiratory conditions), sulfate concentrations did not seem to play a significant causative role.

This was an extremely carefully done study with access to excellent data, yet notice some of the things it did not reflect:

- The effect of long-term exposure to air pollutants (unless you believe that current pollution levels in '79 were very highly correlated with readings in earlier years *for the subjects of the study*)
- The effect of pollution experienced at places other than the subjects' homes— places such as commuting routes and work and shopping locales
- Any interplay between small particulates (or any other air pollutants) and sulfates

I hope this begins to tell you how hard it is to do health-effects epidemiology.

The effort to obtain a so-called dose-response function for pollution-caused ill health is a difficult first step. But to go further we need to be able to value that ill health. And this is where we run up against a basic flaw in the averting-cost (and curing cost—the cost to return to a well state) methodology that must be acknowledged before proceeding. The problem is most obvious and serious in the health area: The cost of disease, as measured by the costs of treatment and time lost to other activities, is only a lower bound on the total damages. Missing is the WTP of the people experiencing the sickness to avoid having the symptoms at all. That is, if air pollution makes it slightly more likely that you will have a cold, or flu, or an asthma attack, you can try to "avert" the effects by staying inside, using more air conditioning, even wearing a surgical mask when outside. And the symptoms of these conditions can be treated at some cost. Your loss of work time, school time, even recreation time may be valued (though this exercise is full of its own problems and pitfalls, as discussed below). But you would be happier not to have been sick at all. Your total WTP to avoid sickness in principle values both "pain and suffering" and the costs of cure. The cost approach being discussed here fails to get at the part of WTP that reflects pain and suffering. The fundamental reason is that you do not have options that allow you to pay individually to avoid the pollution effect. It's not an analogous situation to substituting an electric drier for a clothesline. Further, it is reasonable to expect this to be a bigger problem the more serious the disease. Skin cancer attributable to loss of stratospheric ozone is potentially far more serious than an extra cold attributable to "too much" ground-level ozone. (Actual suffering plus anxiety about ultimate outcomes both count here.)

This same sort of problem exists, but seems likely to be less serious, where material damage is involved. Thus, for example, where house gutters must be replaced more often because of acid rain, the cost of the actual material and work fails to reflect the "hassle factor." The homeowner would be WTP something more than cost to avoid the entire episode: discovering a problem, such as a leak; finding potential contractors; taking bids; checking up on work; . . . . These are all interruptions and annoyances to life, though they are hardly on the scale of the anxiety produced by an incident of skin cancer.

While the above consideration is the most serious problem with the averting/curing cost approach to benefit estimation, there are other difficulties as well. One is worth noting, especially because something very like it will come up when we talk about using travel cost to value places or experiences. Here it appears as the question of how to value time "lost" to sickness, (e.g., Portney and Mullahy's "restricted activity days" [Portney and Mullahy, 1986]). At one extreme, valuing these can be seen as equivalent to valuing pain and suffering—WTP to avoid them. But sticking with the cost notion, it is at least conceptually possible to obtain a lower bound on their value. For any particular person something is given up when sickness causes the need to stay at home, possibly to stay in bed. That something may be hours at work and hours of recreation; or hours at school and at play; or hours fighting household entropy by cleaning, cooking, running errands, and doing laundry. Costing all of these is difficult, even those that seem closest to the market, such as work time. For starters, a sick day may not cost the worker anything at all because of sick leave. It may cost the employer something in lost output, providing a substitute, and so on. But what this amounts to is highly job and firm specific. Usually the work the individual would do is accomplished by someone else at slightly greater expense or later by the same person, when she or he returns to work. In the latter case, again, there may be a small increase in cost to the employer due to delays, but the real cost is unlikely to be as high as the wages for the sick period would imply. And when the lost activity is play or work around the house, the problems of costing are much greater. While these losses might reasonably be thought to be included in statements of WTP to avoid the sickness entirely, in the absence of those numbers a costing approach by itself becomes quite arbitrary.

One final comment. The beginning of this discussion used a diagram in which a MWTP function for "quality of life" appeared. This device was meant to stand for whatever demand is appropriate to the problem at hand: miles of driving per year; healthy days per month or year; items of clean, dry laundry per period, and so on. As already noted, in the short run the demand may be almost completely inelastic, as when miles of driving are implied by commuting route and days of work per period. Or we may think it reasonable to assume infinite elasticity, as we might for health days. But the greater the elasticity, the larger the cost savings from higher quality, everything else equal, as the simple sketch in Figure 7.12 illustrates. Here (a) is the benefit measure corresponding to cost reduction $mc_0 \rightarrow mc_1$ when demand for the "quality of life" measure is inelastic. $(a + b)$ is the measure when demand

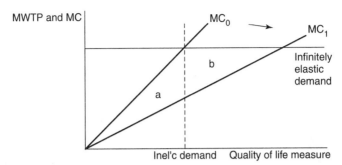

Figure 7.12 Varying Price Elasticity of Demand for a Quality-of-Life Measure. MWTP, marginal willingness to pay; MC, marginal cost.

is infinitely elastic. Intermediate elasticities give intermediate benefit measures. But finding these demands will be difficult, and it may often be convenient to assume zero elasticity.

TRAVEL COST AND ITS RELATION TO ENVIRONMENTAL QUALITY

The use of travel cost as the basis for valuing places that are not themselves priced was suggested about four decades ago and has since become a routine tool of analysis for several U.S. government agencies, especially the Corps of Engineers. Once again, the idea is simple: The (recreational) value of a place, such as a reservoir or forest, is revealed by how many people travel how far to visit it, because the cost of travel is the cost of a visit. Thus, observations of travel cost correspond to observations of price per visit; and the number of visits, say per year, is the quantity purchased. (See Box 7.5 for a quick summary of the technique.)

As with every one of the indirect techniques, beneath the superficial intuitive appeal lurk many problems and disputes—some without "correct" answers. Just to give you a flavor for these, here is a partial catalog:

- Where and how to gather the necessary data. Most often, actual users are interviewed at the site. But it has been argued that it would be better to interview random samples of the population where they live. (And if the goal is to value a prospective place—a reservoir that might be constructed—there is no existing place at which to interview users.) This raises questions of how far out to go in distance terms, a question with answers necessarily specific to the place in question, and in any case, not discoverable except through the interview process itself.

- What functional forms to fit to the data on use and travel cost from the interviews—linear, semilog, log-log, or more general.

BOX 7.5

Travel-Cost Demand Curves

Travel-cost demand functions are derived from data on visitation to the place of interest from distance-based zones around the place. Usually these are thought of as annular rings, as in Figure 7.13

Thus, after sampling users at the facility or prospective/possible users in the zones, we would have data on numbers of visitors (per year, say) from each zone; their characteristics in the usual socioeconomic terms, such as gender, age, education, income; perhaps some special information relevant to the decision to visit the site in question, such as the outdoor activities they engage in and their experience with similar sites; and, of course, the travel cost implied by the location of the person relative to the site. For simplicity here I will just proceed as if each person in zone 0 were d_0 miles from the site, etc. This travel cost is then given by $C_{R0} = 2cd_0 + t_cT_0$, where c is the cost per mile of travel (almost always the variable cost of using a car); t_c is the per hour cost attached to travel time (recall the earlier discussion of costing time); and T_0 is the number of hours required for the round trip from the center of zone 0. Similar formulae apply to the other zones.

Using these data, a visitation rate equation can be fitted using standard regression techniques. This would give: $V_i = f(C_{Ri}, Y_i, \text{Ed}_i, \ldots)$ where V is visitors per year per 1,000 residents of a zone with center distance d_i, and characteristics Y_i (income), Ed_i, education, etc. This, in turn, allows us to predict visitors per year from each zone, V_i. To see the final step, we plot some hypothetical data from the work described so far for just four zones and four travel costs in Figure 7.14.

For simplicity it is shown as a straight line with equation:

$$C_R = 25 - \frac{V}{50}$$

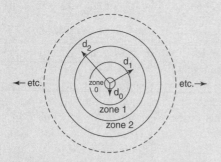

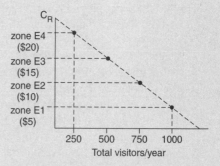

Figure 7.13 Population "Rings" Surrounding a Site to Be Valued

Figure 7.14 A Simple Visitation Function by Zone

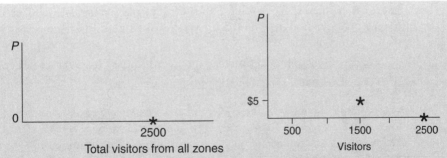

Figure 7.15 Total Visitation at Zero Entry Fee

Figure 7.16 Reduction in Total Visitation with Introduction of a $5 Fee

Now look at the site. If there is a zero admission fee, total visitors are given by the sum across all the zones at current travel costs. For our fou r zones, that sum is $1000+750+500+250=2500$. So the first point on the demand function is (0, 2500). (See Figure 7.15.)

Imagine that an admission fee is now to be charged. Let it be $5. This can be seen as an addition to each zone's travel cost. With it, travel cost from zone 4 becomes $25 per visit, and no one is predicted to visit from that zone. The total of visits at the $5 fee is then 750 (from zone 1) + 500 (from zone 2) + 250 (from zone 3) + 0 (from zone 4) = 1500. This is a second point on the demand function. (See Figure 7.16.) Continuing this way, by increasing the hypothetical addition to travel cost (the hypothetical entrance fee) we get: at $10, 500 (from zone 1) + 250 (from zone 2) + 0 (from each of zones 3 and 4) = 750; at $15, 250 (from zone 1) and 0 from all the others; at $20 additional, zero from all zones. Thus, the demand function in represented in Figure 7.17.

There is, by the way, nothing magical about the $5 increments. One dollar could just as well have been used. But, if the original zones are "$5 wide," as are the ones in the example, nothing is gained in information terms by using a $1 step.

Then the total WTP (per year) for the existence of the site is the area under the TC demand curve. If there were costs involved in managing and maintaining the site for the visitors, the net annual benefit of having the site would be the WTP minus the annual cost.

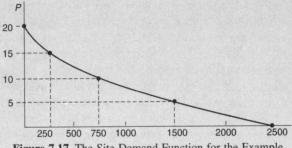

Figure 7.17 The Site Demand Function for the Example

- How to cost the time spent traveling.[6] [See the previous section, and think about the added consideration that travel for recreational purposes may sometimes be fun rather than pure cost.]
- How to deal with the influence of other sites to which people might also travel.
- How to deal with multiday and multipurpose trips.

But what is most important in the context of this course and topic is not exactly how to do travel-cost work. Rather it is: How can travel cost be useful for estimating the benefits of environmental quality improvements? The answer seems to be in two ways, one of which corresponds to the weak complementarity method; the other of which is closely related to the cost-shift approach of the previous section.

In the first of these, a change of environmental quality shifts the demand curve for the site or sites. For a well-defined site that has undergone a known change in quality—with before and after travel-cost surveys—this is a fairly straightforward idea. The problems for which benefit estimates are usually needed seldom are so conveniently defined, however. Consider:

- A policy generally will affect many sites. Indeed, a policy that affects the water quality of all the water bodies in a state, region, or nation will stretch the notion of site far beyond its breaking point. How do we define "sites" for a river with many access points and no barriers to travel by boat along it? Or for a large lake?

- Very often the benefit question is couched in the future tense—what *will* it be worth to achieve some proposed quality change? Since there will be no actual experience with—no actual users of—the hypothetically changed quality, the benefits must be based on a generalization of what is known from existing sites of varying quality with other relevant characteristics known. If this reminds you of "hedonics" you are probably starting to get the hang of things. The idea behind "hedonic travel cost" is to use data on existing but varying quality, controlling for other characteristics, to estimate the aggregate WTP for a prospective change affecting many sites. (You might want to remind yourself of some of the problems with hedonics. But you will definitely want to remember that there are problems—*and* that the implied data requirements are very large.)

The other way travel cost has been used amounts to a variant of the cost-of-producing-quality-of-life approach just discussed. An example comes from Clifford Russell's and William Vaughan's *Freshwater Recreational Fishing: The National Benefits of Water Pollution Control* (1982), in which the benefits of the Clean Water Act, as they result through freshwater recreational fishing, were estimated for the entire conterminous United States. This approach uses the household production framework, within which families (or their modern equivalents) are seen as producing for themselves goods and services, using their own time and skills, purchased goods and services, and unpriced natural resources. In the case of recreational fishing, the households combine time, equipment for travel and fishing, and sites at which to fish to produce fishing days.

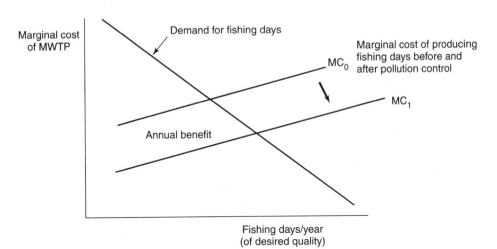

Figure 7.18 The Benefits of Pollution Control Accruing Through Recreational Fishing— Where the Control Is Seen as Reducing Costs

Improvement in water quality has its effect here by increasing the quality of fishing (in terms of types of species present; or, at the extreme low end, by allowing some hardy species to live in what was fishless water) at sites all over the country. This reduces the average travel time and distance, hence cost of producing days of recreational fishing for the average fishing family, whatever type and quality of fishing they seek. (See Figure 7.18.[7]) This way of using travel cost does not depend on identification of particular sites but only on the notion that everyone faces an array of sites of varying qualities and distances from his or her home. The effect of water pollution control is to improve everyone's "portfolio" of fishing opportunities by reducing travel cost to sites of particular qualities. But only this average effect for the randomly chosen family is taken into account—not actual sites visited. It also was used before actual quality changes had been recorded—thus it predicted the benefits—using the pre-pollution-control variation in water quality to predict the response to improvements that would, in general, raise quality everywhere.

GENERAL COMMENTS ON INDIRECT METHODS OF BENEFIT ESTIMATION

The undeniable advantage of these methods is that they make use of actual consumer decisions to buy or to do one thing rather than another. When the decisions are made there is no element of the hypothetical, nor is there any reason to think that the people involved are revealing anything other than their true preferences among the choices available. A further strength of the methods is their intellectual foundations, constructed over many years of work by some really excellent economists and econometricians. If you wanted to embark on an hedonic, travel-cost, or averting-cost study, you would have a very large amount of reading to do; and from it you would learn at least how to get started, what pitfalls to watch out for, and how the data you gather could be dealt with. You would also discover that some important problems have no correct solutions; but you would at least have the arguments on all sides available and could make an informed choice of a way to proceed. Indeed, you could learn a very great deal from just one large and careful book— A.M. Freeman's *The Measurement of Environmental and Resource Values* (1993), which is as close to a conceptual bible as environmental economics offers in any subfield.

What you would not find anywhere is, however, equally important. And the largest hole, to my mind, is the lack of a correspondence between policy-related questions and the indirect methods. Thus, for example, if you were asked, as an employee of or consultant to some government agency, to produce benefit estimates for a pending regulatory decision about changing a National Ambient Air Quality Standard, or the rules for Superfund site cleanup goals, or for a past decision such as the definition of "Best Available (wastewater) Treatment" technology under the Clean Water Act, you would have a big problem on your hands. First you would have to identify all the routes by which the benefits might accrue to society. Then you would have to try to identify an indirect benefit estimation method that could, at least in principle, produce numbers for each route. In doing this, you would have to be careful that you weren't going to be either double counting or missing some benefits. At this point, you would have to be sure that you were able to translate the policy change into changes in ambient environmental quality—what people experience and what drives the generation of benefits. (Also notice that some policy changes are couched directly in ambient quality terms, but refer to lower limits on acceptable quality. Thus a careful benefit estimate requires effort to identify the actual pattern of quality across a region or along a river. Finally, you would have to figure out where to get the necessary data: secondary sources, such as surveys compiled for other purposes; original survey work; or some kind of calculation, as of costs avoided, based on scientific or engineering knowledge. Table 7.2 contains a sketch of such a process and its problems for the water quality example. The two biggest problems noted there are:

- the possibilities for overlapping and "underlapping" estimates
- the lack of any way to get at nonuse benefits via indirect methods

Box 7.6 describes an effort to add nonuse to use benefits in the case of the Tuolumne River dam controversy in California. And finally, it is worth emphasizing that each benefit route estimate would require its own (extensive) data and would present its own conceptual and econometric conundrums, so that the entire effort could require several person-years of effort in the parallel projects and even then would probably take at least a couple of years to do.

TABLE 7.2 Benefit Estimation by Indirect Methods: The Case of Changing the Technology-based Standards Under the Clean Water Act

Routes to Benefits	Possible Methods
Recreation	
Fishing	⎫ Hedonic travel cost
Boating	⎬ or
Swimming	⎭ Travel-cost reductions in household production framework
Water as backdrop to other recreation	Housing hedonic prices or some version of travel cost
Health	
Drinking water	Reduced cost of treating raw water to drinking water standard
Contact recreation	(See swimming above)
Water and aquatic ecological systems as inputs to production	
Process and boiler water	Reduced cost of intake treatment
Commercial fisheries	Increased profit or reduction in costs of maintaining catch
Nonuse	
Idea of generally cleaner water	⎫
Protection of rare aquatic species	⎬ No indirect methods but see Box 7.6
Keeping future generations' option open	⎭

Cautions

Fishing/boating tend to go together. Data may not distinguish purpose of boating days; or boating days may frequently have multiple purposes that cannot be disentangled.

Swimming benefits may be largely, though not entirely, due to decreased risk of infection from water contact, creating another overlap. Some part of any hedonic benefit estimate based on prices of houses on or near water bodies subject to quality improvement will reflect recreation and some part aesthetics.

Freshwater commercial fishing in natural water bodies is a very small activity and the resource is generally treated as open access. (No one *owns* the fish or the space so all involved have an incentive to catch as much as they can.) Profits tend to be zero at whatever level of activity is undertaken.

Connecting Treatment Technology to Ambient Conditions

Requires a system of water quality models covering all natural water bodies in U.S. These must begin with pre-regulation pollution discharges and resulting quality. Changing technology definition changes discharges over several pollutants (e.g.: biochemical oxygen demand, fertilizers such as nitrates and phosphates, particulate matter, oil and grease [that make floating sheens and scums and harm wildlife], and toxics such as chlorinated hydrocarbons). The new predicted discharges must be transformed into changed ambient quality and associated aquatic ecosystem conditions (e.g.: algae, insects, plants, fish—by species).

These observations provide a useful jumping-off place for the next chapter, which deals with the so-called direct methods of benefit estimation. These speak to the problems just identified, and this is perhaps *their* greatest strength. But they present their own problems, all traceable ultimately to the fact that they involve taking seriously people's answers to hypothetical questions about future behavior.

Box 7.6

The Tuolumne River Preservation Study

Rob Stavins was asked, in the early 1980s, to do a study of the benefits and costs of a pair of hydroelectric and water supply dam/reservoir combinations proposed for the Tuolumne River in northern California. While the details of the river's situation and uses at the time of the proposed development, and of the motivations of the opponents of the proposal (led by the Tuolumne River Preservation Trust) all make interesting reading, my interest is only in the technique Stavins used to estimate nonuser values for the river.[8] I will also, therefore, spend no time on how Stavins obtained the user values, which, as you will see, were built upon to get to the nonuser numbers.

Briefly, Stavins looked at:

1. The benefits of the development in terms of cheaper electricity; of increased firm yield of water for out-of-basin users; and of recreation on the new reservoirs (fishing and boating): B_D

2. The costs of the dams and the associated equipment required to produce the benefits in (1): C

3. The costs in terms of benefits lost because of the developments: B_P

The question was: did B_D exceed $B_P + C$ or not?

The user benefits to be lost were based on white-water rafting use and amounted to about $3.6 million per year. But Stavins wanted to obtain a benefit attributable to nonusers—those who might want to bequeath a Tuolumne with at least some uncontrolled stretches left; those who valued the survival of the mule deer, whose winter habitat would be disrupted; and those who generally believe preservation is a good idea in the face of ignorance of long-term ecological consequences of development (see Chapter 13).

To get at these values he first found in the literature nine studies that purported to estimate the ratio of per household nonuse to use values. ("Purported" because there is now substantial agreement that this is not really possible without a very elaborate survey and sample procedure.) The average of this ratio from the studies was 0.6, with a range of 0.47 to 1.39 (a factor of about 3).

Now came the difficult part. Without the time or money to find the actual population of nonusers who nonetheless would value the preservation of the river, Stavins ingeniously settled on Sierra Club membership as a "proxy." His calculation looked like this:

(1) For California
         User value (consumer surplus) lost per California user $184/yr

Nonuser/user value ratio 0.6
Implying annual value per nonuser $110/yr
Sierra Club membership: 130,840 in California
Implying a California nonuser value of $14.46 million/yr

(2) For other parts of the United States
User value (consumer surplus per non California user) $393/yr
Assumed nonuser/user value ratio 0.45
Implying annual value per nonuser of $177/yr
Sierra Club membership outside California: 215,460
Divided by 2 (to be conservative): 107,730
Total non-California, nonuser value $19.05 million/yr

(3) Total annual nonuser value: $33.50 million or
almost 10 times the user benefit $33.50 million/yr

The ultimate comparison using "levelized" values after allowing for growth in demands and discounting were:

B_D = $187.9 million/yr

C = $134.2 million/yr

B_P = $80.0 million/yr (of which $72.0 million was attributable to nonusers)

So, the project failed the benefit-cost test on the basis of Stavin's analysis:

$187.9 million
−134.2
− 80.0
$−26.3 × million

Without any nonuser benefits, the project would have passed the test, so the choice of the ratio of nonuser to user benefits per person mattered. But even more important was the guess at market extent for those benefits.

CONCLUSIONS AND REMINDERS

In this chapter you have had an introduction to the ways environmental economists have thought of using market data—data generated by consumers making decisions to do or buy something—as a source of information on how much they value actual or prospective changes in environmental quality. Several of these methods rely on the notion of complementarity—the shifting up of demand functions for certain activities or places or goods when environmental quality improves. The original, general idea was described and then related to hedonic analysis of house prices and hedonic use of the travel-cost method. The other broad approach looks at the cost of producing something, such as recreational fishing or health or automobile transportation. For several such costs, improving environmental quality can be seen as shifting the marginal cost function down, and the benefit comes from the implied savings.

Each method tends to be data intensive and to involve choices among techniques and assumptions, no one of which is "the" right one. And this means that an estimate of the value of some actual or hypothetical change is really a point taken from the distribution of possible results implied by looking across all the choices. This is inconvenient for the analyst, perhaps, but it does not mean there is anything wrong with the approach.

More serious in the context of actual policy analysis is the observation that for many, perhaps most, policy problems, there is unlikely to be a set of indirect benefit estimation techniques that captures all the benefits (or damages) and that does not overcount some of them. A related point is that there is, currently at least, no nonarbitrary way to estimate benefits accruing to nonusers via indirect methods.

NOTES

1. Another use of the hedonic technique is to estimate willingness to pay for less risk (greater safety) in work situations. This is done using data on wages and job characteristics, including the safety measure of interest. I do not go into detail on this application, but many of the same problems and *caveats* apply.
2. "Net" because it reflects the entire market affected by the quality change. Some house prices may fall. Also note that when we look at the problem this way, both parts of the weak complementarity requirement seem very likely to apply. That is, it seems likely that there is some price at which any particular consumer's demand for housing defined by a set of characteristics such as size, quality of finishes, number of bathrooms, etc. would be driven to zero. And at zero consumption of such a house, the quality of the air around any one house would be of no interest to the nonconsumer. (See Box 7.2)
3. If this intuition does not immediately appeal to you, try the following thought experiment: Assume you are buying a new car and can choose from a set of models that are all the same except for their quickness of acceleration, measured as seconds, to go from zero to 60 miles per hour. You might be willing to pay $1,000 to reduce this time from 14 seconds to 12 seconds, but less to reduce it from 11 seconds to 9 seconds.
4. It should be noted that although the errors introduced by these imperfections are generally random, nonrandom errors will be introduced by the continuous movement, or the expectation of movement, of market forces in any one direction, resulting in biased marginal implicit prices.
5. Economists have developed a framework for this kind of analysis called "household production" that, in effect, looks at the household (family) as a firm using time and purchased goods to produce services such as health, recreation, and "wellness" for its own consumption.
6. For a thorough discussion of costing the time spent traveling for recreation purposes, see Elizabeth Wilman's paper in the *Journal of Environmental Economics and Management*, Sept. 1980.

7. While this brief description sets out the conceptual basis for the Russell/Vaughan estimates, the actual calculations were different because of the availability of particular kinds of data—on participation in recreational fishing, for various kinds of fish, across the states. In effect, the benefit in the diagram was approximated by, first, estimating increases in participation (whether and how much) attributable to the lower average distance to water of desired fishing quality; and then combining these with estimates of consumer surplus per day created by the several types of fishing, the latter based on a different data set entirely, but also involving use of travel cost demands for types of fishing.
8. The details are most accessible in a "Case Study" used in the Kennedy School of Government at Harvard. "Saving the Tuolumne," C15-86-701.0 of 1986, attributed to Joseph Kalt and José A. Gomez Ibañez.

REFERENCES

Freeman, A. M. 1993. *The Measurement of Environmental and Resource Values.* Washington, D.C.: Resources for the Future.

Kalt, Joseph, and José A. Gomez Ibañez. 1986. "Case study: Saving the Tuolumne." Kennedy School of Government, C15-86-701.0. Cambridge: Harvard University.

Mäler, Karl-Göran. 1974. *Environmental Economics.* Baltimore: Johns Hopkins University Press for Resources for the Future.

Portney, Paul, and John Mullahy. 1986. "Urban air quality and acute respiratory illness." *Journal of Urban Economics* 20(1):21–38.

Rosen, Sherwin. 1974. "Hedonic prices and implicit markets: Product differentiation in pure competition." *Journal of Political Economy* 82(1):34–55.

Russell, Clifford S., and William J. Vaughan. 1982. *Freshwater Recreational Fishing: The National Benefits of Water Pollution Control*, Washington, D.C.: Resources for the Future.

Wilman, Elizabeth. 1980. "The value of time in recreational benefit studies." *Journal of Environmental Economics and Management* 7(3):272–286.

8

DIRECT METHODS OF BENEFIT ESTIMATION

When Paul Samuelson formulated the theory of public goods back in the 1950s he included some observations on the prospective difficulties of determining MWTP schedules for such goods (Samuelson, 1955). In particular, he ruled out the appealing notion of simply asking people, on the grounds that it would not be in the interest of respondents to such questions to tell the truth. He concentrated on the incentive to understate WTP produced by a situation in which payment will be required and will be related to stated WTP, while the good, once provided, will be provided to all regardless of their responses—the essence of publicness. The resulting temptation, to understate, counting on others to respond with high enough bids that the good is actually provided, he labeled "free riding." The combination of impeccable source and compelling internal logic of this observation kept all but a handful of economists from pursuing direct questioning for decades; and the idea that people will answer WTP survey questions dishonestly ("strategically") remains a very big worry for economists.

Nonetheless, experimentation with direct questioning began at least as early as the 1960s, with a recreation valuation study by Jack Knetsch and Bob Davis, involving both WTP questions and the application of travel-cost methodology (Knetsch and Davis, 1966). In the middle and late 1970s, impatience with the practical limitations of the more economically respectable methods of the last chapter led to some small-scale but wide-ranging experimentation with the direct approach.[1] The increasing demand for damage and benefit estimates created by new laws and presidential executive orders stimulated much more work in the 1980s. And, as mentioned in Chapter 6, the Exxon Valdez grounding and oil spill in 1989 was an immensely important event for this field, with millions spent on obtaining damage estimates using direct methods and on critiquing those methods. There is by no means universal agreement about what has been learned from these years of work, but the executive summary of my interpretation is that:

- There is not much evidence in the literature that people systematically understate their WTP for hypothetical public goods. If anything, there is evidence of overstatement.

- There is substantial evidence that the single greatest difficulty facing application of direct questioning is people's inability to know what their true WTP is for unfamiliar and difficult-to-understand "goods" such as changes in environmental quality.

- One result of this "cognitive" difficulty is that people seem to resort to fairly rough rules of thumb for picking responses.
- These rules of thumb are often sensitive to small, even irrelevant, details of the survey instrument and may be disappointingly insensitive to highly relevant details.

The net result is more than enough controversy to keep a generation or two of environmental economists, interested psychologists, and decision theorists busy. And the pages of the important field journals are full of ingenious efforts to probe for weak spots, suggest improvements, and invent or adapt quite different, but still direct, approaches.

In this part of the text, I shall first look a little more carefully at the traditional economic concern—strategic responses. We'll see there is more to it than the free-riding possibility, but that even early on the evidence from experiments was that at best (or worst) few people seemed to be acting this way.

Then I shall turn to what should be logically the prior concern—with people's *ability* to answer WTP questions, especially where unfamiliar and complex environmental goods are concerned. We shall see that there are two problems here: ability to know your WTP in the current, hypothetical setting; and ability to know how you would feel in a future "real" situation.

These concerns will lead fairly naturally into a look at some of the troubles that plague the practioners of direct valuation today and to some of the proposals for improvement in methods.

STRATEGIC RESPONSES

Early on it was recognized that "free riding" was not the only possible strategic response to WTP questioning and that, if people were going to conceal true preferences, how they did so would likely depend on the situation they faced in the survey. The major possibilities are captured in a two-by-two table with cells depending on the influence on survey responses of (a) whether or not the good is to be provided and (b) how the size of the individual respondent's payment for the provision will be determined. See Table 8.1.

BOHM'S TV EXPERIMENT

One of the most impressive pieces of evidence probing these a priori expectations was also one of the earliest in the entire field. This was an experiment done in Stockholm in 1972 by Peter Bohm, an imaginative and ingenious Swedish economist.[2] It involved asking questions about willingness to pay to see a new TV program made by two famous Swedish television humorists. The experiment was conducted by the Swedish TV and Radio Broadcasting authority, and the subjects were first given an amount of money for participating. This amount (50 Swedish kroner [SEK] or then

TABLE 8.1 Incentives in Answering Direct Willingness to Pay Questions

	If Provision of the Public Good:	
If the Respondent's Payment:	**Depends on the Survey Results**	**Does Not Depend on the Survey Result**
Depends on her/his response	An interesting challenge— might even try to tell the truth despite publicness	Incentive to "underbid" (i.e., free ride)
Does not depend on her/his response	Incentive to overbid	No incentive even to think about the question very hard

about $10), was larger than all but 1 of the 211 responses to the WTP question, and about six times as large as the mean bids turned out to be.

The central feature of the experiment was the division of the total experimental group into six distinct subgroups on the basis of the relation between their responses and the payment they would make to see the show. They were told this payment would be due if the total bid by them and by "many other people" also answering the questions totaled at least 500 SEK, the "cost." The expectation was that by varying the incentives to misrepresent, the experiment would produce a range of WTP numbers that would include the "true" WTP. (This, of course, depended on keeping the group subsamples similar in all relevant ways, such as education, age, and probably income.)

The six subgroup "treatments" were the following:

Subgroup	Payment arrangement
I	Pay what you say.
II	Pay a fraction of what you say, equal to the cost of providing the show divided by the group's total stated WTP.
III	Pay an amount made uncertain by an intervening random process in which methods I, II, IV, and V are equally likely.
IV	Pay a fixed amount, independent of stated WTP.
V	Pay nothing.
VI(1)	Simple polling question; no mention of cost or payment.

For the first five groups, provision of the good—seeing the show—was made, at least in prospect, dependent on the total stated WTP of the group exceeding the cost of provision. (The good, getting into the theater to see the show, was thus made "public." Either everyone enjoyed it together or no one did.) Thus, in terms of Table 8.1, the arrangements, in effect, involve only the first column. There was no full-bore incentive offered for free riding. Nonetheless, the expectations were that the groups' WTP would be ordered in the following way because of the payment arrangements[3]:

$$WTP(IV, V) > WTP(III) > WTP(II) > WTP(I)$$

To provide a benchmark valuation of the good on offer, the sixth group, after answering a purely hypothetical question, was presented with an auction of the individual right to see the show. (The good was "privatized" for them.) The group WTP revealed by this mechanism was considered a priori to be the accurate WTP. I refer to this treatment as VI(2).

In the event, the experimental results revealed no statistically significant differences in the mean stated WTP amounts for the groups subject to "treatments" I through V. To many economists, and I include myself here, this has seemed particularly powerful evidence against systematic misrepresentation—"particularly powerful" because the good being asked about, while not itself familiar (being unseen), involved familiar "stars" and so must have been as well "understood" as anything in the future can be. So we cannot say here, as we can in so much environmental survey work, that people couldn't realistically be expected to know what they were bidding on.

There were, however, significant differences between the mean of responses to the *purely hypothetical* question—VI(1) in shorthand—and the means for treatment I and III (both at 1% significance), IV (at 6%), and the pooled results for all treatments I through V. In each case the hypothetical response means (from VI(1)) are *higher*. These differences are consistent with the prediction in Table 8.1, and are what Bohm and others have seized on to argue that the experiment provides, in effect, the opposite of support for direct questioning methods. That is, when payments are involved, even uncertain (III) or fixed (IV) payments, the exercise remains rooted in reality for the participants, and they answer with something like care. Even in V, where no payment was involved, respondents were anchored in reality by the contingent nature of the decision that would be made about the show. (Recall that more than 500 SEK, it was said, had to be bid by all the people taking the survey for the group to see the show.) Bohm has argued, and continues to argue, that only in situations of such reality anchoring can questioning techniques be useful for public policy.

He has said a good deal more besides, including suggesting what he calls the "interval method." Here, in what he calls a nonhypothetical setting, incentives for overstatement and understatement are systematically employed so that a range of WTP estimates is produced. Then, if the revealed WTP using the understatement incentives were greater than the cost, it would be strong evidence that the project is very likely worth doing, whereas if responses to questions including the overstatement incentives fell short of the cost, the opposite conclusion might confidently be reached—at least from the efficiency point of view.[4]

But it is worth lingering a bit longer over this important experiment. It seems to me that one very interesting question involves something that did *not* happen—

TABLE 8.2 Integer-Valued Bids in Bohm's Experiment

| | *Number of "Bids" at Integer Values Out of Total Bids in Relevant Interval* | | |
Bid (SEK)	From I–V	From I–VI(2)	In Interval (SEK)
5	39[a] (of 50)	55 (of 70)	4.6–6.5
10	<u>29</u> (of 29)	<u>54</u> (of 54)	8.6–10.5
Total	68 (of 157)	109 (of 211)	(all bids)

[a] My estimate, calculated as 55/70 × 50.

the responses to V, where seeing the show was said to be contingent on the total of bids but no payment was going to be required, were *not* higher than those to I through IV, where payments were required. It is only by assertion that V is not hypothetical; and indeed the contingent nature of the showing would seem to make the setup perfect for eliciting overstatements. What was it about the question that produced the observed result? One candidate is the information about cost. All the treatments I through V involved telling the respondents what the cost of the showing was (500 SEK) and thus presenting them with a target, as it were.

Granted this was a very fuzzy target, since they knew only that in order to see the show they, together with "a large number of people sitting in several rooms like this in this building," would collectively have to bid over 500 SEK to see the show. But looking at Bohm's report of the bids in his 1972 article we find the following interesting results. (See Table 8.2) That is, about 43 percent (68/157) of responses from groups I through V might be said to have reflected a simple calculation of how much would have to be bid if the "large number" of subjects involved were 50 (producing 10 SEK) or 100 (producing 5 SEK). Further, 12 or 13 (of 13 in the interval 12.60–17.50) bid 15 SEK. Another 5 (of 5 in the interval 17.60–22.50) bid 20 SEK. Four (of 5 in the interval 22.60–27.50) bid 25. And 1 (of one in the interval 27.60–32.50) bid 30. So a total of 90 of the 157 responses involved 5, 10, 15, 20, 25, or 30 SEK. Four of those amounts are consistent with whole numbers of participants and the respondent's guess at what bid would be necessary to get to 500 SEK.)

Now, it is true that the purely hypothetical responses also tended to clump at the amounts divisible by 5. But with even less by way of a target, their variance was greater. The standard deviations of the subgroup means were:

I	6.11
II	5.84
III	4.11
IV	4.68
V	6.24
VI(1)	7.79
VI(2)	6.84

Since the lowest bid allowed for was zero but there was no upper limit, greater dispersion will tend to produce a higher mean.[5] This is the essence of the so-called hypothetical bias. But we see here that "hypothetical" ought to be considered a relative rather than an absolute condition.

It seems to me that the problem uncovered by Bohm has nothing much to do with strategic misrepresentation. Rather he simply showed early on that people who have only a vague idea of what something is worth to them will grasp at relatively weak straws to provide answers that are honest if not necessarily meaningful.

"INCENTIVE-COMPATIBLE" MECHANISMS

In the days when strategic responses were seen as the biggest threat to the usefulness of WTP surveys, a good deal of intellectual firepower was trained on the target of designing so-called incentive-compatible demand-revelation mechanisms. The challenge was to structure the payment mechanism so that individuals facing it would recognize an incentive compatible with telling the truth. The simplest such mechanism with which I am acquainted involves the following rule:

> Each person in the relevant group will be taxed, if the public good in question is provided, an amount equal to the difference between the cost of provision and the sum of the stated WTPs for all the *other* members of the group.

Thus, for person i in a group of N people asked about WTP for a public good Q that could be provided to all of them:

If the good is provided it must be true that:

$$\sum_{j=1}^{N} WTP_j = \sum_{j \neq 1}^{N} WTP_j + WTP_i > C(Q)$$

and i's tax will be:

$$T_i = C(Q) - \sum_{j \neq 1}^{N} WTP_j$$

So *each* person is, in effect, put in the position of being the decisive "vote" on provision. If $\sum_{j \neq i} WTP_j < C(Q)$, a high enough stated WTP_i will push the bid total over the top and create for i (and for each other person, since all are treated symmetrically) a tax bill equal to the difference between what others are willing to pay and total cost.

To see that overbidding, at least, is not a conservative strategy, let's look at a simple numerical example. Assume the following "facts":

Cost of public good provision $= 100$

WTP for public good of person $i = 15$

Using the tax rule above produces the following payoff matrix for person i; I provide numbers for only five bids, an "accurate" one (15) and two others on either side of the accurate one. The unknown (source of uncertainty) is the sum of the bids from the other people. Let me call that z. Payoffs are in two parts: provision (1 for provided, 0 for not), and tax bill. (See Table 8.3) Using a conservative rule of picking the bid strategy that produces the least bad of the worst results in the right-hand column leads person i to be indifferent between underbidding and bidding accurately.[6] But person i rejects overbidding under this rule, since overpaying for the good is worse than not getting it and paying no tax.

It is important to emphasize that this mechanism depends for its power on actual payments being collected. As a hypothetical question it is no different from any other formulation, though more complicated to state. But as a "real" mechanism it suffers from at least three flaws[7]:

- It would strike any politician asked to approve it as bizarre and, probably, any prospective subject as ridiculous or threatening.
- It has been shown to be manipulable by strategic coalitions of individuals, even though individuals "playing" alone find it optimal to tell the truth.
- The taxes collected could be as small as zero (if every $N - 1$ size subset has total WTP $\geq$ cost) and never greater than C (if the sum of all N WTPs is exactly equal to C).

UNCERTAINTY

The power of the simple incentive-compatible mechanism just discussed depended on uncertainty about what other people would bid. Bohm's subgroup III also faced uncertainty, where the outcome depended on choice of payment rule plus own bid (for I) and own bid plus bids of others (for II), if the sum of all bids led to provision of the show. The idea in the Bohm experiment is that there is no clear strategy for misrepresentation in group III, and that trying to devise such a strategy would involve difficult calculations, especially if they have to be done quickly in one's head. So truth-telling might well be seized on as the best readily available alternative.

TABLE 8.3 Person i's Payoff Matrix

| | Sum of Bids from Others (z) | | | | | | |
	100	95	90	85	80	75	70	Worst Result for Each Bid
Underbid (5)	1, 0	1, –5	0, 0	0, 0	0, 0	0, 0	0, 0	(0, 0)
Underbid (10)	1, 0	1, –5	1, –10	0, 0	0, 0	0, 0	0, 0	(0, 0)
Accurate bid (15)	1, 0	1, –5	1, –10	1, –15	0, 0	0, 0	0, 0	(0, 0) = (1, –15)
Overbid (20)	1, 0	1, –5	1, –10	1, –15	1, –20	0, 0	0, 0	(1, –20)
Overbid (25)	1, 0	1, –5	1, –10	1, –15	1, –20	1, –25	0, 0	(1, –25)

This approach has been adopted, in somewhat fuzzier versions, by many practitioners and experimenters; one way or another people are left wondering, it is assumed, how their responses will affect their payments. The fuzziest approach simply asserts that if the project (or policy) in question is done (or adopted), the bill will be paid by some combination of higher prices and taxes. Thus, adding uncertainty is a theoretically respectable way of trying to deal with the economist's traditional worry. But it is interesting to note, by way of introducing a bridge to the next major problem area, that adding uncertainty makes the respondent's problem of deciding how to respond *more* difficult. This may seem a less attractive way to proceed if the big difficulties with WTP surveys are seen to lie in the lack of knowledge and rapid calculating ability of lay respondents, rather than in the cleverness and self-interest of those same people.

COGNITIVE DIFFICULTIES AND LACK OF KNOWLEDGE

To put the contrast a bit more starkly and simply than is entirely accurate, those who come to WTP surveys from a background in psychology do not worry about respondents concealing their true preferences. Rather they are trained to doubt that respondents can *know* those "true" preferences, either in the sense that they can do the hypothetical internal computations to value some unfamiliar and often complex good or service in the survey setting; or in the more important sense that they can predict how they would *actually* want to answer if the hypothetical became real. To some extent this conditioned view is based on classic work that has had the same status as Samuelson's dictum on free riding. One tremendously influential study done in the 1930s, for example, showed that overnight accommodation keepers were unable (or possibly unwilling) to predict how they would actually behave when faced with the (then-difficult) decision of whether to rent a room/cabin to a Chinese couple (Lapiere, 1934).

More recently, and at least as persuasively, research on the shared frontier of psychology, decision analysis, and economics has shown that people confronted by such survey questions as: What would you be willing to pay to fix problem *x*, or avoid problem *y*, or achieve good outcome *z*?, in effect make it up as they go along (or, said less informally, "construct their preferences" in the course of the interview).[8]

This pervasive difficulty of answering WTP questions, particularly when the goods or services to be valued are unfamiliar, subtle, uncertain, distant in time or space, or complex and multidimensional, seems to me to lie behind many of the problems that environmental economists struggle with in trying to apply direct survey techniques to get at benefits or damages. My partial but none the less daunting catalog of those problems would include:

1. Hypothetical bias—the problem observed by Peter Bohm when, *without any incentive to do so*, people facing hypothetical WTP questions tend to overstate, insofar as we have benchmarks against which to hold their responses.

2. The "embedding effect" (or size invariance of responses). Here respondent's stated WTP seems almost invariant with the size of the hypothetical effect asked about, be it numbers of birds saved from oil pollution or numbers of lakes with higher water quality on account of some policy.

3. The difference between mean WTP results obtained from similar samples using open-ended (what are you WTP?) and "dichotomous" (are you willing to pay W?) questions. (The latter are generally higher.)

4. All of the above may be related to something that has come to be called the "warm-glow effect"—that people appear to derive some pleasure from announcing that they *are* WTP some amount for what must be (because it is being asked about) a worthwhile environmental result. That is, people in the survey setting may finesse the actual question and focus instead on the act of responding and on how differences in that act make them feel.

The links here may be along the following lines: The respondent has no real idea what his/her WTP for some described environmental effect is but has no doubt that this effect is basically desirable. For such situations people may be able to pull a number out of the air that seems adequate as a statement of good will—and that thus produces a warm glow. That statement may then be difficult to revise up or down if the quantity of the good in question is somehow varied. At the same time, the desire to make such a statement of good will pushes the respondent to say "yes" to a take-it-or-leave-it suggested amount (a yes/no, dichotomous question) because leaving it (saying no) seems to imply the possibility that the respondent does not, in fact, recognize the value of the hypothetical good.

5. The effects of survey instrument details that "should" be irrelevant for the fully rational, fully informed person. Examples here include:

a. Choice of "payment vehicle" (how any hypothetical cost will be paid), taxes, prices, donations, or whatever. It seems that in the United States, WTP is lower when taxes are the proposed vehicle; in Europe, the opposite is true.

b. Effects of question order, particularly as related to a series of WTP questions. Here, the first items tend to get the high expression of WTP.

c. "Yea-saying." Here respondents are found to say yes to questions, whether to "please" the interviewer or to minimize effort or for some other reason.

Notice that if lack of knowledge, forethought, and quick calculation/introspection capability are recognized as the great bar to making direct questioning approaches really useful contributors to policy and project analysis, then two related conclusions seem to follow:

• It is self-defeating, even foolish, to think that asking difficult questions without providing some previous information is a good way to proceed.

• In the course of providing the information and asking the questions, the survey itself will help the respondent "construct" his or her preferences.

These observations make economists very uncomfortable, first because they seem to leave the door open to manipulation by the unscrupulous, and second because the whole notion of preferences constructed ad hoc runs counter to the thoroughly rational homo economicus, mentally equipped for any situation or question with pre-existing preferences to be called on at will.

SOME OTHER CHALLENGES FOR DIRECT QUESTIONING METHODS

Whether you are inclined to believe that the major problems are those flowing from too much or from not enough knowledge and calculating ability, you need to recognize several other challenges in the WTP survey game.

First, there is a well-documented unease among some fraction of respondents with the very idea of putting money and environmental goods and services on the same scale. In my experience this unease is most obvious and acute among those who care most strongly about the environment. It seems that they would like to have the environmental "cause" treated as symmetric with the basic "values" (see Chapter 6) of society and not as just another more-versus-less trade-off decision in which money becomes a useful common denominator. People who feel this way are likely to refuse to respond or to respond with a protest amount (very high or very low, which may or may not be discoverable as such by data analysis).

A second problem, probably related to the first, is our apparent inability to get people to answer willingness-to-accept (WTA) (compensation) as opposed to WTP questions. The reason this is a problem is itself twofold. First, in cases in which a policy or project would in effect take away "rights," even if only de facto rights of usage, the affected parties should, ethically, be asked about what compensation they would require to accept the loss (WTA). And second, there is a priori reason to expect an accurate estimate of WTA to exceed a WTP measure for the symmetric but opposite change of situation.[9]

But respondents appear to object to the idea of compensation as being in the nature of a "bribe" to accept an immoral outcome. Their objection often takes the form of very high "bids" (high stated required compensation); much higher than seems supportable on the basis of the so-called Willig bounds or the Randall–Stoll version of them for public good quantity changes. Michael Hanemann (1991) has suggested that these statements are in fact consistent with theory when lack of available substitutes for the "lost" goods or services is taken into account. But there is still no confidence that answers to hypothetical WTA questions mean even as much as answers to WTP questions.

A third challenge is closely related to the concept of nonuse damages or benefits as legitimate parts of the aggregate damages or benefits from environmental changes. To avoid a long and complex discussion and taxonomy of the nonuse idea, let us just agree to let this phrase refer to the effects "enjoyed" by people who neither use nor think they might *ever* use the good or service in question. Thus, you might be WTP something to help ensure the survival of the great, exotic ecosystems of eastern Africa without ever having been there, and having no idea of ever going there. Your motives for this might be subtle and complex, involving judgments about human society's stewardship obligations and the desire to hand on such systems to future generations. Or this might be another warm glow effect but one not identifiable as such by an outside observer.

The question raised in starkest terms by nonuse benefits or damages is: Whose preferences (WTP) count? Or, said in economic jargon: What is the "extent of the (hypothetical) market"?[10] There is both a practical and an ethical dimension here. Practically, there is no way to know the answer in advance. By setting generous limits for the population to be surveyed, one can lower the probability of leaving out some contributions to aggregate damages or benefits. But setting generous limits increases survey costs; if particular levels of sampling error are to be maintained, the number surveyed must increase. The ethical problem is to determine who *should* count. To pick up on the earlier example, should your feelings about East African wildlife count in any analysis of Kenyan or Zimbabwean wildlife policy? After all, you are not in a position to make a contribution to offset the cost to peasant farmers of protecting elephants who trample crops, destroy fences and houses, and even kill people.[11] Similarly, someone in Germany might express WTP to know that there will never be a new dam in the Hells Canyon of the Snake River in the U.S. Northwest. *Should* that be relevant to any benefit-cost analysis? For an example of a study that provides food for thought about non-use benefits and the "extent of the market," see Box 7.6 on the Tuolumne preservation benefit study.

In the next section I turn to direct approaches that require inference of WTP from responses to questions about *vectors* of situation characteristics.

CONJOINT ANALYSIS

Conjoint analysis (CA) encompasses a number of indirect hypothetical methodologies that are widely used by market researchers in the evaluation of new products and markets.[12] These multiattribute, preference-elicitation techniques are based on the premise that commodities can be viewed as bundles of various attributes (recall "hedonics"). In CA studies, respondents rank or rate a series of these bundles in which some or all of the different attributes are allowed to vary. From these rankings or ratings of the different bundles, marginal rates of substitution between the different attributes can be estimated. By including price as one of the attributes, these marginal rates of substitution can be translated into WTP for changes in attribute levels.

There are four different kinds of multiattribute elicitation formats used in CA. The first of these is *dichotomous* or *contingent choice*, where respondents are simply asked to choose their most preferred alternative from two or more choices with differing levels of attributes. Some contingent choice studies force respondents to choose one of the alternatives and some allow respondents to reject all. Dichotomous choice contingent valuation (Are you willing to pay W or not?) is essentially a special case of dichotomous choice CA, where the study is limited to two alternatives, one being the status quo and the other variation in only two variables, price and the environmental quality. Relaxing these restrictions allows CA to emphasize tradeoffs among hypothetical alternatives over the purchase of an environmental amenity. Some have argued that this change in emphasis deflects emotional stress and, as a result, is less likely to generate protest or symbolic responses. Dichotomous choice CA has been used to estimate WTP to preserve different kinds of undeveloped land, to take recreational fishing trips, preferences for locating landfills, and for reducing health risks.

A second form of CA, *contingent ranking*, asks respondents to rank a set of hypothetical alternatives from "most preferred" to "least preferred." Contingent ranking has been used to evaluate the demand for electric cars and WTP for improved visibility at national parks and for improved water quality. A third form of CA, *contingent rating,* asks respondents to rate a set of hypothetical alternatives on a numerical scale. The difference between ranking and rating is that the latter asks respondents to supply information about *how much* they prefer one bundle to another. Since the responses to a contingent rating survey contain more information than the responses to a contingent ranking survey, some authors have asserted that contingent rating is the superior exercise. However, these assertions assume that the two methods are equivalent in terms of the "accuracy" of the preferences elicited, and this assumption is unproven. Contingent rating has been used to estimate WTP for different attributes of salmon fishing and waterfowl hunting.

A fourth type of CA is *graded pair* or *pairwise rating.* In graded pair surveys, respondents are shown two alternatives and are asked to show their preference for one of the products by choosing a number within a set of numbers, say from 1 to 7, where 1 represents the strongest possible preference for one good and 7 the strongest possible preference for the other good. The exercise is then repeated a number of times with different hypothetical alternatives. In addition to estimating the demand for electric cars, pairwise rating has been used to estimate WTP to avoid the adverse effects of electricity generation and to achieve health benefits from improved air quality.

CA is perceived as having a number of potential advantages over CV. For one thing, respondents are not required to monetize environmental goods or services explicitly. As one author put it:

> Finally, [CA] offers some significant practical advantages over [CV]. Respondents are generally more comfortable providing qualitative rankings or ratings of attribute bundles, which include prices, rather than dollar valuations of the same bundles without prices. In de-emphasizing price as simply another attribute, [CA] minimizes many of the biases that can arise in open-ended [CV] studies when respondents are presented with the unfamiliar and often unrealistic task of putting prices on non-market amenities. (Mackenzie, 1992).

Stated differently, CA focuses respondents on marginal tradeoffs between attributes as opposed to stating a maximum WTP. A second advantage is that CA allows a more detailed evaluation of the alternatives. Like dichotomous choice CV, CA is believed to present a more realistic, familiar setting for respondents[13] and to be free from strategic bias (though I have tried to persuade you that strategic bias is unlikely to be a big problem, anyway). Finally, if, as some researchers believe, the ability to "accurately" answer hypothetical questions about unfamiliar goods improves with reflection or examination of preferences, such that responding to a survey can be viewed as a dynamic learning process, then the greater number of elicited responses in CA may allow more room for this dynamic learning process to occur. This last potential advantage, though, is offset by a potential disadvantage—that people will tire of answering questions and, thus, the "accuracy" of their responses will decline as the survey progresses.

Although early evidence on CA is mixed, it seems clear that the indirect hypothetical methodologies will be the focus of much of the future development of nonmarket benefit estimation:

> In addition to willingness to pay, contingent purchases, and contingent policy referendum methods, we are now seeing an explosion of contingent ranking and contingent choice experiments. We can in the near future expect to see contingent resource compensation experiments in which the relative values of different kinds of resource services are compared directly, rather than mediated by money measures. This proliferation of methods is desirable, and can confidently be expected to continue. (Randall, 1997)
>
> Hypothetical market methods appear to have a substantial role to play in securing a fuller incorporation of environmental considerations into public decision making. For many environmental goods, they seem to offer what is effectively the only way forward. Within this context, [CV] and [CA] should be seen as variations on a theme. They share many of the same strengths and weaknesses; overcoming problems with one will often help overcome equivalent problems with the other. (Pearman, 1994)

A TECHNICAL PROBLEM

There is one important *technical* caveat involved with all the CA methods and with yes/no (so-called referendum) versions of CV. The fact that a respondent does not directly give a WTP estimate for herself or himself means that there must be an intermediate *inferential* stage in the benefit estimation process. This stage takes the yes/no or ranking or rating information from the survey results, embeds it in an assumed structure of preferences and errors in the response "mechanism," and uses econometric techniques to tease out the desired WTP answer. The problem with all this is that the final answer is, in general, quite sensitive to the choices made at each step of the structuring and teasing-out process.

It would go beyond the limits of this text to discuss this problem in any depth, but a fairly simple example will give you an idea of how serious it can be. This example is based on the simplest technique—the referendum CV—requiring inference of WTP. In such a study, each respondent answers yes or no to a question: Would you be (are you) willing to pay W for the described environmental change? Since across the sample, different values are posited for W, the data from such a survey has, at its heart, a set of observations of the form:

Posited W or "Bid"	% Agreeing they would pay W (accepting "Bid")
W_1	P_1
W_2	P_2
:	:
W_M	P_M

If the W_i above are ordered so that $W_1 < W_2 < \ldots < W_M$, then we expect $P_1 > P_2 > \ldots > P_M$, subject to random response error and the systematic influence of such independent variables as income, education, and preexisting environmental position. The analyst faced with data of this sort can choose from among roughly a dozen methods for inferring the relationship between probability of the respondent accepting the "bid" presented her or him and the size of that bid. The resulting relationship implies a mean WTP for the project or policy being asked about that may be attributed to the population as a whole or to parts of that population as distinguished by particular characteristics. Then to complete the benefit side of the cost-benefit analysis, the inferred mean WTP(s) is (are) multiplied by the number of individuals assumed to be fairly characterized by that number (or each of those numbers).

To illustrate how much difference in final results can be produced by different choices of economically respectable estimation methods, I have reproduced here as Table 8.4 a simplified version of a table reporting such a range of results for an actual project being considered for a Latin American country by one of the multinational lending agencies. (Vaughan et al., 2000)

The project involved building sewers and wastewater treatment plants with the aim of improving ambient water quality in a river flowing through a major industrial city. Under preproject conditions, this river regularly had periods of zero dissolved oxygen, with attendant problems of noxious smells over reaches within the city itself and much longer reaches that were of no recreational value at any time because of poor water quality (smell, turbidity, lack of aquatic life, and generally disgusting appearance). The WTP figures were sought by describing the project and its predicted effects on the river's quality and then asking the respondent if she or he would be willing to pay an amount W_j that varied across the sample of people interviewed. That sample was divided between people living close to the river, who could be expected to care a good deal about its condition, and those living farther from it, who could be expected to care less.

In the table, all the numbers are in the local currency, with the first two columns

TABLE 8.4 Ranges of Per-Household WTP and Resulting Cost-Benefit
Results Produced by Alternative Estimation Methods

Methods Briefly Described	WTP per Household per Month (local currency)		Net Present Value of Project (10^6 currency units)	
	Close to River	Far from River	Optimistic Assumptions (see text)	Pessimistic Assumptions (see text)
Linear function; assumes acceptance is 100% at zero bid	9.73	6.16	684	310
Graphical method; no function estimated; observed data points connected	9.42	7.09	704	322
Linear function; same assumption as (1); plus assumes acceptance is zero above max. bid offered	7.65	5.03	501	202
Alternative graphical method to (2)	6.07	4.51	376	128
Linear function; no assumption about 100% acceptance level so this can be negative	4.74	−1.27	−96[a]	−38[a]
Log function; no assumption about bid intercept	4.66	1.46	153	−4
Log function; bid intercept = income of average household	3.49	1.23	67	−55
Graphical method to obtain median rather than mean	3.33	1.83	83	−46
Nonlinear function; bid intercept = income median, not mean	3.21	0.63	24	−81
Log function as in (7) median, not mean	2.34	0.61	−34	−115

[a] Negative WTP for far-from-river subsample set to zero in net benefit calculation.

reporting on the inferred WTP per average household per month for the close and far (from the river) populations respectively. These WTP numbers are ordered in decreasing size of the estimate for the close subsample. Notice that the ratio of highest to lowest estimate is over 4 for the close households and about 10 for the far households. Notice also that one technique that gives a WTP estimate near the middle of the range for the close subsample produces a *negative* monthly WTP for the far group. That is, the method infers that this group would, on average, want to be *compensated* if the project were built. If this were the only result that had been calculated for this group, it could be very troubling, for the simple implication is that a significant group does not look at this as a desirable project, perhaps because they anticipate some sort of negative externalities. (Though what these could be in this case is very hard to see.) It is also possible that these respondents were, on average, cynical about the possibility that the predicted good effects were ever going to be achieved and were expressing their cynicism in their responses. But since we have in this case quite a few other positive estimates of mean household WTP on the part of this group, we can see that this is best taken to be an extreme result of the particular choice of estimation method represented by that row of the table.

One way of thinking about how the choice of estimation method can lead to such large differences is as follows: The range of "bids" (the Ws) offered to the sample may not sufficiently tie down two important parts of the relationship between bid level and probability of acceptance. The first is the level of bid that allows for 100-percent acceptance. For example, the lowest bid offered in the survey might be 0.5 unit per month, and that might be too high to be accepted by all those offered it. This leaves open the probability axis intercept for the estimated relationship. The other key point is the bid level that drives acceptance to zero—the intercept of the relationship with the bid axis. Figure 8.1 provides a sketch of the problem emphasizing these two uncertainties. Together the uncertainties, in turn, leave uncertain how much of the relationship's "weight" is to be found in the region of negative bids. Only two possibilities are illustrated to keep the sketch simple, but one of these has a substantial weight in the negative WTP region.

The last two columns of the table illustrate how large the effects of this relationship uncertainty can be for the overall project (or policy analysis). In the first of these columns the underlying assumptions about the timing of project construction (hence how soon benefits begin to be accrued) and about whether some "extra" benefits from the generation of electric energy by the project are actually enjoyed are optimistic.[14] In the second they are pessimistic. You can see that the uncertainty about project acceptability resulting just from the uncertainty about the bid/probability of acceptance relationship is significant. Under the optimistic assumption, almost all the

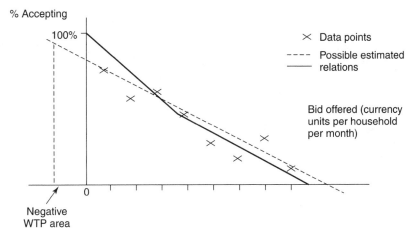

Figure 8.1 A Sketch of the Uncertainty About Function Shape: Probability of Acceptance Related to "Bid" Offered. WTP, willingness to pay.

methods produce a positive present value of project net benefits. But under the pessimistic assumptions only four of ten of the methods do.

Of course the choice of method is not itself a matter of chance. Armed with information like that in the table, the analyst could choose a method of inference that would be most likely to give a high mean WTP estimate. That is, sensitivity of results to estimation method choice becomes, in the practical world in which project proposers have a stake in getting the project funded, susceptibility to manipulation via strategic choice of that method.

This technical problem does not exist in what might be (and has been) called the "conventional" contingent valuation method. Thus, we arrive at another trade-off:

Conventional CVM may involve problems with responses to direct questions about WTP (protests, ignorance, confusion). But the responses, once obtained, do not have to be econometrically "massaged."

The "conjoint analysis" methods may get around the challenges of obtaining responses because they never ask the questions most likely to provoke protests, show up ignorance, or trigger confusion. But those responses are only translatable into WTP via techniques that themselves determine the answer, and among the set of which choice is arbitrary.

THREE FINAL, PRACTICAL PROBLEMS

Three other practical problems for use of any direct questioning technique have already been mentioned: sample size and sampling method, and survey format. The first of these can be "solved" by making assumptions about the standard deviations in responses to key questions and picking an "acceptable" confidence interval for the conclusions of the study.[15] But this is not a course in statistics, and I leave the technical details to others, observing only that most rules of thumb are based on the usual opinion survey problem, where key questions are of the yes/no variety for which a priori standard deviations can be calculated on the basis of the number sampled and the a priori probability of one of the answers. These easy answers usually do not apply to WTP surveys. *How* to sample depends on details about the society within which the sampling is to take place. In most OECD countries, random telephone dialing will produce random sets of people who can be interviewed over the phone, mailed surveys, or visited (if they agree). But in countries with relatively few phone lines per 100,000 people, this technique will produce a sample biased toward more income (or influence).[16]

A final, very important practical choice is that of survey type—phone, mail, person-to-person interview, or group interview. To go into the advantages and disadvantages of each would take us rather far afield. So only a few, to some extent obvious comments will have to suffice. Phone interviews are cheap and quick but depend on the survey involving information that can be adequately conveyed orally. Mail surveys give more scope for the transfer of information by allowing for graphs, charts, and still pictures. They are usually reckoned more expensive than phone surveys and involve "nonresponse" bias problems since, without the goad of another person (the interviewer) present or on the phone, more people are likely to simply fail to respond—and these will tend to be those who care least. In-person interviews, one-on-one, are ideal, giving maximum scope for information transfer, especially if computers can be used. But they are substantially more expensive than the other methods. Group "interviews" in suitable settings can have some of the information transfer advantages of the one-on-one interview at less expense. But there are always the risks that the study team will lose control of the group dynamic or that burning questions of clarification will go unasked because of shyness. In short, there is no single right answer to the how-to-survey question.

AN ATTEMPT AT A BOTTOM LINE ON DIRECT QUESTIONING TECHNIQUES

At the end of the day, I think that we have no real alternative to trying to improve direct questioning techniques. The two major reasons have already been stated:

- Indirect methods do not match the problem settings that have to be addressed. Underlapping and overlapping are unavoidable and not correctable, even when only "use" benefits or damages are sought.

- Nonuse damages or benefits are both real and ethically important, though where to draw the line around "relevant" nonusers will remain an enormously difficult question in any real situation.

But the problems posed by the hypothetical nature of most of these studies, in combination with the limited knowledge and calculating abilities of lay respondents (ordinary people, as opposed to experts), are themselves enormously difficult. Attempts to improve on the current situation will, it seems to me, have to involve at least the following:

- Some agreement on how and how much to inform respondents about unfamiliar problems before asking them questions. This will have to involve finding out what puzzles each person and addressing the puzzlement. The old ideal of steamrollering over confusion by rereading (not even restating) the question to maintain survey purity will have to be modified for complex and unfamiliar situations. At the same time, the technology of conveying information will have to be improved. The printed word and the reproduced still photo can only carry us so far. Both these observations suggest to me that the future lies with interactive computer graphics and questions on highly portable computers.

- Better ways will have to be found to get to the ultimately interesting question of WTP (or (WTA) for some environmental change. Perhaps the answer will lie with adapting conjoint analysis from marketing, or the stated preference method from transportation, or multiattribute utility techniques from decision analysis. All these methods are designed with vector problems in mind. And most of the biggest valuation challenges of the future are likely to involve such problems, where multiple dimensions of an environmental feature or component, such as an ecological system, can all change more or less independently so that no single dimension can be seized on as the key to valuation.

NOTES

1. As already mentioned, this early work was supported by U.S. EPA, thanks almost entirely to the adventurous spirit and farsightedness of a single employee.

2. Bohm does not interpret his results as I do, and indeed finds it upsetting that this experiment has become something of a rock in the foundation of people's optimism about the prospects for direct questioning techniques. I will try to make clear where and why I think we differ, but if you are interested in pursuing this further, see Bohm, "Estimating the Demand for Public Goods: An Experiment," 1972, and "CVM Spells Responses to Hypothetical Questions," 1994.

3. Because of the way "null hypotheses" are stated for testing, the "null" here was that payment rules I–V would yield identical WTP estimates.

4. See below for some very important qualifications even to these modest hopes, especially on matters of the "extent of the market" for a real good and the role of nonusers and their WTP.

5. Neither clause of this sentence is necessarily true. Some people might well require a payment for sitting through a half-hour TV comedy show. But this possibility does not appear to have been pointed out to the experiment participants, an oversight common in WTP surveys, where the "goodness" (or "badness") of the plan, project, or policy in question is usually assumed. And even when bids are truncated at zero, greater dispersion does not logically *imply* a higher mean. (As a simple counter example calculate the means and standard deviations for the two sets of bids: [3, 3, 3, 3] and [1, 2, 3, 4]).

6. Not having/not paying is equivalent for person i to having the good and paying the tax of 15. Recall that this is the definition of WTP, from Chapter 6.

7. An alternative version of this mechanism would have respondents pay a tax equal to their stated WTP if and only if the sum of WTPs over all respondents exceeds the cost of provision. This also provides a "truth-telling" incentive but has the flaw of allowing the collection of tax totals much greater than the cost of provision. How to deal with such surpluses would be a difficult question in itself, since returning them to respondents in any way related to amounts bid would introduce a new and destructive incentive to overstate.

8. For those interested in following this up, a few good initial sources are: Robin Gregory, Sarah Lichtenstein, and Paul Slovic, "Valuing Environmental Resources: A Constructive Approach," 1993; Charles Harris, B. L. Driver, and William J. McLaughlin, "Improving the Contingent Valuation Method: A Psychological Perspective," 1989; and David Schkade and John Payne. "How People Respond to Contingent Valuation Questions: A Verbal Protocol Analysis of Willingness to Pay for Environmental Regulation," 1994. There is, of course, a strong link here to the problems people have in dealing with uncertainty, discussed in Chapter 12.

9. Robert Willig (1976) produced a limit on the difference between WTA and WTP when the change involved was in the price of a marketed good. Because his interest was actually in the size of the difference between the correct, Hicksian (compensated) surpluses and consumer surplus from a Marshallian (ordinary, uncompensated) demand curve, the result is indirect. Willig's limits on the fractional error involved in using consumer surplus, S, instead of WTA or WTP from compensated curves, are:

$$\frac{S}{M} \cdot \frac{\underline{E}_m}{2} \leq \left| \frac{S - \text{WTP}}{S} \right| \leq \frac{S}{M} \cdot \frac{\bar{E}_m}{2} \quad \text{and similarly for} \quad \frac{\text{WTA-}S}{S}$$

where M is income and E_m is income elasticity of demand, the underline indicating the smallest and the overline the largest value in the interval. The difference,

$$\frac{\text{WTA} - \text{WTP}}{S}$$

then would be greater than zero, indeed greater than S/ME_m, and for his results to apply at all, this expression must be ≤ 0.10. This result was extended to quantity changes by Randall and Stoll. See Robert Willig, "Consumer's Surplus Without Apology," 1976, and Alan Randall and John Stoll, "Consumer's Surplus in Commodity Space," 1980.

10. I say "starkest terms" here because there is always a problem of identifying the "right" population to sample when doing WTP surveys, even if only use benefits or damages are at issue. This is because there is no easy or automatic way to identify prospective future users. For a small, local effect or resource this population may still be fairly widely spread. For a major national or international site or effect, the appropriate population could be spread around the world.

11. Some people who care deeply about such real problems are striving to find practical ways to allow U.S. citizens, for example, to make contributions to African wildlife preservation via the formation of U.S. nonprofit, tax-exempt organizations the purpose of which is to support particular overseas efforts, such as former ranches now run as elephant and rhino preserves in Kenya and other East African countries.

12. This terminology is borrowed from the marketing and transportation literatures, at least partly because no alternative has been proposed. The authors who do not use this label generally confine their analysis (and terminology) to specific methodologies within this category, e.g., contingent choice, ranking, rating, etc. Conjoint analysis has become an increasingly popular approach to modeling consumer preferences for multiattribute choices. For example, almost two decades ago, Cattin and Wittink (1982) estimated that more than 1,000 CA applications had been reported.

13. "Contingent referenda and contingent choices among specified attribute-price combinations both mimic familiar consumer decision processes. While economists view prices and quantities as mathematically dual (and the conventional [CV] approach makes that duality explicit), consumer perceptions are unencumbered by this theoretical framework. Price is simply another attribute of the good in question. Surveys structured in accordance with such perceptions may avoid many of the protest and strategic biases that afflict [CV] studies" (John Mackenzie, "A Comparison of Contingent Preference Models," 1993). "Among alternative [CV] structures, a principal advantage of the paired comparisons approach is that, in many cases, respondents find that choosing among alternative commodities is among the most natural and frequently experienced decision environments, compared to directly evaluating individual characteristics. For example, people have routine exposure to this kind of choice in their purchases of market goods, where

they often choose between products that are similar, but not identical" (James Opaluch et al., "Evaluating Impacts from Noxious Facilities: Including Public Preferences in Current Siting Mechanisms," 1993).

14. The energy would be generated by allowing water transfer downhill from the dirty river to a nearby basin through a generating station. This transfer had been stopped because the river water was too dirty.

15. There is a much better, though more elaborate and expensive way to choose an optimal sample size in a particular policy or project context. It involves taking a small initial sample, doing the sorts of calculations just summarized, and estimating the likelihood and cost of making a wrong decision—doing something that would actually fail the CB test or failing to do something that would actually be worth doing. Then, based on an estimate of how fast increasing sample size would reduce the expected costs of being wrong and the cost of adding respondents, it is possible to decide on the best size of an addition to the original sample.

16. To sample in Seoul, Korea, for example, where phones are commonly shared by several families, we had to develop a spatial rule based on picking neighborhoods at random, finding the neighborhood head-man's house, and sampling some number of doors to the right or left of it.

REFERENCES

Bohm, Peter B. 1972. "Estimating the demand for public goods: An experiment." *European Economics Reviews* 3:111–130.

———. 1994. "CVM spells responses to hypothetical questions." *Natural Resources Journal* 34:37–50.

Cattin and Wittink. 1982. "Commercial use of conjoin analysis: A survey," *Journal of Marketing* 46(3):44–53.

Gregory, Robin, Sarah Lichtenstein, and Paul Slovic. 1993. "Valuing environmental resources: A constructive approach." *Journal of Risk and Uncertainty* 7: 177–197.

Hanemann, W. Michael. 1991. "Willingness to pay and willingness to accept: How much can they differ?" *American Economic Review* 81:635–647.

Harris, Charles, B. L. Driver, and William J. McLaughlin. 1989. "Improving the contingent valuation method: A psychological perspective." *Journal of Environmental Economics and Management*, 17:213–229.

Knetsch, Jack, and Robert Davis. 1966. "Comparisons of methods for recreation valuation." In *Water Research*, edited by A. W. Kneese and S. C. Smith. Baltimore: Johns Hopkins University Press for Resources for the Future.

Lapiere, R. T. 1934 "Attitudes vs. actions," *Social Forces* 13:230–237.

Mackenzie, John. 1992. "Evaluating recreation trip attributes and travel time via conjoint analysis." *Journal of Leisure Research* 24(2):171–184.

———. 1993. "A comparison of contingent preference models." *American Journal of Agricultural Economics* 61(3):593–603.

Opaluch, James, Stephen Swallow, Thomas Weaver, Christopher Wessells, and Dennis Wichelns, 1993. "Evaluating impacts of noxious facilities: Including public preferences in current siting mechanisms." *Journal of Environmental Economics and Management*, 24(1):41–59.

Pearman, Alan. 1994. "The use of stated preference methods in the evaluation of environmental change." In *Valuing the Environment*, edited by Rüdiger Pething. Dordrecht, the Netherlands: Kluwer Academic Publishers.

Randall, Alan. 1997. "The NOAA panel report: A new beginning or the end of an era?" *American Journal of Agricultural Economics* 79(5):1489–1494.

—— and John Stoll. 1980. "Consumer's surplus in commodity space." *American Economic Review* 70(3):449–455.

Samuelson, Paul A. 1955. "A diagrammatic exposition of a theory of public expenditures." *Review of Economics and Statistics* 37:350–356.

Schkade, David, and John Payne. 1994. "How people respond to contingent valuation questions: A verbal protocol analysis of willingness to pay for environmental regulation." *Journal of Environmental Economics and Management* 26(1):88–109.

Vaughan, William J., Clifford S. Russell, Diego J. Rodriguez, and Arthur C. Darling. 2000. "Uncertainty in cost-benefit analysis based on referendum contingent valuation." *Impact Assessment and Project Appraisal*, June, Vol 18, pp 125–137.

Willig, Robert. 1976. "Consumer's surplus without apology." *American Economic Review* 66(4):589–597.

POLICY INSTRUMENTS I
Some Basic Results and Confusions

In the next two chapters I shall be concentrating on what economics has to say about alternative ways of trying to achieve given policy goals in complex settings. The classic situation, and the one to which many important results apply fairly straight-forwardly, is pollution in a region, where many separate dischargers ("sources") af-fect the levels of quality experienced by "consumers" of air and water (ambient environmental quality or AEQ, for short). One of the oldest research questions in the field amounts to asking: In this setting, what is the best way of influencing the behavior of the sources to achieve a given (politically chosen) level of AEQ?[1] As we shall see, there is no simple answer to this simple-sounding question. Once we recognize the several dimensions on which policy instruments can usefully be judged, we find that picking a "best" instrument would require somehow compar-ing the importance of the dimensions, for no single instrument scores highest on all of them. Indeed, we shall also find that for some important dimensions we do not even have the tools necessary for making formal judgments about better and best performance.

Along the way, we shall also find new and interesting policy instruments that do not fit very well into the judgment game—the provision of information being the most important. For these, our current level of understanding is very limited.

The material is divided between the two chapters roughly as follows:

- Chapter 9 is confined to the basics—looking at the classic regional pollution con-trol setting and largely sticking to efficiency concerns (both static and dynamic). Unavoidably, however, even these basics will raise questions about institutional capabilities.

- The next chapter (10) looks both at some concerns outside pollution control effi-ciency and at some instruments for which making efficiency statements is more difficult.

NARROWING DOWN

"Environmental policy" is a phrase with a very wide range of possible meanings, potentially encompassing any policy that impinges directly, or even indirectly, on the natural world. For example, we do not need to stretch to file each of the following under this label: mining law; water law; policies on the acquisition and management of local, regional, and national parks; highway design and construction rules; policies concerning the control of disease vectors such as mosquitos and rodents; and urban and regional planning. Perhaps the most obviously environmental policies, however, are rules for the control of point and nonpoint sources of air, water, and solid waste pollution and standards for ambient environmental quality at every geographic level from the local creek to the global shield of stratospheric ozone.

Similarly, the range of possible environmental policy instruments is fully as wide as the range of concerns they might be used to address—from mining royalties for public lands, through irrigation water pricing, park access fees and permits, highway tolls and traffic rules, . . . to the roughly ten policy instrument types commonly mentioned with respect to the management of pollution and resulting ambient environmental quality (as discussed and listed below). To make this discussion of instruments manageable itself, some limits have to be imposed on what will be covered. And the most straightforward limits are those separating pollution concerns from the rest of the spectrum. This approach has the advantage of focusing attention on the set of problems and approaches most frequently discussed in the environmental economics literature, though it necessarily leaves undiscussed many fascinating and difficult issues for environmental and resource economists.

To see that there is still plenty to discuss, even after limiting the chapter to pollution-type problem settings, note first, in Table 9.1, how many different kinds of situations fall under the pollution control heading, where we take account of only the four source types defined by two distinctions: point versus nonpoint and fixed location versus location moveable by the responsible party. Both these features have implications for which policy instrument types are in fact most likely to be relevant to which problem, in particular because the distinctions are key to defining the relevant monitoring task. Second, consider Table 9.2 in which are listed ten instrument

TABLE 9.1 Examples of Pollution Management Settings

	Discharge Location(s)	
Type of Discharge	**Fixed**	**Moveable by Source**
Point	Municipal sewage Industrial process wastewater Combustion wastes from boilers and process units Irrigation return flow via drainage tiling	Containerized toxics (solvents, acids, etc.) Batteries, tires, auto hulks
Nonpoint: area or line	Farm and forest runoff Home heating Highway construction runoff	Spray-can emissions Auto exhaust

TABLE 9.2 Instruments of Environmental Policy

1. Prohibition (of inputs, processes, or products)
2. Technology specification (for production, recycling, or waste treatment. An example in the U.S. is the rules for construction of landfills that specify the details of the liners and water collection systems and how gas generated is to be dealt with)
3. Technological basis for discharge standard[a]
4. Performance specification (discharge permits)[b]
5. Tradable performance specification (tradable permits)
6. Pollution charges[c]
7. Subsidies: (i) lump sum for capital cost; (ii) marginal for desired results[d]
8. Liability law provisions
9. Provision of information: (i) to polluters (technical assistance); (ii) to investors, consumers, activists (e.g.: U.S. Toxics Release Inventory); (iii) to consumers (green product or process certification, or green labeling more generally)
10. Challenge regulation and voluntary agreements

[a] In technology-based standard setting, the amount of pollution allowed is determined via an engineering study of a group or class of sources, such as refineries of a certain size range, with a particular product mix, in which a legally designated technology is applied on paper to a calculated uncontrolled pollution load. The result of this exercise is an achievable discharge amount per unit of source size, which is taken to be the required standard for the source type.

[b] Performance specification can be based on any of a number of rules or methods, from uniform percentage reduction by all sources, to modeling that determines the cheapest way to attain a given ambient quality standard. Performance standards may refer to inputs (e.g., place a limit on the sulfur content of fuel oil burned in a boiler) or outputs (e.g., place a limit on SO_2 coming out of the smoke stack from the boiler).

[c] Like performance standards, charges may, in principle, apply to the input of something, such as sulfur, that is transformed into a pollutant (SO_2) or to the pollutant itself. Agricultural inputs, such as fertilizers and pesticides, may be subject to a special sales tax as they are in Denmark. This amounts to a pollution charge on their use, since they would never be purchased except to be "used" and use involves "discharge" onto fields, orchards, or forests.

[d] A deposit-refund system, for example for drink containers, is a self-financed marginal subsidy for container return.

types that among them span the range of possibilities to be found in the economics and policy literatures.

Now, the prospect of slogging through the forty cells of the implied options table to try to identify happy matches of instrument and problem is a daunting one, because behind each judgment would necessarily lie considerations on multiple dimensions of comparison. (See Table 9.4) A substantial fraction of the literature in this area, especially the less formal and mathematical part of the literature, has tended to simplify the task in two ways:

- to divide the instruments into two blocks, one referred to as "command and control" (CAC) and the other as "economic incentives" or "market-based instruments" (EI or MBI)

- to minimize the importance of some of the distinctions in Table 9.1 by assuming that perfect monitoring (usually implicitly costless as well) is possible

Generally, the definition of the MBI class of instruments includes tradeable permits, pollution charges, liability provisions, and subsidies; or four of the ten instrument types in Table 9.2. Thus, implicitly, the phrase "command and control" is taken to include approaches as disparate as product prohibitions, technology-based discharge standards, and challenge regulation.[2] Now, any label that is this inclusive is unlikely to be useful. But at least as important as its imprecision is the connotational baggage carried by "command and control," for the phrase harks back to descriptions of the centrally planned economies of Eastern Europe and the Soviet Union. Production quotas were "commands," and price signals lost any meaning because of "controls" over every phase of production and distribution, from choice of technology to quotas for "retail" outlets. The result was at best dismal economic performance. The implication seems clear: command and control is no way to run a railroad, or a steel mill, . . . , and certainly not an economy or an environmental policy. Arguments about the best choice of policy instruments therefore begin with the conclusion prefigured if not absolutely set in stone.

However, returning to the problem of the CAC label for all the non-MBI options, it will be worthwhile to begin by sharpening up the relevant distinctions. To that end, consider the following pair of choices that designers of policy must make, implicitly or explicitly, in crafting a strategy for managing an environmental problem caused by the actions of a group of economic actors, the "sources":

1. Those parties may or may not be ordered to achieve particular *results* relevant to the problem (e.g., to discharge no more than some fixed amount of pollution per period of time).

2. The parties may or may not be told *what* exactly to do—*how to achieve* whatever it is that they do achieve (e.g., to install equipment type x or to burn fuel type y).

Together, these choices imply another two-by-two matrix table (Table 9.3), into which the instruments from Table 9.2 can be placed. Several observations about this new table are worth stressing. First, only the upper left-hand cell, in which parties are told both *what* to achieve and *how* to achieve it, seems to qualify as "command and control" in any useful sense. Second, a very important instrument in U.S. environmental policy, technology-based standards (on discharges of water pollution) specify *what* is to be achieved but not how. The distinction between "technology-based" and "technology specification" has often been lost sight of in critiques of existing policy choices. Third, even some instruments commonly included under the MBIs can be used in ways that involve specifying how to proceed if not what to achieve. This is true of liability when a standard of care is specified and can be used as a defense in a lawsuit for damages. It is also true of subsidies, when these are tied to particular technologies, for example. Thus, while the economist's enthusiasm for MBI rests heavily on the range of choices they generally leave to regulated parties, it is necessary to be careful and to recognize that not every way of structuring instruments that involve exchanges of money rather than the issuing of bureaucratic "licenses" need involve both freedoms—to choose what and how.[3]

TABLE 9.3 An Alternative Taxonomy of Environmental Policy Tools
(numbers are from Table 9.2)

	Specifying *What* Is to Be Achieved	Not Specifying *What* Is to Be Achieved
Specifying *How* to Achieve Whatever Is Achieved	#1 Prohibitions #2 Combining technology specification with ⇓ #4 Performance standards (this combination is used for auto exhaust regulation in the U.S.)	#7(i) Subsidies (lump sum for particular equipment) #8 Liability provision (with minimum standard of care) #9(i) Technical assistance (focused on particular technology)
***Not* Specifying *How* to Achieve Whatever Is Achieved**	#3 Design (technology-based) standards #4 Performance standards #10 Voluntary agreements and challenge regulation	#5 Tradable permits #6 Pollution charges #7(ii) Subsidies (marginal, open-ended) #8 Liability provisions (without minimum standards of care) #9(i) Technical assistance (not focused on particular technology) #9(ii,iii) Information reporting

BASES FOR JUDGING AMONG INSTRUMENTS

Even though this chapter will concentrate on efficiency basics, it will be useful to put all the cards on the table at once by listing the much broader array of criteria that are suggested by the literature on instrument choice. This is done in Table 9.4, where twelve criteria are divided into five groupings: static concerns, dynamic concerns, general institutional demands, political dimensions, and perceived risks (to agency and to the regulated parties). The table also contains indications of where the main discussion of each criterion is to be found.

STATIC EFFICIENCY

We might as well plunge right into the subject by looking at the longest and most tangled (but by no means most difficult) line of argument—that concerning the attainment of static efficiency (maximum net benefits, or minimum costs of achieving some goal, in an unchanging world). The material will be presented in both algebraic and graphic form wherever that seems both possible and desirable.

TABLE 9.4 A Synthesis of Criteria Against Which to Judge Policy Instruments

Static Concerns
  1. Efficiency (Chapter 9)
  2. Information/computation demands (Chapter 9)
  3. Relative ease of monitoring and enforcement (Chapter 10)

Dynamic Concerns
  4. Flexibility in the face of exogenous changes (Chapter 9)
  5. Incentive for environment-saving technical change (Chapter 9)

General Institutional Demands
  6. Agency: honesty, technical capabilities (including data gathering, model building and solving, monitoring and enforcement, and revenue handling) (Chapter 9)
  7. Regulated parties: experience in markets, reliance on government regulations to protect markets, technical skills (including controlling discharges via production and treatment processes and making decisions about processes, products and inputs) (Chapter 10, briefly)

Political Dimensions
  8. Distributional implications (Chapter 10)
  9. Perceived ethical message (Chapter 10)
 10. Perceived fairness (Chapter 10)

Perceived A Priori Risks
 11. To agency: failure to achieve goals, freezing current technology for too long, possible perverse responses (Chapter 10)
 12. To regulated parties: false convictions, "ratchetting down" of requirements (chapters 9, 10)

A CHARGE ON EMISSIONS

Taking up the idea that originated with Pigou, early advocates of the use of effluent or emission charges (e.g., Kneese and Bower, 1968) assumed that the government knew *the* marginal damage function, that the function applied to every source, and that it was, in fact, a constant. Then it was easy to show that charging the marginal damage as the per-unit cost of (tax on) discharging the damaging pollutant produced the socially optimal level of pollution at least cost. The marginal costs of all dischargers, assuming they respond rationally, would be equal to the common marginal damage. Most importantly, though, the authority needed to know *nothing* about the dischargers' costs.

Algebraically, assume we have N polluters, each with a function relating cost of pollution control effort to discharge, $C_i(D_i)$. Further assume that the regional damage function (DR) is linear and of the form:

$$DR = \alpha(D_1 + D_2 + \ldots + D_N)$$

The first-order conditions for an optimum (where the sum of costs and damages is minimized) are $-C_i' = \alpha$ for every I. This is derived as follows:

Minimize:

$$\text{Damages} + \text{costs} = DR + \sum_{i=1}^{N} C_i(D_i)$$

Requires:

$$\frac{\partial DR}{\partial D_i} + \frac{\partial C_i(D_i)}{\partial D_i} = 0 \text{ for all } i$$

which in turn gives N expressions:

$$\alpha + C'_1(D_i) = 0$$

If α is known, the policy problem looks very simple indeed.

Graphically, for any one discharger, the total and marginal graphs look like Figure 9.1. It is not hard to visualize the total regional problem in this simple setting. We could just relabel the "Total" figure to make the horizontal axis total discharge. Then α(total discharge) is the total damage function and the $C(D_i)$ curve becomes the sum of the costs of achieving any particular total discharge level *when the responsibility for discharge reduction is allocated efficiently among the sources*. (This last phrase is necessary because there is an infinite number of ways of allocating a total of regional discharges among the N sources. But in general only one of these is efficient—the one that equalizes marginal costs. This comes up again just below.) The marginal graph could be drawn to show each source (Figure 9.2).

A small variation on this first-best case begins to hint at some of the problems found in more realistic situations. Thus, assume the damage function is nonlinear but still separable, so that each source can still be dealt with independently. It is then still possible to imagine the authorities announcing a charge schedule for each discharger such that the socially optimal pollution level is arrived at without either

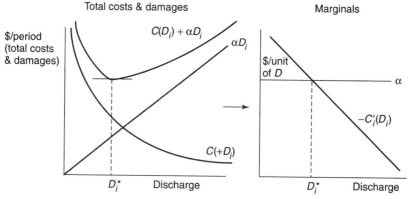

Figure 9.1 Costs and Damages for a Single Pollution Source. C, cost of pollution control effort.

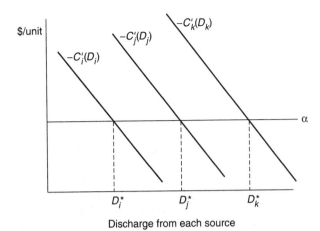

Figure 9.2 Marginal Costs and Damages for Several Sources. The discharge axis is scaled so that it is appropriate for each source separately.

knowledge of discharge control costs or the use of trial and error. Thus, let the damage function be:

$$D_R = \alpha[D_1{}^2 + D_2{}^2 + \ldots + D_N{}^2]$$

Then the FOCs are of the form:

$$-C_i{}'(D_i) = 2\alpha D_i$$

Then at the optimum the charge level for each discharge would be different unless every cost function is the same.[4] But those levels still could be found by simply announcing a marginal charge *schedule* that was the same for each discharger. No other knowledge would be necessary for the authority. It is important to be clear about how such a marginal charge schedule would operate and about one key assumption that has been left implicit. First, the schedule is of the charges that apply to each unit as discharge increases. So, if the schedule were $2\alpha D_i$, the total charge for D_i units would be $(2\alpha\, D_i)D_i/2 = \alpha\, D_i{}^2$. Graphically, the total amount of the charge at any level of discharge would be the triangle under the marginal charge schedule out to that level (see Figure 9.3). The implicit assumption is that there is enough monitoring and enforcement effort that the source cannot cheat, that is, discharge more pollution than it pays for. This is *not* a trivial assumption, but it is almost always left implicit in the literature.

Finally, there are reasons for thinking that trial and error *itself* may not be a very good idea. These are taken up later in this chapter.

This is not so easy to graph for the full regional problem, but the damage function separability allows us to pull out each source individually, as in Figure 9.4. Notice, however, that if the damage function is not separable, this straightforward

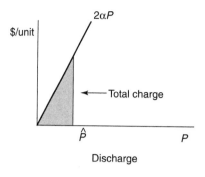

Figure 9.3 An Emission Charge Increasing with Emission Level

strategy will not work. If, for example, DR were of the form $\alpha[D_1 + D_2 + \ldots + D_N]^2$, marginal damages for the ith source are $2\alpha[\Sigma D_i]$, and no schedule of charges independent of the discharges of sources $j \neq i$ is possible. To obtain an optimal solution requires knowledge by the agency of all the sources' cost functions for discharge reductions.[5]

So far the discussion has focused on what to do when a damage function is available and marginal damages by source are calculable. The recognition that we did not then (the early 1970s) have, and likely would not have in the foreseeable future, information on marginal or total damage functions led economists to try to salvage the argument for charges and simultaneously bow to evolving U.S. policy by examining their use in encouraging the meeting of politically set (not necessarily economically optimal) ambient quality standards.

William Baumol's and Wallace Oates' "The Use of Standards and Prices for Protection of the Environment" (1971) is the classic reference here. And their main result, already mentioned in Chapter 4, appears to retain the economy of central-

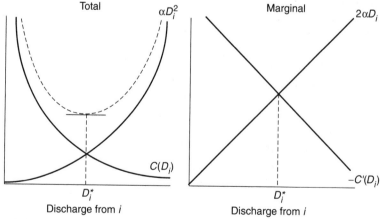

Figure 9.4 Nonlinear Damages from a Single Pollution Source. C, cost of pollution control effort.

ized information needs that was part of the appeal of the earliest case. Thus, if ambient environmental quality depends only on the sum of the regional discharges,

$$AEQ = f(D_1 + \ldots + D_N) \text{ where } f \text{ is linear.}$$

And if $AEQ \leq \hat{S}$, a standard, the first-order conditions for cost minimization imply equal marginal cost at each source:

$$-C_i' = \lambda f'$$

for all i (where λ is the multiplier or shadow price, from the constrained optimization problem) analogous to the damage function case with equally weighted discharges.

Now trial and error again looks possible: Pick a charge. Observe AEQ. Raise the charge if the standard is violated; lower it if the AEQ is too good. Continue until the standard is just met. No knowledge of discharger cost functions is required; a result that rests on the equality of marginal costs required for the optimum in this situation. This is simple and apparently elegant, but not, in fact, very helpful case. Again, leaving aside practical difficulties, the major problem is that this type of connection between discharges and ambient quality is a very special one—the "mixing bowl" of Chapter 4—a situation in which ambient quality can be taken to be uniform and affected the same by a unit of discharge from any of the sources. Location of the sources does not matter. As soon as that very special assumption is relaxed, the beauty of the argument on conserving information begins to be stressed.

Note, however, that while location does matter in the usual regional problem it does not for global problems, such as greenhouse gas accumulation in the atmosphere and ozone depletion in the stratosphere. So trial and error, relying on equalizing marginal costs at sources, might be a useful idea after all, for certain global problems.

When location does matter, but we are only interested in quality at one place, the regional problem becomes:

$$\text{Min}_{D_i} \Sigma_i C_i(D_i) - \lambda(f(\beta_1 D_1, \beta_2 D_2, \ldots, \beta_N D_N) - \hat{S})$$

where the β_i are "transfer coefficients," as discussed in Chapter 4.

Then the FOCs are of the form:

$$C_i' = \lambda f' \beta_i$$

so that at the least-cost solution the sources' marginal costs in general differ according to their differential impacts (the β_i) on AEQ where it is being measured and compared with the standard.

So it is true that if there really is only one point at which AEQ is of interest, the optimal charges bear a fixed ratio to each other. Trial and error is not out of the question in principle when the agency knows the β_i and all the cost functions are conveniently shaped (do not exhibit falling marginal costs of additional removal anywhere). A graphic demonstration of the result showing unequal charges on discharges is found in Figure 9.5.

But as soon as there is more than one point at which AEQ is of interest, the FOCs take the following form (assuming for convenience strict equality of the constraints):

$$C'_i = \gamma_1 f_1' \beta_{i1} + \gamma_2 f_2' \beta_{i2} + \ldots + \gamma_j f_j' \beta_{ij}$$

where the notation β_{ij} means the transfer coefficient relating source i to ambient monitoring point j.

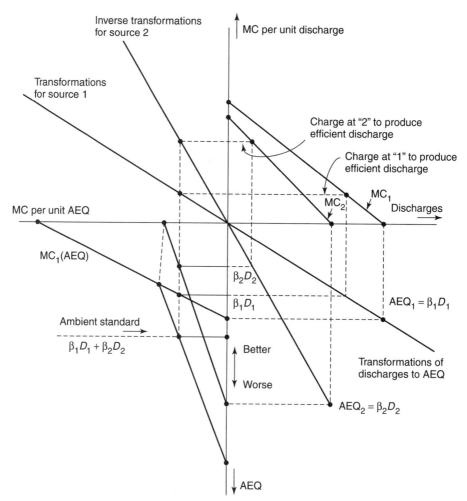

Figure 9.5 Charges on Discharges When the Policy Goal is AEQ and Location Matters. MC, marginal cost; AEQ, ambient environmental quality; D, discharge.

Taking ratios does not get rid of the multipliers. And since these are just the shadow prices of the constraints, it is intuitively clear that their failure to disappear implies a need for knowledge of control costs at the sources.[6]

The following discouraging results apply:

- From any starting charge vector there is no straightforward rule for varying the charge vector elements that guarantees a move toward the optimum.
- Even if a feasible charge vector is found by luck, there is no reason to think it is optimal.
- There is no way to choose among a set of feasible charge sets, were these discovered, in the absence of observations on dischargers' costs.

These observations give rise to a useful if also discouraging rule: Obtaining static efficiency in the general case, with exogenously given ambient standards, requires that the charge-setting agency have knowledge of all control cost functions as well as a complete characterization of the natural world systems that connect discharges and the points at which compliance with the ambient quality standards is required.[7]

Before going on to relate these results to their duals in the world of discharge permits and then to discuss matters concerning time, it is worth pausing to point out that even if trial and error were in theory a possible way to find an optimal charge set, it would not follow that this was a good idea, for trial and error can be very costly when fixed capital is at stake. This is not just because of the overbuilding penalty either. It will often be true that getting to removal level x by first building to remove $x/2$ and then adding another $x/2$ capability will be more expensive than going to x directly. And to find the error is not the work of a short period, but would require long enough for every source to adjust and for measurements of AEQ to have been numerous enough to reduce standard errors to some acceptable level.

MARKETABLE PERMITS: THE DUALS OF CHARGES

In the context of a regional pollution control model, emission charges and discharge standards are "duals." This is just another way of saying that the cost minimization program produces an optimal set of discharge levels and their shadow prices. Making permitted discharge amounts tradable among sources in effect takes advantage of this duality to bring into being one or more market prices, the real versions of the shadow prices that fall out of such models when standards are imposed. And it should not be surprising that results related to the efficiency and required information characteristics of marketable discharge permits can be understood as the duals of the results set out in the previous section. Thus:

- The simplest sort of tradable permit scheme, in which discharge amounts are traded within a region but without restriction, will involve a single equilibrium price, the analog to a single charge level. This, in general, cannot be a statically efficient way of meeting a desired ambient quality standard, though it will produce the *total* amount of permitted discharge at the lowest aggregate cost.

• An ambient standard could be attained efficiently using an ambient quality (reduction) trading system. In this, sources would have to hold portfolios of rights to reduce quality (increase pollution) at some finite number of monitoring points in the ambient environment. Each point would constitute a separate market with, in general, a separate price. Those prices, in turn, would translate into different implied prices for changes in discharges via translation through some agreed-on natural world model that predicted ambient pollution levels from discharges by sources.

Thus, obtaining static efficiency in meeting desired ambient standards using an ambient-quality permit system would involve more complex trading and decisions on the part of sources—the analog to the information and computation intensity implied for the agency by the need to find individually tailored charges.

One new problem comes up in the static marketable permit case: hot spots. That is, unless the initially allowed total of permitted discharge is small enough, there will always be possible trades that could concentrate discharges in such a way as to result in violation of the ambient standard somewhere. Strategies proposed to guard against this eventuality have the effect of either (or both) complicating the trading schemes or reducing the efficiency of the permit market by fragmenting it. Thus:

• If there is only one monitoring point of interest, trades can be required to take place at "trading ratios" defined by the relative impact of each party to the trade on that point. Thus, an amount of discharge being sold by (moved from) a source with a small effect on the monitoring point to one with a large effect would be reduced by the ratio of those effects. This would have the effect of producing individualized prices and would be analogous to the situation described under charges for a single monitoring point.

• If there are many monitoring points and "slackness" in the constraint set, it will not in general be clear, in the absence of real-time intervention by the agency running a regional model, what the correct "trading ratio" should be for any particular trade.

• Subregionalization of discharge permit trading markets (restricting the possible set of trading partners by some distance-based decision rule) will make each market less likely to function in the desired competitive way and will mean that the regional total of discharges is not attained at lowest cost in equilibrium.

The matter of transaction costs has recently been examined formally by Robert Stavins (1995), and his conclusions—that taking them into account reduces the attractiveness of permit schemes and, in particular, that there exists a danger of overselling such systems when the details have been ignored—reinforce the points being made here.

"Second Best": What Can Be Said?

It seemed to some of the early enthusiasts for emission charges that, even if they granted the objections and caveats so far outlined, it would still be more desirable (more nearly lowest cost) to have in place an emission-charging scheme of some kind than to use another instrument such as nontradable permits, unless these were chosen to be the duals of the efficient charges. But it can be shown that no such general notion of "second bestness" holds. For example, a comparison of a uniform charge and a nontradable discharge permit (standard) defined by applying a uniform rollback percentage to unregulated discharge levels reveals that which of these instruments produces the lower regional resource cost of meeting an ambient standard depends on the details—on the shapes of the sources' cost functions and how they are located relative to the monitoring point.[8] (See Russell, 1986.)

CONTRASTING THE STATIC AND DYNAMIC CASES

The ability to say anything at all about static efficiency and the choice among policy instruments rests on a generally persuasive and accepted model of the static situation. This model usually includes the following central assumptions:

- that each source knows its static marginal-cost-of-discharge reduction function
- that the impact of the source on the relevant policy target is known (in the general case this means that transformation functions, mapping discharges into ambient conditions, are assumed to be known)
- that the policy instrument is understood by the source as it is by the analyst
- that monitoring and enforcement are costless, but sufficient effort is expended to ensure compliance with permits or perfect reporting of discharges for effluent charge billing

None of this stretches credulity, at least the credulity of environmental economists, very far. It is worth reemphasizing, however, that the optimality or otherwise of any particular set of charges, or other instruments, is not something straightforwardly *observable* in monitoring data. To show that a particular policy instrument choice induced the static optimum would require either "experiments," in which instruments were varied and removal costs and remaining damages were observed at all the levels (a search of the regional response surface); or collection of sufficient information on cost and damage functions as well as on the regional natural systems so that a regional optimizing model could be constructed and solved to find the optimum (assuming only one exists, to avoid an even longer digression).

Things look quite different when the setting is dynamic and the goal is to produce even roughly analogous efficiency results that would involve the *paths* of alternative instrument values (charges, permit terms) over time. Instead of an unchanging set of sources producing a fixed output level, we confront in general a changing set, with sources entering and leaving the region, varying in size and in location, and changing both production and pollution control technology. These changes can be both endogenous (reactions to environmental policy) and exogenous (reactions to changes in tastes, incomes, factor availability, and technology that have nothing to do with that policy). Optimal instrument *paths* over time can in principle be determined for particular assumptions about the standards to be met and the nature, size, and timing of the shifts; about the costs of adding increments of capacity; and indeed about how the sources see the problem they have to solve—whether they anticipate change or treat each instrument value as if it would be unchanging.

This is a complicated problem, with many possible sets of assumptions and, almost certainly, with many possible different orderings of instrument efficiencies, even ignoring endogenous technological change. Rather than create the dynamic models, perform the calculations, and assess the results, economists have tended to content themselves with observing (with more or less sophistication) that marketable permits have an advantage in the dynamic setting because the permit prices do automatically adjust, rising if the number or size of sources grows, falling if capacity disinvestment is going on or if marginal costs of discharge reduction are falling. This automatic adjustment feature reduces the need for continuing agency intervention such as would be needed to try to maintain an efficient charge set under changing conditions. The latter would require new data, new computations, and new charges imposed to meet every change, even simple inflation. This would stress the bureaucratic system. But it is worth remembering that the automatic adjustments of the permit system are not, in general, maintaining a lowest cost solution—just an equal-marginal cost solution. Further, the trades that constitute the adjustments *can*, though they do not *have* to, lead to hot spots.

The mention of changing marginal costs of discharge reduction brings up the second dynamic problem, one even more difficult for the profession to deal with in a convincing way: endogenous technical change—change driven by the path and level of the policy instruments themselves. To deal convincingly with instrument comparisons in this setting would require a convincing model of the process of induced technical change. This model would have to allow the determination of an optimal path of instrument values for particular assumptions about standards, sources, and so on, as above. But it would also have to reflect the costs of searching for successful innovations, including the costs of failures.

Given these challenges it is not surprising that the relevant published research avoids the efficiency question and explores instead the simpler question of which instrument provides the *largest* incentive for seeking and adopting technical change that is directed at reducing discharges. Roughly speaking, all conclude that the instruments that require continuing payments for discharges create larger incentives than those that do not. This seems commonsensical and can be illustrated with a simple figure (Figure 9.6) that contrasts the incentive attached to an emission charge with that from a permit that is not marketable. D^*_0 is both that level of discharge chosen by the firm facing the charge and the standard set for the no-payment case.

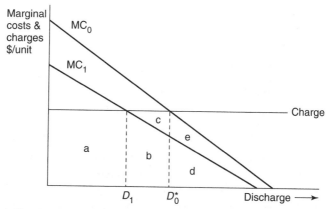

Figure 9.6 A Simple Comparison of Incentives to Adopt a Technical Improvement That Lowers Marginal Costs

MC_0 is the marginal cost of discharge reduction in the base case. MC_1 is the function to which marginal cost might be lowered by technological advance. D_1 is the level of discharge after the advance, *under the charge*. (See Table 9.5.) Net savings attributable to technological advance:

$$\text{Charge:} \qquad c + e$$
$$\text{Standard:} \qquad e$$

The published analyses go beyond this of course, and there seems to be agreement on an unambiguous ranking for instrument types (in declining order of incentive size). This is:

1. Permits auctioned each year
2. Emission taxes and subsidies
3. Permits issued free but marketable (the usual U.S. approach)
4. Performance standards (nonmarketable permits)

TABLE 9.5 Cost Savings from Innovation Under Two Different Policy Instruments

		Resource Cost of Discharge Reduction	Charge Payment
Initial situation	Charge	$d + e$	$a + b + c$
	Standard	$d + e$	0
Situation after technical advance	Charge	$b + d$	a
	Standard	d	0
Savings attributable to the advance	Charge	$e - b$	$c + b$
	Standard	e	0

A WORD ABOUT SUBSIDIES

Subsidies—payments to pollution sources—have played a large part historically in U.S. policy. But these have been nonmarginal, construction subsidies. That is, the burden of meeting new standards for discharge cleanliness for municipal wastewater (and storm water) discharges was spread around over urban and rural residents of the United States by a system of national and state subsidies that paid, at times, up to 75 percent of the capital costs of meeting the new requirements. Because there was never enough money available to meet all the requests in any given year, the system became, in effect, a cause and legitimator of delay. To the extent the subsidies had other effects, economists would claim that those effects must have been to increase treatment plant size or sophistication (or both) relative to the undistorted optimal response to the regulations (discharge permit allowances).

But subsidies can also be of the marginal variety. In fact, in terms of the comparative statics results for a single discharger, a marginal subsidy for discharge reduction achieved is symmetric with a per-unit charge for discharge. But there are at least three reasons for doubting the wisdom of using marginal subsidies as a general pollution control strategy. For my money, the most telling is that in order to have a meaningful per-unit subsidy, we have to know the base discharge level—that level from which discharges are reduced to qualify for the subsidy. This means having good baseline information; and the incentives for the dischargers will be to exaggerate their baseline discharges in order to capture a greater subsidy. This is a monitoring problem, but a rather different one from finding out what *current* discharges actually are. (It becomes really difficult for new sources joining the system.)

A second reason arises from the observation that though, at the margin, the subsidy and charge are similar, the subsidy raises firms' profits relative to the situation with either a charge or a simple standard. This will tend to draw more firms into the market, thus increasing total discharges and production associated with any particular product. There is the possibility, then, that long-run industry expansion will result in a net increase in discharges.

The third reason for doubting that marginal subsidies are a generally good idea is that to pay the subsidies, the government will have to impose taxes elsewhere. These taxes will be both economically distorting (recall the deadweight loss problem for sales or income taxes and see the next chapter on the "second" or "double" dividend) and politically expensive, using "chips" that might well be better used in some other way such as improving health-care financing or welfare system incentives.

There is, however, one form of per-unit subsidy that avoids almost all of these problems and that is, in fact, widely used around the world. This is the "deposit-refund" (D-R) system for "returnables." Most common is a D-R approach to packaging, especially beverage containers. When you buy a drink in a can or bottle (glass or plastic) in many countries and in some states of the United States, you pay a deposit that is usually in the range $0.05 and $0.25 depending on where you are and the container's material and size. When (if) you return the container to a legitimate receiving facility (usually another store where the same beverages are sold), you get your deposit back as a reward.

Seen in this light, the D-R system amounts to a self-financed (by the deposit) system of subsidy for good behavior. The self-financing feature does away with the second and third objections above. And the fact that you have to buy something to become eligible for the subsidy means that there is almost no way you can lie about the original position from which the subsidy is calculated. ("Almost," because if the subsidy were large enough it might pay someone to create containers only in order to "return" them. This "counterfeiting" could also happen in some of the other situations mentioned below as candidates for D-R application.)

The really interesting features of D-R, however, are not tied to its identification with a subsidy. Rather, there are two advantages created here that can be enormously useful in real problem settings. First, the subsidy changes the burden of proof in the matter of undesirable disposal. So, for example, catching someone throwing a soda can out of a car window is most unlikely. And to really "catch" someone, the act has to be witnessed. It is not worth the expense of trying to match up already discarded cans to those who drank from them and then tossed them, even if this might be possible in theory via fingerprints. The D-R system means you (the buyer) have to "prove" (by returning the container) that you did *not* use an *undesirable* form of disposal (such as littering).

The second desirable feature of the D-R system is that even if you toss your container (or other item subject to a refund), someone else can collect the subsidy by "correcting" your act—by picking up the can or bottle and returning it. This effect is what I call a "decentralized" incentive for desired behavior.

And, as hinted above, D-R is applicable more widely than to beverage containers. Examples of products for which it is being or might be used include: auto hulks; lead-acid, mercury/cadmium, or other dangerous batteries; lubricating oil; and solvents for retail commercial or industrial use. (See Table 9.6 for some real examples of D-R systems in Europe.)

A SUMMARY TO THIS POINT

This brief look at static efficiency results and at two dynamic considerations (there being no comparable efficiency results available in that setting) leaves us with some reason to take the economic incentive approach seriously and to prefer it to non-marketable permits (simple emission standards). But the case for either charges or marketable permits is by no means overwhelming.

1. To capture the static efficiency result of a charge with given AEQ standards to be met, the agency will have to have a comprehensive model including information on all dischargers' marginal costs of discharge reduction and on the regional environment.

TABLE 9.6 Deposit-Refund Systems in Europe[a]

Current	Proposed
France	
For a short period (1979–80) there was a charge on lubricants used to subsidize the rerefining industry. This was later replaced by a system of regulatory controls designed to provide regenerators with waste oil at low cost.	None.
Germany	
Waste oil charge. A levy is raised on all lubricants put on the market and the proceeds of this levy are used to provide financial assistance to waste oil collectors in order to facilitate recovery. This levy (and the subsidy scheme) was phased out gradually up to 1990. The scheme has helped to set up an established collection and recovery industry, and oil prices are now sufficiently high that the value of waste oil itself provides an incentive to recycling.	There are recurring proposals for a charge on beverage containers. The suggestion of its introduction has been used to encourage industry to operate container recovery and reuse systems.
Norway	
Deposit/refund on beer and mineral water containers. Deposit-refund system on automobile bodies. Deposit paid as part of import duty on new cars. (In 1979 this amounted to 1% of sales price.) Refund paid at any of 100 collection points.[b]	Charge on heavy metal batteries. Charge on chlorofluorocarbons.
Sweden	
Charge on beverage containers. This was introduced in 1973, and intended to reduce the use of nonreturnable beverage containers. In 1997 it amounted to about $0.75 for large plastic water and soda bottles.	
Vehicle scrapping deposits. Since 1976 a charge of Skr. 250 has been made on sales of new cars. When a car is delivered to an authorized scrap dealer, the final owner receives SKr. 300 and all liability to car tax comes to an end.	Charge on heavy metal batteries. Charge revenue will be paid to a collection and recycling company that will in turn offer an incentive to consumers to return used batteries.

[a] Adapted from Table 3.6(a) in *Environmental Resources Ltd.,* "Cost Effectiveness: Experience and Trends," prepared for the government of the Netherlands, June 1984.

[b] Organization for Economic Cooperation and Development (OECD) 1981. *Economic Instruments in Solid Waste Management.* Paris, OECD.

2. For efficiency to be maintained, charges must be continually adjusted for exogenous change in the regional setting, including especially entry and exit of sources (and changes in the size or costs of continuing sources). This means revising the model and rerunning it regularly.

3. Marketable permits allow the achievement of static efficiency only if the permits are for the degradation of AEQ at particular points in the environment.[9] Tradable (marketable) permits to discharge in their simplest form give equal marginal costs of discharge reduction, which in turn imply least cost only when location of

sources relative to the monitoring points doesn't matter (as it does not in the greenhouse gas/climate change setting).

4. But marketable permits do at least adjust "automatically" to exogenous change in that the price of discharge rises if demand shifts up and falls if it shifts down.

5. Unrestricted trading of discharge permits can lead to "hot spots"—violations of ambient standards at points in the regional environment—because of the concentration of discharges at particular sources.

6. There is no second-best result that says that any economic incentive is better than any standard where both have the same AEQ result.

7. In the long run, the chances of finding "environment-saving" new technologies are increased by using either emission charges or marketable permits—especially if the latter involve the payment of "rents" every period to the issuing agency.

8. There is no general *dynamic efficiency* result comparing the instruments that is analogous to the static result.[10]

Thus, where you come down at this point in the continuing debate will depend on how you weight continuing institutional demands versus increased incentives for technological progress and "automatic" price adjustment (even if the prices are not themselves the optimal set). You pays your money and you takes your choice. The next chapter will show that things are even more complex than they appear at this point, however.

NOTES

1. Recall that in Chapter 5, the optimization problem, "Find the lowest-cost way of meeting a given set of AEQ goals," was taken as a fallback from regional cost-benefit analysis. It was pointed out there that the solution to the actual mathematical problem would produce "shadow prices" for pollution discharges that could be interpreted as the charges on emissions that would encourage rational dischargers to act consistently with the lowest cost solution. This chapter elaborates on the question, Are such charges the best way to try to influence discharger behavior?

2. There is currently some disagreement about how to classify the provision of information in this twofold scheme. Just below you will see where I classify it.

3. It is worth noting, anticipating later comments about risks for bureaucrats in instrument choice, that tradable permits do involve an aggregate specification of *what* is to be achieved. This sets an upper limit on the aggregation of discharge rights by any single source and thus puts a limit on how bad quality can be made at any point. The facts that total allowed discharges are limited and that dischargers are very likely to have different marginal costs for reducing discharges, strongly suggest that any single discharger faces an upward sloping supply curve for rights. This differentiates a tradable rights scheme from a pure emission charge instrument, in which the "supply" of *allowable* discharge amounts will be completely elastic.

4. For example, let the i discharger's cost function be $c_i(D_i) = Z_i - B_i D_i$ (so $C_i = 0$ at Z_i/B_i). Then at the optimum, $D^*_i = B_i/2\alpha$ because $\partial C/\partial D_i = -B_i$ and $\partial DR/\partial D_i = 2\alpha D_i$ and their

sum must be equal to zero. The charge level (the marginal charge) is $2\alpha D_i = B_i$ and the total charge paid is $\alpha D_i^2 = \frac{1}{2}(D_i)(2\alpha D_i) = B_i^2/4\alpha$.

5. Announcing this sort of charge schedule could not work as part of a trial and error process because each source would have to know all other sources' discharges in order to know what to pay.

6. In reality (and as noted in Chapter 5) these regional models are programming problems, in which it is required that quality be at least as good as the standards at some finite set of points. This actually complicates even more the prospects for trial and error, since different points become binding constraints (and have nonzero shadow prices) at different vectors of discharges.

7. Actually the problems of comparison on which even the simple static efficiency results are based are worse than generally admitted to. This is because our programming approaches produce quality *no worse* than the standard at every modeled point. In general, however, the pattern of just-binding and nonbinding constraints will be different for different patterns of discharges. Thus we are not really fulfilling the conditions for judging outcomes on the basis of cost only, that is, the "outputs" of the alternatives are not, in fact, equal. If we knew the benefit function we would be able to demonstrate which pattern was optimal by the test of minimizing costs plus damages. See Kerry Smith and Clifford Russell, "Demands for Data and Analysis Induced by Environmental Policy," 1990, for a discussion and illustration of this point.

8. The rollback factor, in a setting of multiple ambient monitoring points, would be based on the size of the reduction in ambient concentration required at the worst such point in order to meet the desired ambient standard. Thus, if $\mathrm{AEQ}_i - \hat{S} > \mathrm{AEQ}_j - \hat{S}$ for all j, then this difference at i is used to define the regional rollback percentage, R:

$$R = (\mathrm{AEQ}_i - \hat{S})/\mathrm{AEQ}_i$$

And for every source k, the permitted discharge $D_{kp} = (1 - R)D_{k0}$ where D_{k0} is the unregulated level of discharge at k.

9. The choice of such a set of points would be a difficult task in its own right, for it would require judging which finite set of points best captured (or protected) the AEQ everywhere else in the region.

10. The closest thing to such a result I have seen has been produced by Hans Gottinger: "In summary, there is no policy regime [instrument choice] that is optimal for all situations. The optimal policy regime will depend on the characteristics of the social damage, treatment function, and production function." Hans Gottinger, "A Model of Principal—Agency Control of Waste Under Technological Progress," 1996, pp. 263–286.

REFERENCES

Baumol, William, and Wallace Oates. 1971. "The use of standards and prices for protection of the environment." *Swedish Journal of Economics* 73(1):42–54.

Environmental Resources, Ltd. 1984. "Cost-effectiveness: Experience and trends." Prepared for the government of the Netherlands.

Gottinger, Hans. 1996. "A model of principal-agency control of wastes under technological progresss." *Environmental and Resource Economics* 7(3):263–286.

Kneese, Allen, and Blain T. Bower. 1968. *Managing Water Quality: Economics, Technology, Institutions*, Baltimore: Johns Hopkins University Press for Resources for the Future.

Organization for Economic Cooperation and Development. 1981. *Economic Instruments in Solid Waste Management*. Paris: OECD.

Russell, Clifford S. 1986. "A note on the efficiency ranking of two second-best policy instruments for pollution control," *Journal of Environmental Economics and Management* 13:13–17.

Smith, V. Kerry, and Clifford S. Russell. 1990. "Demands for data and analysis induced by environmental policy." In *Fifty Years of Economic Measurement: The Jubilee of the Conference on Research in Income and Wealth,* edited by Ernst Berndt and Jack Triplett. Chicago: University of Chicago Press.

Stavins, Robert N. 1995. "Transactions costs and tradeable permits." *Journal of Environment Economics and Management* 29:133–148.

POLICY INSTRUMENTS II
*Other Considerations and More
Exotic Instruments*

The previous chapter concentrated on the first five criteria for judging policy instruments as summarized in Table 9.4. The first part of this chapter will go over the three broad categories of criteria not so far covered: general institutional demands (beyond data gathering, modeling, and computation), political dimensions, and perceived risks. The second part of the chapter will look beyond the standards-versus-charges debate and discuss three (at least apparently) quite different instruments; the imposition of ex post liability for environmental damage; the public provision of information on products, processes, or dischargers; and the encouragement of voluntary agreements via "challenge regulation."

COMPARING INSTRUMENTS: OTHER CONSIDERATIONS

GENERAL INSTITUTIONAL DEMANDS

THE AGENCY

Running any environmental policy involves challenges for the responsible executive agency. We have talked about the special challenge implied by the task of finding and maintaining a set of efficient emission charges. But we have so far neglected another pair of very big challenges: monitoring and enforcement. Only in Chapter 11 will we spend time on the nuts and bolts of this challenge, such as finding out how often to monitor, how to use the information developed by previous monitoring, and how to structure penalties. For now, let us confine ourselves to discussing how the major alternative pollution control instruments differ on this criterion of judgment.

One extreme view that can be found in the literature is captured by the following quote: Charges (sometimes MBI more generally) are "self-enforcing" because they "harness the commercial self-interest of [the regulated parties]" (Deutsch Gesellschaft für Technische Zusammenarbeit, 1995, p.1).

The thinking behind this generic proposition appears to run along the following line: Given that regulated parties face a particular negative incentive (such as a charge per unit discharge) and given that they are rational, they will react in a way that the charger (the environmental agency) intends. And nothing has apparently been said about the agency having to do any monitoring. This is implicitly or explicitly contrasted with a discharge limit (standard, permit) that can be violated and will be in the absence of monitoring and enforcement. The problem with this reasoning is the word "face." As used in the logic of the sentences it must mean not just that the parties know what the charge per unit is, but that the agency can, with some probability, know what the party actually discharges and hence its correct bill for the period. In the absence of such a capability on the agency's part, the source is free to set its own bill by declaring its own discharge level. The charge becomes merely a penalty for telling the truth rather than announcing falsely low numbers. In short, the agency's chore for monitoring and enforcing a charge is the same as the chore it would face under any choice of policy tool that involves quantity discharged per unit time, whether as a limit or as the basis for a bill.

Thus, whenever the instrument is aimed at controlling discharges, the agency will have to make some effort to measure (monitor) discharges. If self-monitoring by sources is required, as it now is across most major sources of air and water pollution in the United States, the agency will have to put some effort into auditing the self-reported results. Violations of standards or misreporting of discharges for purposes of charge billing will have to be punished.

Auditing of self-reporting is complicated by the ephemeral nature of the act of polluting. That is, it is very difficult, indeed one might well say practically impossible, to determine what source "i" discharged yesterday unless a measurement device was in place then. So an "audit" cannot have the same meaning as an IRS audit of the paper trail that defines a person's income. Continuous monitoring devices do help here, but there still must be a way to check up on them to see that they are operating properly and have not been tampered with.

It must also be noted that marketable permits do complicate the monitoring problem by adding the requirement for real-time updating of agency records for trades so that each source is evaluated relative to the proper requirement. But that aside, the monitoring and enforcement problem context here is not really different from that for charges or for nonmarketable permits.

This does not mean that there are no differences among the instruments of Table 9.2 in terms of the relative difficulty of the monitoring jobs they imply. Nor does it rule out, in particular settings, finding ways to change the monitoring chore. As already discussed, if the problem to be addressed is litter (solid waste "emissions" from autos and pedestrians) monitoring is made difficult by the sheer number of "sources" and the fact that the emissions are ephemeral, infrequent, and random events. But a subsidy per item turned in to a "proper" place in effect puts the burden of proof on the "sources," who must show, to claim the reward, that they did not jettison bottles or cans. If this subsidy is self-financed it becomes the refund in a deposit-refund system. Something similar may be achieved by using a "presumptive charge"—a charge that will be of a particular size unless the charged party can prove it deserves a lower one.

But in some very important cases, the difficulty of monitoring makes the policy-design problem especially difficult. Water pollution from "nonpoint" sources such as farms and managed (fertilized) forests is the archetypical case. Measuring the pollution load from any specific farm is either very expensive or essentially impossible with currently available technology. This is because the "discharges" do not, in general, come out of one or a few pipes.[1] Rather, discharges occur in what amount to sheets of water moving over and through the soil and carrying soil particles to which are attached fertilizers and pesticides. The amount of the discharge varies in time with rainfall (or irrigation) intensity and in space with topography, soil type, and cropping. Obtaining a legally persuasive measure of discharge per unit time from a specific activity does not now seem possible. And the option of measuring the loads after they hit the water courses would only give load per farm or forest unit per unit of time if there were an extraordinarily unlikely match-up between activities and streams. In the general case, there will be more than one source upstream of any in-stream monitoring point. Or else, if the point is interior to the farm, there will be discharges not being measured that enter below the monitoring point.

In these circumstances, many ingenious notions for policy instruments have been suggested. Of these the presumptive charge—with burden of proof falling on the farmer to obtain a lower charge—seems most promising to me.[2]

One final type of institutional demand on the agency is that for honesty or freedom from corruption. This demand is ubiquitous where public policy is concerned, but seems to have differential force in the instrument-choice setting as between charges and permits. Charges can bring large amounts of money into the charging agency. There will always be the temptation to try to conclude side deals that reduce a source's charge payment in exchange for some payment, smaller than the reduction, to a bureaucrat in a position to ratify the smaller charge.

THE SOURCES

As far as the sources go, the demands of good management cover most of the needs of the alternative instruments. But marketable permits will work only to the extent that the sources are familiar and comfortable with actually negotiating market transactions. This may be a problem for sources that are or have until recently been government enterprises themselves. (See Chapter 16 for comments in the developing country context.)

PRICES, ETHICS, AND POLITICS
IN ENVIRONMENTAL POLICY

For economists, prices are signaling devices through which decentralized actors on the economic stage communicate about tastes and desires, capabilities and sacrifices. The information efficiency of the market economy resting on these signals is a thing of beauty to many, if not all, in the profession. But the world at large does not necessarily share this view. For many, it seems that prices symbolize greed and the exclusionary aspects of markets. These people observe that those ideals and conditions that are valued most are not priced—for example, freedom, religious expression, the everyday glories of the ambient environment. For these people, prices may be a necessary part of reality, but they are not a part to try to expand. Applying them in environmental management may be compared with putting a price on a sunset—free marketeering run amok. Indeed, the notion of pollution prices strikes some of the extreme opponents as analogous to selling licenses to murder. This connotation is one part of the overall political problem faced in trying to bring MBI into use in actual policy. In the early days of this argument, the opponents used the phrase "license to pollute" to condemn the charging idea. Economists were understandably baffled, for permits, given away free, seem more deserving of that label than charges. It appears in retrospect that the word "license" in this context was intended to be thought of in terms of a different one of its definitions: "excessive or undue freedom or liberty."[3]

Another part of the political dimension of instrument choice involves that same revenue that featured above in the discussions of incentives to improve technology and of the need for agency freedom from corruption. There are two sides to this political consideration: one arises from the paying side and one from the receipt side, as is usually the case with taxes. First, however, let me note that, for a long time, the political role of charges was concealed behind economists' rather facile tendency to dismiss such payments as "mere transfers." That is, since no resource or service flows changed hands in the direction opposite the charge payments, they held no implications for society's welfare. Whether they were "spent" on resources and services by sources of pollution or by government was of no particular interest.[4]

The first counter observation is that for the pollution sources this is of very great interest, for these are real, out-of-pocket costs and may be just as large as the resource costs of reducing discharges to adjust to the charge levels.[5] These payors can be expected to prefer a system of free permits, marketable or not, to a system of charges (or periodic permit fees) aimed at achieving the same level of ambient quality.

Some MBI enthusiasts will point out here that the increase in efficiency achieved by use of charges could leave room for charge payments with everyone still better off. This assertion is empirical and cannot be dismissed on a priori grounds. But, for its truth to make a *political* difference, not only would polluters in the aggregate have to be better off; this aggregate result would have to be achieved via making most individual sources better off, not by having one or two of many sources benefit immensely and all others lose out.

A second thread to the charges-as-significant-revenue argument is still quite new in the literature, and so suffers from some confusion of terminology and assumptions. This thread sees charge revenue as a replacement for other tax revenues, to the society's advantage. The advantage comes because the charge is a tax on a "bad" activity so does not create a deadweight loss, while the other sources of government revenue—certainly the major sources—involve taxing "goods" (labor services as producer input, or goods and services as they are sold).[6]

This prospective benefit of using emission charge revenue as a replacement for other sources of revenue is known as the "double [or second] dividend," the first dividend being the reduction in pollution.

To make sure we are really talking about a second dividend from an environmental policy instrument and not a first dividend from a tax reform, the rules of the game say that we have to operate, in theory at least, in the context of what public finance people call an "idealized second-best tax system," with equality of marginal deadweight losses across all taxes in use. (Almost needless to say, this is a very difficult condition to check on in the real world.) Further, the relevant comparisons are with two alternative policy approaches:

• having the revenue-raising environmental policy instrument but redistributing the revenue within society by means of those old economist favorites, lump-sum payments

• achieving the same (optimal) environmental goal using a standard or a free but marketable permit so that no revenue is raised

Under these restrictions and within the required comparison, the nature of the second dividend can be illustrated by a simple graph, shown in Figure 10.1, where GMAC is the, by now familiar, marginal pollution abatement cost function with G for "gross" appended to emphasize the distinction with the net version; MD is the marginal damage function for the pollution, here assumed constant; and NMAC is the net marginal abatement cost function—that reflecting gains from reducing other, distorting taxes such as the income tax. Then P_R is the original or regulatory optimum pollution level, while P_{DD} is the optimum level taking account of the "double dividend."

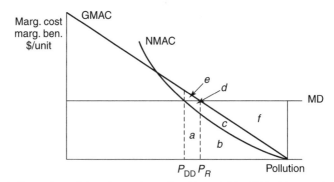

Figure 10.1 Illustration of the "Second (or "Double) Dividend." MAC, marginal pollution abatement cost; G, gross; N, net; MD, marginal damage; P, pollution; R, regulatory; DD, double dividend.

Under the original or purely regulatory (nonrevenue) approach, the net benefit of setting the goal at P_R is $f = b + c + f - (b + c)$. When a tax per unit of pollution equal to MD is charged, and the revenue is used to reduce other, deadweight loss (DWL)-producing taxes, there is an additional benefit to society. This is reflected in NMAC. When this tax recycling benefit is taken into account, there is a new optimal goal P_{DD}, and the net benefit is now $c + d + f$, with $c + d$ equal to the "second dividend." Or, summarized as a simple table:

With tax recycling

Gross benefit (WTP) for P_{DD}: $a + b + c + d + f$

Gross costs of P_{DD}: $a + b + c + d + e$

Tax recycling benefits: $c + d + e$

Net costs: $a + b$

Net benefits: $a + b + c + d + f - (a + b) = c + d + f$

e is not an environmental benefit, so that element of gross costs of pollution control cancels the tax benefit of recycling that revenue element.

A question that may well occur to you is why NMAC is drawn so that the marginal tax recycling benefit eventually goes to zero. The straightforward answer is that the marginal *tax revenue* must go to zero in the situation graphed. Thus, if GMAC equals $G - aP$, with G the intercept on the vertical axis and $-a$ the slope, the following holds: Because a tax $= MD$ calls out pollution equal to $(G - MD)/a$,

$$\text{Tax revenue} = \text{tax} \times \text{pollution} = MD\left(\frac{G - MD}{a}\right) = \frac{GMD - MD^2}{a}$$

The marginal revenue of the tax is:

$$\frac{\partial(\text{tax.rev.})}{\partial MD} = \frac{G - 2MD}{a}$$

and this is zero at $MD = G/2$. For MD above G/2, the marginal tax revenue is negative and so must be the marginal second dividend. (Does this marginal revenue result remind you of anything in intermediate micro?)

This suggests the possibility of another situation, with relatively high marginal damage function (Figure 10.2). The "second dividend" is $c - (d + e)$, arrived at as follows:

Original net benefit: $d + e + f$ (net benefit of attaining P_R by imposing a standard)

Gross benefit of P_{DD}: $b + c + e + f$

Gross cost of P_{DD}: $b + c$

Tax recycling benefit: $c - e$

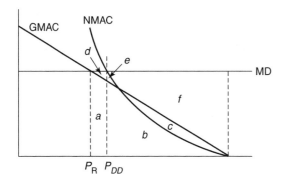

Figure 10.2 The Double Dividend with High Marginal Damages—an Illustration. See Figure 10.1 for explanation of symbols.

Net cost of P_{DD}: $b + e$ ($= b + c - [c - e]$)

Net benefit of P_{DD}: $f + c$ ($= b + c + f + e - [b + e]$)

Difference in net benefits: $f + c - (d + e + f) = c - d - e = c - (d + e)$

OTHER DIMENSIONS OF JUDGMENT

Three of the criteria noted in Table 9.4 of the previous chapter have hardly been mentioned so far. They are perceived fairness and perceived risks, either to the regulating agency and its public or to the regulated parties. One reason that more has not been said is the difficulty of saying anything that fits very neatly into a text in economics. So this section will be short and impressionistic.

PERCEIVED FAIRNESS

The word "perceived" is important here because fairness is almost always in the eye of the beholder. It is seldom that situations are so stark that what is fair can be agreed on by all hands—those who will pay are likely to think they are paying too much; those who benefit are likely to think they should receive a greater benefit. This observation doesn't carry us very far where policy instruments are concerned, but the same phenomenon can be anticipated. So, for example, if the sources existing when a policy starts receive, in effect, free permits, which they later can sell to new sources who want to begin producing, this will look fair to the existing sources (after all, their previous decisions were made in a context without pollution control laws) but unfair to those contemplating a new business. Over time this discrepancy between "new" and "old" becomes a normal part of reality and only a problem for the economist because of the bias against new technology that it embodies. Similar remarks might be made if a new spatially differentiated set of emission charges, designed to produce a politically given AEQ standard efficiently, were introduced. In the beginning, those who had, under the zero charge situation, opted for what turns out to be the high charge location, could be expected to see the system as unfair.

One sort of policy instrument that may seem unfair to more than those subject to it is the instrument that penalizes previously legal behavior after the fact. Superfund is such a policy instrument—a version of liability that applies to disposal decisions made when such decisions were legal. While no one would argue that nothing should be done about contaminated Superfund sites, many might say that fairness would require that society collectively take responsibility for its previous ignorance and resulting laxity. (Notice the difference between penalizing previous disposal actions and regulating or pricing all future actions.)

PERCEIVED RISKS

To the Agency: Fear of Failure to Attain Environmental Change

The political path of emission charges has always been made even rockier than it deserved to be by a vague but real fear among environmentalists, politicians, and some agency officials that, faced with a charge, sources might well simply pay it and continue to pollute. This, it seems to me, results from confusing personal with firm behavior. Thus, faced with an increase in cigarette or liquor taxes, an individual may rationally exhibit nearly zero elasticity of demand, consuming as much of each as before the tax. This is more likely the larger the individual's income and the smaller the importance of drinking and smoking in his or her pretax budget. So trying to cut down on smoking through very large increases in cigarette taxes risks (a) having an effect largely on the poor and (b) not having a very large aggregate effect.

But firms do not *enjoy* pollution in the same sense that individuals enjoy smoking or drinking. Firms have to view a pollution charge as they would the price of any other input to their processes. If they do not, their *irrational* behavior puts them at risk of bankruptcy in the longer run. So this particular version of the risk of policy failure seems more than a little unreasonable, though it may seem real enough to many who share it nonetheless.

A rational but somewhat esoteric fear concerning the effect of particular instrument choices revolves around the possibility that the agency does not, in fact, have an accurate view of the firms' marginal costs. This fear is usually illustrated by reference to a situation in which the agency is aiming at optimality—equating marginal costs and marginal damages—and using either a charge or a standard as the policy instrument. Thus, in Figure 10.3, the agency knows that the firm causes marginal damages MD and *thinks* the firm's marginal cost is MC_{EX}. It can either set a standard, P^*, or a charge, e^*, for optimality in this situation. But what if it is wrong with respect to the marginal costs? The figure shows the losses for each instrument choice and for a higher and lower marginal cost curve. P_{HI} and P_{LO} are, respectively, the firm's response to the "optimal" charge e^* when its actual marginal cost is MC_{HI} and MC_{LO}. The shaded areas labeled C_{HI} and C_{LO} are the resulting social losses—the losses associated with picking the *wrong charge*. The losses resulting from setting P^* as the standard are the shaded areas labeled S_{HI} and S_{LO} for the two possible actual MC functions. Note that the losses are areas between MC

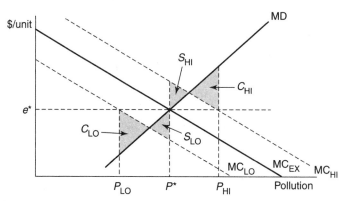

Figure 10.3 Possible Losses due to Ignorance (on the Agency's Part) of Marginal Costs. MD, marginal damages; MC, marginal cost; P^*, pollution standard; e^*, apparently optimal charge; EX, expected by agency; S_{HI} and S_{LO}, losses from being wrong about the cost function when using the standard, P^*; C_{HI}, and C_{LO}, losses from being wrong about the cost function when using the charge, e^{**}

and MD functions from actual to optimal levels of pollution. The real optimal levels are at the intersections of MD with the two possible MC functions, MC_{HI} and MC_{LO}. These levels are not labeled in order to keep the diagram less cluttered.

What if the MD function has a different slope, the one above being rather steep? In Figure 10.4 MD is quite flat, the MC functions have roughly the same slope as before, and the relative sizes of the losses have been reversed. S_{HI} and S_{LO} are now larger than C_{HO} and C_{LO}.

Can you see why this reversal in the ordering of possible loss sizes makes intuitive sense? It has to do with the "shape" of the instrument as it relates to the "shape" of MD.

What if the uncertainty concerned the marginal damage function—a likely situation? Can you convince yourself that the two instruments perform equally well or badly in that case (that the S and the C areas are the same)? Why is that?

It is, of course, possible to design instruments that fail in the sense of producing little or no effect on the problem addressed. Superfund seems to qualify for such a label, since the incentives built into it have pushed everyone involved into lengthy and expensive litigation over who will ultimately pay for cleanup rather than encouraging actual cleanup work. (Although if you think of it as part of a complex of laws "designed" to discourage generation and disposal of toxic wastes, the complex certainly seems to have been effective in changing ongoing behavior.)

One other area of actual failure, though not one that creates the same political problem as Superfund, is in the design of incentives for seeking and adopting technical advances for dealing with pollution. Both the choice that mandates looser dis-

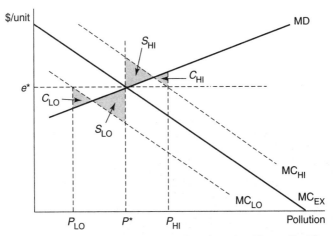

Figure 10.4 Losses When the Marginal Damage Functions Are Flatter. See Figure 10.3 for explanation of symbols.

charge standards for existing than for new sources, and the requirement that the technology bases for discharge standards for water pollutants be "rachetted down" to reflect technological changes, create incentives that work against innovation. (See Box 10.1 for the rachetting-down case—a version of the strength-of-incentives demonstration from the previous chapter.) But the discouragement of new technology does not show up as clearly as the failure to clean up known Superfund sites. We don't know what we're missing, as the saying goes, so we are not inclined to get upset about it.

Risks for the Public from Instrument Choice
To a very large extent the risks for the public of instrument choice are just the other side of the risks for the agency just discussed. That is, the agency worries about certain outcomes because those outcomes will harm the public in obvious ways and subject the agency to political criticism and bad publicity. So there are two basic kinds of risk—failure to achieve the desired change, and failure to achieve whatever is achieved at lowest cost, whether in the short or longer run. As already pointed out for the case of fears about the effectiveness of emission charges, the two risks may not both be thought to be avoidable by the same choice (the liquor tax example). Trade-offs may seem to be necessary in some circumstances. This is just one more simplification in what I hope you are persuaded is a very complicated problem setting.

At this point, the chapter shifts gears and looks at three varieties of policy instruments that are quite different from those examined so far. (Though we shall see that there are strong theoretical connections between liability provisions and standards and charges.)

Ratchetting Down

In "ratchetting down," the standard that must be met is tightened to take account of new technology. In Figure 10.5, MC_0 is the marginal cost function before an innovation; MC_1 the marginal cost function afterward. Let e^* be the *level* of marginal cost implied by the original standard, P_0. Without rachetting down, the cost savings from finding and adopting MC_1 is area c. Because ratchetting down is an imprecise idea, to graph it we have to pick some particular definition; the graph uses the definition: Pick the new standard such that the marginal cost of control is the same before and after the innovation. Then the new standard will be P_1 and the new costs $a + b$. The incentive to innovate is $c - a$, which looks to be negative in this illustration. Other definitions would produce other results. For example, if the ratchetting rule were to equalize *total* costs before and after, the incentive would clearly be exactly zero.

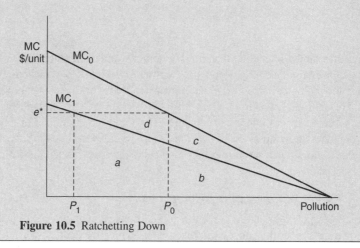

Figure 10.5 Ratchetting Down

BEYOND ADMINISTERED PRICES AND STRAIGHTFORWARD REGULATIONS

LIABILITY PROVISIONS

Liability provisions relevant to the management of environmental quality can arise either from the common law of torts or from statutory law that imposes particular liabilities for particular events on classes of parties. These provisions have two related functions: ex post they result in the collection of damages or restoration costs or some combination of these (however defined and measured) when an act is committed or an event happens. Ex ante, the (uncertain) prospect of paying the damages or restoration costs provides an incentive to the potentially liable parties to take care.

The rules that surround the finding of liability, particularly under statute law when the statute writers are in control, can also vary. An especially important distinction here is between a strict liability rule, under which taking precautions to prevent the act or event in question is no defense against being found liable, and a negligence rule, under which taking some amount of care (perhaps not known ex ante with certainty) is a complete defense against being held liable. Another distinction of importance is between what we might call a standard apportionment rule for assessing damages to a jointly responsible group of parties and the joint and several liability approach that allows recovery of the full damages from as few as one of the responsible parties. Finally, sometimes the party(ies) assessed damages under joint and several liabilities is (are) allowed the right of contribution. That is, they may then sue other responsible parties to force them to share in the payment of damages.

Beyond the above very basic distinctions, there is the huge body of accumulated and refined common law that has the effect of ruling that branch of liability provisions out as a reliable tool for routine environmental management. As a mere economist, I cannot improve on Donald Dewees' 1992 conclusion in this regard:

> The characteristics of tort doctrines for redressing environmental harms that operated a century ago continue to exclude recovery for many environmental harms. Equally important, it is often impossible to prove that a given defendant caused the plaintiff's harm, rendering even favorable doctrines useless. The cost of the tort system precludes its use except for major harms, and with plaintiffs receiving as little as one-third of the total cost of the tort system it is a terribly inefficient means of compensating victims or deterring polluters.
>
> These considerations suggest that tort is most effective for local pollution problems involving a single polluter and very substantial damage, and is of little significance for pollutants dispersed in low concentrations over a large area, or discharged in a developed area with many other pollution sources, including most air and water pollution problems. (Dewees, 1992, p. 162)

In contrast, *legislatively established* liability provisions have clearly made a difference to source behavior, particularly in the areas of oil spills and the handling and disposal of toxic wastes generally.[7] The laws involved include the Outer Continental Shelf Lands Act amendments of 1978, Comprehensive Environmental Response, Liability, and Compensation Act (CERCLA), 1980 and 1986 amendments), Resource Conservation and Recovery Act (RCRA), and the Clean Water Act Amendments of 1987 (CWA) (the "complex" of laws referred to just above). The key features of the laws and their implementing regulations appear to be:

- the assignment of strict liability for discharges or spills (taking precautions is not a defense).

- the spelling out of methods of calculating the natural resource damages for which parties are liable (even where the methods do not meet economists' standards of conceptual correctness).

- explicitly assigning to federal and state governments roles as trustees of the damaged resources.

- using joint and several liability under Superfund (CERCLA), which creates potentially enormous liabilities for parties to disposal activities that, even if legal at the time, turn out later to have contaminated and damaged resources. (Recall the discussion under "fairness.") It also has led to substantial litigation expense involving the government, insurance companies, and other potential contributors to cleanup costs.

Other features of the environmental problems themselves seem also important to the observed effects. First, even though there are many of them, Superfund sites and oil spills are discrete spatially or temporally. They are not routine, continuing, and diffuse. Second, it is usually possible to identify the party responsible for a coastal oil spill or at least one "potentially responsible party" for a Superfund site. (Even for quite old sites, there are likely to be records or at least local memories that give investigators sufficient leads.) Third, the contamination evidence tends to disappear slowly, if at all.

Now, it is important to note that this broad instrument type can be dealt with in the static efficiency context analogously to standards, charges, and marketable permits. That is, we can use a priori models based on standard economic assumptions about the behavior of firms (and government agencies or litigators, where appropriate) to analyze the relative efficiency of different types and combinations of specific provisions. Indeed, there is a substantial literature sufficient to justify several months of thoughtful investigation in its own right. Nonetheless, some useful conclusions can be suggested even within this text.

SINGLE-PARTY PROBLEMS

When the problem at issue involves the behavior of a single party (e.g., a single potential creator of an isolated spill), in the absence of uncertainty about the outcome of litigation to collect the damages the party subject to a strict liability rule has the incentive to behave in a socially optimal manner. These assumptions create a situation exactly analogous to the elementary but classic notion of controlling environmental damages by levying a tax on discharges that equals marginal damages at the socially optimal control level. Here, however, the *source* is assumed to know the total damage function as well as its costs of control ("taking precaution" in the language of the liability literature).

If we relax the very strong assumption of no uncertainty, we begin to see the practical difficulties that, here as elsewhere, stand in the way of attaining the elusive optimum. Two sources of uncertainty, as referred to by Dewees in the long quote above, are:

- possible inability to establish causality because of lack of scientific knowledge
- possible inability to establish causality because of time lags between event and observed effect

Another source of uncertainty arises under a negligence standard (where taking a "proper" level of care is a defense against liability) because the source may be unsure where courts will actually place the "proper" standard and hence whether it will be liable at all. Dewees, in the piece quoted from, adds to this list other impediments to the use of liability litigation at all, such as statutes of limitations and limits on the actual recoverability of damages (e.g., bankruptcy protection).[8]

Whatever the source of the uncertainty about actual liability, it is generally modeled via a probability expression, so that the source is assumed to minimize costs of precautions plus *expected* liability for damages. Under quite plausible assumptions about relations between damages and precautions and between the probability of paying damages and taking precautions, even a single source will take less than optimal care under uncertainty. This provides an opening for a complementary use of ex ante regulation to supplement ex post liability. It has been shown that such a complementary approach can produce optimal caretaking, with the ex ante regulation itself specifying less than the socially optimal level of precaution. (For example, Segerson, in 1990, developed a system of complementary regulations and liability aimed at protecting groundwater from pesticides.)

SEVERAL-PARTY PROBLEMS

When the environmental problem being dealt with involves more than one party contributing to the damage, as, for example, is true in most standard regional pollution situations, we run into additional problems with liability as a policy instrument.

First, and conceptually most interesting, is the problem raised for incentives by knowledge among the parties that their total damage liability can never exceed actual total damages. This implies, in the usual formulations, that a single party will optimize its response, not to the total expected damage, but to that source's expected *share* of total expected damage. This means that less care will be taken by each source than is required for the socially optimal solution—the one corresponding to a centrally calculated set of optimal emission charges, to carry forward the analogy with the last chapter.[9] See Box 10.2 for an illustration.

This may sound like a case for joint and several liability. Surely under that doctrine the trustee can pin the full damages on *some* single party. True, but not necessarily helpful. If the problem—the potential Superfund site, for example—is correctly understood to be jointly created, then it must be true that every source must believe itself to be potentially liable for all the costs *and* to believe that all other sources face the same situation. But the government's litigators in such a joint and several case have the incentive to single out one or two responsible parties who are likely to be able to pay the ultimate judgments. Those parties and the others will likely know who is who a priori. Thus, in solving the optimization problem about

---

> **BOX 10.2**
>
> ## The Problem of Shared Liability for Damage
>
> Here is a simple model that illustrates the problem with shared damage liability—
> that it filters through to the marginal damage in the first-order conditions.
>
> Assume there are two parties, 1 and 2, who jointly cause damage by discharg-
> ing a pollutant in quantities P_1 and P_2. The total damage caused is a function of the
> sum of the two pollution amounts, as each is altered by the natural environment.
> This alteration is captured by constant "transfer coefficients," α_1 and α_2. So dam-
> ages are $f(\alpha_1 P_1 + \alpha_2 P_2)$. Each party can reduce the quantity it emits at a cost given
> by $C_1 = g_1(P_1)$ and $C_2 = g_2(P_2)$ respectively.
>
> In this situation, the social optimization problem is:
>
> $$\min_{P_1, P_2} [f(\alpha_1 P_1 + \alpha_2 P_2) + C_1(P_1) + C_2(P_2)]$$
>
> and the necessary conditions for its solution are:
>
> $$\text{For 1: } C_1'(P_1) + \alpha_1 f' = 0$$
> $$\text{For 2: } C_2'(P_2) + \alpha_2 f' = 0$$
>
> If shared liability were used as a policy instrument here, and the parties were as-
> signed shares in the responsibility for total damage, S_1 and S_2, with $S_1 + S_2 = 1.0$,
> party 1, for example, faces the problem:
>
> $$\min_{P_1} [S_1 f(\alpha_1 P_1 + \alpha_2 P_2) + C_1(P_1)]$$
>
> for which the first-order condition is:
>
> $$C_1'(P_1) + S_1 \alpha_1 f'' = 0$$
>
> and similarly for 2:
>
> $$C_2'(P_2) + S_2 \alpha_2 f'' = 0$$
>
> So the marginal damage each source sees as its responsibility is incorrect from the
> social point of view.

caretaking, one or a few parties will have incentive to take more care than their socially optimal levels because they will have to assume that some other subset of
sources will not take care at all.

The other broad approach to liability, a negligence standard, can be used to give
sources an incentive to take at least some level of precaution against the event. If a

negligence standard is specified with certainty (e.g., use of double-hulled ships for coastal oil shipments), then unless the expense of meeting this standard exceeds the cost plus expected damages of the individually optimal solution to the joint problem, each source will find it optimal to meet that standard.[10] With full knowledge of the joint damage function as a function of the care taken by each party, and each party's costs of taking care, the regulators or legislators could specify a negligence standard that would correspond to the social optimum. This same unrealistic set of assumptions, in the standard pollution control problem, would allow the regulator to set socially optimal discharge (performance) standards. Far more likely is an arbitrary (from the social point of view) standard that is either too loose or too strict. In general, then, we can see that liability provisions, while open-ended and future oriented in their incentive effects, suffer from infirmities analogous to those we find with charges and performance permits where static efficiency is concerned. In the real, complex situations of most interest, a very large amount of knowledge has to be available to regulators, and they have to apply individually tailored implications of that knowledge to the sources. On the other hand, the open-ended and future-oriented character of liability may be considered valuable in its own right. Dynamic efficiency, as has repeatedly been said, is very difficult to explore because endogenous change is poorly understood. But if one finds the dynamic incentives of charges—toward environment-saving technical change—attractive for routine emissions, then the similar potential for liability to affect isolated decisions about disposal and general precautions against accidents may also seem desirable.

The perceived fairness or unfairness of liability provisions seems to me to be related to several features of the actual systems just discussed under uncertainty:

- Uncertainty, negligence standards, and standards of proof. The outcome of liability litigation is never certain. This interferes both with efficiency and fairness, with both classic types of errors being perceived in outcomes. Sometimes the "obviously" guilty escape scot free, while in other cases the apparently innocent are stuck holding the bag.

- Strict liability. This approach in effect gives no credit for taking precautions when those fail to be enough to prevent an event that causes damage. This seems unfair on its face, though it may improve the efficiency properties of the provisions.

- Joint-and-several liability and litigation strategy. This may be the most contentious element of Superfund. It strongly encourages the government to go after one or a few parties that can be expected to be able to pay. But in some cases it may result in suits that seem patently unfair, as when a small municipal source becomes the target because its records happen to be accurate and accessible; or when a small company is sued because other sources can either not be identified or have gone out of business.

- Ex post changes in the rules. This is by no means a necessary part of a liability system, but it does appear to be a feature of Superfund. Many, and not only those sued for damages, will find it unfair when the fact that an action complied with the regulations in effect when it was taken cannot be used as a defense against current liability for the damages ultimately attributable to it. There would seem to be *collective* responsibility for permitting the action in the first place.

THE PROVISION OF INFORMATION

There are several possible ways that government agencies may use information as a tool of environmental policy. These differ in terms of the target group and the route hypothesized to exist between the information and an effect on the actions of polluters (or others affecting the environment). A summary and introduction to the methods and their targets is found in Table 10.1, below. The text to follow will go into more detail and point out the difficulties.

TECHNICAL ASSISTANCE

This policy tool is as old as environmental policy. It is built on the assumption that government is better placed than firms and farms (and even smaller governmental units) to assess the state of the art of pollution control technology. Thus, technical assistance shows polluters what is possible and what it costs. To think that this will lead to lower pollution discharges is to believe that ignorance of these possibilities

TABLE 10.1 Providing Information: Options for the Agency

Method	Information Provided To	Information Provided About	[Apparent] Hypothesized Connection to Action
Technical assistance	Firms, farms, other government agencies (polluters)	Available technologies (treatment, cleanup, process enhancements, "cleaner" inputs)	Makes up for ignorance of what pollution control possibilities exist, their costs, etc.
Product or service analysis/certification	Consumers of products and services	Products, services, companies	Allows consumers to choose most environmentally responsible consumption patterns or choose firms that make "green" products
Emission inventories or other info on actions of firms/farms themselves	Investors in firms; possibly consumers of products and services	Environmental behavior of firms	Gives investors warning of possible future problems; allows consumers to choose to deal with "responsible" firms

is the key to current behavior. It may be, especially if we are talking about the behavior of small enterprises, unable to afford an environmental engineering staff or major consultancy, and faced in any case with some incentive to reduce discharges. But trying to make a case for technical assistance to large, sophisticated polluters is to contradict the case for emission charges and other economic incentive approaches. One of the reasons those approaches are praised is that polluters are supposed to know better than the pollution control agency what the pollution-reduction "frontier" looks like and how to get to it.

Note that providing technical assistance is not the same as supporting basic research into pollution-related processes, such as the identification of microbes that can detoxify chlorinated hydrocarbons. Because basic scientific information is a public good, government provision is often the most direct way to deal with market failure—the failure of private markets to provide a socially desired quantity. But, at the level of applied technology, there are market forces pushing for "getting the word out" on existing processes and possibilities.

Finally, it is important to repeat that technical assistance makes most sense when polluters face incentives or regulations that push them to keep on reducing discharges.

PRODUCT OR SERVICE ANALYSIS AND CERTIFICATION

This policy tool can be seen as building on the provision of information about products and services, usually by nonprofit organizations, and aimed at what we might call the private-good aspects of the items reported on. In the United States, Consumers Union has been providing this kind of service for decades, testing and evaluating everything from automobiles to health insurance, from spaghetti sauces to toaster ovens, and from movies to plumbing fixtures. The idea is that no single family has either the money or the time to try out all the alternatives for any of these products or services. In the absence of outside information each family will make choices on the basis of accident, hearsay, or, at least, incomplete trials. This is clearly more of a problem for "big-ticket" items such as cars and refrigerators than for packaged food. And the information is more valuable, because most difficult for the individual family to obtain, when the dimension reported on is some form of reliability—as in the absence of automobile breakdowns or the service from an insurance company's claims-processing department—where there is an element of randomness, and rational choice is best based on a large sample of *past* performance.

In the case of environmental information, the range of possible consumer interests is large. Some of these have both private and public dimensions. As examples, think about:

- picking agricultural products on the basis of methods used in their production (e.g., whether chemical pesticides are used on fruits and vegetables; whether cows are given artificial hormones to increase milk production; even whether the animals are allowed to lead roughly "natural" lives. The first two of these are examples of mixed private and public concerns. The third seems clearly "public").

• picking appliances on the basis of their energy efficiency (information now required to be provided for major appliances in the U.S.) Again, this involves both private (energy bills) and public (pollution discharges at power plants) aspects.

• picking packaged foods on the basis of recyclability of their packages.

A first and obvious question for an economics course is: Why would any consumer be willing to pay more to buy a tiny amount of some public good that will benefit many? Why not ignore the information and "free ride" on what any more public-spirited citizens might do? Assuming that problem away, however, leaves us with other questions. For example, focusing on one aspect of a product may blind consumers to other dimensions of its environmental "performance." An attempt to bring all these dimensions together is called "life cycle analysis" (LCA). This is the name given to efforts to quantify *all* of the environmental impacts of a product (or service, at least in principle) from the initial extraction of raw material to the final disposal of the residuals left after use.

On the surface, this may sound like the ultimate in information, allowing the consumer to make fully informed purchasing decisions. But beneath the surface plausibility lie at least three serious problems. First, there is inevitably an element of arbitrariness in the design and conduct of an LCA. Where, for example, should the cycle start? With the raw material itself? Or with the construction of the raw material extraction and processing equipment? Or with the raw material extracted to build that equipment? The possibilities for going back through the chain are, in principle, endless, though the payoff becomes smaller and smaller as we get further from the good at direct issue.

A second definitional problem exists whenever the "time lines" of different products producing the same service are different. The best place to see this is in a comparison between, say, recyclable milk bottles (glass) and disposable milk cartons (waxed cardboard). What is the product here? Not one half gallon transported one time from store to home. Rather, the product has to be defined in terms of the number of trips the average glass container can make. (And, of course, the environmental impact of the between-trip cleaning of the bottles has to be included in the analysis.) For a good as complex in use as an automobile, arriving at a useful definition of "the product" has to be arbitrary—so many miles of transportation at particular speeds and temperatures for a particular number of people, for example, since all these features affect pollution emissions. And then there are the service and repair activities over the period chosen, with *their impacts*.

The third problem, though, seems to me most serious both conceptually and practically. To see it, think about the milk container example, in a particularly simplified form. The relevant items might be:

Glass Product	*Paper Product*
Manufacturing	Manufacturing
Sand, etc. mining and transport	Logging and wood transport
	Papermaking
Melting, refining, pouring of glass	Cardboard coating—
	cutting, forming (the coating probably is purchased from a specialty chemical firm and comes ultimately from crude oil)
Bottle Transport	*Container Transport*
(milk transport)	(milk transport)
Bottle Cleaning	*Container Disposal*
Bottle Reuse	
(milk transport)	
Ultimate Bottle Disposal, or Recycling	

Each of these major steps involves the generation of different environmental impacts, at different places, over different time periods. Thus, mining of glass raw materials is totally different from logging or from crude oil extraction. Glassmaking is nothing like papermaking or petroleum refining in terms of pollution loads generated, except that they all use energy. Further, the plants involved will almost certainly be in different places. Transport of the containers may involve similar modes but different routes to the "average" consumer (another more or less arbitrary choice). And milk bottle washing and sterilization, with ultimate disposal of broken or weakened bottles, is totally different from the landfilling or incineration of empty waxed-cardboard cartons, though both may last for many years in covered landfills.

Given complete but "raw" information on this comparison, the consumer has to be able to supply her or his own weights for all the different impacts in order to arrive at a judgment of which product is least harmful. The alternative, having the weights supplied by the analyst, perhaps based on elaborate damage estimation, magnifies the arbitrariness. (And, if you paid attention to the discussions of damage estimation capabilities in chapters 7 and 8, you would have to be skeptical of the numbers in any case.)

So LCA can produce vast quantities of numbers, but those numbers (a) are always open to challenge on the grounds that they are based on arbitrary and ad hoc assumptions, (b) are not generally comparable across alternative products, and (c) cannot be transformed into single, comparable "impact" numbers without difficult, essentially arbitrary, and (let us admit) unreliable conversion into some sort of damage estimate.[11]

That said, policymakers appear to be interested in consumer information provision, and other questions have to be addressed, even if the information itself focuses on one or two dimensions of alternative products, such as packaging recyclability or production process toxic use. For example, several options exist for the source of such information. These include a government agency; the producer (with or without external "monitoring"); a consortium of producers, such as an industry association; or an independent nonprofit, such as Consumers Union. The choice here involves differences in credibility of the information as well as the extent of private information on production details that has to be shared outside the firm.

Further, the information may take the form either of a simple certification that a product meets some minimum standards or the provision of quite complete data about the actual levels of "performance" attained. (The same difference, for example, as between a "heart-wise" symbol for some food product and a complete list of ingredients.)

INDICATORS OF ENVIRONMENTAL PERFORMANCE BY FIRMS

There have long been efforts by environmentalists to influence the future environmental behavior of firms by publicizing their current behavior. These generally involved efforts to exploit public records, such as self-reported air and water pollution discharges, especially if these include permit violations.

These efforts, more or less inevitably, were spotty in coverage and difficult to sustain. Therefore, they hardly constituted a serious test of this use of information as a policy tool. But in 1986, with the Emergency Planning and Community Right-to-Know Act, the U.S. government launched a serious effort that has already begun to produce data on and analyses of effects. This open-ended experiment—for it seems very unlikely that the effort was systematically designed to achieve any particular end—is the Toxics Release Inventory (TRI). By some accounts, the origin of TRI was in Congress' frustration with the glacial pace of EPA's progress in regulating toxic discharges. (To be fair to EPA, this pace was the product of the complex process required by the laws created by Congress, a process that involved, first, a formal "listing" of a compound as "toxic" on the basis of the threats it posed; and second, the publication of discharge limitations. The basis for a "toxic" listing is generally the possibility that the compound causes or promotes chronic disease, especially cancer.)

When the TRI was created, only about half a dozen of the tens of thousands of emitted substances that might be expected eventually to qualify for listing and regulation had been successfully handled. In the TRI legislation, Congress originally took it on itself to say that a list of 300-plus compounds would be subject to the emission-reporting rules. This number was more recently increased to include more than 600 compounds.

Any source emitting more than some very small amount per year of each compound is required to report annually to EPA on its emissions. (These are self-reports, are not necessarily based on measurements, and are not checked [audited] for accuracy by EPA.) EPA is then required to publish a compendium of the reports and to make available all the information it receives. The first year of discharge reporting was 1987; EPA's publication, each spring, involves the reports from two years before. So, as of June 2000, there were twelve year's worth of reports and backup documents in the public domain.

It seems beyond question that Congress wanted the TRI to influence emitter behavior. But it is not entirely clear why or how legislators expected this to happen. Three major possibilities seem to be that:

- Consumers could react by not buying the products of firms with very large emissions (or emissions of particular compounds that consumers feel, rightly or wrongly, are especially bad).
- Activists and politicians could use the information to turn up the heat on polluters at the state level, perhaps even passing state laws that regulate what EPA had not yet gotten to.
- Investors could "punish" emitters, either on moral grounds or because the TRI was taken to be a signal of future costs, such as possible future Superfund liability. This punishment would occur through the stock market, with the stock prices, and hence the values, of some firms driven down in anticipation of future lower profits.

Of these possible routes to effects, the first seems least likely to work. While some consumers might be outraged to learn that plant x of firm y is a large emitter of some solvent (a chlorinated hydrocarbon, say), it is not so clear what they would do about it *as consumers*. For most consumer purchases outside autos and appliances the identification of brand labels with companies, let alone with specific plants, is not easy. A large, diversified, consumer goods firm such as Sara Lee, for example, sells many brands of packaged foods, only the bakery products in this range being called by the company's name. It also sells leather products and underwear for men, women, and children. How many consumers identify Coach luggage, wallets, and handbags with Sara Lee?[12] Or Haynes underwear? If not many do, then there are only a limited number of ways for those consumers to "punish" Sara Lee should it show up badly in TRI.

More likely, but harder to substantiate empirically, is that TRI is, in effect, a handy tool for environmentalists to use in pushing for stricter state-level laws on industrial toxics use and emission. This was certainly how the Tennessee Environmental Council (TEC), through its Toxics Program, tried to use the information. Consistently, TEC would point out in the early 1990s that Tennessee ranked near the "top" of the fifty states in terms of total toxic emissions, as a prelude to its suggested legislation that would have required firms to do a sort of toxic-reduction planning exercise.

But the route to effects that has been systematically investigated is via investors and stock market values. And the results so far obtained are at least promising. These results may be summarized as follows:

- Stock prices of firms have responded to TRI publication, at least in the early years.[13] There was no simple relation between the amount of discharge reported and the size of the stock price "correction." If anything, and somewhat tautologically, the biggest movements seem to be associated with firms for which the TRI data could be said to be a "surprise," that is, firms not thought of as having toxics problems.

- The firms that take the largest stock price "hits" tend to *report* the greatest reductions in toxics releases in subsequent years. (Since the reports are unaudited, it is slightly risky to equate them to actual discharge reductions; but only a complete cynic would dismiss all reported reductions as fabrications.) (If you are interested, see Konar and Cohen, 1997.)

Thus, TRI seems to have had some effect: anecdotally through providing a bigger stick to environmentalists, and systematically shown via stock price responses and their effects on firms' reported efforts to clean up. The next question, however, is: What can be said about even the stock-price route that is normative? Or, in other words, can we say anything about information as a policy tool that is even roughly parallel to the comments in this and the previous chapter on static and dynamic efficiency, incentives for technical change, and so forth?

For starters, what would have to be true for discharge information to produce efficiency, either in the sense of minimizing the sum of damages and the costs of avoiding them, or of minimizing the costs of meeting given ambient quality goals (both in the absence of other regulations or economic incentives)? For the first version of efficiency, the information would have to make the firm "see" and react to its appropriate marginal damage function. For the second version of efficiency to apply, the information would have to make the firm "see" and react to an analog to an emission charge schedule—a penalty per unit of emission that the firm could expect to pay via changes in its value. How likely is either of these outcomes?

First, we can see that the information actually provided by TRI is not what would be needed by investors to form an accurate judgment on the firm's current damages or on its likely future liabilities. The R in TRI, "release," makes it clear that what is being reported are discharges. But damages (or future liabilities for past damages) depend on the *effects* of the discharges. Those effects in turn vary depending on release location relative to people (or things) who might be harmed. A very large release of a particular compound hundreds of miles from any population center could have a smaller damage result than a much smaller amount released in the midst of a major city. To transform discharges into risks, one needs information on the *fate* of the chemical in the natural environment and on the resulting *exposure* of people and things to the harmful ambient concentrations. Actually, the way TRI tends to be used, the connection between information and relevant risk is even more tenuous than just suggested. There is a tendency to focus on *total* emissions from a plant, company, or state, aggregated over compounds. This makes for good publicity it seems, but certainly not for good risk analysis. Finally, we can see that even if the information actually available were better matched with needs for damage-relevant data, there is no guarantee that filtering this through the stock market process will produce either (a) a good approximation to possible damages or (b) something the sources will see as their future liability functions, or some other relationship that should be responded to. Thus, it seems unlikely that information as a policy tool can be shown to produce efficient results.

Even so, there may be advantages to using information to try to influence the behavior of dischargers. Most important, the institutional demands are small—though with the TRI they are probably too small because no effort is made to audit the self-reports of dischargers. But simply publishing data on discharges takes almost no technical skill or training. Were those data to be transformed into something closer to associated risk, using models of the natural-world processes and exposure/effect relationships, the task would be much larger. But one might argue that it would still be easier than developing and defending regulatory standards, such as those based on technology definitions or on chosen AEQ standards.

Other advantages may be seen in dynamic flexibility, since no adjustments need be made except to report the changed discharges, and perceived fairness. After all, telling the public about the pollution loads to which they are exposed can hardly be called unfair, though sources may argue that the responses of press and environmental groups to the information is out of proportion to the real risk and is thus unfair. (Note that if some sources get "too much" bad publicity under this argument, others are likely to be getting too little. They are unlikely to point this out.)

CHALLENGE REGULATION

Challenge regulation is an interesting response to the constraints of the regulatory environment.[14] Theoretical discussion tends to assume that the regulatory agency has *indisputable* power in the enforcement of *well-defined* environmental statutes. But many policy provisions are not well defined. For example, technology-based standards, by definition, leave the door open for costly disputes between agency and sources (usually through the courts) concerning what forms of technology usually constitutes compliance. Paul Portney has observed:

> Whenever legislation provides general guidance that must be translated into specific terms at the discretion of the bureaucracy, there will be many opportunities for legal challenges to bureaucratic decisions in which it can be argued that the bureaucracy misinterpreted the legislative intent, failed to give adequate weight to particular evidence, exceeded its authority, failed to utilize its authority, and so forth. (Portney, 1978, pp. 54–55)

Second, the notion that agencies possess indisputable power is usually false. The burden of proof of noncompliance usually falls on the agency. This burden means agency time and resources must be spent to gather evidence that will survive court scrutiny—this can be a rather expensive and drawn out process. Even if the evidence seems compelling, though, there is no assurance that judge or jury will rule in favor of the agency.

Within this environment, sources possess a degree of "power" in determining the final regulatory outcome. This means environmental regulation is a process of dialogue, of action and reaction, between agency and firm. Any efforts that make firms feel they are excluded from the process will only increase their recalcitrance, thus raising the costs of enforcement. The desirability of including firms directly in policy decision making is positively related to the potential disruption they can cause.

Challenge regulation is a way to "include" sources in the process. The agency "challenges" sources to voluntarily achieve a given standard. This approach has two advantages. First, sources are in no way forced to participate, thus little animosity should exist between them and the agency. Second, participating sources determine *how* the standard is met. This allows the final outcome to be sensitive to market and technological constraints.

When agents are *perfect* volunteers (i.e., there are no threats of action by the agency against those who do not participate), moral suasion is the only instrument needed to achieve environmental improvements. Policy practice, however, shows that moral suasion is far from sufficient. For example, researchers have concluded that voluntary arrangements with farmers for agricultural pollution control have had little impact on total farm runoff. Economists, at least, tend to expect that sources need a much stronger incentive to participate in emissions reduction programs.

Implicit in the working relationship between the source and the regulator are certain protocols the former knows it has no power to challenge and overturn (i.e., the authority of the agency to put in place *some* type of pollution standard). The source must accept and act upon the premise that a certain level of pollution abatement will have to be implemented. Maintaining a policy regime that is flexible is in the interest of the source, and this is achieved through cooperation with the agency. Polluters who make life difficult for the agency may motivate regulators to increase their policing power and impose on firms costlier methods of control.

If the agency "challenges" dischargers to voluntarily achieve new, more stringent standards, this is likely to be seen as a signal that regulators will, in the near future, be seeking to further reduce emission levels on a mandatory basis. Sources can either "pay the piper" now by agreeing to cooperate with the agency, and enjoy the advantage of a flexible regulatory program, or pay later by waiting for the agency to force the environmental improvements. It is arguable that polluters will typically choose the former because, from the source's point of view, there are penalties associated with the loss of voluntary compliance status and these penalties can be considerable. These can include plant shutdown, bad publicity, and refusal to renew operating permits.

In practice, challenge regulation is a new instrument in U.S. policymaking. EPA's 33/50 program is the most visible use of this policy tool. Initiated in 1991, the policy "challenged" participants (who volunteered) to reduce transfers and emissions of seventeen toxic chemicals by 33 percent by the end of 1992 and by 50 percent by the end of 1995. Seema Arora and Timothy Cason published an evaluation of the program's initial outcome (Arora and Cason, 1995). Although in their sample from the universe of invited firms they found only about 13 percent of the firms actually agreed to participate, those who did participate tended to be the largest firms with the highest pollution levels. Successful participation by these firms would offer significant overall reductions in the release of target chemicals.

These observations suggest two issues concerning the fairness of challenge regulation. The fact that firms meeting the "challenge" enjoy short-term improvement in their image means firms that have previously met (or have no need for) reductions gain no visibility. To address this asymmetry, the government could publicize a list of "clean" firms who are "ahead of their time." Another fairness issue arises over the influence of participating on future standards. Firms with large R&D programs or political influence, through participation, could enhance their ability to define new statutes, putting at a disadvantage smaller firms that cannot afford program participation.

Challenge regulation offers *sources* the ability to achieve the standard desired by the agency at lowest cost—the government does not mandate the adoption of a treatment technology that might not be appropriate for certain sources. Each firm determines its own solution to the problem (or "challenge"), just as with an efficient emission charge. It is important to note, however, that the standard itself may not be socially efficient, and this is almost certainly true for 33/50. For example, more environmental improvement might be achieved at the same cost by decreasing emissions at some plants by 70 percent and at others by 30 percent than by decreasing emissions by 50 percent for all. So, the efficiency of the *overall* policy depends on how the "challenge" is structured, even assuming complete participation. More to the point, if only 13 percent of the sources of some problem actually volunteer, then whatever is being achieved is only a shadow of the overall goal.

If, over time, the government desires to maintain the effectiveness of challenge regulation, then it must devote resources to policies that bridge the gap between the environmental goal and the environmental outcome of a challenge regulation previously enacted. If, after 33/50 expires, enough pollution reduction has not been achieved, then the EPA will have to implement stricter policies (in accordance with the *original* goals of 33/50) for those who did not volunteer and successfully complete the program. This should encourage a higher level of voluntary participation when the next challenge regulation is offered. If future participation is higher, the effectiveness of low-cost challenge regulation strategies increase, and the costs of "filling the gap" decrease.

CONCLUDING COMMENTS AND REMINDERS

This chapter has covered a wide range of subject matter, divided into two broad areas. The first area involved additional considerations useful in thinking about the choice between market-based instruments and some alternative regulatory approach. The list included institutional demands, especially monitoring capability of the environmental agency; the political difficulties raised by trying to introduce "prices" into environmental policies, both those of message and those arising from the actual flows of money; the interesting matter of the "second dividend" that, under certain circumstances, can be claimed for policy instruments that result in a flow of money to the agency; the general problems of perceived fairness and of perceived risk, especially the risk that an agency or government may perceive that a particular instrument may fail because of perversity on the part of the regulated parties or because of ignorance on the agency's part. It seems to me especially interesting to realize how many different roles *prices* on pollution, however defined, play beyond the original static efficiency concerns from Chapter 9. On what most would agree is the plus side, those prices are the source of an extra dynamic push toward environment-saving innovation and, potentially, of a second dividend. But they are also the source of political objection based on the claim that it is simply wrong to create markets that explicitly price the environment. Further, especially if prices are supposed to be set and maintained to achieve static efficiency, the requirements for their calculation imply large data collection, modeling, and computation demands on the capabilities of the agency.

The second major chapter part took us beyond the common comparison of market-based and more traditional regulatory instruments. First, we considered the possibilities for relying on liability law and saw that there were many parallels, as to both strengths and weaknesses, with the by-now-familiar approaches, especially in the matter of inducing socially efficient choices by regulated parties. In general, liability law, without statutory interventions that impose minimum standards on care taking, will be a weak basis for policy. As a supplement to other approaches, however, it can be quite powerful. A key distinction in thinking about liability and policy is between single- and multiple-party problems, with the latter much the more difficult.

A second, fairly recent innovation in policy is the use of information as a way of influencing behavior. Two variations on this theme seem especially interesting: informing consumers about product characteristics and informing investors about firm behavior (probably as a proxy for the firm's store of potential future problems). We saw that empirical research had found significant effects of TRI data publication on later toxics discharges by some firms—in particular, those whose stock prices were most affected by the release of the TRI data. Consumer-oriented information about the public aspects of products might be expected to have considerably less effect because no single consumer can notice an environmental effect attributable to her or his consumption decisions. Nonetheless, there has been a considerable amount of work put into "life cycle analysis" of consumer product environmental implications, and some time was spent explaining why the results of such analyses may be less useful than enthusiasts seem to understand.

Finally, challenge regulation and the related business of devising voluntary agreements between agency and regulated party were very briefly examined. Here the central question for an economist is: Why would any firm volunteer to do more than is currently required of it? Answers to that question depend in general on there existing a credible threat of *some* agency requirement to take additional costly action in the future, a threat that may be made less immediate or less costly if the firm cooperates now.

One general observation seems especially worth keeping in mind. It is that, while some of the newer ideas in the policy-instruments world seem interesting and to hold out some potential advantages—such as small institutional demands made by the use of a public information approach—it is often hard to do empirical analysis of their actual effects on environmental quality and even more difficult (almost impossible in most cases, I would say) to create a persuasive a priori model of their operation that would put their analysis on a symmetric footing with the analysis done for the "classic" instruments.

NOTES

1. In irrigated areas of the West, there may in fact be systems of drainage in place to slow or prevent soil salination. These do collect irrigation return water polluted by fertilizers and pesticides, and the ultimate discharges to water bodies from even quite large farms may be coming from a small number of "points."
2. A sort of collective responsibility scheme suggested by Kathleen Segerson seems related to the liability approach discussed below. But it will not be assessed here. Anyone interested can look at J. Miceli and K. Segerson, "Joint Liability in Torts," 1991.
3. Still one of the best, probably *the* best, statement of this general position, as well as other arguments against the environmental use of emission charges is to be found in Steven Kelman's book, *What Price Incentives?*, 1981.
4. This view assumes that there is no intrinsic interest in the size of the public, as opposed to the market sector. But since such fractions are often part of country comparisons, as indicators, for example, of general business friendliness, this may be an incorrect assumption, even before the considerations below come into play.
5. This was true for the steel and petroleum refining industries according to the pollution control models constructed at Resources for the Future in the 1970s, e.g., Clifford Russell, *Residuals Management in Industry: A Case Study of Petroleum Refining*, 1973, and Russell and William Vaughan, *Steel Production: Processes, Products and Residuals*, 1976.
6. As a reminder, the following simple graph shows the deadweight loss created by imposing a proportional sales tax on a good.

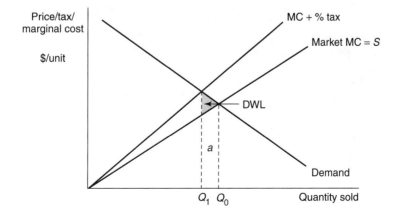

The tax reduces the quantity sold from Q_0 to Q_1, reducing resource costs by (a) but also reducing producer and consumer surpluses by the triangle labeled DWL, as compared with the undistorted market outcome.

7. "Clearly" is meant in a strictly informal sense. For example, a regular reader of the *Wall Street Journal* has, over the last decade, been exposed to dozens of articles dealing with the economic woes of commercial hazardous waste handling and disposal companies. These firms added incineration capacity in response to the perceived "crisis" of the mid-1980s, only to find volumes of such waste generation declining annually.

8. The "threat" of bankruptcy as a way for a responsible party to escape ex post liability is an argument for adding criminal penalties to those of the liability system.

9. If each source really faced a situation in which full damage recovery could be imposed on it, then the possible total recovery would be the number of sources times total damages.

10. The double-hulled example is not at all farfetched. This is a regulatory (not a negligence) standard from the Oil Pollution Act of 1990. It has apparently resulted in a few foreign oil shippers refusing to send their tankers into U.S. ports. Others are reorganizing into a set of single-ship companies to limit liability losses.

11. Peter Kennedy, Benoit Laplante, and John Maxwell, "Pollution Policy: The Role for Publicly Provided Information," 1994, discussed circumstances under which public provision of information about environmental effects of consumer goods will help attain social efficiency as opposed to those under which it will make matters worse. Their work assumes that the information is accurate, that it has been "predigested" or transformed into scalar form, and that those who react are those being harmed.

12. Since this was written, Sara Lee has spun off Coach, but the point remains.

13. The method used is called "event analysis" and it looks at stock price changes just before and just after the "event"—TRI publication here—as contrasted with the projected stock price path based on past stock performance.

14. Challenge regulation generally involves voluntary acceptance of the challenge, so that this section will also be about the approach called "voluntary agreements." These are currently of great interest in Europe and are the subject of a major international research effort.

REFERENCES

Arora, Seema, and Timothy Cason. 1995. "An experiment in voluntary environmental regulation." *Journal of Environmental Economy and Management* 28(3):271–286.

Dewees, Donald. 1992. "Tort law and the deterrence of environmental pollution." In *Innovation in Environmental Policy*, edited by T. Tietenberg. Aldershot, Hants, England: Edward Elgar.

Deutsch Gesellschaft für Technische Zusammenarbeit. 1995. *Market-based Instruments in Developing Countries*. Eschborn, Germany: Author.

Kelman, Steven. 1981. *What Price Incentives?* Boston: Mount Auburn.

Kennedy, Peter W., Benoi Laplante, and John Maxwell. 1994. "Pollution policy: The role for publicly provided information." *Journal of Environmental Economics and Management*, 26(1):31–43.

Konar, Shameek, and Mark Cohen. 1997. "Information as regulation: The effect of community right-to-know laws on toxic emissions." *Journal of Environmental Economics and Management*, 32(1):109–124.

Miceli, J., and Kathleen Segerson. 1991. "Joint liability in torts." *International Review of Law and Economics* 11(3):235–249.

Portney, Paul. 1978. *Current Issues in U.S. Environmental Policy*. Washington, D.C.: Resources for the Future.

Russell, Clifford S. 1973. *Residuals Management in Industry: A Case Study of Petroleum Refining*. Baltimore: Johns Hopkins University Press for Resources for the Future.

————— and William J. Vaughan. 1976. *Steel Production: Processes, Products, and Residuals*. Baltimore: Johns Hopkins University Press for Resources for the Future.

Segerson, Kathleen. 1990. "Liability for groundwater contamination from pesticides." *Journal of Environmental Economics and Management*, 19(3):227–243.

11

MONITORING AND ENFORCEMENT

So far in this text we have pretty much ignored monitoring and enforcement, except for some comments in the instruments chapters on ease or difficulty of these tasks under alternative instruments and on changing the burden of proof through instrument choice. But at the same time, we have in effect been assuming, quite unrealistically, a sufficient effort to obtain compliance with standards (if those are in place) or proper charge payments (if those are the instrument of choice). And, even more unrealistically, we have been assuming that this is being achieved without cost. This chapter makes some amends for this previous lack of realism by describing the overall problem more carefully and then going into the more formal, but still quite simple, economics of the problem of the regulated party (the discharger) and that of the public agency.

First, however, we need to make sure we know what the basic words mean.

• *Monitoring* is the general word for efforts to find out what the regulated parties are doing and how what they are doing compares with what they are either (a) supposed to be doing or (b) self-report that they are doing.

The common, generic, though by no means simple, monitoring problem is the measurement of actual discharges from a point pollution source per unit time. But catching a litterer or a "midnight dumper" of toxics in the act is also a monitoring problem.

• *Enforcement* refers to the actions taken, usually on the basis of monitoring evidence, to reward desired or (more usually) to penalize undesired behavior. Most generally, enforcement activities include sending "notices of violations"; levying automatic, administrative penalties; filing civil legal actions that seek (usually larger) money penalties; and obtaining criminal indictments of individuals deemed responsible for violations. In the literature, "enforcement" almost always shows up as a penalty or penalty function. Sometimes there will be uncertainty involved, as with a probability of successfully imposing a penalty (to reflect the uncertainty of legal proceedings). And a full account of the enforcement problem involves a cost of the penalty's imposition, with cost perhaps related to severity of punishment.

CHARACTERISTICS OF VARIOUS M & E SETTINGS

You have read enough by now to have some sense for the wide variety of situations encompassed under the phrase "the monitoring and enforcement problem." Table 11.1 is an attempt to capture this variety by looking at three dimensions: the characteristics of the actions to be monitored; the characteristics of the monitoring instruments available; and the characteristics of the enforcement system, including assignment of responsibility for monitoring and of burden of proof based on monitoring results. Some comment on the range of situations represented by combinations of these characteristics may be helpful as background to a discussion of general requirements for M & E system design.

ACTIONS

I have already noted that point sources (smokestacks, wastewater outfalls) present a much simpler challenge than nonpoint pollution sources. But another type of source might be called point but moveable in time or space (or both). Thus a small dry-cleaning plant in a large city might accumulate a few barrels of spent (dirty) dry-

TABLE 11.1 An Overview of Some Monitoring and Enforcement Issues

Characteristics of the Actions to Be Monitored	Characteristics of the Monitoring "Instrument"	Characteristics of the System
Source Type Fixed: Know where to monitor, not necessarily how • Point • Nonpoint Moveable: Could happen anywhere	Precise Imprecise: High type I and/or II error	Burden of proof on: • Government agency • Regulated party • Third party (as in 3rd party enforcement suits and liability/tort law)
Impact/Discharge Type Storable Immediate impact: "Generation" followed immediately by impact on environment, as gas from boiler Ephemeral: Must be caught in the act Imprinted: Action can be discovered/reconstructed/ attributed later	Require entry Remote	Monitoring done by: • Government agency • Regulated party • Third party Penalty: • Fine • Jail • Reputation • Other Forum for penalty Setting: • Administrative • Special hearing body • Court

cleaning solvent per month or quarter. If legal disposal becomes very expensive or administratively onerous, the plant manager may be tempted to find a quiet place with a storm-sewer grate for midnight dumping of the burden. This poses a problem close to that of littering from cars, though with much more serious potential consequences.

The "moveability" of the solvent is closely linked to its "storeability," which is a matter largely of volume but also of other characteristics of the potential discharge. For example, it would be enormously difficult and expensive to "store" combustion gases from a boiler. The very attempt would affect the efficient operation of the boiler; the technology for cooling the gases would be a challenge; and even with cooling, the volume needed for storage would be huge. Wastewater from an industrial plant or a city falls somewhere in between the dry-cleaning and the boiler examples on the storeability measure. Storage for normal volumes could probably be provided at reasonable expense. Indeed, that is the essence of some discharge reduction techniques such as settling ponds. But a common problem for older cities is that their sewers carry both normal flows *and* storm water from streets. This produces huge volumes during brief periods and, in many cities, results in the need to discharge these "combined sewer overflows" during big rainstorms. Building larger, temporary storage is one solution to this problem. Building separate sewers for stormwater and household/commercial/industrial wastewater is another. But for monitoring, the ability of sources to store discharges can present a new problem rather than a solution, since discharging might then be done when it was clear to the source that monitoring effort was low.

Also linked into this complex of characteristics is the distinction between ephemeral and what I call "imprinted" actions. Throwing a beer can out of a moving car is the archetypical ephemeral act. Unless the authorities have nothing better to do than look for and try to find matches for fingerprints, or unless each can is to be numbered and sales recorded by number, if the act is missed so is the chance of punishing it. The contrast, as suggested by the beer-can numbering scheme, is to acts involving "imprinting." For liquids this could involve seeding with tiny amounts of radioactive tracer materials, each unique to particular users or transporters. For example, crude oil can be seeded before it is loaded onto a tanker so that discovered spills can be traced to the source without observation of the act of spilling itself. Some wastes may be naturally tagged because they have unusual, even unique, characteristics. This might be true of some specialty metal-plating wastes.

MONITORING INSTRUMENTS

The technology available for monitoring at any one time is important in defining the difficulty and expense of the task. The ideal monitoring instrument is one that is always in place, measuring without error, and recording constantly in a way the source cannot tamper with, so that the results can be looked at by the agency at its convenience. Such an ideal machine converts an ephemeral into an imprinted act.

Real monitoring instruments never have all these features. There are, for many pollutants, in-place, constantly operating methods of measurement. (An example is a device that shines a strong light through a smokestack from one transparent port to another to obtain an estimate of the level of particulate matter in the emitted gas.) None of these instruments is without error, and the harsher the environment in which they operate, the more susceptible they will be to breakdown. Any of these could be wired to record their measurements, even at some remote spot, accessible only to the agency. But the output might still be tampered with by a skilled and determined source.

There are also instruments that can remotely measure (with error) the amounts of particulates and of certain gases contained in stack gases. This means that entry to the source's premises and access to the stack are not required for monitoring. Earlier instruments were designed for what is known as "initial compliance" testing—finding out whether a source's equipment is *capable* of producing discharges that meet its permit terms. In the initial compliance setting it is in the interests of both source and agency to have accurate, precise measurements.[1] So access was granted without any fuss or delay. But in *continuing* compliance monitoring, sources may have an incentive to be difficult about access. Anticipating such difficulties, it has become common for state monitoring people to give prior notice of visits. This destroys a key element of the desirable system—surprise. Advance notice may allow sources to adjust from not complying to complying so that monitoring is essentially a useless exercise.[2] But access and cooperation make the use of the older monitoring methods feasible.

I shall come back to the economic implications of measurement errors and resulting errors of inference later in this chapter.

OTHER CHARACTERISTICS OF THE SYSTEM

We discussed in Chapter 9 the problem of burden of proof in the context of choice of instruments; and noted that changing from a penalty to a reward can be a way of shifting that burden. After we have discussed errors of inference we'll be in a better position to see formally how such a shift affects a monitoring and enforcement system. For now let me just point out that in some situations the law may effectively put a burden of proof on a third party if that party can sue to enforce standards, force penalties to be paid for past violations, and so forth.

Similarly, the monitoring itself can be done in the first instance by the agency, the source, or some third party. "In the first instance" is inserted because even though self-monitoring and self-reporting is a common provision of U.S. environmental law, the responsible agency cannot entirely disregard the possibility of false reporting. There must be some nonzero probability that false reports will be caught and punished. But producing such a probability via "auditing," in the absence of the ideal-recording, continuous-monitoring instrument is very difficult, as already pointed out. The essence of the problem is that, unless the "auditor" measures the same event (same discharge over the same time span), the case to establish false reporting will be tenuous. But again, unless monitoring is completely unobtrusive, the source will know when it is occurring, and only an inept source will falsify its report for the audit period.[3]

The choice of prospective penalties is a very interesting part of the problem. In almost all of the work in this chapter, I shall be using money penalties, as in fines for violations. But there are a couple of linked problems with confining any system to this option. The first is that there is an upper limit, though perhaps it is not very well defined, on the size of money penalties that will be credible. Fines that are really enormous relative to the benefit to the source of not complying (or to the damage caused by noncompliance) may not be taken seriously by judges or juries though they may appear to make a reduction in monitoring effort possible (see below for the algebra). The second problem is bankruptcy. This helps make fines that are very large relative to a firm's size not credible. If a huge fine would drive a firm into bankruptcy, it will probably not be used, either because it would not seem "fair" or because, if levied, it would never be collected.

In these common circumstances, economists have shown that introducing jail-time as part of a suite of penalties can be very useful. The down sides here are that jail-time requires a criminal conviction, which in turn means proof of the violation beyond a reasonable doubt, while civil penalties (fines) depend on the "preponderance of the evidence" supporting the conclusion that a violation has occurred; and that imprisoning someone costs society real resources. Collecting a fine is usually assumed to be costless.

Another enforcement tool, related to the use of information on firm behavior as a policy instrument, is the ability to influence the general reputation of sources. By publicizing violations, even in the absence of more than token fines, it is possible for the agency to create costs for troublesome sources.

Finally, as should already be clear, the nature of the available penalties to a large extent influences the forum in which proof of violation must be achieved. In general, the burden of proof will increase as the forum changes from administrative hearing, to civil law court, to criminal court. And burden of proof is an excellent proxy or predictor for the *cost* of enforcement.

ELEMENTS OF A MONITORING AND ENFORCEMENT SYSTEM

Building on the discussion of the previous section we can specify some of the elements of a system of M & E.

• The regulation or charging scheme must be enforceable. In particular it must specify or imply something that is actually measurable and impose a requirement against which measurements can be compared. Compliance with a discharge standard is enforceable in that sense. So is accurate payment of an emission charge. But a requirement that a source "do its best" is not, because "its best" is not defined.

• The technology must be available for measuring the behavior at issue—discharges most commonly, but installation of required equipment or compliance with a ban on a particular input are other possibilities. As pointed out in a previous chapter, technology does not allow currently for routine measurement of nonpoint-source water pollution discharges.

• The technology should have known precision and accuracy, and it should be possible to estimate the probabilities of the two key errors: type I, in which the agency falsely finds violations, and type II, in which the agency falsely identifies violation as compliance.

• The source should not be able to control what is measured by adjusting its discharges after finding out that monitoring is or will be taking place. The most important element here is surprise.

• There must be a credible process for passing from an observed violation to a penalty. This can be administrative, civil, or criminal, depending on the penalty involved. But there must be consistency in the sense that the burden-of-proof demands of the process (forum) can't be more stringent than can be met by the monitoring method.

• The penalty at the end of the process must be credible. We cannot try to enforce pollution control laws by threatening to execute offenders. No one, on either side, would believe that such a penalty would ever be imposed.[4]

SOME SIMPLE ECONOMICS OF MONITORING AND ENFORCEMENT

Assume, for a start, that the cost of monitoring and enforcement can be taken to be a constant, independent of the discharge target specified. Now let's take a second look at the problem first encountered in the review chapter—minimizing the sum of damages from discharges and the costs of preventing discharges. The M & E costs may be treated as analogous to those of preventing discharges. But the effect of including them is nil. Algebraically, the two problems are:

Original:	*M & E costs constant:*	
min $D(D) + C(D)$	min $D(D) + C(D) + M$	(11.1)
FOC: $D'(D) = -C'(D)$	FOC: $D'(D) = -C'(D)$	
defining D^*	defining D^*	

Because M is a constant with respect to D, it does not change the optimum level of pollution. Graphically, this same result is shown in the first panel of Figure 11.1.

If, on the other hand, the cost of M & E is higher the greater the discharge re-

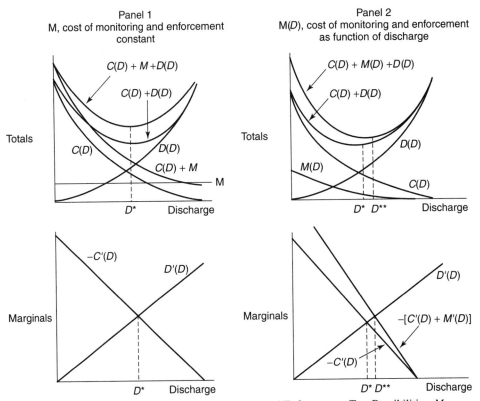

Figure 11.1 Bringing in the Cost of Monitoring and Enforcement: Two Possibilities. M, monitoring cost; C, cost; D, discharge.

duction from the unregulated level (the smaller D), the optimal solution is changed. Algebraically we now have:

$$\min D(D) + C(D) + M(D)$$
$$\text{FOC: } D'(D) = -C'(D) - M'(D) \tag{11.2}$$

and optimal D will increase. This is shown graphically in the second panel of Figure 11.1.

FINDING $M(D)$

So far we have just assumed that we know $M(D)$, the M & E cost consistent with maintaining D as the discharge level. But to see how such a function might be derived it is necessary to take a look at the problem faced by a pollution source. Again we shall start at the simplest end. Take a firm that has a linear $C(D)$ function and faces a discharge standard, $\hat{D}$. In the absence of any M & E effort, the optimal choice for the source is to ignore the standard and to discharge the amount designated as D_0 in Figure 11.2

But now allow for M & E effort (E) played out as:

- a probability that the agency will find a violation if it occurs,

$$M(E)\left(\frac{\partial M}{\partial E} > 0\right)$$

- a fine imposed for the violation, F.

Three levels of the resulting *expected penalty $M(E)$ F* are shown at the right of the graph in Figure 11.2 as additions to the source's zero cost of maintaining P_0. At effort level E_3, resulting in detection probability $M(E_3)$, the source will find it optimal to meet the standard, spending $C(\hat{D})$ to do so. In this simple setting, the source will comply if $M(E)F > C(\hat{D})$; otherwise it will violate. (Because $M(E)F$ is constant with respect to D, the minimum sum of compliance cost and expected fine is found at the "corners," $\hat{D}$ or D_0.]

A slightly more complicated setting involves a fine that varies with the level of violation, that is,

$$F = F(D - \hat{D}) \quad \text{with} \quad \frac{\partial F}{\partial D} > 0$$

Then for varying $M(E)$ and a variety of forms for $F(\ )$, we can get a range of solutions to the source's choice problem. Just a few are sketched in Figure 11.3.

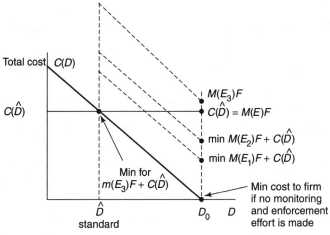

Figure 11.2 A Very Simple Version of the Firm's Compliance Decision Problem. C, cost; D, discharge; E, M & E effort; F, fine.

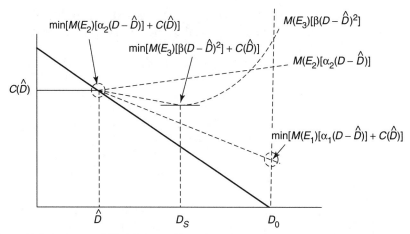

Figure 11.3 An Array of Slightly More Complicated Firm Compliance Problems. $M(E)$, Probability of catching a violation as a function of effort; E, effort put into monitoring; D, discharge; C, cost of discharge reduction; β, scaling factor. α_1, α_2, slopes of linear fine functions

Notice that for linear fine functions, the compliance decision is again 0,1. That is either $M(E)F(D_0 - \hat{D})$ is $> C(\hat{D})$ or it is not. But with a nonlinear fine function, such as $\beta(D - \hat{D})^2$, there can be an optimal level of discharge for the firm that lies between the standard and the unregulated level. This is the level at which $M(E)\beta(D - \hat{D})^2 + C(D)$ is a minimum.

In principle, then, a pollution control agency, responsible for a number of sources and interested in the problem of minimizing the sum of damages, costs of discharge reduction, and costs of monitoring and enforcement effort, could determine two functions:

$C_E(E)$ = cost of putting effort, E, into monitoring and enforcement; and

$P(E)$ = discharges from "its" sources resulting from E level of effort *and* a given fine structure.

To be clear about this problem you need to be sure you understand the following:

• Stating it this way assumes that only the total discharge from all the sources, called P here, matters to damages.

• The function $P(E)$ is found by repeated solution of the choice problem for each source and thus depends on agency knowledge of control costs for each source.

• $P(E)$ also assumes that the total effort, E, is spread over the sources in such a way as to minimize the cost of attaining any particular total discharge.

• No account is taken here, explicitly or implicitly, of the effect on one source's behavior of its observation of the treatment of any other source. It is assumed to know what $M(E)$ (the probability of detection) will be and to be aware of $F = f(D - \hat{D})$. But it does not adjust what it thinks it knows on the basis of what it sees happening to other sources. ("Encouraging the others" is an important justification for many harsh penalties. But it is very hard to model because it depends on perceptions of the sources and how these are adjusted as information is obtained.)

THE SOCIAL PROBLEM ONE MORE TIME

With the above information in hand, our agency is in a position to solve the following social optimization problem: $\underset{E}{\text{Minimize}} \ [C(D(E)) + C_E(E) + A(D(E))]$, where I use $A(D)$ for damage, to avoid confusion with D, for discharge.

The FOC for this is:

$$\frac{dC}{dD} \cdot \frac{dD}{dE} + \frac{dC_E}{dE} + \frac{dA}{dD} \cdot \frac{dD}{dE} = 0$$

Or, written as the analog to the simpler early result:

− Marginal damages = marginal costs of control + marginal costs of M&E effort:

$$-\frac{dA}{dD} \cdot \frac{dD}{dE} = \frac{dC}{dD} \cdot \frac{dD}{dE} + \frac{dC_E}{dE} \qquad (11.3)$$

Graphically, Equation (11.3) may be represented as in Figure 11.4.

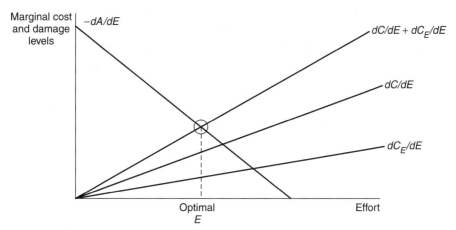

Figure 11.4 Optimal Effort (E) When Effort's Effects on Damages and Control Costs (C) Are Known

Finally, another equivalent formulation is:

$$\frac{DA}{dD}\cdot\frac{dD}{dE} + \frac{dC}{dD}\cdot\frac{dD}{dE} = -\frac{dC_E}{dE}$$

This way of writing the condition shows us that the net marginal benefit of pollution control, expressed per unit of M & E effort, must equal the marginal cost of that effort.

MONITORING AND COMPLIANCE AS A DECISION UNDER UNCERTAINTY

Before introducing errors of inference into the M & E picture it will be useful to develop a slightly different way of looking at the problem faced by a source of pollution. First, let us take the errorless problem and construct a decision tree (Figure 11.5). The first two branches of the tree are the source's two possible decisions (going back to the simple zero/one, constant or linear fine setting): comply with or violate the standard. From each of these branches sprout two more—whether or not the source is monitored. Each branch is labeled, and probabilities, where applicable, are supplied. To the right of the branches are the costs and fines applicable if

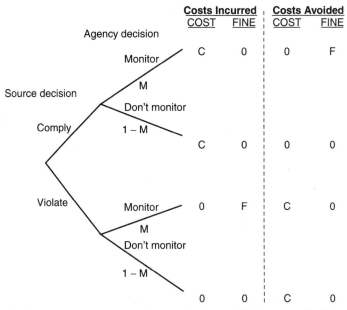

Figure 11.5 A Decision-Tree Version of the Monitoring and Enforcement Problem. M, probability of being monitored; C, cost of compliance; F, fine for discovered violation.

a source travels all the way out a particular branch, as well as the opposite version of the costs—the costs avoided by traveling out that branch. It is important to understand that in this formulation monitoring, when it is done, is perfect. No violation is missed if monitoring occurs when a violation is going on.

The question for the source is, which strategy gives the *lowest expected value* of costs plus fines incurred or the highest total expected costs avoided—complying or violating. Here are the comparisons:

Incurred Costs

$$E(\text{comply}) = M(C + 0) + (1 - M)(C + 0) = C$$

$$E(\text{violate}) = MF$$

Compliance is optimal if $E(\text{comply}) < E(\text{violate})$ or $C < MF$. This is the same result as found in the graphical presentation in Figure 11.5. For avoided costs (benefits) the question is turned around.

Avoided Costs

$$E(\text{comply}) = M(F) + (1 - M)0 = MF$$

$$E(\text{violate}) = M(C) + (1 - M)C = C$$

Compliance is optimal if $E(\text{comply}) > E(\text{violate})$ (Remember, these are benefits), that is, if $MF > C$. So, either way, if $C < MF$, compliance is optimal. For a given F and C, this relation defines the necessary M to ensure compliance:

$$M^* \geq \frac{C}{F} \qquad (11.4)$$

All this assumes that if monitoring occurs while a rule is being violated, the violation will be discovered; and that if compliance is being achieved when monitoring occurs, the monitoring will correctly find the source in compliance.

And one last thing. Implicit in this presentation is the idea that the decision to comply or to violate and the probability of being monitored apply over some period, which could be a day or a week or something shorter or longer. At the end of a period the source gets to decide again and the agency presents it with the same (or a new) probability of being monitored. This period notion is not important here but becomes so when the source faces time under different monitoring regimes according as it is found in compliance or violation. In those circumstances, the source will anticipate future periods in making its decision about current compliance.

INTRODUCING ERRORS OF INFERENCE

In the real world, with errors of measurement and with imperfect discharge control by sources, there are two possible outcomes to each monitoring event: correct and

TABLE 11.2 Possible Outcomes of Inference with Imperfect Monitoring

	Inference Outcome	
Compliance State	**Correct Inference**	**Incorrect Inference**
In compliance	Compliance found	Violation found (false positive)
In violation	Violation found	Compliance found (false negative)

incorrect decision on the compliance status of the source. And, since there are two possible compliance states, there are four possible outcomes or findings (see Table 11.2). It is customary to use the Greek letter α for the probability of a false positive and β for that of a false negative. ($1 - \beta$, the probability of correctly identifying a violation, is often called the "power of the test.") Seen as branches in a tree diagram, with probabilities, the possibilities look like those in Figure 11.6 (given that monitoring occurs).

The source of the α and β and the link between them can be understood from the following, simplified setting. For a source trying to comply with its standard, assume a distribution of measurements is possible, because of measurement error

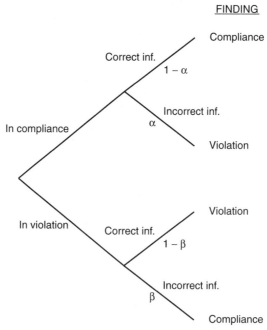

Figure 11.6 An M&E Game Decision Tree with Uncertain Inferences (Inf.). α, probability of a false positive; β, probability of a false negative.

and the source's own inability exactly to control its discharge. Let this distribution be roughly normal around some mean that is less than $\hat{P}$, the standard (call it $\hat{P} - \partial$). If, on the other hand, the source has chosen to violate, assume it has only one choice of by how much to do so. That choice leads to a new, higher distribution of possible discharge measurements, also roughly normal, but centered at a mean of $\hat{P} + V$. This situation is sketched in Figure 11.7.

Now the agency can pick a reading for the pollution measurement, above which the source is deemed to be in violation and below which it is deemed to be in compliance. Such a magic number is indicated on the sketch as D (for decision). For this choice of D, the hatched area to the right of D and under the compliance distribution is equal to α. The other hatched area is β. It is the area to the left of (below) D and under the violation distribution of readings. You can see that by moving D to the right you would reduce the probability of false positives but in the process *increase* the probability of false negatives. The only way to decrease both is to reduce the variance of the measurement distributions by improving technology (of monitoring or of source control or both) or by taking more measurements to reduce the variance of the resulting mean value for P. This narrows the distributions of possible readings under each assumption of compliance status.

This simple diagram allows us to see what changing the burden of proof amounts to. The key concept is that of a "null hypothesis," which the party responsible for the burden of proof has to disprove. The agency-burden null hypothesis is that compliance is occurring. The source-burden null is that a violation is occurring. In such problems it is *customary* to pick α, the probability of falsely disproving the null, to be some low level, such as 5 percent, and to let β fall where it may. In the diagram in Figure 11.7, we were representing the agency-burden situation. If $\alpha = 0.05$ and $\beta > \alpha$, then shifting the burden to the source would move D to the left, increasing the probability of finding a violation—including the probability of falsely finding one.

Now let's go back to the source's decision problem, with errors of inference this time but otherwise identical to the version cost-incurred above. The new decision tree is shown in Figure 11.8.

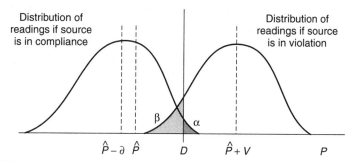

Figure 11.7 A Graphical Illustration of Errors of Inference in Monitoring. P, pollution standard; D, decision re violation; V, violation; α, probability of a false positive; β, probability of a false negative.

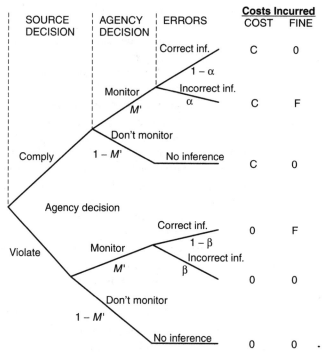

Figure 11.8 A Decision Tree Reflecting Errors of Inference and Payoffs. Inf., inference; M', monitoring probability.

Notice the following:

1. The monitoring probability has been labeled M' to make it clear that it will in general be different from the one derived from the errorless setting for the same C and F.

2. No inference is necessary (or possible) if no monitoring is done.

3. The fine under comply/monitor/incorrect inference is the only apparent difference from the earlier problem setting, except for the two extra branches.

The source's decision, seen as an expected value problem, now is the following:

$$E(\text{comply}) = M'[(1 - \alpha)C + \alpha(C + F)] + (1 - M')C = C + M'\alpha F$$

$$E(\text{violate}) = M'[(1 - \beta)F]$$

So compliance will be optimal [$E(\text{comply}) < E(\text{violate})$] if $C + M'\alpha F < M'(1 - \beta)F$], or

$$M' > \frac{C}{(1 - \alpha - \beta)F} \tag{11.5}$$

TABLE 11.3 Monitoring Probabilities Required to Inspire Compliance with Varying Errors of Inference and Fine Sizes

		Errors	
Fine Sizes[a]	$\alpha = 0; \beta = 0$	$\alpha = .05; \beta = .20$	$\alpha = .1; \beta = .4$
$F = 2C$	0.5	0.67	1.0
$F = 5C$	0.2	0.27	0.4
$F = 10C$	0.1	0.13	0.2

[a] Fines are expressed as multiples of compliance costs.

So α and β work in tandem to increase the monitoring probability required to produce compliance (in the "one-play" decision) for given levels of C and F. To get a feel for how important this might be take a look at the sample values of M' in Table 11.3.

So, introducing the $\alpha = 0.05$ and $\beta = 0.20$ errors increases the required probabilities of monitoring by about 30 percent over the errorless situation. Doubling these levels results in another 50-percent increase, so that the probabilities in the third column are twice those in the first.

Since errors are always present, they must be part of the actual decision process even if we ignore them sometimes in our models. They have an important political dimension, as well. False positives create outrage among regulated parties. (Of course the falseness of a false positive is itself a matter of assertion.) False negatives, if suspected, may create a symmetric antagonism, this time among the population at large and possibly among the parties making good faith efforts to comply. This means that the setting of decision rules, by which monitoring results are interpreted, is a delicate political activity—not only a scientific exercise.

CONCLUSION AND REMINDERS

Taking monitoring and enforcement into account complicates the problem of how to implement environmental management laws. These complications include matters of technical concern, such as whether a particular rule can be monitored and what levels of precision and accuracy are attainable at what costs. There are also legal questions, such as whether "surprise" monitoring is possible (either because entry of a monitoring team, arriving unannounced, is not preventable by the source; or because monitoring can be done remotely, without permission of the source). Neither can politics be avoided, for there are questions about the fairness and credibility of penalties for violations that will be fought out in this arena; and the decision rule for finding a violation at all will also have political overtones. By comparison, the economics of at least the simple situation seems fairly easy to come to grips with. But if you want to take a wider, more complex view (for example, by taking account of the effect on many sources of imposing a penalty on one source), the challenge on the economic side grows vastly greater.[5]

Two more generally useful tools to take from this chapter are: first, how to set up a decision problem, such as the firm's compliance or violation choice, in a tree diagram. This can help by forcing you to think systematically about who gets to make which choices and what string of choices leads to what outcomes. It is often, then, very easy to write down expected value relations. Second, the notion of errors of inference is far more widely useful than just as part of the monitoring problem. In Chapter 13 we will run into it again as part of a discussion of shifting the burden of proof in a situation of uncertainty as part of a regulatory strategy.

NOTES

1. Accuracy here deals with lack of bias of the mean measurement relative to the "true" but unknowable discharge. Precision deals with the size of the random measurement error. The result of monitoring can be accurate and imprecise, inaccurate and imprecise, inaccurate and precise, or both accurate and precise. Both are usually determined by using the methods on artificial samples with known characteristics.
2. There is a complex legal dimension to all this that I do not have the expertise to deal with. The case law particularly deals with when unannounced visits or remote measurements are acceptable in the context of regulatory needs.
3. There are other possibilities than simultaneous measurement, but each has its own problems. For example, one might try to infer discharges from information on inputs and outputs, using materials balance. But this can work only when the timing of input use and of outputs (and discharge) is well defined and understood *and* when the discharges of interest are related in a simple way to the inputs and outputs. (SO_2 in stack gas, for example, comes from the sulfur in the fuel burned. When coal is the fuel, some sulfur will end up in the ash that collects in the furnace and the net loss will be up the stack as SO_2.)
4. At a conference once, when I was presenting a paper on ways to use information on previous violations in defining current monitoring probabilities, and thus to save money, a member of the audience said: "Why all this fretting over monitoring cost? Why not just shoot the violators?," implying that this way would lead to lower required monitoring probabilities. This was said only half in jest.
5. One way of complicating the problem has been mentioned in a previous footnote—using a source's past record of (inferred) compliance to define, for some period at least, either its monitoring probability or its fine. If you are interested, see C. Russell, "Game Models for Structuring Monitoring and Enforcement Systems," 1990.

REFERENCES

Russell, Clifford S., 1990. "Game models for structuring monitoring and enforcement systems." *Natural Resource Modeling* 4(2):143–173.

12

DEALING WITH RISK
The Normative Model and Some Limitations

This chapter will begin with a brief review of normative (or, as they are sometimes called, "rational") models for decision making in conditions of risk and uncertainty. From that foundation I shall move on to examine the tensions between this benchmark and the most common perceptual and operational approaches exhibited by the public at large. These tensions may be thought of as arising from three broad classes of influence:

- Problems created by our ways of approaching life generally and the results of our response to actual experience with risk or to communications about risk that reach us from our friends, neighbors, colleagues, or the media
- Limitations on our ability to think as the detached experts say we should
- The conditions in which we find ourselves when called upon to make such decisions

Before we proceed, let me return very briefly to matters of terminology. I said in Appendix 3.I that the old distinction between risk and uncertainty is no longer generally observed and that I feel free to use the two words interchangeably. However, I also mentioned another problem that is often hard to detect: variation in the meaning of the word "risk" itself. For example, when I speak of "risk aversion" and "risk seeking" as descriptions of preferences, I shall be referring to a feeling related to the dispersion of outcomes and the changing value of the marginal unit of gain or loss across the range of outcomes. Often in the technical literature, however, "risk" means something even more specific. Sometimes it means the probability of contracting a disease (as in, "the cancer risk of smoking is . . ."); sometimes it means the chance of death or some other serious health damage for a randomly chosen member of a population from a cause or activity (as in, "the risk from Superfund site x is 10^{-5}"); sometimes it means the number of deaths per year from a cause or activity; and sometimes it means a complex amalgam of the characteristics of an activity—its riskiness—as perceived by lay people. So you must be alert for variations in the meaning of "in risk" other sources of information.

RATIONAL MODELS FOR DEALING WITH RISK

Let me begin by assuming that our interest in risk arises from the necessity of choosing among alternative programs, policies, or projects when the outcomes that follow from the choice are partly determined by events over which we have no control and that, indeed, appear random to us. To illustrate, let me be more specific and assume that we are required to choose among three alternative projects (A, B, C) competing for investment dollars. Further, assume that the actual results from choosing any one of the projects depend on which of many alternative possible "states of nature" (1, 2, . . . , n) is actually experienced. Thus, these states are exogenous to our choice but, jointly with that choice, determine the net benefits accruing from it. Also assume we have quite complete information, including an estimate of how likely each state of nature is to occur,[1] and estimates of the payoffs (net benefits) that accrue when a project is chosen and a state of nature occurs. Thus, we have at our disposal information about what *could* happen, depending on how we choose. The payoff information might be summarized in a matrix of payoffs like that in Table 12.1. Here, I have assumed that we know what the probabilities of nature's choices are. For this example, we know that event 1 has a 50 percent chance of occuring (probability = 0.50); event 2 has a 30 percent chance of occuring (probability = 0.30); and event 3 has a 20 percent chance of occuring (probability = 0.20). Where these probabilities might come from will be discussed later. For now, we can think of them as reflecting historical experience, as might be the case if A, B, and C were alternative flood control projects and 1, 2, and 3 were weekly rainfall totals. The probabilities are shown in the row below the payoff matrix in the table.

The fundamental problem of choice under uncertainty may be thought of as arising because, in general, no project will have payoffs in all states that are at least as large as those of any other project choice. If such a project does exist, there is surely no point in doing other than choosing it. But in the inconvenient "real" world, such a trivial version of uncertain choice is rarely seen. Thus, in the above payoff matrix, we can see that no project dominates in that sense. A is the best choice if we are certain nature will choose event 1. C is the best if we know in advance that event 2 will occur, and B would be best if we knew that nature was going to choose event 3. But, the essence of risk is that we do *not* know.

TABLE 12.1 Matrix of Payoffs (Net Benefits) and Related Information

	Project	Nature "Chooses" a State or Event			Worst for Each Project	Best for Each Project
		1	2	3		
We choose a project	A	7	5	−3	−3	7
	B	2	−10	9	−10	9
	C	−2	6	6	−2	6
Probabilities		0.5	0.3	0.2		

How do we decide which project to undertake then? In brief, we have to seize on one state of nature or one payoff for each project, or we have to summarize all the information we have into one number per project. Some alternative rules:

• Look at the worst result for each project and pick the project that gives the least serious of these worst outcomes. Picking the project that gives the "least-worse" result is very conservative and puts a limit on our losses. (This would lead us to choose C.)

• Pick the project that gives the best of the best results. This is a very aggressive strategy and ignores the possibility of a truly horrific loss. (This leads to B in the example.) Neither this method nor the previous one makes any use of the probability information we assumed to be available.

• Another option is to create a summary measure using all the available information. Called the expected value (and already introduced in Appendix 3.I in Chapter 3), it is calculated for each project using the probabilities and net benefits. The expected values of the net benefits in Table 12.1 are as follows:

$$E(\text{Project A}) = .5(7) + .3(5) + .2(-3) = 3.4$$

$$E(\text{Project B}) = .5(2) + .3(-10) + .2(9) = -0.2$$

$$E(\text{Project C}) = .5(-2) + .3(6) + .2(6) = 2.0$$

And by this criterion, project A is best. (In general each of the criteria may lead to a different choice of "best.")

As I note below, the expected value criterion can be elaborated for cases in which the gap between maximum losses and maximum gains is so large that we might want to weight losses more than gains (or even vice versa). It is also possible to elaborate on the methods that seize on one particular payoff, and indeed, we can even decide what to do by trying to anticipate how badly we will feel (how much we will "regret" our choice) when our decision is actually stacked up against nature's choice.

In the little example in Table 12.1, the regret matrix would be as represented in Table 12.2. These entries are calculated from the original payoffs by first look-

TABLE 12.2 The Regret Matrix for the Example in Table 12.1

Project	State of Nature 1 2 3	Max. Regret by Project
A	0 1 12	12
B	5 16 0	16
C	9 0 3	9

.

ing down the net benefits for each given state of nature. That is, start with state 1. The best choice of project if 1 turns out to be the actual state is A. If we had chosen that project we would have no regrets if state 1 turned up. So it gets a zero regret. If we had chosen B, we would be 5 units worse off than we could have been—so that is the value of our regret. And the choice of C would produce a regret of 9 if state 1 turned up. The same procedure is used for states 2 and 3. The final column lists the worst (largest) regret value for each project. The "minimax-regret" choice criterion says to choose the project that produces the smallest of these largest regret values. In the example, that is project C. It is not possible to characterize the regret criterion as conservative or aggressive. It is, however, possible to point out that minimax regret has one disturbing characteristic: the ranking of any two projects is, in general, dependent on what other project possibilities are available. In this simple example, if project B were declared impossible and removed from consideration, the new regret matrix would be as reprented in Table 12.3. Now A and C have the same result in regret terms, whereas when B was "allowed" or "relevant," C was preferred to A. This failure of choice to be independent of which other alternatives are relevant and which irrelevant is a reason to be wary of regret as a basis for choice.

Going back to the expected value criterion, observe that there are several ways to understand what it means, any one of which may be helpful to any particular person. If we begin by asking how we might use all available information, we can see that this technique seems an intuitively sensible answer. We have weighted our information about the possible results using our information about the relative likelihood of our experiencing any particular result. If, on the other hand, we think about the problem as though we could repeatedly run an experiment in which we choose and then nature chooses, and finally we observed a result, the criterion just discussed can be seen as our best predictor of the average of all the results observed in that series of experiments.

In this latter connection, however, it is important to note that this "expected value" measure is not a prediction of the result that will actually be observed in any particular experiment. That is, if we have a single decision to make, the expected values of the alternatives are not predictions of outcomes but simply agreed upon criterion values for ranking the decision alternatives. One very easy way to understand the difference between prediction and expected value is to think of rolling a fair die (one of a pair of dice). We can predict with certainty only that the result will be a 1, 2, 3, 4, 5, or 6 on the top face. We can "predict," as we do in games involving dice, that some particular face will come up, but we have only one chance

TABLE 12.3 The Regret Matrix When Project B Is Not Available

Project	1	2	3	Max. Regret
A	0	1	9	9
C	9	0	0	9

in six of being right in a particular trial. On the other hand, the expected value of the operation "toss one die and record the top face" is $(6 + 5 + 4 + 3 + 2 + 1) \div 6 = 3.5$. This can *never* be the result of *any* single trial of tossing the die. But if we toss the die 1,000 times, record the value of the top face each time, add the results, and divide by 1,000, the result will be very close to 3.5.

It is easy to construct examples in which agreeing to use the expected value criterion leaves us very uncomfortable. It is also possible that sometimes people will be uncomfortable with the notion of a probability distribution over outcomes. Therefore, let us briefly consider these two areas of discomfort.

WEIGHTING OUTCOMES

In some applications, even government agency applications in which gains are not personal and bankruptcy is not a possibility, decision makers may want to put a greater weight on large losses (e.g., losses of life from a toxics accident) than on large gains (e.g., cheaper transportation of a toxic via a new route). In such circumstances, it is possible to introduce another weighting function—economists often refer to it as a "utility function"—that is tailored to the feelings of the decision maker in question. Or it may be instructive to try several different weighting functions and see how sensitive the implied choice of project is to the choice of function. A typical weighting function displaying the conservative bias known as "risk aversion" is concave to the results axis—that is, it increases as results increase but at a slower and slower rate. Such a function is displayed in Figure 12.1.

How can we determine what an appropriate weighting function looks like (for a particular person in a particular situation)? Here is an example keyed to the Corps of Engineers. But you can easily see how to change the words.

Consider that you are responsible for an investment decision in which the possible outcomes under different choices by you and different "calls" by nature can range from a gain of $7.2 million to a loss of $400,000. The specific project might be a lock and dam repair or construction of a small dam designed for water supply and recreation. The range might reflect, in the former case, the losses resulting from not doing anything on the one hand and the time gains at maximum predicted travel levels on the other. For the dam, the loss might result if there were no demand for either the water or the flat-water recreation; while the large gain might result if a new planned bedroom community were built very near the dam site. You call in a consultant and ask her to help you construct at least one possible utility function—yours.

To construct a utility scale for you, as decision maker, your consultant would first "anchor" the scale at 0 and 1; 0 being the worst end and 1 the best end. Then she would ask you questions of the following form:

If you faced an investment opportunity giving a $7.2 million payoff with probability P_B and a $400,000 loss with probability P_W, how much would you be willing to invest? (Subscript B here stands for "best" and W for "worst".)

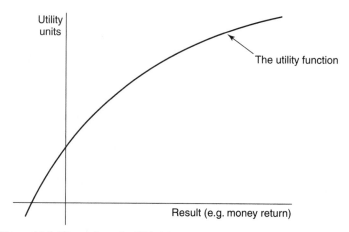

Figure 12.1 Illustration of a Weighting Function for Outcomes Under Risk

By varying P_B (and thus P_W, since $P_B + P_W = 1$) she could get you to trace out your utility function for payoffs *in the assumed range*. The mathematics of this result are simple:

$$U(\text{WTP}) = P_B(U(\$7.2 \times 10^6)) + P_W(U(\$-400 \times 10^3))$$

where WTP equals your expressed willingness to pay. Since $U(\$7.2 \times 10^6) = 1$ and $U(\$-400 \times 10^3) = 0$, we get:

$$P_B = U(\text{WTP})$$

Thus, say she offered you a chance to invest in a project with a 50- percent chance at the high payoff and a 50-percent chance at the low payoff. Let's assume that you thought $375,000 an acceptable price but $425,000 unacceptable. Then, approximately:

$$U(\$400,000) = 0.5.$$

Similarly, for $P_B = 0.25$, suppose you would enter the investment only if you were paid up front $200,000 (so your WTP $= -\$200,000$). And for $P_B = 0.75$, say you would pay as much as $2,000,000, so $U(\$2,000,000) = 0.75$. Then, your utility function would look roughly as shown in Figure 12.2. In this example, the numbers show a very sharp decline in marginal utility. As it happens, the underlying utility function in this can be approximated by:

$$U(\text{payoff}) = \log\left(\frac{\text{payoff} \times 10^{-3} + 500}{100}\right) = .53 \log (\text{payoff} \times 10^{-5} + 5)$$

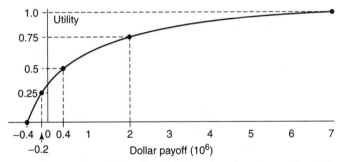

Figure 12.2 A Risk-Averse Utility Function Based on Answers to Simple Questions

This pattern of utility weight is consistent with the purchase of insurance at a premium exceeding the expected value of the loss from the insured-against event (see Figure 12.3(a)). It is not consistent with purchasing lottery tickets that cost as much as the expected value of the winnings (see Figure 12.3(b)). (Playing a lottery bespeaks "risk-seeking" preferences, since the tickets cost more than the expected value of your winnings.)

From Figure 12.3(a) we see that the money equivalent of the expected utility of the gamble over losses is more negative than the expected *money* value (EMV) of the loss. (Probabilities of ½, ½ are used for ease in presentation.) Thus, paying a premium greater than the expected value but less than the dollar equivalent of the expected utility loss is a good deal for the buyer of insurance. Conversely, in Figure 12.3(b) the risk-averse utility function implies that the money equivalent of the expected utility of the gamble between gains O and D (½ chance at each) is less than the expected money value of the gamble. Only if it cost less than P_L to play the game would this individual do so. And most gambles, certainly those run by profit making "houses" and state agencies, cost *more* to play than the expected value. So many people must not be risk averse when facing a lottery-style gamble—a tiny chance at a very large amount of money.

Now, what about probabilities? It may seem to be one thing to talk about probabilities where coins and dice are concerned, something slightly different where local rainfall and stream flow are the states of nature, and quite another when we have to cope with a question of possible failure of a complicated mechanism (e.g., failure of a nuclear power plant cooling system). In the first case, probabilities are determined by simple physics and the shapes of the chance determiners (e.g., we ignore the infinitesimal probability that a tossed coin will land and stay on its edge, and we argue, a priori, that unless it has been tampered with, either side down is equally probable). In the second case (hydrologic), we can look at quite long historical records, at least we can in most places in the industrial economies. Using more or less sophisticated techniques we can extract the information in that record and obtain estimates of the relevant process probabilities—for example, a continuous probability density function for daily rainfall or stream flow someplace.

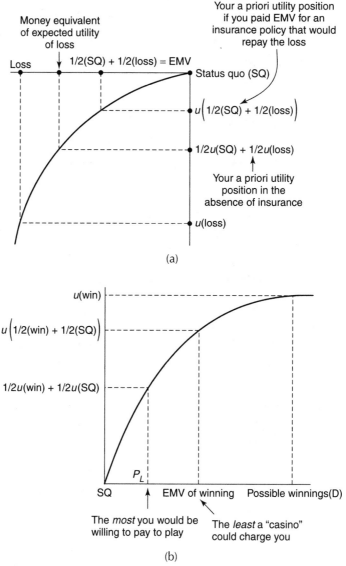

Figure 12.3 Risk Aversion, Potential Losses, and Potential Gains. (a) Insurance; (b) Lotteries. EMV, expected money value.

But in many important decision contexts we have either no record or a very short record, while simple physics will not carry us very far. Does it make sense even to talk about, let alone to use, probabilities in such cases? Many, though by no means all, of those who have thought deeply about this subject believe that answer is yes, it does make sense not only to talk about but also to use probabilities, even when these are "subjective"—based on judgment and experience rather than on physical laws or data. In complicated cases, such as the nuclear plant failure possibility, it may be necessary to break down the path to failure (decompose the risk) into small steps that different individuals can wrap their minds around, and later, to combine many judgments into an overall probability that all the failures necessary to produce a major accident would occur.

There is also an established method for updating subjective probabilities as experience and information accumulate, Bayes' theorem (see below for a brief discussion of how it works and what sort of results it gives). The usual *prescription* for decision making in the presence of risk is to maximize the expected utility represented by the possible outcomes, using the available probabilities.

COGNITIVE PROBLEMS WITH RISKY DECISIONS

Understanding of the cognitive limitations of individuals' use of the normative, rational model of choice under uncertainty has been developing for at least thirty-five years, though examples illustrating those limitations have existed since the eighteenth century. The size and richness of the literature in this field pose their own problems—how to do the literature justice; how to make connections among at least a few of its many dimensions; how to reconcile some of its apparent contradictions; and how to draw from it practical lessons. The approach taken in this section will be to use the structure of the rational model to organize a catalog of phenomena that have troubled thinkers in this field and to discuss:

- How people define, estimate, and manipulate probabilities (recall that subjective probabilities are generally accepted as part of rational decision making)
- How people interpret, and especially how they weight, the possible outcomes in an uncertain situation (recall that subjective "utility" weights are also an accepted part of rational decision making)
- What sorts of decisions people make when confronted with actual choice situations, whether in or out of the laboratory

NOT-SO-RATIONAL MODELS: WHY DO WE CARE?

I have emphasized that the description above is fundamentally normative (prescriptive)—a matter of what we ought to do when we make decisions under risk. But I will set out below some examples from the considerable body of evidence suggesting that individuals do not always, or even usually, follow this prescription. Now, let's just ask why this is a problem worth our time.

In the context of purely personal decisions, no one but the decision maker stands to lose from the use of a flawed version of the normative model. If an individual wants to gamble on coin tosses while assuming the coin in question has a memory and a will, that is his business. (Economists may be upset because this calls their entire model of the rational, self-seeking individual into question, but hardly anyone else will care.) If another individual allows small differences in the words used to describe her problem to influence her decision, she pays whatever price is involved. But the number of decisions that are purely personal is surprisingly small, once we begin to take account of the many forms of interdependence implied by such features of modern society as crowded streets, buildings, and highways; public (tax) financing of much health care; and welfare programs aimed at preventing the worst ravages of total poverty. In such societies, driving while drunk, for example, endangers not only the driver but also others on the road, and the cost of any care required for resulting injuries would likely be shared generally across society through insurance premiums or such programs as Medicaid. So even what might seem on the surface to be a private decision about taking risks can have diffuse social consequences. Therefore, all citizens have, in principle, an interest in how those decisions are made. They would, if they were asked, presumably say that accurate information and sound methods should be used.

An agency charged directly with the spending of public money to achieve public ends has an obligation to use accurate information and sound methods in dealing with the uncertainties that face it. But its decisions cannot in general be made and imposed unilaterally. It therefore has an interest both in understanding how the private citizens with whom it interacts make their decisions and in encouraging the use of the best available methods and information by those citizens.

Concern about disconnections between expert or agency assessments and those of lay people has inspired a substantial amount of literature. Much of this literature has a tone in which condescension and frustration seem mixed in equal parts. "Why can't they be more like us?" expressed Professor Higgins' frustration with the ways of women; it might stand for the technocracy's feelings toward the public's ability to deal with risk.

Two points, however, must be stressed by way of putting this concern in perspective. First, not everyone who qualifies as a "public" decision maker—certainly not every legislator or executive or regulatory agency head—also qualifies as an expert in understanding uncertainty. Thus, this individual human frailty is doubly a matter for collective concern. But second, and at least as serious, there are reasons to be concerned even about the experts in our public decision-making structure. Consider the following:

• Sometimes expert expressions of confidence (of the low probability of hazard) seem to be related to political and financial pressures to keep programs on track. For example, NASA's official estimate of the probability of shuttle failure, 1 in 100,000, was wildly different from the recorded rate of 1 in 25 or 1 in 50, depending on the calculation used.

• Even in more mundane and familiar settings, experts may be quite unreliable judges of risk. William Freudenburg (1988), for example, reported on studies of the inability of physicians to diagnose disease from case histories and examinations and on the inability of geotechnical engineers to predict correctly the height of an embankment that would cause a clay foundation to fail.

And even when bias and lack of skill are both absent, experts may face very fundamental constraints on their ability to deal with risk. For example, philosophers of science talk about "interference effects" that may occur when technologies are combined in new ways. It may be impossible to predict when such effects will occur and what form they will take.

Thus, there appear to be several difficulties even with expert risk assessments. Whatever rules of thumb the lay public may use to assess the assessors, it would be surprising if there was collective agreement to put a "decision weight" of 1 on expert predictions of risk. Since in many of the situations that form a backdrop for the "we-us" lament there is at least some reason to see corporate or agency self-interest served by low levels of risk prediction, much higher levels may well enter individual calculations with nonzero weights. In the presence of such fundamental defects in our knowledge, skepticism and conservative rules of thumb may seem only prudent, even to educated, objective, and unemotional members of the public.

The final nail in the coffin of hope for rational public decisions about risk has been thought to be that even if there were no a priori rational grounds for devaluing a particular risk assessment, the public would still in a sense be unreachable. The combination of faulty understanding of risk, flawed manipulation of new information, and tendencies to try to take the probabilities out of risk would form too powerful a block to learning. While this may yet prove to be so, there are fragments of evidence that, at least where people see their self-interest immediately involved, careful attention to the details of risk communication can make a useful difference.

PROBLEMS WITH PROBABILITIES

In the rational model, individuals are supposed either to draw their probability information from objective facts (such as the shapes of coins or dice, or records of events such as rainfall) or to construct their own probabilities from their subjective judgments (such as one might do by looking at the sky in the morning and judging how likely rain is that day). In either case, for any but the simplest situations, these same individuals should manipulate the probabilities in ways that are consistent with some of the fundamental rules of probability theory.

Understanding Independence of Events

Some individuals do not appear to be able to take seriously the independence of events. Thus, some individuals will argue vigorously that tails must be more likely on the next toss after heads has come up five or six times in a row. It seems that people are inclined to attribute memories to dice and coins as an outgrowth of a misunderstood version of the law of large numbers. Analogously, people often seek comfort or certainty by attributing weather events such as floods and tornadoes to some sort of extra worldly intelligence or to a cyclical process. The general effect of such beliefs is to lower the subjective probabilities people hold for repetition of events that have just happened or for events that have recently happened frequently relative to some notion of the long-run mean occurrence rate. Operationally, the most important manifestation of this is probably the belief, often widely shared within groups that have experienced a natural disaster such as a serious flood, that a repeat performance "can't" occur for a long time.

Incorporating New Information

Another major technical error that has been observed in the handling of probabilities is with updating in the face of new information. Rational individuals who use subjective probabilities should also use Bayes' theorem to update those probabilities when they are given relevant new information.

Updating subjective prior probabilities (or for that matter, objective prior probabilities) using Bayes' theorem can be illustrated with an example given by Emanuel Parzen in his 1960 statistics textbook. Assume the prior, perhaps subjective, probability is 0.005 that a randomly chosen person has a disease attributable to a toxic chemical. Further, suppose that there is a test available that correctly diagnoses the disease, when it is present, 95 percent of the time. The test also correctly says a person is free of the disease 95 percent of the time when it is applied to a disease-free person. Finally, suppose a random person is tested and the test says she or he has the disease. What should be the doctor's new estimate of the probability that the person has the disease? Bayes' theorem says that the new probability should be:

> The prior disease probability times the probability of a positive test given presence of the disease (0.005 × 0.95) divided by the sum: The probability of a positive test given the presence of the disease times the prior subjective probability of disease *plus* the probability of a positive test given that the disease is not present times the prior probability of no disease (0.95 × 0.005 + 0.05 × 0.995). So the new adjusted probability that the tested person has the disease should be: 0.00475 ÷ 0.0545 = 0.087.

Observe that the test result should cause the doctor to revise his or her initial probability estimate all the way from 0.005 to 0.087, a multiple of over 17.

There are at least two problems with lay (and even expert) behavior vis-à-vis this prescription. First, Bayes' theorem is simply not well known, and even those who have heard of it, and possibly even used it in a statistics class, are unlikely to have developed any true familiarity with its operation. Second, its results appear to be counterintuitive in many situations. You may find this true for the example sketched above, where the prior probability estimate is very low and the ability of the test to detect the condition at issue is very high. Thus, in the example, many lay observers (and even professional ones) might be tempted to say that if such a "good" test gave a diagnosis of disease we "ought" to take it more seriously and revise the probability of failure to something closer to 0.95. This might be called a tendency to overweight "diagnostic" information, relative to previously held notions.[2]

Estimating Subjective Probabilities

Whether people at large can or cannot manipulate probabilities, it does not seem that they are very good at estimating them in the first place. Daniel Kahneman and Amos Tversky (1981) and others have discovered that individuals without special training or expertise tend to overestimate the probabilities of very rare events (such as deaths by exotic causes) and to underestimate the probabilities of more common events. Even where outside information on probabilities is available, individuals will tend to supply their own subjective version, in which low-probability events are treated as more probable and higher-probability events as less probable than the information supplied would indicate. This is shown schematically in Figure 12.4. Here "decision weights" may be thought of as subjective probabilities supplied by the experimental subjects while "probability" refers to objective or expert likelihood estimates for the same phenomena. If the experimental subjects were perfect judges of probabilities, the "decision weight" line would coincide with the 45° line. That is, the estimated decision weights would equal the probability estimates.

It is not clear whether this phenomenon arises from a fundamental difficulty in coming to grips with very small numbers such as 10^{-6}, or because very rare events are brought to our attention when they happen while more common events bask in relative obscurity. What is clear is that if we have reason to doubt people's ability to get the magnitude of probabilities right, then it is very hard to work backward from observed decisions to infer the implied weighting pattern for outcomes. This is a subject I mention again in the next subsection.

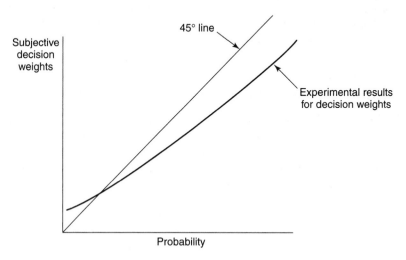

Source: D. Kahneman and A. Tversky, 1982. "The Psychology of Preferences," *Scientific American*, 246: 160–73

Figure 12.4 Decision Weights Related to Probabilities

The Dominance of Sensational Information

Even in this very general look at probability problems, it is necessary to mention a couple of other phenomena that are sometimes discussed under this heading but that may be interpreted in other ways as well. In particular, the tendency of laypersons to fasten onto the sensational may or may not be part of a cognitive problem. Sensational information is, almost by definition, very available information. For most purposes, in most activities, of most ordinary lives, it is not worthwhile for individuals to spend scarce time or money in seeking out information on which to base a probability estimate. If something pops up, ready to hand, it may well make sense to use it. If this makes us overestimate the probability of being murdered by devil-worshiping cultists, it is probably not a problem for anyone. But if it makes many people overestimate the chances of being harmed by toxic chemicals from a Superfund site, then we do have a collective problem.

The Role of Expert Judgments

In the matter of expert judgment and its role in subjective probability formation, we have to keep in mind that citizens of modern, free democracies hear constantly from experts who disagree about everything under the sun: whether or not a little drinking is good for you; whether paper or Styrofoam cups are easier on the environment; whether an interest rate cut by the Federal Reserve Board is currently desirable; whether we should try to introduce a greater element of parental choice into public education. What has to be clear to the observer of this cacophony is that, for every issue, at least one of the sets of contesting experts is wrong. The trick is knowing who they are in advance. In the absence of costly (in time and money) investigations of who is most likely to be right in any given situation, rules of thumb such as "split the difference" or "go with the group with whom you agree on other matters" can certainly not be ruled irrational.

PROBLEMS WITH WEIGHTING OUTCOMES IN UNCERTAIN SITUATIONS

I have said that in some situations, particularly those involving widely dispersed uncertain outcomes, individuals may rationally want to apply nonlinear weighting schemes to the outcomes in addition to taking account of probabilities. Other than our expectation that anything called "utility" ought to increase as the underlying outcomes improve, however, we cannot judge the "correctness" of patterns displayed in actual situations by lay or expert individuals. But it is usually hypothesized that most people in most situations in their daily lives are risk averse. As discussed above, this pattern of utility weighting is consistent with the purchase of insurance at a premium exceeding the expected value of the loss from the insured-against event. It is not consistent with purchasing lottery tickets at prices above the expected value of the winnings.

There is, however, some evidence that, at least in laboratory settings, individuals use utility-weighting schemes that are risk averse for gains and risk seeking for

losses, certainly an odd, though not an irrational, pattern. The pattern and its implications are illustrated in Figure 12.5. Again, probabilities of ½, ½ are used in the
illustrated gambles (over gains A and B and over losses C and D). We observe that
the person would not want to play even a fair game (the money equivalent of the
expected utility of the payoffs

$$P_G < \tfrac{1}{2}\, A + \tfrac{1}{2}\, B);$$

but neither would she buy insurance

$$|P_L| < |\tfrac{1}{2}\, C + \tfrac{1}{2}\, D|.$$

If this pattern were widespread, we would commonly not see insurance purchased against catastrophic losses, but neither would we see much activity in the
lottery (or numbers) business. Thus, the fact that we do see lines outside of stores
selling state lottery tickets when the prizes become very large, and that we see people buying at least some kind of insurance suggests that the laboratory results may
not be terribly good guides to reality. (Admittedly, the insurance purchases are generally required as conditions for obtaining a mortgage or registering a car, and the
requirement may exist *because* of the disinclination of people to buy insurance vol-

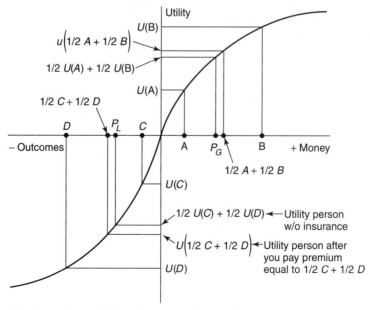

Figure 12.5 The S-Shaped Utility Function and Its Implication. See text for explanation of
symbols.

untarily.) Newer forms of insurance, often not required, such as flood insurance, do seem to be widely neglected by consumers.

Observe also that in trying to infer subjective weighting schemes from actions we run into an identification problem of sorts. If we believe that individuals take any account of both outcomes and (subjective) probabilities, we cannot disentangle the "cause" of observed decisions. For example, an individual could have risk-averse preferences but still buy lottery tickets if that individual systematically overestimated the chance of winning the grand prize. (And such systematic overestimation is what "feeling lucky" is all about. See Figure 12.6.) Here, the prospective gambler estimates the chance of winning as ½ rather than the correct ¼. The person whose perceptions are sketched here would play the "game" or buy the lottery ticket for A and B, even at prices somewhat higher than the expected money value. But this is not the result of being a risk seeker. It is the result of misperceiving the probabilities—thinking that winning B is twice as likely as in fact it is.

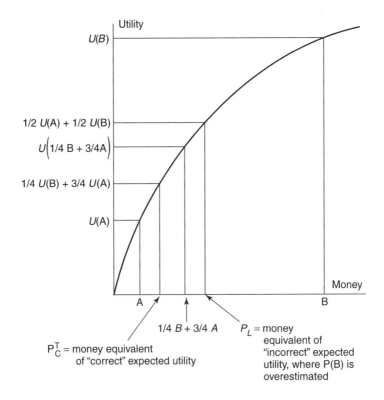

Figure 12.6 Feeling Lucky. U, utility.

PROBLEMS WITH OBSERVED JUDGMENTS IN RISKY SITUATIONS

The last subsection referred to certain patterns of decision that have been observed in the debate about cognitive limits on individuals' ability to deal with uncertainty. It is almost always difficult to say, outside a laboratory setting, what these patterns are evidence of, since subjective weights and probability estimates may reasonably be thought to interact in the decision process.

Within laboratory settings, however, researchers can better control the information and incentives that lie behind decisions under risk. And in such settings, or in closely related survey research, there is evidence of actual logical failures in individual's risk-related decision processes. Here are three kinds of problems:

- The paradoxes, exemplified by the "Allais paradox," in which revealed decisions violate one or another fundamental axiom of the rational model
- Framing problems, in which irrelevant features of the problem or its presentation seem to change people's choices
- "Preference reversal," in which stated preferences over generalized "lottery tickets" (explained below) contradict the stated prices for which the subjects say they would be willing to sell the same "tickets"

The Allais Paradox

The Allais Paradox involves a combination of logic and empiricism demonstrating that individuals faced with uncertain, lottery-type decisions violate what is known as the "independence axiom." That is, when individuals choose between two lotteries (mixes of probabilities and outcomes) they do not focus only on the differences but also take account of the similarities. The following way of visualizing the paradox is attributed to Robin Dawes (Pool, 1981). Imagine an urn filled with 100 balls, divided as follows: 89 red balls, 10 blue balls, and 1 black ball. Now imagine that four different games of chance (referred to here as "lotteries") have been created on the basis of this urn. In each lottery, the payoff obtained by the player is determined by which color ball is drawn from the urn. In the experiments, the subjects are each asked to make two choices: between lotteries A and B and between C and D, where the payoffs for each lottery are as described in Table 12.4.

Logically, the only difference between the two *choices* is the result of drawing a red ball. In both A and B a red ball gets you a million dollars; in both C and D it

TABLE 12.4 Lottery Payoffs

Ball Drawn	Probability	Outcomes			
		Lottery A vs. Lottery B		Lottery C vs. Lottery D	
Red	.89	10^6	10^6	0	0
Blue	.10	10^6	2.5×10^6	10^6	2.5×10^6
Black	.01	10^6	0	10^6	0

gets you nothing. The differences between A and B themselves are exactly the same as between C and D. Therefore, someone who prefers A to B should also prefer C to D and vice versa. But empirically there is a very widespread, if not unanimous, choice of A over B and D over C. Thus, the choices A versus B and C versus D are not "independent" of the similarities between A and B and C and D. The million dollars in A *and* B when a red ball is drawn make a difference to the choice *between* A and B; and similarly for the 0 in C and D.

We can tell stories that explain this behavior, such as invoking the notion that the prospect of the certain $1 million in A produces a new status quo. Then, the choice between A and B is interpreted as a choice between a 10/11 probability of adding $1.5 million and a 1/11 probability of "losing" the $1 million that is notionally in hand. In the C versus D choice there is no change in status quo accepted implicitly, so the (unlikely) zero event is not translated into a loss. But story or no story, the real situation does *not* involve a change in the status quo, and the commonly observed pair of choices is irrational. It bespeaks problems with handling choice under uncertainty that go beyond difficulties with probabilities and odd subjective utility patterns.

Response to "Framing" of the Risk

"Framing" problems arise when the words used to describe alternatives under uncertainty are changed—without changing the substance of the choice—and produce a change in the preferred alternative. A classic example, attributed to Amos Tversky and Daniel Kahneman, goes as follows:

> "Imagine that the United States is preparing for the outbreak of a rare Asian disease, which is expected to kill 600 people. Two alternative programs to combat the disease have been proposed, and the scientific estimates of the consequences of the programs are as follows: If program A is adopted, 200 people will be saved. If Program B is adopted, there is a 1/3 probability that 600 people will be saved and a 2/3 probability that no people will be saved. Which of the two programs would you favor?" The majority response to this problem is a risk-averse preference for Program A over Program B.
>
> Other respondents were presented with the same problem but a different formulation of the programs: "If Program C is adopted, 400 people will die. If Program D is adopted, there is a 1/3 probability that nobody will die and a 2/3 probability that 600 people will die."
>
> The majority choice in this problem is risk seeking: D over C. The certain death of 400 people is less acceptable than a 2/3 chance that 600 people will die. (Tversky and Kahneman, 1981)

Since A and C are mathematically identical, as are B and D, the observed differences in choices exhibited in these experiments means that we are not dealing here with purely rational thought. Clearly, the choices are at least in part emotional responses to the different pictures conjured up by "deaths" and "lives saved." In the first version, the reference point or status quo is implicitly 600 deaths, while in the second framing, the reference point becomes zero deaths. Thus, in one case respondents are thought to be evaluating "gains" and in the other "losses." But again, the fundamentals of the given problem are explicitly gains, because we are told that in the absence of any intervention, 600 lives will be lost. The two interventions both improve on that base case, at least in expected value terms.[3]

Preference Reversal

"Preference reversal" is said to occur when contradictory answers are given to two different questions concerning choices among a single set of alternative "lottery tickets." Again, a classic example should help make clear how the reversal arises and what it means. David Grether and Charles Plott (1979) provided a simple graphic one in their important paper on this phenomenon.[4]

Imagine that you can choose between playing two games, P and D, with darts (see Figure 12.7). In P, the dart board is a circle with a single radial line. A dart is thrown by a blindfolded person (with nonetheless a guarantee that it will hit the interior of the circle). If it hits on the radial line, you will receive nothing. If it hits anywhere else, you will receive $4. (Clearly this is a near-certain $4.) The alternative board, D, is divided into two areas by a pair of radial lines. One area, covering 40 percent of the circle, will produce a $16 payoff if the dart hits it. The 60-percent area produces a zero payoff when hit. The subjects who are presented with these two games are asked to say which one they would prefer to play and to assign a money value to each, usually thought of as the price for which they would sell the right to play the game if they held it. Consistently, over actual experiments, a large proportion of those presented such problems say they prefer the P game but assign a higher dollar value to the D game.

As in the previous two examples, we see a clear problem with the logic (or rather the illogic) that must lie behind this contradiction. It comes down to this. If you prefer P to D you ought to require being paid a higher price to give up P if you owned the right to play it than you would require to give up D if you owned the right to play it.

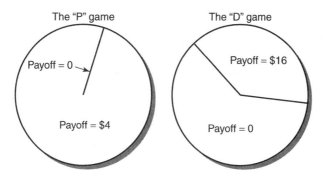

Figure 12.7 Dart Board Patterns for the Preference Reversal Experiment

Grether and Plott, in their own preference reversal experiments, worked very hard to eliminate any conditions that might allow the reversal phenomenon to be argued away as rational (e.g., they tried to make the gamble payoffs large enough so that they could assert that serious efforts were being made by the experimental subjects to make correct judgments. They also designed the pattern of payoffs so that increasing wealth as the experiment proceeded would not be a potentially distorting factor). Further, they attempted to control for a set of competing noneconomic theories of decision making under risk with the aim of ruling out as many of these as possible. In this latter regard they could not in the end rule out one possibility related to a previously discussed problem, the effect of framing. That is, they could not rule out the possibility that decision makers seize on "anchoring" information such as probabilities in one case and payoffs in another for reasons that have little to do with the quantitative substance of the gambles in question, but more to do with the language and context of the experiment (or real decision). If this is the source of the problem, it becomes very difficult to understand in any general way what people think they are doing when they make uncertain choices. Even more disturbing is the prospect that once some understanding is developed, manipulation would, in principle, become extremely easy.

There is, however, another side to the literature on preference reversal, which unfortunately remains to date a bit obscure. The principal source of this other side is Peter Bohm at Stockholm University, and his contribution has been to move the experimentation out of the laboratory and to increase by a factor of several hundred the significance of the payoffs involved in the P and D games. In Bohm's first experiment (Bohm, 1994), the P and D "lotteries" were defined by used cars. The "P-car" was a model known for reliability but with very modest performance. The "D-car" was sporty, but had a reputation that suggested a significant probability of a serious breakdown. The subjects were university graduate students who were in the market for a car. These were real cars and were actually given away at the end of the experiment, but Bohm could not afford to give each participant a car, so the gamble on the cars themselves was, in effect, embedded in a more complex lottery that determined who received a car. Thus, the payoffs were large and real, though not certain for any individual.

From the subjects who chose to participate, Bohm extracted rankings of the cars as well as stated willingness-to-sell prices. He found no preference reversals (Bohm, 1994). In another nonlaboratory experiment, this one involving real-world lottery tickets, Bohm and Lund (1993) found that 11 percent of the subjects exhibited preference reversal, a considerably smaller percentage than has been found in the laboratory exercises. This suggests that the laboratory results may actually include an element of minimizing decision costs in the face of rather trivial rewards despite the efforts of experimenters. This, in turn, suggests we should be doing additional research before using preference reversal evidence as part of an argument for the widespread existence of serious cognitive problems in individuals' ability to deal with uncertainty (or for the larger "failure" of the microeconomics foundation of choice rules and theory).

SOME CONCLUSIONS

Once individuals have attended to and filtered external information concerning risky decisions, they are in a position to process what has survived. The literature on risk perception and the actual behavior of people in the face of uncertainty—whether the task be guessing at probabilities or choosing among alternative "gambles"—compares the evidence of such processing with the benchmark of the normative model set out at the beginning of the chapter. In general, the conclusions of that literature find individuals wanting. In summary:

- They neither judge nor manipulate probabilities correctly.
- They seize on spectacular information and dismiss the judgments of experts.
- They often exhibit or rather appear to work from utility-weighting schemes that would lead toward very nonconservative behavior, though in other settings they seem to favor explicitly conservation options.
- They are prone to inconsistency and even blatantly irrational decisions in the face of real, albeit unfamiliar or not very weighty choices.

On the other side, it must be acknowledged:

- Generally, being good at probability estimation is probably not very important to success or even survival of individuals.
- Spectacular events are easy to learn about. The commonplace, beyond that in our own lives, must be sought out.
- Subjective utility-weighting patterns can and, in general, should look different for different outcome ranges. Laboratory experiments can only cover a tiny part of the range people see in everyday life.
- The restricted range of laboratory experiments involving actual rewards and the hypothetical nature of questions probing such apparent contradictions as the Allais paradox may very well imply that much of the observed intentions and behavior represent minimum effort at decision making.

NOTES

1. It is not essential that either the relevant possible states of nature or their likelihood be independent of project choice, but it is certainly simpler for this review.
2. Another way of thinking about the intuition that the new probability—that reflecting the results of the test—ought to be 0.95, is as a rejection of the original probability. If, for example, that original estimate had been 50/50 for the chance of disease being present, 0.95 would be the appropriate posttest probability. But even if the original failure probability had been 0.25, the appropriate posttest probability would be 0.864, nearly as large as the test's ability successfully to identify the disease.

3. Tversky and Kahneman (1981) attribute the result to the S-shaped utility (outcome-weighting) function already discussed. But there is also considerable similarity between this sort of "framing" problem and the reaction of subjects to the Allais paradox gambles. Both seem to involve unacknowledged, and in a logical sense unjustified, shifts in the assumed status quo.
4. Grether and Plott also report on the rather large psychology literature—even up to that date—that had explored this phenomenon. See D. Grether and Charles Plott, "Economic Theory of Choice and the Preference Reversal Phenomenon," 1979. *American Economic Review*.

REFERENCES

Bohm, Peter, and H. Lind. 1993. "Preference reversal, real world lotteries, and lottery-interested subjects." *Journal of Economic Behavior and Organization* 22:327–348.

Bohm, Peter. 1994. "Behavior under uncertainty with preference reversal: A field experiment." *Empirical Economics* 19:185–200.

Freudenberg, W. R. 1988. "Perceived risk, real risk: Social science and the art of probalistic risk assessment." *Science* 242:44–49.

Grether, David M., and Charles Plott, 1979. "Economic theory of choice and the preference reversal phenomenon. *American Economic Review*, 69(4):623–638.

Parzen, Emanuel. 1960. *Modern Probability Theory and Its Applications*. New York: John Wiley & Sons.

Pool, R. 1981. "The Allias paradox." *Science* 242:512–513.

Tversky, Amos, and Daniel Kahneman. 1981. "The framing of decisions and the psychology of choice." *Science* 211:453–458.

13

RISK ANALYSIS AND RISKY DECISIONS
Some Applications

In this chapter I'd like to go a bit beyond the classical but quite abstract material of the previous one. But this is not a course in risk analysis or decision theory, so the "bit beyond" will really amount to a sampling of topics intended to give you the beginnings of a feel for the field, especially that part of the field to which economists have made contributions that seem to me to provide especially good fodder for thought. First, there will be a brief definition and discussion of risk management and risk analysis, with an illustration of the sources of uncertainty about the human health damages from a particular kind of toxic chemical accident. That sort of damage will be explored a little further by investigating how a small change in the probability of death in a year plays out to define expected loss of life from such an accident. Then a generic risk management strategy, shifting the burden of proof, will take us back to material discussed in Chapter 11, but will put a slightly different twist on it.

At that point the scene will shift to a risk topic for which we usually have neither good probability nor good damage (or benefit) information—the preservation versus development (destruction) decision for places or ecosystems. There I will concentrate on contrasting the approaches of three groups—Rob Mendelsohn from Yale's Forestry School and his collaborators, John Krutilla and his coauthors at Resources for the Future; and Richard Bishop and one of his students at the University of Wisconsin.

RISK ANALYSIS AND RISK MANAGEMENT

These two pairs of words have come to be used to define the spectrum of activities, usually in the public policy arena, undertaken to make explicit the uncertainty faced by society and to try to formalize at least our preparations for the ultimate, inevitably political decisions that have to be taken to deal with it.

Now, "risk management" is no different in principle from other social decision problems, though by making the uncertainty dimension explicit, we do challenge the system more. This is because decision makers like to be able to pretend that the systems they deal with are determined and certain so that when they decide x, y and z will follow as the night the day.

Risk analysis, on the other hand, is a blanket label for a set of techniques that are aimed at informing risk management decisions by making explicit the uncertainties and providing one or another *summary* of complex situations. At one end of a risk analysis continuum are efforts to identify outcomes, causal factors, susceptibilities, and associated probabilities. At the other are the normative rules for using the information developed to identify (technically) most economically desirable (or least undesirable) courses of action, as discussed in the previous chapter.

The identification of pathways of failure (as of a nuclear power plant) or accident (a spill of crude oil) or routine exposure (to the emissions from municipal incinerators burning plastics, batteries, etc.) is at the heart of risk analysis (RA). And, in a sense, our ignorance about every stage of these pathways is a large part of the reason for the underlying uncertainty—though not the only reason, for natural-system variations play a part as well.

Schematically, much RA work involves characterizing the range of outcomes and associated probabilities for situations of the general type sketched in Figure 13.1. At each stage, we are talking either about:

- ignorance of exact mechanisms (groundwater transport, how the body handles chemicals, how ecosystems work) or
- dependence on stochastic events (accidents, weather, distribution of susceptibility in population)

or both simultaneously.

Often we are also talking about long time periods so that underlying conditions can change, as in land use, location of containment, even climate.

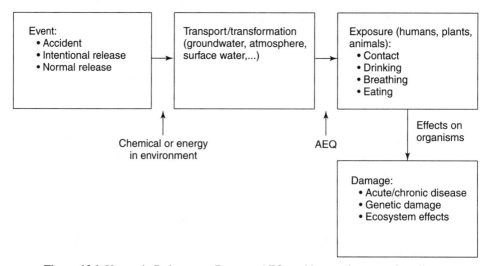

Figure 13.1 Uncertain Pathways to Damage. AEQ, ambient environmental quality.

PROBABILITIES AND TIME

it is often said that probabilities are "unitless," but that is only true if we confine ourselves to single trials, for, implicitly, the probability of a head is per-coin toss. One can easily enough construct event trees for multiple coin tosses and find, say, the probability of a head (at least one) in, say, three tosses. This is easy because only one path gives no heads—and that has $P_{TTT} = (\frac{1}{2})^3 = \frac{1}{8}$. So P (at least one head) $= \frac{7}{8}$.

Extending the notion that probabilities are "per trial" allows us to deal with more complex situations, such as ones in which accident or early death or some other important but unlikely event is involved and where we have an estimate of the probability of an event for one trial period, say a year, but would like to know a lifetime probability for a person exposed to the possibility. For example: Say we "know" that chronic exposure to chemical x creates an *increased* probability of early death (before the expected age at death) of .001 per year. (The trial period is a year of life.)

Let's say you are 40 and your expected age at death is 80. What is the added probability of death earlier than 80? Well, it is 1 minus the probability of *not* dying before 80 because of the new higher probability. So for two years, the probability can be diagrammed as shown in Figure 13.2. Extending this idea over the forty years of expected life of the example, a 40-year old, the probability of the path L, L, . . . , L to 80 is $(.999)^{40} = .961$ or ΔP(death before 80) $= .039$, the increased probability of dying before the "normal" (expected) age.

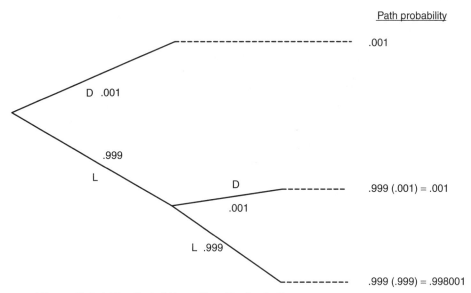

Figure 13.2 A Two-Period Event Tree. D, die; L, live.

Another way of thinking about the results of such "risks" (that word again) is in terms of the expected reduction in years of life that they cause. This approach is illustrated by a slightly different extension of the life and death event tree shown in Figure 13.2. In Figure 13.3 I have added information about the years of life lost for each "death event" to go with the probability of that event. (These "years lost" are still based on the "normal" expected lifetime of eighty years.) The probability of losing zero years of life is, then, $(.999)^{40}$, as already noted, and the expected years of life lost by a single person chronically exposed to this chemical is:

$$E(\text{YLL}) = 40(.001) + 39(.001)(.999) + \ldots + 1(.00\ 1)(.999)^{39} + 0(.999)^{40}$$

or, in compact form:

$$E(\text{YLL}) = \sum_{t=0}^{40}(40 - t)(.001)(.999)^t$$

The answer is 0.769 or about three-fourths of a year of expected life lost per person exposed at this level. This same sort of calculation could be done for a person

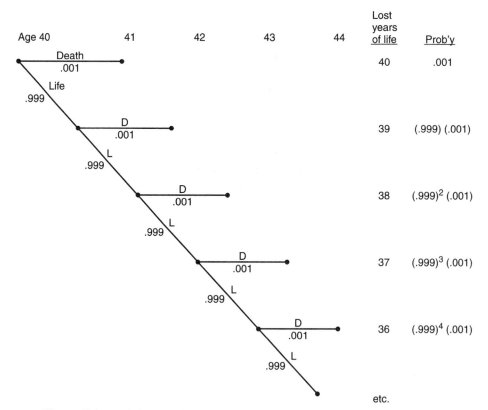

Figure 13.3 A Life/Death Event Tree

of any age. (The expected age at death would be different for each age.) And the results for a population of exposed individuals could be obtained by adding the results using the distribution of current ages. To shortcut this fairly tedious procedure, an approximation could be obtained using an average current age, and the expected lost years of life for a "representative person" could be calculated.

It is worth emphasizing at this point that discussions of risks that involve loss of *expected* years of life through *possible* early death are not always couched in careful language. A common though not very helpful expression you will find is "lives saved" (or, on the bad side, "lives lost"). For example, "Following policy X— as in shutting down all municipal incinerators—will save Y lives per year" (or two lives over twenty years, or whatever).

I label this as not very helpful since it does not really tell us what we are gaining or losing with any precision. No human lives can be permanently "saved." All are "lost" eventually. And even the qualification, lives "saved" per year, which may be taken to refer to early deaths postponed, isn't entirely helpful if there is a question of the age of the population whose early deaths are avoided. For example, if a choice had to be made between immediately cleaning up toxic waste site A or site B it would be relevant to know that, say, the population exposed to A consisted of young children in the main, while those exposed to B were residents in an elder-care center.

I hasten to add that taking such differences into account does not inevitably commit anyone to saying that the life of a child is "worth more" than the life of someone aged 80. But it does at least make explicit that there are differences in outcomes from different choices of how to use scarce resources. The "lives saved" rhetoric tends to obscure this. Years of life saved makes the physical differences explicit without touching on the "value-of-a-life" problem.

THE BURDEN OF PROOF AS A RISK MANAGEMENT STRATEGY

In the monitoring and enforcement chapter, I discussed the problem raised by errors of inference for deciding about violations of regulations. The same conceptual mechanism can be used to understand how society can try to anticipate and "manage" risks through the placement of the burden of proof.[1] That is, it makes a difference, because of the customary scientific approach to "proof," whether the agency charged with responsibility for safety, or the proponent of a project or chemical that carries some risk of future damage, is assigned the burden of proof for its version of "the case" for or against.

To tie things down, let's look at the problem of deciding whether a new chemical should be allowed into general production and commerce. (This might be a new pesticide, an intermediate chemical for making some plastic, or an industrial solvent that poses a threat to stratospheric ozone, for example.) As part of the safety testing procedure, the pesticide will be checked in the lab for its mutagenicity capacity using some bacterium as the test medium. (The compound is applied to colonies of the bacterium and the number of mutations to the bacterial DNA are counted. This has been used as a surrogate for the cancer-causing potential of chemicals.) For a number of reasons, not the least of which is the difficulty of making such counts with precision, the numbers of mutations found can be represented by distributions—one that applies if the chemical is "benign" (not a mutagen and hence unlikely to be a causer of cancer); and one that applies if the chemical is "harmful." Deciding between the two possibilities is much the same problem as deciding between compliance and violation: a count of mutations is chosen above which the conclusion is "harmful," and below which the conclusion is "benign." But unless the distributions from which the counts are drawn are quite "tight" relative to the distance between their means, there will be nonzero chances of being wrong in both ways—letting through a harmful chemical because the mutation count happens to be low, and rejecting a benign chemical because the actual count happens to be drawn from the high part of the benign distribution. Figure 13.4 below will remind you of the situation.

At this point, however, we have to refine the definition of the test to include the "null hypothesis." This, in turn, defines a customary level of type I error probability (α), which is now the probability of rejecting the null hypothesis when it is true. So, if the "null" (for short) is that the chemical is benign, α is the area under the benign distribution above the decision level for the mutation count. Conversely, if the null is that the chemical is harmful, α is the area under the harmful count distribution to the left of the decision level.

How does this help? There are two pieces of the puzzle required yet. First, it is customary to assign the null hypothesis in such a way that the party with the burden of proof has to operate with the null that is *un*favorable to the result we can presume it would "like" to find. Thus:

Burden of Proof	*Null Hypothesis*
Agency	Chemical is benign
Proponent of chemical	Chemical is harmful

Second, it is customary to require the setting of the decision level so that α has some small value (0.01, 0.05, or 0.10 are common). Then if, as is often the case, β

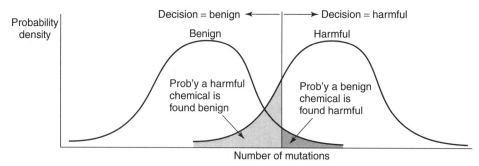

Figure 13.4 Errors of Inference About the Safety of a Chemical

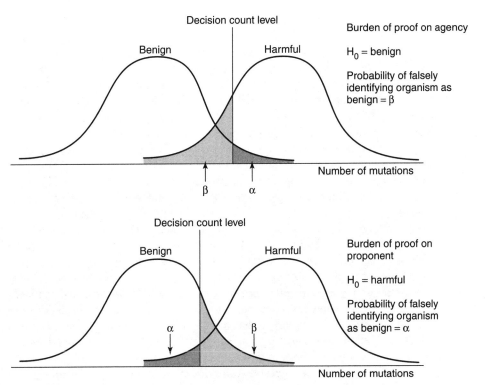

Figure 13.5 Shifting the Burden of Proof: Chemical Safety

(the probability of accepting the null when it is false) is greater than the customary α, shifting the burden of proof to the proponent will make the hurdle for introduction of the chemical higher (the decision count level lower), and vice versa.[2] This is illustrated in Figure 13.5.

IRREVERSIBLE DECISIONS, IGNORANCE, AND THE TECHNIQUES FOR INFORMING DECISIONS

As human power to interfere in the environment has increased with technology and sheer numbers of humans, the general problem we might call the irreversible decision seems to have become more important and to be faced more frequently (though we sometimes can't be entirely sure we *are* facing it). One version, where it seems we can be sure, is the destruction of a plant or animal, either through gathering or hunting to extinction or through destruction of habitat. Another is the introduction of a very long-lived radioactive waste product to the general environment.

But consider the building of a dam across a river. Here "irreversible" is not necessarily an absolute, forever, outcome. A dam can eventually be removed, at some expense, and the river in (a long) time will return to something like its original condition. (This has started to happen in the United States, where old dams that are judged no longer particularly useful are being dismantled. Usually the justification is to allow unimpeded movement of fish.) Similarly, radionuclide half lives (the time to a halving of their particle emissions per unit time) can vary from hours to hundreds of centuries. At some point on that scale, effects look irreversible to humans who, after all, have only had written history for a very few thousand years. Species loss is forever with current technology, though in the future a Jurassic Park technology could give us more options in some cases.

But the species loss example suggests that our catalog of "irreversible" actions has another interesting dimension as well—how sure we are that the event has occurred. The dam is obvious. The nuclear waste is detectable even if the initial event was an accident and even if that accident was unobserved. But species loss can be highly speculative. The extreme in this regard is the assertion that, by logging a particular piece of tropical rain forest, we will destroy some number of species, most of which are only present by inference since they have yet to be observed and identified. It seems somehow less speculative to say that species S_1 has been driven to extinction because no individual of that species has been seen for T years. But it is virtually impossible to say that a particular plant or beetle does not any longer exist, when we could never be sure of its range in the first place.

The above paragraphs suggest that the risk-analytic dimensions of irreversible decisions may include any one or more of the following:

- *whether* the irreversible event will, in fact, occur as a result of our doing (or not doing) something
- the *extent of the irreversibility* or (said more directly) how long it might take to return the affected natural systems to their status quo before the action (should that be undone) or accident
- the *damages* from the irreversible event (or the benefits of avoiding it) compared with the benefits of the action that is at issue

Economists tend to have most to say about the third of these problems; and it will be worth looking at three ways that have been suggested for dealing with damage uncertainty as a way of drawing together several threads from the text. One of these concentrates on trying to estimate the losses that can be anticipated from the action, using indirect damage-estimation methods. Implicitly, these damages are taken to be *certain if* the action is taken. Very little attention is given to possible uncertainty about them or about other losses that we might be missing because of less than full understanding of the physical consequences of the action (here, logging a rain forest). The second way rather elegantly finesses the damage-estimation problem by asking the question: How large would just the first year's damages have to be to justify giving up the net project benefits that we can estimate in our current state of knowledge? The third is an attempt to specify conditions (and decision rules) under which it would be enough to know the relative sizes of the development benefits and the damages from the irreversible action. This third technique is the only one of the three that *looks* as though it deals explicitly with risk, though you will see that through what is called "sensitivity analysis" the second technique is actually showing us a range of possible outcomes to which probabilities could be attached.

MENDELSOHN: DAMAGE ESTIMATION FOR TROPICAL RAIN FOREST LOSS

Robert Mendelsohn's approach to trying to capture what may be lost through rain forest logging concentrates on the identification and valuation of the *what* (Tobias and Mendelsohn, 1991; Balich and Mendelsohn, 1992; Mendelsohn and Balick, 1994). It treats the outcome—the loss—as certain. The method is to measure, for representative areal samples of the forest, a variety of benefits that would be lost for a very long time, if not forever, were logging to be undertaken. Table 13.1 contains a summary of such results drawn from several of the papers published by Mendelsohn and his colleagues. These preservation values (output sustainable from undisturbed forest) fall into three groups: recreation, known commodity harvests, and speculative commodity harvests. According to Mendelsohn's numbers, the sec-

TABLE 13.1 Valuing Rain Forest Areas: Preservation (Sustainable) vs. Development

Preservation Values	$/Hectare
A. Recreation (using travel costs/actual visitors)	1250
B. Known commodities (local market prices, measured quantities from test plots)	
1. Traditional medicines	560–3330
2. Other nontimber products	6330
C. Speculative commodities	
1. Possible modern medicines (expected values at world prices)	50–1000
Totals[a]: Most optimistic A+B+C (high end)	11910
More conservative B only (low end)	6890
Most conservative B1 only (low end)	560

Development Values	
A. One cutting followed by pasture use	3960
B. Continuing logging	3180

[a] Optimism here has two dimensions. One is which figure is chosen when the Mendelsohn group offered a range. The optimistic choice is the high end. The other is the extent to which the routes to benefits conflict. The optimistic choice is that they do not.

ond category looks potentially most important, at least given current knowledge. It is important, in this connection, to note that not all the sustainable uses are probably *simultaneously* sustainable. Recreation may conflict with harvesting, for example, while providing an input for a modern medicine might involve a more obvious, long-term change in the forest than the gathering of traditional medicinal materials.

At the bottom of the table are the comparable "development" benefits—logging and subsequent use as pasture and continued logging alone. Assuming logged-over forest can be used as pasture gives a development benefit of about $4,000 per hectare. Continued logging is estimated to produce only $3,000/hectare. The highest possible sustainable or preservation benefit, assuming all uses could occur on the same hectare, is about $12,000/hectare, or about three times the "development" benefit. The lowest preservation benefit that does not involve speculation about unknown modern medicines assumes a low value for traditional medicines and no other uses (no tourism, no modern drugs). This preservation benefit is only about 15 to 20 percent as large as development benefit. So even in this fairly narrow and carefully worked out case, the issue still must be considered in doubt, because a great deal depends on items about which there is lingering uncertainty, such as use compatibility and what would happen to local market prices for traditional products as incomes increased because of other policies.

One could take the Mendelsohn numbers and create an explicitly risky decision context by attempting to characterize the probabilities associated with the uncertainties. For example, we could convene a panel of experts who would try to arrive at consensus about which uses might be compatible and which would probably be incompatible. Further, an effort could be made to associate some probabilities with the *ranges* of benefits given for traditional and modern medicines. For example, the modern medicine range might be seen as so speculative that the best we could do would be to say that *all* the possible numbers are equally likely. (That is, the so-called probability density function would be "uniform" [flat] between 50 and 1,100.) We could even do this for numbers that look certain in the table, such as that for "other timber products," since we should be suspicious of apparent certainty in this context. Having assigned probabilities to combinations of uses and to ranges of values for the uses, we could harness the power of computers to run what are called "Monte Carlo" simulations in which the computer would make "draws" from all the sets of possibilities and calculate the benefit total per hectare associated with that draw. At the end of several hundred or several thousand runs, the machine would be able to give us a plot of the results, which would probably look a lot like a probability density function. Our choices for the distributions of possibilities would have a very big influence on the exact shape of this outcome summary, but we might expect to find a single peak somewhere in the range $1,000–$6,000/hectare as in Figure 13.6. The expected value would be available and might well turn out to be very close to the predicted development values. This would not make any particular decision easy, but would have the salutary effect of reminding us of the challenge created by our ignorance.

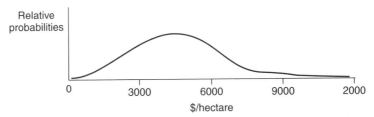

Figure 13.6 A Hypothetical Probability Density Function for Values per Hectare

KRUTILLA: WHAT WOULD DAMAGES HAVE TO BE IN YEAR ZERO?

John Krutilla was the author of an early and justifiably influential paper, "Conservation Reconsidered" (1967), that made a case for rethinking what "conservation" is or ought to be about in a world with changing incomes and tastes, when technological change can lower the cost of producing marketed goods but not of reproducing natural systems and sites. His conclusion, in broad terms, was that the traditional "conservation," saving the commodities provided by nature (wood, minerals, water for hydropower or irrigation, for example), should be supplanted by a newer conservation concentrating on natural sites, scenes, and experiences. These are the irreplaceable natural products for Krutilla, while the path of human technology has been toward substituting for the commodities—plastic, metal, and concrete for wood; plastic and the more abundant minerals for the scarcer ones; fossil fuels for water power).[3]

Krutilla was given a chance to put his ideas into real policy practice when he was appointed an expert advisor to a "special master," himself appointed by the Supreme Court, to make a recommendation in a case involving a proposed damming of the Snake River in its Hells Canyon area. Two dams were proposed to be built on this, one of the last great undeveloped hydropower sites on the continent—and in the deepest gorge on the continent. Krutilla was asked to advise on the economics of the build/not build decision.

Krutilla's approach (Fisher et al., 1972) to the problem began with the justification for building the dams in the first place—that they would produce electricity more cheaply than the alternative, fossil fuel or nuclear power, over the life of the dam—that is, over the 100 years before the storage pool would collect so much silt that the dam would be useless. He and his colleagues estimated what this saving would be, given the generation of power each year, for every year over the horizon.[4] Because Krutilla believed that technological progress would continue increasing the efficiency of the alternative generation methods, his group modeled this increase by lowering the cost advantage of the dam in steps, assuming that three generations of power plants would have to be built to span the life of the dam. Schematically, this part of the approach is shown in Figure 13.7, where T_1, $T_2 - T_1$, and $T_3 - T_2$ are the life spans of the fossil plants and $T_3 = T^*$, the life of the dam. (See Appendix

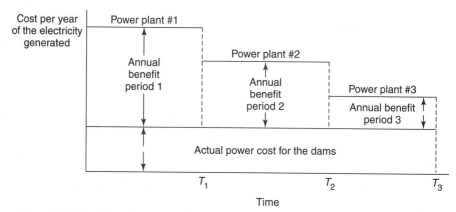

Figure 13.7 Declining Cost Advantage (Benefit) of Hydro Power over Nuclear Power with Advancing Nuclear Plant Technology

3.I about present values where projects have unequal lives.) Then the benefit attributable to building the dams was:

$$B_D = \sum_{t=0}^{T_1} \left[\frac{Ann.Benefit_1}{(1+r)^t} \right] + \sum_{t=T_1+1}^{T_2} \left[\frac{Ann.Benefit_2}{(1+r)^t} \right] + \sum_{t=T_2+1}^{T_3} \left[\frac{Ann.Benefit_3}{(1+r)^t} \right]$$

The other half of Krutilla's argument for a new conservation was that demand for the unique and nonreproducible sites and experiences of nature-based, outdoor recreation would increase, even as technological advance made nature-based *commodities* cheaper. His group built this into the Hell's Canyon problem through, in effect, straightforwardly shifting out a single demand function that was intended to include all the recreation and aesthetic "services" of the undammed canyon (fishing, hunting, camping, white-water rafting). The key to the approach, in the face of ignorance of exactly what this demand curve looked like or would look like in the future, was that the Krutilla group concentrated on building a shift mechanism that could be used to explore alternative assumptions about this demand growth. What they could ask was the question: If the net benefits of recreation on the free-flowing river and canyon are $1 today, what will they be in every year out to T^* under alternative assumptions about demand growth?

Then the present value of that stream of annual benefits could be calculated; and, the key question becomes: How large would the benefits of preservation have to be today for that stream to exceed the benefit from the dam? If B_P equals the present value of the stream of preservation benefits, based on *a single dollar* of benefits in year zero, this question might be written as finding the solution, k, to the equation:

$$kB_p = B_D$$

k is then how large the first year's preservation benefits would have to be to justify denying the license to build the dams. Notice that built into the approach are several dimensions of possible "sensitivity analysis," which is to say, several ways of exploring the implications of our ignorance—the major source of uncertainty here:

- The rate of technological progress in the alternative power generation technology can be varied. This determines the sizes of the cost differences in the alternative cost diagram, and hence B_D.
- The rate of growth of the future value of a current dollar's worth of recreation benefit in the undisturbed canyon can be varied. This determines B_P.
- The discount rate, r, can be varied.

Krutilla did not do a formal analysis such as the one just proposed for the Mendelsohn work. But the whole method was devised to deal with ignorance of the benefits of preservation by reducing the ultimate build/do-not-build choice to the decision about the reasonableness of one number, k, the "necessary" recreation benefits attributable to the canyon in the first year of the hypothetical period of the dam's life. While even this number was not known for certain, its reasonableness could be judged by reference to some fragmentary data on visits by recreationists, what was being paid for hunting days of the type available in the canyon, similarly for fishing days, and so forth.

Had Krutilla wanted to formalize this approach in a more obviously risk-analytic framework, it would not have been hard to do. In effect, he could have constructed, using the same sensitivity analysis mentioned above, distributions of B_D and B_P corresponding to some distribution of possible values of the underlying assumed rates of change—in technology and in recreation demand. This could have been done for many possible values of r. Then a distribution of *required* k's would be obtainable, again for given r. For example, the resulting density function for the k's might be roughly normal, as in Figure 13.8. This would allow a slightly more

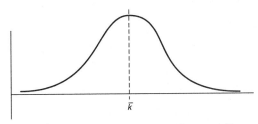

Figure 13.8 A Hypothetical Density Function for the Necessary Recreation Benefits in the First Year

formal look at the question: How likely is it that initial year benefits are large enough to justify the do-not-build decision?

Finally, it is worth emphasizing again the asymmetry inherent in irreversible decisions and what it implies for caution. If the decision *not* to build the dam seems justified for the initial year involved in this analysis, that still leaves open the possibility that circumstances or knowledge will change over time and make building the dam look desirable in a later year. The option to build remains open so long as do-not-build is chosen today. Once the dam is built, the option of *not* having the dam is closed for a very long time by human standards.[5]

READY AND BISHOP: IRREVERSIBILITY AS A GAME

Richard Ready and Richard Bishop modeled the irreversibility decision problem as a game (Ready and Bishop, 1991). Constructing the payoff matrix for such a game put them up against the same problem of ignorance as that faced by Krutilla and that worked on by Mendelsohn. But their attempt at a solution involved a third route. They tried to see if, within the game structure, and using specified game solution rules (such as the conservative minimax loss or maximin gain), they could reach conclusions based only on the *relative* sizes of the potential preservation benefits and known development benefits.[6] (If "development" is chosen, the preservation benefits cannot be enjoyed and vice versa.)

They actually developed two different games, which may sound very much the same when first described, for the difference between them arises from a subtle but important difference in when information is assumed to become available and what options are open when it does. In both games, the decision to be made is whether to "develop" or "preserve" some resource, where the development option entails extinction of some species. In both games there is uncertainty about future events that might be thought to affect the future value of the species to society. This uncertainty, in their choice of setting, involves a "deadly disease like AIDS," and the possibility that the species in question manufactures a protein that may become the cure for the disease. The differences between the games, called "insurance" and "lottery," are summarized in Table 13.2. As for notation, I will use B_P for the benefits to society of having the species *and* having it hold the cure, *in the presence* of the disease. B_D will be the benefits of the development that will lead to the species' extinction. $B_P > B_D$ *is assumed.*

Ready and Bishop constructed the payoff matrices from the point of view of *losses*—what is given up by the decision made. And these losses are measured in

TABLE 13.2 Comparing the Insurance and Lottery Games

Game	What Is Certain to Occur	What Is Uncertain
Insurance	That species holds cure	Whether disease outbreak occurs
Lottery	That disease will occur	Whether species holds cure

TABLE 13.3 Loss Matrices in the Insurance and Lottery Games of Ready and Bishop

Insurance Game	Uncertain Events			
	Disease Outbreak Occurs	No Outbreak	Maximum Loss	
Develop	$B_P - B_D$	$-B_D$	$B_P - B_D$ (loss)	
Preserve	0	0	0	*choice*

Lottery Game	Species Holds the Cure	Species Does Not Hold the Cure		
Develop	$-B_D$	$-B_D$	$-B_D$ (gain)	*choice*
Preserve	$-B_P$	0	0	

each case relative to a base situation. In the insurance game the base is the situation with preservation but no outbreak of the disease. In the lottery game the base is preservation but the species does not turn out to hold the cure.

The loss matrices the way Bishop and Ready write them are listed in Table 13.3. (Minus losses are gains.) First, we see that if we adopt the decision rule that takes the action leading to the lowest maximum possible loss (minimax loss), we would choose to preserve in the insurance case and to develop in the lottery case. Why the differences in matrices and chosen action? The answer, in my words, is as follows:

- In the "insurance" setting we *know* about the curative capability before we decide on the species' future. B_P *as a loss*, therefore, will occur if we develop and if the disease occurs. The simplicity of this decision situation might be clearer with a different choice of base, so just below the base has been moved to "Develop/No outbreak."[7] Here all entries are losses (see Table 13.4). If you preserve, you give up B_D. If you develop, you know in advance you will give up B_P if the disease occurs.

- In the "lottery" setting, *if* you choose to develop, the species is assumed to have disappeared *before* you know about its curative property or lack of same. Thus, there is no penalty in the cell that corresponds to develop/species holds cure. Since we cannot know, we cannot reasonably penalize ourselves as though we knew— so goes the argument. Again, we can rewrite the loss matrix with a different base,

TABLE 13.4 Changing the Base in the Insurance Game

	Disease Outbreak Occurs	No Outbreak	Max Loss	
Develop	B_P	0	B_P	
Preserve	B_D	B_D	B_D	*choice*

TABLE 13.5 Changing the Base in the Lottery Game

	Species Holds Cure	Species Does Not Hold Cure	Max Loss	
Develop	0	0	0	*choice*
Preserve	$B_D - B_P$	B_D	B_D	

which may help you to see what is going on. In Table 13.5, the base has become "Develop/Species does not hold cure."

Does this bother you? If it does, what could you do about the structure of the decision problem that would help? The extreme possibility would seem to be to refuse to play the lottery game. That is, to refuse to decide on preservation or extinction until you knew about the promise, or lack of it, of every species. The problem with this answer is that it makes an unrealistic demand on our knowledge. We do not even know all the species that are "out there"—in a given piece of tropical rainforest, for example. And even for the species we have identified, we cannot know the possible properties of every protein they "manufacture," in large part because we don't understand all the mechanisms of life and disease. To refuse to play the lottery game is to refuse to touch any part of nature for an indefinite period, until huge increases in knowledge have been achieved. This may not seem too onerous to those of us sitting in the industrial (or postindustrial) world, where B_D may involve some furniture hardwoods or some addition to world copper supply. But B_D might look really large to the country owning the resource in question. And the real problem might better be seen as how to make it worthwhile for such countries to go slow, to give at least some chance for knowledge to catch up with development capabilities.

CONCLUDING COMMENTS

This chapter has looked at several separate topics, all of which are related to risk analysis and risk management. In no way is this a complete survey of either field of endeavor, or even a systematic introduction. But my hope is that you will see here that risk analysis and management are connected to other parts of the text, such as monitoring and enforcement with errors of inference accounted for, and the estimation of damages and benefits. What changes with explicit recognition of risk is how we combine the underlying tools to help make sense of the environmental challenges we face.

An important technical notion to take away from this chapter is that different approaches are available for trying to come to grips with risky decisions, even ones in which our ignorance is profound. Fundamentally, the choice is between trying to characterize that ignorance via probability distributions, using computers to generate distributions for the net results of alternative decisions—not just expected values; and relying more heavily on point estimates but taking a conservative game-based approach to their use. The Ready and Bishop "lottery" version of this approach brought us squarely up against the cost of our ignorance and forced us to consider what might be reasonable responses to it.

NOTES

1. It is very important to understand that managing risk almost never means eliminating it. It is a matter of balancing risk and reward. But just as in other areas of public decision, society can adopt *processes* that it trusts, and those processes may or may not involve explicit balancing themselves.
2. It is worth noting that the Toxic Substances Control Act, which deals with exactly this type of situation, places the burden of proof on the proponent. So do the Federal Insecticide, Fungicide and Rodenticide Act; and the Food and Drug Administration legislation for drugs and foods additives.
3. With the advantage of hindsight, one might say that Krutilla's notions of the promise of technology and changing input structure were a trifle optimistic. For there have been waves of concern about running out of petroleum, and the global climate change question involves the products of fossil-fuel combustion as central threats. In his work described below in the text he also relied on the then-current optimism about nuclear fission as prime mover for electricity generation. And, on the other side, it is not hard to find people who will argue that our ability to "create" experiences, at different levels from the Disney World to the "virtual" cyberspace variety, means that the only nonreproducible part of the "real" natural experience is the knowledge that it is "natural"; and this knowledge cannot be obtained from "inside" the experience but only from what we are told before or after.
4. Nothing is said here about the origin of this power "requirement." It is taken as given, and only "cost effectiveness" is at issue.
5. Krutilla and his colleagues pursued the more difficult questions hinted at here in a series of subsequent books and papers. If you are interested, look at: Anthony C. Fisher, John V. Krutilla, and Charles Cicchetti, "The Economics of Environmental Preservation: A Theoretical and Empirical Analysis," 1972. and Kenneth J. Arrow and Anthony C. Fisher, "Environmental Preservation, Uncertainty, and Irreversibility," 1974.
6. Bishop had earlier published a paper in which preservation did seem to be justified if we could be confident only that the potential benefits of preservation promised to be greater than the benefits of development. Ready and Bishop showed that this model was faulty.
7. Changing the base in this way involves, arithmetically, adding B_D to the entry in every cell, which leaves zero in the base.

REFERENCES

Arrow, Kenneth J., and Anthony C. Fisher. 1974. "Environmental preservation, uncertainty, and irreversibility." *Quarterly Journal of Economics* 88(2):312–319.

Balick, Michael J., and Robert Mendelsohn. 1992. "Assessing the economic value of traditional medicines from tropical rain forests." *Conservation Biology* 6(1):128–130.

Fisher, Anthony C., John V. Krutilla, and Charles Cicchetti. 1972. "The economics of environmental preservation: A theoretical and empirical analysis." *American Economic Review* 62(4):605–619.

Krutilla, John V. 1967. "Conservation reconsidered." *American Economic Review* 57(4):777–786.

Mendelsohn, Robert, and Michael Balick, 1994. "The value of undiscovered pharmaceuticals in tropical forests." Working Paper. New Haven, Conn.: Yale School of Forestry.

Ready, Richard C., and Richard C. Bishop. 1991. "Endangered species and the safe minimum standard." *American Journal of Agricultural Economics* 70:309–312.

Tobias, Dave, and Robert Mendelsohn, 1991. "Valuing ecotourism in a tropical rain-forest reserve." *Ambio* 20(2):91–93.

14

DEVELOPMENT AND ENVIRONMENT
Descriptive Statistics and Special Challenges

If you look only at the more or less abstract microeconomics contained in the previous chapters, your response to this chapter and the following might well be: What's the point of having separate chapters on developing countries and the environment? Unless we assume something drastically different about the behavior of individuals or firms, environmental economics ought to look pretty much the same, no matter what the average income of those people or the technical sophistication of the technology and products of those firms. And yet, reading about developing countries and their environments in newspapers and other wide-circulation sources can't help but give you the feeling that something very different *is* going on. The tone taken by developing-country leaders often seems to be: The environment is a policy issue for rich countries. We are too poor to afford the luxury of fretting about pollution. Indeed, we see pollution as now-developed countries *used to*—as evidence of desirable industrialization and growth. Similarly for forests and other natural resources. We want to use them, not save them to make rich people feel better.

To complicate the scene, there is another side to the public debate that stresses how bad the environmental problems of developing countries really are: how many children die because drinking water is polluted due to poor sanitation (no sewers, no wastewater treatment even if there are sewers, no reliable household water supplies with intake treatment to kill bacteria and parasites); how bad air quality is in the large cities of the developing world; how massive deforestation leads to soil loss and downstream flooding. Implicitly or explicitly, this side is saying: Only idiots or evil people would ignore these massive damages for the sake of growing money income by 8 percent per year instead of 6 percent per year.

If environmental economics applies so straightforwardly in the developing world, and if the damages created by policy neglect (or actual encouragement of resource exploitation) are so huge, why the rhetorical dismissal of environmental protection by less-developed country leaders? Or, if there really are "special challenges" in dealing with LDC environmental policy from the economics point of view, what are they and what role do they play in provoking or at least allowing the ongoing shouting match?

Certainly there are two practical challenges for the text. The first is to provide at least a rough and ready understanding of what "growth" and development are all about and how and why they proceed (at least as economists see it). The second is to suggest the sizes and shapes of differences between "developing" and "developed" (or "industrialized") countries. Without these bits of background the flavor of these next several chapters might well be too bland. But I hope that with the background will come a sense for just how high the stakes are for the developing world—hence the decibel level of the shouting—and yet how intricately the environment really is tied up in the long-run processes at issue. So, the next section will discuss growth and "sustainability," and the one following will try to provide the flavor of the differences between the developed and the developing worlds, using data from a sample of countries from around the world.

TRYING TO UNDERSTAND ECONOMIC GROWTH AND SUSTAINABILITY

Our society is obsessed by economic growth and the measurement paraphernalia that is required for judging how well we are doing, whether there are storm clouds on the horizon, how long the current spurt has lasted, and what it has meant for different parts of society. It is probably the single most important yardstick we apply to political leaders in deciding how well they are doing. And we even seem to have become sophisticated enough to realize that our economy will be healthier if other economies are also healthy, so we even worry about macro and micro economic policies of our major trading partners. Somewhere well down the list of our concerns, at least in the absence of highly visible "crises," is the growth, or lack of it, being experienced in what used to be called the "Third World"—the countries of Africa north of South Africa, the non-oil-producing Middle East, much of Asia, and much of Central and South America.

We were not always so self-consciously interested in growth. From the time European growth "took off" in the late eighteenth and early nineteenth century until the middle of the twentieth century, the "average person" might spend a lifetime adjusting to growth and change or helping cause it, but probably almost no time reading or fretting about the immediate prospects or immediate past of his or her economy. (Not that economists ignored the phenomenon; just think of Adam Smith, who published *Wealth of Nations* in 1776.) The breadth and intensity of interest that we take for granted today, though, seem to have their roots in the economic cataclysm of the Great Depression of the 1930s; the subsequent war-related recovery of the 1940s; and the long-term booms, only occasionally interrupted, of the five following decades. Not only economists, indeed even politicians, have been interested in what went wrong in the 1930s, what went right during and after World War II, and especially whether we were and are at the mercy of random events or can act to keep economies growing.

If the first spur to obsession was fear of the repeat of the 1930s, the second, it seems to me, could be said to have been the nearly simultaneous observations that (a) after WWII we appeared to take conscious steps that succeeded in setting the devastated economies of Western (noncommunist) Europe at least, back on the growth path; and (b) that the countries clamoring for and receiving independence from their European colonial masters in the 1940s through 1960s seemed ripe for the same treatment. They were poor and lacked industry. Couldn't the industrialized world just create a "Marshall Plan" for the rest of the world and watch all the national flowers bloom as we had watched Europe recover?

Even though the answer to this last question has turned out to be no, the multi-decade effort to understand how and why of modern economic growth has produced valuable insights and lessons for the makers of policy—and not just macro economic policies—around the world. Because most of the theory work has ignored the relationships among the economy, the environment, and natural resources, however, most of the obvious lessons are not directly relevant to a text dealing with development and environment. The relatively new offshoot of the concern about growth, usually called the "sustainability" question, is clearly relevant, though, and worth at least brief examination. And to set the stage for that examination, it will be useful to see what the models of economic growth look like even in the absence of specific concern with environment and resources.

ECONOMIC GROWTH, THE ACCUMULATION OF CAPITAL, AND TECHNICAL CHANGE

From the earliest days of modern growth theorizing there has been special interest in capital—the machinery of industrial production that so obviously sets the modern economy apart from its premodern ancestors. Machinery, embodying new technologies, for example steam engines for transportation, pumping, and powering textile looms, certainly seemed to be at the heart of the Industrial Revolution of the late eighteenth and early nineteenth century. And this identification of economic growth with a growing (and changing) capital stock has continued since.

One of the earliest efforts to understand and formalize the connection, jointly attributed to Roy Harrod (1948) and E. Domar (1947), is a model that looks directly and only at the capital-to-output relation. Indeed, the fundamental building block of the Harrod–Domar model is the capital-output ratio, which is assumed constant. So, letting K stand for aggregate capital and Y for aggregate output, this building block may be written as $g = K/Y$. The constancy of this (assumed) relation is exploited by observing that to achieve an increase in Y, ΔY, an increment to K, ΔK, will be required, and $\Delta K = g \, \Delta Y$. But to get any addition to capital, there must be savings, and savings is taken to be a fraction of income, $S = sY$. Then, since $\Delta K = $ investment = savings = sY, for there to be growth, $sY = g \, \Delta Y$ must be true. Or:

$$\frac{\Delta Y}{Y} = \frac{s}{g}$$

which says that a society's income growth rate is determined b/y the interplay of the fraction of income it saves and the capital-to-output ratio—what might be called its capital intensity. So, for example, if $g = 3$ and $S = 0.1$, $\Delta Y/Y = 0.033$. Since g

could be seen as given by the prior path of technological development, the policy variable here is the savings rate. The higher that could be pushed, the faster aggregate income could grow. One way to increase saving in developing countries was thought to be to squeeze it out of exporters, often the agriculture sector, which was exporting commodities such as sugar, coffee, tea, cotton, or bananas. The trick was to force the exporters to sell to a government "marketing board" relatively cheaply. The board then sold the commodity on the world market, and the government pocketed the difference for use as investment capital in its "growth plan." Another source of "savings equivalent," as we might call it, would be foreign aid. And the Harrod–Domar model might be seen as an early theoretical justification for aid— jump-starting the growth process using the savings of other nations to substitute for what was not yet available domestically.

But the H-D model is based on rigid technology, takes no account of labor, and ignores the problem of maintaining macro economic equilibrium in which consumption plus savings (ignoring exports and imports) equals production. What has come to be called "neoclassical" growth modeling attempted to fix these shortcomings via a production function in which labor and capital both contributed and could be substituted. The convenient and common choice is the "Cobb–Douglas" form:

$$Y = zK^\alpha L^{1-\alpha}$$

On this functional form, see Brown, 1987. Now, income will grow at a decreasing rate as a function of K alone (see Figure 14.1). It is easy to manipulate the time derivatives of this aggregate production function to show that:

$$\frac{\partial Y/\partial t}{Y} = \alpha \frac{\partial K/\partial t}{K} + (1 - \alpha) \frac{\partial L/\partial t}{L}$$

or, in the common notation that uses a dot for a time derivative:

$$\frac{\dot{Y}}{Y} = \alpha \frac{\dot{K}}{K} + (1 - \alpha) \frac{\dot{L}}{L}$$

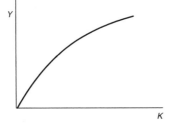

Figure 14.1 Income as a Function of Capital in the Neoclassical Growth Model

The growth of output per unit of labor, which is usually written as $y = Y/L$, is:

$$\frac{\dot{y}}{y} = \frac{\dot{Y}}{Y} - \frac{\dot{L}}{L} = \alpha \frac{\dot{K}}{K} - \alpha \frac{\dot{L}}{L} = \alpha \frac{\dot{k}}{k}$$

where $k = K/L$ = the capital-to-labor ratio.[1]

In the long-run *equilibrium*, however, the capital/labor ratio, k, is a constant. So long-run *equilibrium* growth in per capita output is zero in this model.

To "explain" the persistence of growth in per capita income and consumption, something else was required. The first such something else suggested was exogenously determined technological progress. The idea was that changing technology made both capital and labor more productive. Mathematically, the production function became:

$$Y = Ae^{ut} K^{\alpha} L^{1-\alpha} \qquad \text{(sometimes written } A(t)K^{\alpha}L^{1-\alpha})$$

and u is the rate of technological progress or, in the second formulation, $\dot{A}/A$. Then in equilibrium, growth proceeds, so that:

$$\frac{\dot{c}}{c} = \frac{\dot{y}}{y} = \frac{\dot{k}}{k}$$

The common rate of per capita "welfare" growth, which we might call z, is: $z = u/(1 - \alpha)$. This line of work is strongly associated with Robert Solow. See, for example, Solow, 1984.

This, then, accounts for persistent growth, but really only by introducing something that itself is unexplained—not a very satisfactory way to proceed for real understanding. Further, if externally determined technical change drives growth, and technology is roughly speaking a public good, available to all countries perhaps after some lag, it seems that all countries ought to be observed to grow at close to the same rate. But nothing like that shows up in the data. The divergences might be explained by differences in "national characteristics"—what you might call the sociology of growth—which, in turn, explains why countries differentially are able to take advantage of the exogenous technical progress.

ENDOGENOUS EXPLANATIONS FOR GROWTH

It is safe to say that economists would prefer to put off as long as possible calling on the nearly tautological "explanation" that countries grow at different rates because they have different national "characters." And in a major intellectual effort to do this, the so-called endogenous growth models were developed over roughly the decade 1983–1995. In these models, private decisions to employ capital and labor in certain processes (technological research and development or the formation of "human capital" through education and on-the-job training) create spillovers to the economy at large.

The version that I think is easiest to come to grips with is that involving investment in human capital.[2] The investment is decided on privately and endogenously because it increases the effectiveness of labor applied in production. But in the process, an effect closely analogous to the exogenous technical change term is "created." Thus:

$h \equiv$ human capital (a stock)

$u \equiv$ the fraction of the potential labor force applied to production of Y

$1 - u =$ the fraction applied to producing human capital

$\dot{h}/h = \delta(1 - u) \equiv v$, where δ is the maximum possible rate of growth of human capital if all labor effort were devoted to its production

Now L is defined as $[uhN]$. So

$$Y = MK^\beta \, [uhN]^{1-\beta}h^\gamma$$

and the last term on the right is the external effect of the human capital investment. Lucas shows that on the balanced growth path,

$$\frac{\dot{c}}{c} = v + \frac{\gamma v}{1 - \beta}$$

and the economy's progress is determined largely by v, the rate of growth of human capital. But this reflects, in turn, an endogenous decision on the amount of effort $(1 - u)$ to put into education and training. This implies both that countries have some control over their destinies in the growth realm and that there is no reason to expect "convergence" of growth rates because country decisions can differ.

The growth model identified with Paul Romer (Romer, 1990, 1994) is more complex, including both human capital and something closer to pure technology (Romer, 1994). The latter is modeled by "designs" for capital goods. The development of these designs is the business of a sector of the economy, the firms in which operate in a monopolistic competition setting, generating profits that reward the research and development they undertake. But it is also true that the development of new designs raises the productivity of the whole research and development sector in the generation of yet more designs. This is the spillover.

A little bit of the math will help to show how this model differs from the others. First, there is a stock of human capital, H, which can be used either in the production of new technologies ("designs," A) or of output, Y.

$$H = H_A + H_Y$$

There is also undifferentiated labor, L.

Capital, K, is given by the sum of the available designs at any one time, A, as follows:

$$K = n \sum_{i=1}^{A} x_i$$

A, then, is the size of the stock of designs, and that stock grows according to the rule:

$$\frac{\dot{A}}{A} = \delta H_A$$

The spillover here is from the individual firm producing a new "design" to the entire design sector. Said another way, $\dot{A}$, for a fixed application of H_A, will be larger the larger the existing stock of technology. This effect of private decisions to do R&D on the overall productivity of R&D done by others creates a growth model that mathematically looks very much like the neoclassical variety but does not imply convergence.

BRINGING IN THE ENVIRONMENT AND SUSTAINABILITY

There is more than one way to tie growth modeling into a concern about environmental quality. One possibility is to add an environmental quality term to the consumer utility function that "values" production and that has been ignored in the above brief discussion of the production-side basis for growth. Increasing production of Y could lead to declining levels of this (public) quality index, and so there would be opposing forces at work at the heart of the model. To make it really interesting, it would have to be possible to apply labor and capital to improving the quality index.

Another possibility, broadly speaking the one that lies behind much of the discussion of "sustainability," at least the economic discussion of that notion, is to distinguish different types of capital. In particular, the sustainability writers identify stocks of nonrenewable natural resources and a stock of environmental quality that can be run down or conserved, in addition to man-made and human capital. Sustainable growth is growth that can be maintained over the long run, though just how long it is reasonable to be concerned with is really an open question. A reasonable way to specify a sustainability condition, though one that ignores distribution questions *within* each time period, is to require that per capita utility be nondecreasing over time. (That is, $u_{t+1} \geq u_t$ for all t, where u is per capita utility.)[3]

The key to sustainability, then, is maintaining the capacity to produce goods and services, which is to say, maintaining the capital stock. But which stock(s)? The subsequent question, the one that tends to separate optimists from pessimists, and "ecological economists" from the more conventional variety, is: Do we have to maintain each type of capital separately, or are all the forms generally substitutable? Can advancing technology (Romer's "designs" or Lucas' human capital) substitute for depletion of natural resources? If it can happen over some range, what are the limits? Similarly for the assimilation capacity of the environment.

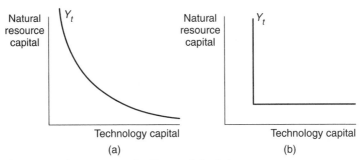

Figure 14.2 Substitution Extremes for Forms of Capital

Using a Cobb–Douglas aggregate production function, and distinguishing different forms of capital within it, amounts to *assuming* that any of the capital stocks can be run down to arbitrarily small levels and utility maintained so long as other forms are beefed up. At the other extreme, a fixed proportions function assumes that for any specified output level, at least some associated level of every capital stock is required. In two dimensions, the contrast is between (a) and (b) in Figure 14.2.

The answer to this large and important question is by no means obvious, even though common sense says that we cannot make something out of nothing. First, the "something" that we use can change with technology, as in the substitution of nuclear for fossil fuel energy. But second, as noted above, since the point is to maintain utility in the long run, the actual goods and services that have to be produced can change as well. For example, travel is a very energy-, material-, and pollution-intensive activity. The technology exists even now to make it less so, but for the even longer run, the technology that is now leading to efficient "telecommuting" may make physical travel a much less important part of the satisfaction of wants.

If one takes substitutability seriously, then the prescription offered by Robert Solow, for "an almost practical step toward sustainability" becomes a guide for both research and policy.[4] This prescription, based on the theoretical work of Solow and others, is to reinvest the "rents" from using up particular stocks of capital in other, substitutable forms. This applies, in particular, to nonrenewable natural resources, such as fossil fuels, as well as to the environment when that is seen as "depletable." As Solow has noted these "rents" are not at all easy to calculate, especially the environmental quality rents, since there are no markets to appeal to for data. But this challenge is exactly what environmental economists have been working and making progress on for several decades. (See chapters 6 through 8 and 15.)

DESCRIBING COUNTRIES AND THEIR HEALTH AND ENVIRONMENTAL PROBLEMS

It will now be worthwhile to pause and look at some data—to try to put some flesh on the bones of the labels "developing" countries and "developed" countries (which

I will often refer to as OECD countries, after their club, the Organization for Economic Cooperation and Development). This will involve setting out selected pieces of data for a selection of countries with different levels of per capita national income, especially data dealing with matters related to pollution and health. The selection of countries has been done to reduce the possibility of data overload while still giving you information that cuts across continents and absolute country sizes as well as across income levels. However, any small selection from the roughly 125 to 150 nations of the world that might be called "developing" will fail to do justice to some dimensions of the vast range of physical and economic "settings" represented. For example, while most of the nations of sub-Saharan Africa have always been relatively poor, some nations, which in current income terms are realistically thought of as developing, used to be among the world's richest. Argentina, for example. Others used to be part of a grouping that the world took seriously as developed nations but that has subsequently been revealed to have been substantially poorer than perceived. The nations that were part of the former Soviet Union are the prime examples here. And yet others have been, except for a hiccough "crisis" in the late 1990s, on a very rapid economic growth trajectory: the Asian "tigers" such as Korea, Malaysia, and Thailand, for example. (Korea has, in fact, joined the OECD club.)

The physical settings of the developing world are just as variable. These range from the low-lying and tropical (e.g., Bangladesh, the West African coastal nations, Guiana, some Pacific island nations), to the Arctic regions of Russia. In between lie mountainous countries (Nepal, Peru), deserts (Mongolia, Chad, Libya), and temperate highlands (Eastern Africa from the Cape of Good Hope to Nairobi).

So it is presumptuous to write about "the" differences between developing and developed nations. On the other hand, it would be tedious to try to slog through every possible specific contrast. And the benefits (if you'll pardon the word) would be most unlikely to outweigh the costs, for any of us. Therefore, in what follows, the "typical" country being discussed can be pictured as toward the poorer end of the income scale and as lying in the tropics (at least its cities; there might well be cooler and hillier hinterlands). It can also be thought of as fairly densely populated, even in the countryside, with a large proportion of its citizens (large by OECD standards) in subsistence (or only tenuously cash-crop) agriculture. From time to time it will be worthwhile pointing out the implications of big differences from this model along any of the dimensions of interest.

INCOMES, POPULATION, AND THE IMPORTANCE OF AGRICULTURE

So . . . on to a look at some indicators of relative poverty and associated characteristics that bear on the relation between a nation's citizens and its physical environment. The indicator on the "wealth"-poverty scale will be gross domestic product (GDP). This measure is discussed below in this chapter, but for now, if you are not familiar with the notion, just take it as the result of trying to measure and add up all the incomes accruing to people, property, and machines in a particular nation and year. To normalize for the absolute size of the nation, the annual total is divided by the population to produce a per-person average. Further, to reduce the importance of local currency value movements, the figures are reported in terms of what is known as "purchasing power parity." The factor used in this conversion is defined as the number of units of a country's currency required to buy a standard "basket" of goods and services that a dollar would buy in the United States.

Table 14.1 contains basic comparative data for thirty-four countries from five continents (counting Central America as separate from South America) that can be called "developing." Eleven of these are from Africa, seven from Europe, three each from Central and South America, and ten from Asia. The samples are roughly proportional to the number of nations coexisting on each continent, but they have not been completely randomly selected. For example, China and India were explicitly

TABLE 14.1 Some Basic Developing Country Comparisons: Economics, Population, Sanitation

	GDP/CAP[a] Prch Powr Parity (1995 $)	Ave. Ann. ROG[b] 1985–1995(%)	GDP fm Agriculture 1995(%)	Proj. Pop. ROG 1995–2000 (%)	Life Exp'y at Birth 1995–2000(yrs)
Africa					
Algeria	5600	0.3	13	2.3	68.9
Burundi	640	0.9	56	2.8	47.2
D.R. Congo	473	X	30	2.6	52.9
Ethiopia	460	3.6	57	3.2	49.9
Guinea-Bissau	800	3.7	46	2.0	43.8
Madagascar	680	0.9	34	3.1	58.5
Morocco	3470	2.6	14	1.8	66.7
Nigeria	1310	3.8	28	2.8	52.4
South Africa	5240	1.1	5	2.2	65.2
Tanzania	670	3.6	58	2.3	51.4
Zambia	990	0.5	22	2.5	43.0
Europe					
Albania	X[c]	3.3	56	0.6	70.9
Bulgaria	4700	(1.6)[d]	13	(0.5)	71.3
Hungary	6680	(0.2)	8	(0.6)	69.0
Latvia	3360	(5.1)	9	(1.1)	68.4
Poland	5430	0.8	6	0.1	71.1
Russia	4820	(3.9)	7	(0.3)	64.4
Slovak Rep.	3600	(0.8)	6	0.1	71.3
Central America					
Belize	5620	6.5	20	2.5	74.4
Guatemala	3290	3.3	25	2.8	67.2
Nicaragua	2430	X	33	2.6	68.2
South America					
Argentina	8450	2.6	6	1.3	73.2
Ecuador	4560	2.7	12	2.0	69.8
Uruguay	6700	3.5	9	0.6	72.9

TABLE 14.1 Some Basic Developing Country Comparisons: Economics, Population, Sanitation (*Continued*)

	GDP/CAP[a] Prch Powr Parity (1995 $)	Ave. Ann. ROG[b] 1985–1995(%)	GDP fm Agriculture 1995(%)	Proj. Pop. ROG 1995–2000 (%)	Life Exp'y at Birth 1995–2000(yrs)
Asia					
Azerbaijan	1460	*X*	27	0.8	70.6
Bangladesh	1380	4.0	31	1.6	58.1
China	2970	9.6	21	0.9	69.9
India	1420	5.2	29	1.6	62.4
Kazakstan	3040	*X*	12	0.1	67.6
Mongolia	2010	0.3	17	2.1	65.8
Philippines	2760	3.4	22	2.0	68.3
Sri Lanka	3290	3.8	23	1.0	73.1
Thailand	7710	9.0	11	0.8	69.3
Turkey	5510	4.3	16	1.6	69.0
Developed Countries					
Denmark	21,990	1.7	4	0.2	75.6
Germany	20,120	*X*	1	0.3	76.7
Italy	20,180	2.1	3	0.0	78.3
Switzerland	24,900	1.4	*X*	0.7	78.6
United States	26,980	2.5	2	0.8	76.7
Japan	21,930	2.9	2	0.2	80.0
So. Korea	11,550	8.4	7	0.9	72.4

[a] GDP, gross domestic product; CAP, per capita. [b] ROG, rate of growth. [c] *X* = unavailable. [d] ( ) around rates of growth indicates negative numbers.

Source: 1998–99 World Resources: A Guide to the Global Environment. New York: Oxford University Press, 1998. Data tables 6.1, 7.1, 7.2.

chosen because they are enormous and often compared with each other. But there should be enough variation among the countries to give you a sense for the ranges of conditions already alluded to. Some observations:

• The African countries, in particular the sub-Saharan African countries, are the poorest group—and in this sample, Ethiopia is the poorest nation. For these countries, per-person GDP estimates are, Nigeria and South Africa excepted, less than $1,000, or less than 5 percent of the comparable figures for the OECD countries. The sub-Saharan African nations also have high rates of population growth, low life expectancies at birth, and high percentages of their economies in agriculture, again excepting South Africa.[5]

• The poorer European countries, without exception refugees, as it were, from the Soviet Union and its system of client states, are five to ten times better off in GDP per capita terms than the poorest African nations. At least over the 1985–1995 decade, however, the trauma of the breakup of the old system left them negative rates of economic growth *and* negative population growth rates. (The pie was shrinking and so were the numbers of chefs and consumers.) Except for Albania, the fractions of their GDPs accounted for by agriculture are small, roughly a fifth of those seen in Africa. And the life expectancy of a newly born citizen would be around seventy years, only slightly lower than the corresponding figure for the OECD countries.

 • The Central and South American countries have per-person GDP figures that have a larger range than those of the poorer European countries but a mean roughly in the same neighborhood. Their citizens also have life expectancies at birth of about seventy years. On other dimensions, however, they are quite different. That is, during the 1985–1995 decade, their economies were growing, not shrinking, and so were their populations. The Central American countries reported on had larger agricultural sectors than the South American, with the latter countries looking more like Eastern Europe in this regard.

 • Asia, not surprisingly given its vast area and the enormous differences in geography, resources, history, and culture across that area, presents us with a very mixed bag. Some countries are as poor in per-capita GDP terms as Nigeria (Azerbaijan, Bangladesh, India), while at the other end of the scale, Turkey and Thailand are as well off economically (on average) as the South American and Eastern European leaders. The rates of GDP growth over the 1985–1995 decade were, for the most part, quite high—the highest in the table for China and Thailand, and still more than respectable for India and Turkey. The importance of agriculture in GDP ranged from a South American or Eastern European 11 percent in Thailand to a Central American, almost African, 31 percent in Bangladesh. Similarly for population rates of growth, though none of the rates was as high as those commonly found in Africa and Central America. Life expectancies were generally lowest in the poorest countries, though Azerbaijan and Sri Lanka confound any temptation to make that relation into a rule.

 • The OECD countries, including the newest member of the club, South Korea, have very low rates of population growth, very small agricultural sectors, and life expectancies at birth between seventy-five and eighty years. Rates of economic growth were modest in the decade reported on compared with the most vigorous Asian economies, but far better than those seen in the former Soviet satellite countries. Incomes per capita, South Korea excepted, are in the range $20,000 to $27,000 per year.

HEALTH AND SANITATION

In Table 14.2 we move from economic and demographic data to comparisons on the health and sanitation fronts. The first two columns show, where the data were available, the percentage of the country's population with access to safe drinking water and basic sanitation (way of handling human waste). The next four columns give some part of the picture on public health—infant and maternal mortality and preva-

TABLE 14.2 Health and Sanitation Comparisons

	% of Population with Access to Safe Drinking Water 1990–96	% of Population with Access to Basic Sanitation 1990–96	1995–2000 Infant Mortality Rate per 1000 Live Births	1990 Maternal Mortality Rate per 100,000 Live Births	Cases of Tuberculosis per 100,000 of Pop. 1995	Cases of Measles per 100,000 Pop. 1995	Population per Doctor 1990–93
Africa							
Algeria	78	91	44	160	49	29	1,062
Burundi	59	51	114	1300	62	244	17,153
D.R. of Congo	42	18	89	870	91	12	15,150
Ethiopia	25	19	107	1400	26	1	X[a]
Guinea Bissau	59	30	132	910	163	49	X
Madagascar	29	3	77	490	80	79	8,385
Morocco	55	41	51	610	110	9	X
Nigeria	51	58	77	1000	12	11	X
So. Africa	99	53	48	230	210	3	X
Tanzania	38	86	80	770	134	11	X
Zambia	27	64	103	940	135	106	10,917
Europe							
Albania	X	X	32	65	19	0	735
Bulgaria	X	X	16	27	37	2	306
Hungary	X	X	14	30	43	0	306
Latvia	X	X	16	40	60	0	278
Poland	X	X	13	19	42	2	451
Russia	X	X	19	75	58	4	222
Slovakia	X	X	12	X	0	0	287
Central America							
Belize	X	X	30	X	28	2	2,028
Guatemala	64	59	40	200	32	0	X
Nicaragua	53	60	44	160	64	0	X

TABLE 14.2 Health and Sanitation Comparisons (*Continued*)

	% of Population with Access to Safe Drinking Water 1990–96	% of Population with Access to Basic Sanitation 1990–96	1995–2000 Infant Mortality Rate per 1000 Live Births	1990 Maternal Mortality Rate per 100,000 Live Births	Cases of Tuberculosis per 100,000 of Pop. 1995	Cases of Measles per 100,000 Pop. 1995	Population per Doctor 1990–93
South America							
Argentina	71	68	22	100	39	2	X
Ecuador	68	76	46	150	69	8	652
Uruguay	75	61	17	85	20	0	X
Asia							
Azerbaijan	X	X	33	22	19	6	257
Bangladesh	97	48	78	850	35	4	12,884
China	67	24	38	95	29	4	1,063
India	81	29	72	570	130	4	X
Kazakstan	X	X	34	80	66	2	254
Mongolia	80	74	52	65	125	23	371
Philippines	86	77	35	280	348	6	8,273
Sri Lanka	57	63	15	140	30	10	X
Thailand	89	96	30	200	77	19	4,416
Turkey	80	X	44	180	37	22	976
Developed Countries							
Denmark	z[b]	z	7	9	9	0	360
Germany	z	z	6	22	15	X	X
Italy	z	z	7	12	10	65	X
Switzerland	z	z	5	6	12	0	X
United States	z	z	7	12	9	0	500
Japan	97	z	4	18	34	X	X
South Korea	93	100	9	130	74	0	951

[a] X = unavailable. [b] z = unavailable but almost certainly close to 100 percent.

Source: 1998–99 World Resources: A Guide to the Global Environment. New York: Oxford University Press, 1998. Data tables 7.4, 8.2, 8.3, and 8.4.

lence of two preventable diseases, tuberculosis and measles. Finally, the population-per-doctor figures give an idea of the availability of health care to someone who does get sick.

Again, some observations:

• While there is considerable variation across the set of African nations reported on, outside of South Africa and Algeria access to safe drinking water and sanitation is limited to about half or less of the population. With the same exceptions plus Morocco, infant (up to one year) mortality rates range from the high 70s to over 130 per 1,000 live births. (Remember, a rate of 100 would mean that 10 percent of babies born die within their first year.) There are similarly wide variations in maternal mortality rates per 100,000 live births. That is, outside of Algeria and South Africa they are high—at or over 1 percent of the live births in Nigeria, Ethiopia, and Burundi and upward of 1 percent in the rest of the countries. Similar evidence of public health problems are found in the tuberculosis and measles figures, when seen against the OECD numbers at the end of the table, though again, the figures vary greatly. Here even South Africa has a big tuberculosis problem; but Ethiopia and Nigeria look very good indeed. Finally, for all the countries reporting data there are very few doctors to serve the population that has the problems—from 8,400 to over 17,000 potential patients per doctor.

• The poorer European countries operate on an entirely different level in the public health sphere, it seems. While no data are available for access to safe drinking water and basic sanitation, the worst European country has a better record (by a factor of almost 2) than the best of the African records in infant mortality. Maternal mortality figures are proportionally even lower. Similarly for the infectious diseases, though for tuberculosis there are substantial overlaps in the numbers of cases per 100,000. Doctors face potentially one-twentieth the case loads of the African doctors.

• Central and South American countries appear to have some more inclusive drinking water and sanitation infrastructure than the African nations. Their infant and maternal death rates are roughly intermediate between those of African and the poorer European nations, while their tuberculosis and measles case loads look rather like the European experience. For only two countries is population per doctor reported, but those two observations are also intermediate.

• Asian countries have rather high reported availability of safe drinking water and somewhat lower levels of basic sanitation (especially in China and India. Nonetheless, their experiences with infant and maternal death are generally much worse than in Eastern Europe. Indeed, the maternal death rates in Bangladesh and India are right in line with the sub-Saharan African experience. Looking at tuberculosis and measles, we find the same pattern, with the Philippine figure for the former the highest of any nation in the table. The availability of doctors varies hugely, from the Eastern European level in the several hundred persons-per-doctor range to the African level of 10,000 or more (Bangladesh and the Philippines).

• There are drinking water and sanitation figures reported for only one of the OECD nations in the table, South Korea, but these are close to or at 100 percent. I think it highly unlikely that any of the OECD numbers can be much below 100 percent for either item. Their public health figures represent the results of a century or more of such investments and other efforts. Thus, infant mortality figures are below 10 per 1,000 live births, even in South Korea; and maternal death rates are below 25 per 100,000 in all countries except South Korea. The numbers of tuberculosis and measles cases are low by comparison with the other countries covered in the table, though South Korea seems to have a TB problem, and Italy a measles one. The number of people per doctor in the three OECD nations for which data are available are actually rather large by world standards; higher, for example, than most of the Eastern European nations reported on.

Overall, it appears that public sanitation and health status improve with increasing income, though by no means in lock step. It is also worth noting that having a lot of doctors does not correlate especially closely with improved public health, though a dramatic *lack* of doctors does go with very high levels of easily preventable deaths of infants and mothers.

IMPACT ON THE ENVIRONMENT

The last data compilation, and in nearly every sense the least satisfactory, concerns human impact on the environment, but predominantly the urban environment and the water courses downstream of urban waste outfalls. Some of the available data are summarized in Table 14.3, and the first observation is that many of the countries we have been "following" to this point are missing—almost all the African nations, all but two from Central and South America, and about half the Asian nations. Beyond that, the data all apply to specific cities, which are by definition subject to special local conditions of weather and geography that influence how a particular pattern of pollution discharges translates into ambient environmental quality.

That said, we can see that some of the poorest nations for which we have data are also creating the greatest *local* environmental stress. For example:

• China has some serious urban air pollution problems—a factor of 3 higher than the next worst for SO_2. Rivers are apparently subject to large human waste loads; the number reported for Qingdao is 90 percent of the population's waste discharged untreated.

• Several other nations in the developing group report annual average SO_2 readings for at least one city that are at or over 100 $\mu g/m^3$: (Bulgaria, Russia, Turkey); Poland comes close behind. But Japan reports 100 $\mu g/m^3$ and South Korea about 90.

• High urban levels of NO_2 (average annual readings from a city) are found in Bulgaria, Argentina, and China. But none of these has a record as bad as that of Italy.

TABLE 14.3 Environmental Quality Data

	Urban SO$_2$ Highest Mean Ann. Reported μg/m^3 (1990s)	Urban NO$_2$ Highest Mean Ann. Reported μg/m^3 (1990s)	Market Share of Leaded Gas 1992–96	% of Waste-Water Treated (city indicated)	% Urban Residents w/n. Garbage Collc. (city indicated)
South Africa	31	X[a]	88	X	X
Bulgaria	96	122	95	71	95 (Sofia)
Hungary	45	51	36	92	100 (Budapest)
Poland	89	79	30	36	97 (Warsaw)
Russia	109	30	50	100	100 (Moscow)
Slovakia	27	27	0	98	100 (Bratislava)
Argentina	3	97	0	X	X
Ecuador	45	X	76	10	70 (Guayaquil)
China	340	136	40	11 (Qingdao)	X
India	49	41	X	10	90 (Bombay)
Philippines	33	X	90	X	85 (Manila)
Thailand	11	23	0	X	X
Turkey	124	46	96	X	X
Denmark	7	54	0	100	100 (Copenhagen)
Germany	18	53	5	80	100 (Leipzig)
Italy	31	248	56	X	X
Switzerland	13	58	13	X	X
U.S.	26	79	0	100 (New York)	X
Japan	100	68	0	X	X
So. Korea	89	62	17	X	X

[a] X = unavailable

Source: 1998–99 World Resources: A Guide to the Global Environment. New York: Oxford University Press, 1998. Data tables 8.5, 8.6, 9.3.

- The sale of leaded gasoline is another indicator of level of care for the environment and the citizenry. By this measure, Bulgaria, Ecuador, the Philippines, and Turkey are behind. But again, Italy does not look so good, with a market penetration of leaded gasoline over 50 percent in the early 1990s.

- Looking at treatment of urban wastewater and availability of garbage collection, we see very low levels of the former in Poland (Warsaw), Ecuador (Guayaquil), China (as noted above), and India. Most of the garbage collection figures are quite high—only Ecuador's falls below 85 percent. This says nothing, of course, about what happens to the collected waste, another shortcoming of the data.

Certainly these data do not support any generalizations about the relation between national income and environmental quality. But they do suggest, particularly in combination with the public health data in Table 14.2, that even for poor countries there are some costs to ignoring the environment. Some nations seem to have recognized this; others not.

BACK TO THE QUESTION OF SPECIAL CHALLENGES

The observations of the previous section bring us back to the question: Why? Why do so many developing country leaders seem to insist on the proposition that the environment is a rich man's game and that any attempt to cure their own environmental ills would come at too high a cost in more traditional economic growth foregone?

There is no single short and simple answer to this question, though neither does the puzzle amount to rocket science. One way of understanding it is to observe that in the absence of efforts to monetize environmental damages linked to development projects and policies, any pronouncements of impending environmental doom are bound to be at a disadvantage. They are, after all, competing for attention in an arena (national income accounting—see Box 14.1) that has been obsessed with monetization for decades. If the debate begins with the projected effect on per capita incomes of adopting policy A instead of the existing policy, then concerns about the effect of A on diesel exhaust particulate emissions, or possible mud slides on the edge of logged-over areas, unconnected to money, may receive very little attention. They become, in effect, just anecdotes about the dark side of development; possibly with long-term cumulative effect on political decisions, but easily ignored in the short run.

So then the question becomes, why haven't the effects been monetized? Largely this is because the methods and data have not been available. In Chapter 15 this is discussed at greater length, but the bottom line for me is that only with the beginnings of the application of direct (survey) methods of damage or benefit estimation in developing countries has it been possible to imagine getting at the effects we are talking about here. The indirect methods, even the techniques that value physical effects such as "dose-response" functions based on epidemiology, simply require too many data—data that have not generally been available in LDCs. If there had been methods available, I think they would have been seized on with enthusiasm. At least in an analogous area, the estimation of "shadow prices" for resources and imports, the development economics profession enthusiastically pursued more and more complex methods. These were aimed at trying to ensure that the distortions found in market prices (e.g., because of import restrictions) were removed, or that the prices lacking, because parts of the fabric of rural life were not monetized, were supplied. The correct "pricing" of environmental effects is, in principle, only a small extension of this effort.

The puzzle is complicated by the fact that, whatever the front-line method of damage or benefit estimation, it is not easy to express the resulting numbers in ways that allow direct comparison with, or adjustments to, the annual per capita income

A Reminder on National Income Accounting

National income accounting is the generic label for that part of macroeconomics that works with definitions and measurement techniques to produce aggregate values for the general concept we might call the "size" of the economy. These values can be measured at different points in the classic "circular flow" schematic of the economy, with the points corresponding to different "concepts" of size. Thus, the size of the economy measured as expenditure uses the value of final goods and services purchased by firms, households, and governments.[6]

$$Economy = C + I + G$$

where C = consumption of households
       I = investment of households
      G = purchases by government[7]

Seen as income of the "factors of production," the economy's size is given by:

$$Economy = W + P + I + R$$

where W = wages and salaries
      P = profits, whether distributed as dividends or retained by firms
      I = interest payments on other than government debt
      R = rent for land, buildings, machinery, and accommodation[8]

These measures, suitably refined to distinguish net from gross and to connect to the rest of the world, have been central to the development of macroeconomics, to the formulation of policy, and, in a real sense, to defining how we view the history of the past half century at least. From the point of view of the environment, however, the usual series have a very large weakness: They do not reflect nonmarket "transactions." So, for example, they do not reflect the damage caused by the pollution emitted by firms and households. Said another way, there would be no penalty from the damage side for making everything the economy made in the dirtiest possible way as opposed to the cleanest possible way, even though we would expect there to be vastly greater damages in the "dirtiest case."[9]

The "green accountants" described in the text would fix this by inserting penalties into the accounts—welfare corrections for pollution effects and for wasteful exploitation of natural resources such as forests and fish populations. (These latter are somewhat more subtle but are roughly penalties for not taking adequate account of the future.)

numbers that are the heart of development planning and analysis. Again, why is this so? The key, it seems to me, is to be found in the Chapter 5 discussion of the way that benefits or damages accrue to a nation. For the most part they accrue at many specific places, through a variety of routes, and to people who live, work, or recreate in those places. To obtain comprehensive national numbers, which could be argued to reflect the overall effect of a national development policy choice, requires some way of getting at all the places, routes, and people, probably via some sort of sampling. But even devising such a sample would be tricky. Without it, benefit or damage estimates for one river valley's water pollution, or one city's air pollution, or one forest's soil instability, are themselves, in effect, anecdotes. In this sense, Table 14.3 is a compilation of anecdotes.

Recently, a substantial amount of effort has been devoted, particularly by people at the World Resources Institute (WRI), to arguing for and demonstrating the feasibility of making such aggregate corrections. For example, in *Has Environmental Protection Really Reduced Productivity Growth*, Robert Repetto and his coauthors first argue for correcting aggregate data relevant to national productivity for environmental costs (or their avoidance) and then demonstrate the suggested method for three economic sectors, electric utilities, pulp and paper, and agriculture (Repetto et al., 1996). The actual corrections have to be called quick and dirty, based as they are on the use of such rough numbers as average marginal damages per ton of power plant emissions taken from specific studies and applied to the entire U.S. sector.[10] But the demonstration helps make the point that the resulting corrections are not likely to be trivial in size.

The idea behind such efforts, almost needless to say, is to make the penalty for ignoring or abusing the environment explicit and directly comparable with (subtractable from) the ordinary gross domestic (or national) product figures. The other side of this coin is that the corrected measure of economic "well-offness" shows up as larger when efforts are made to reduce pollution or protect natural resources, such as forests.

DOES RISING INCOME LEAD TO BETTER ENVIRONMENT AND THUS TO SUSTAINABILITY?

The monetization of the damages resulting from neglect or actual abuse of the environment, should it prove practical, can be expected at least to clarify the relationship between the environment and economic development. It may or may not lead to different policies, but there is something to be said for substituting facts for rhetoric. Another line of factual inquiry, which has excited the environment-and-development field because of its promise of shedding light on the key question, involves looking at the *actual* relationship between national income (as conventionally defined and without correction for pollution) and some nonmonetized (physical) measure of the severity of environmental damage being done.[11] Usually this analysis is based on cross-section data (data from many countries at a single point in time) and necessarily reflects a substantial smoothing enterprise. For example, the income variable is usually average per capita income. The environmental variable may be explicitly averaged, as by taking all reported hourly ambient SO_2 concentration readings for a country in the year in question and calculating their mean; or implicitly averaged, as by using total annual SO_2 emissions for the year corresponding to the income data.

The result of statistical estimation of the relationship

$$\text{Pollution} = f(x_1, x_2, \ldots, \text{income}, \ldots, x_N)$$

where $x_1, \ldots, x_N$ are other hypothesized influences on pollution, is frequently, though by no means always, found to have an inverted U shape in the income/pollution space (see Figure 14.3). This has come to be called the "Environmental Kuznets Curve" (EKC).[12] The EKC was found in the earliest studies for ambient levels of the air pollutants, SO_2 and suspended particulate matter, with turning points in the range \$3,000 to \$5,000 of per capita GDP. (Looking back at Table 14.1, we see that these levels are found in North Africa, much of Eastern Europe, Central America, and the poorer parts of South America and Asia.) Later studies have used emissions data, which avoids the idiosyncratic nature of the relations between emissions and ambient results across countries due to climate, weather, and geography. These studies have also tended to find significant EKCs for air pollutants, including SO_2, NO_x, particulates, and carbon monoxide (CO). Other, more aggregate measures of environmental stress, such as energy use and traffic volumes, do not display this result, but instead increase monotonically with income.

The simple-minded way to look at this empirical relationship is as evidence for the notion that, eventually, income growth will, one way or another, tend to "fix" environmental problems. *How* this works is of less interest in this view than the fact that it *does* appear to "work." The quotation marks and the words "appear to" are not-so-subtle hints that this relationship may mean a good deal less than meets the eye. For example, it may be that every country has its own relationship between income and environmental "abuse," but that none of these looks anything like the EKC. Two sample possibilities are sketched in Figure 14.4. If you recall the discussion of the identification problem in Chapter 3, you may detect a conceptual similarity here. That is, the cross-section Kuznets curve can be seen as analogous to the

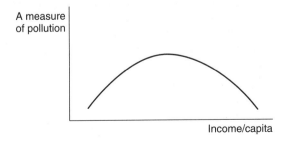

Figure 14.3 A Typical Environmental Kuznets Curve

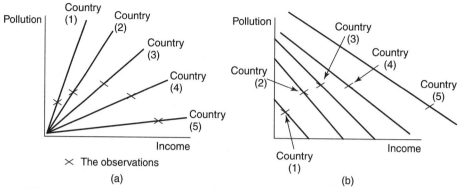

Figure 14.4 Underlying Country-by-Country Relationships That Could Lead to an Environmental Kuznets Curve for a Cross-Section Sample of Countries

result of regressing market data on quantity purchased per period on price data from the same period. In the absence of other data, we have no information on the underlying relationships that led to the equilibrium points actually observed. Trying to project the quantity that will be purchased at some price in a future period is very risky, since the causal relations—demand and supply in that case—are unknown. Similarly, projecting environmental abuse or quality on the basis of future income is also risky in the absence of an understanding of what lies behind the observed points.

More to the point, and more realistically, there is no mechanism that can account for any *automatic* travel along an EKC during the process of development. Not that influences pushing in this direction are lacking. For example, as I have already noted, with increasing income generally come increasing leisure and better access to transportation. All these tend to make outdoor recreation, often in contact with nature, increasingly important. This tends to make people more interested in the environment and more willing to pay to have it "cleaner." Then there is lengthening life span and the accompanying shift in causes of death—generally away from infectious diseases and toward what we might call the afflictions of aging, especially heart disease and cancer. These conditions seem to be related both to personal lifestyle and to chronic exposure to some kinds of pollution. This can focus attention on other aspects of the environment, especially on air pollution and drinking water protection. There may even be a sort of emulation effect at work here. As income rises, a nation may collectively decide it *should* behave more like other high-income nations. And these tend to be aggressive in their approach to environmental protection. (In the case of Eastern Europe, this emulation is a required part of the process of qualifying for membership in the European Union.)

It has been pointed out in critiques of the EKC notion that whatever the *causes* of efforts to improve environmental quality, one of the techniques available so far to countries growing richer has been the availability of poorer countries with resource endowments that encourage them to, in effect, "import" the richer countries' pollution. That is, some of the dirtier industries, especially mining and raw materials processing, are now disappearing from the richer countries but becoming more important to the poorest ones. Because, eventually, there will be no place left to take on this "job," there may be a limit to the ability of nations to reduce pollution, or at least the costs of doing so will become more obvious for later entrants into the game.

But the most important point, in any case, is that conscious political decisions and effective follow-up actions are required to produce a change in environmental direction. A more useful reading of the EKC evidence, then, is that a series of such decisions seems to have been a part of the development process; at least it has played out over the past half century. These decisions involve different specific problems at different levels of economic and technological development. The first items to have to be faced are likely how to handle the human waste from people in urban areas and how to provide safe drinking water to those same people. In some countries there will also be big problems caused by population pressure on forests and other not-yet-developed land. Later, industrial and agricultural pollution will become relatively more important, as will the residuals from energy use and conversion—for example, SO_2 and NO_x from fossil fuel-fired electric generating plants, and lead, unburned hydrocarbons, and CO from transportation.

CONCLUDING COMMENTS

In this chapter I have attempted to give the reader at least a sketch of the environment/development connection by presenting a subset of available data for a sample of developing and developed countries. Beyond the lesson that poor countries really are very poor indeed in money-economy (classic national income accounting) terms, we saw that their citizens face some immediate environmental threats, in particular via contact with and use of water contaminated by human waste. These, in turn, are reflected in high levels of infant and, to a lesser extent, maternal mortality. (The latter may better be seen as a result of low availability of medical care.)

At somewhat higher levels of per capita income, the worst problems of this direct sort seem to be attacked, and the related measures improve. New stresses appear, however, as energy use increases, and the literature exploring the so-called Environmental Kuznets Curves suggests that these may not be dealt with until incomes get into what might be called the medium range—about ten times higher than the lowest levels but still only a fifth or so of the OECD averages.

At every stage there is a desire to increase and sustain the growth of money incomes as traditionally measured, with all that such incomes imply for consumption possibilities. The way success in this game is measured does not count what is happening in the environment, except in a haphazard and sometimes even perverse way. The movement to "correct" the national accounts for environmental public goods and bads attacks this part of the problem head on and is making progress and converts. But this is not something that can be done easily or straightforwardly by just gathering a little more data or inferring something from available market data (as the value of housing services is imputed to homeowners on the basis of housing prices and market rents). Rather, there must be an effort to measure damages from pollution, deforestation, erosion, and other environmental stresses caused by human actions. This immediately brings us up against the techniques of damage and benefit estimation as discussed in chapters 6 through 8 but now applied in quite exotic settings. It is to these applications that I turn in Chapter 15.

NOTES

1. Much of the neoclassical growth literature is easier to read if you see the following:

$$\frac{\partial(K/L)/\partial t}{K/L} = \frac{L\partial K/\partial t - K\partial L/\partial t}{L^2} \cdot \frac{L}{K} = \frac{\dot{K}}{K} - \frac{\dot{L}}{L}$$

2. This version is usually associated with Robert Lucas ("On the Mechanics of Economic Development," 1988).
3. This formulation begs more than intra-time-period distribution. For example, it assumes we have some sort of fix on what will give future generations utility. But if anything seems certain it is that we cannot know this, at least not in great depth and detail. Tastes will change as changing technology opens up new consumption options, and more of the same things we consume today is unlikely to be the optimal consumption package for tomorrow.
4. This was the title of a talk given by Solow in 1992 at Resources for the Future (Solow 1993).
5. The relative importance of agriculture in these countries does not imply the existence of a large modern farming sector. Rather it results from imputing incomes to subsistence farming families or farmers on the edge of the cash economy. That is, there are a lot of people in agriculture in these countries, but they are, for the most part, the poorest of its citizens.
6. Firms purchase both final and "intermediate" goods. The former are investment goods such as machinery and buildings. The latter are purchased current inputs to the production process. All government purchases are defined to be "final."
7. This ignores "net exports" and the connection to the rest of the world more generally.
8. Homeowners are deemed to pay rent to themselves, so this "imputed" rent shows up in both C and R.
9. Things are not quite so simple when we dig a little deeper, however, for there are *market* transactions that *will* reflect the choice between dirty and clean; but these do not consistently push the aggregate measure in the direction that a damage penalty would. For example, on the one hand, investment in pollution control equipment and payments to its operators would tend to make the "clean" aggregate larger than the dirty one. But on the other hand, the damages could lead to consumer purchases, as of health services to fix pollution-related conditions, or of extra tires, paint, and metal house gutters necessitated by pollution damage shortening the lives of these items in normal use. These effects would push in the wrong direction.

10. WRI is not alone in efforts to bridge the gap between the familiar monetized national accounts and the environment. The World Bank, for example, in 1997, published *Expanding the Measure of Wealth: Indicators of Environmentally Sustainable Development.* The Bank's interest, however, in this publication at least, is in "indicators" (or index numbers) rather than in strict monetization on the WRI model.
11. The environmentally relevant data in tables 14.1 through 14.3 may have already suggested to you the possibility of such an investigation. The data used by those who have followed this line of inquiry are not so very different from those you have seen.
12. Simon Kuznets, a Nobel prize winner, was a macro and later a development economist who specialized in very careful accumulation and analysis of data on national income and related measures. The original "Kuznets curve" with this shape involved per capita income and a measure of income inequality. That is, Kuznets found that inequality appeared first to increase and then to decrease as national income grew.

REFERENCES

Brown, Murray. 1987. "Cobb–Douglas functions." In *The New Palgrave Dictionary of Economics,* edited by John Eatwell, Murray Milgate, and Peter Newman. London: Macmillan.

Domar, E. 1947. "Expansion and employment." *American Economic Review* 37(1):343–355.

Harrod, Roy F. 1948. *Towards a Dynamic Economics.* London: MacMillan.

Lucas, Robert E., Jr. 1988. "On the mechanics of economic development." *Journal of Monetary Economics* 22(1):3–42.

Repetto, Robert, Dale Rothman, Paul Faeth, and Duncan Austin. 1996. *Has Environmental Protection Really Reduced Productivity?* Washington, D.C.: World Resources Institute.

Romer, Paul M. 1990. "Endogenous technological change." *Journal of Political Economy* 98(5):S71–S101.

———. 1994. "The origins of endogenous growth." *Journal of Economic Perspectives* 8(1): 3–22.

Solow, Robert Model. 1984. "Perspectives on growth theory." *Journal of Economic Perspectives* 8(1):45–54.

———. 1993. "An almost practical step toward sustainability." *Resources Policy* 19(Sept.): 162–172.

World Bank, 1997. *Expanding the Measure of Wealth: Indicators of Environmentally Sustainable Development.* Washington, D.C.: The World Bank.

15

Estimating Environmental Quality Benefits or Damages in Developing Countries

In the previous chapter I discussed the influential movement pushing for an expanded definition of national income accounting that reflects nonmarket effects of development policies and activities. We might label that the macro impetus to developing and using benefit or damage-estimation methods in the developing country context. There is an accompanying micro-level push as well, which seems to me roughly analogous to the one experienced in the United States from almost two decades of presidential pressure, via executive orders, for the wide application of cost-benefit analysis to policy decisions. That is, the push comes, in a sense, from the top, not the bottom. In the case of developing countries, this "top" is generally the multinational lending agencies such as the World Bank and the Interamerican Development Bank. The latter, for example, requires that all loan proposals include cost-benefit analyses. When the loan involves a project, such as a wastewater treatment plant for a city, that directly affects environmental quality, the estimation of environmental benefits is clearly going to have to be a major focus of the proposal preparation effort. But it is also true that damage (or benefit) estimates are required if a project with a nonenvironmental purpose, such as a road or hydroelectric dam, is projected to have significant side effects on the environment.

The previous chapter also listed some reasons to expect that the relations among population, economy, and environment will be different in developing countries from those found in the OECD world. These included lower incomes, less recreation time, less access to transportation, poorer health status, more people in agriculture—often the peasant or subsistence variety—and a relatively greater role for resource extraction. These differences imply that there may be corresponding differences in the relative importance of specific sources of (or routes to) benefits or damages. As just one fairly obvious example, we would expect the recreation benefits of water quality improvement to be less important relative to other benefit routes in the "typical" developing country than in the typical OECD country. (The most important "other" route would likely be health effects.)

The remainder of this chapter is divided into two major sections. The first discusses methods and the second goes over results. The results of interest include a comparison between developed and developing countries in the relative importance of particular broad benefit or damage routes, and a catalog of developing country results aimed at giving the reader a slightly better feel for the ground being covered.

BENEFIT ESTIMATION METHODS FOR THE DEVELOPING COUNTRY SETTING

In chapters 6 through 8, two broad classes of method were distinguished: indirect and direct. The former methods have long been considered to have the advantage of being based on people's actual choices ("revealed preferences" in economics jargon) in market settings. The tricks are, first, to connect the market setting to the environmental benefit or damage setting and, second, to find the necessary data from the market and to manipulate it in ways consistent with underlying consumer theory and its own structure so that the output is convincing. The direct methods involve asking hypothetical questions more or less directly "about" the environmental project, policy, or action of interest.[1] These methods therefore generate their own data as they go along. The discussion that follows concentrates on assessing the usefulness of these techniques in the developing country setting. For more discussion of the mechanics of each technique refer back to Chapter 7 (indirect) or Chapter 8 (direct).

HEDONICS

The hedonic method is based on the premise that a good (or service) can be defined as a bundle of characteristics or attributes that together determine the price of the good via the demand for and supply of the characteristics in the good market. For example, the price of a residence can be viewed as a function of its size, age, physical condition, proximity to schools or places of work, quality of the environment in which it is located, and so on. Similarly, the wage paid for a job can be expressed as a function of, among other things, the risk of injury associated with the job. These functions are called "hedonic price functions." Once estimated, these functions may be used to generate implicit marginal prices for each of the individual characteristics of the good. Of special interest to us, of course, is the implicit marginal price of environmental quality (or prices, if more than one dimension is investigated).

Even to get this far with hedonics requires data and some confidence that three key assumptions are fulfilled by the market situation generating the data. These assumptions are:

- The market involved (housing or labor) is assumed to be in equilibrium. This is to say that everyone has had a chance to adjust so that MWTP and MC are equal for every individual across all the characteristics. Since at any time there are people trying to buy and others trying to sell houses or labor services, this is never actually true. The practical question becomes: How far from equilibrium does a particular market seem to be?

- Second, buyers and sellers are assumed to be aware, and to "appreciate" the effects, of the environmental quality characteristic(s) of interest. This is symmetric with the requirement that, for example, buyers and sellers know how far a house is from schools and shopping, how many fireplaces it has, and so on. It is also symmetric with the requirement that workers and those hiring them are aware of the hazards posed by any particular job.

- Third, there is assumed to be a sufficiently wide variety of choices on all characteristics that no one is stuck in a "corner solution." That is, if a consumer wants a housing "bundle" that includes three bedrooms, two fireplaces, a large lot, low pollution, and modest distance to the central business district, it must at least be possible to find alternatives that allow trading off along each dimension, including price, of course. There cannot be absolute unavailabilities—for example, no houses with fewer than four bedrooms on lots over certain square footage within some distance of the central business district.

As already noted, these are problematic, even in OECD market settings. Thus, both sellers and, even more likely, buyers, may be unaware of elements of environmental quality or the implications of those elements for their quality of life.[2] And there may, in fact, be "missing choices." Most important, all three assumptions seem less likely to be fulfilled in developing-country applications. That is, developing-country markets are more likely to be regulated in ways that prevent attaining equilibrium. For example, only a few favored builders of houses may be allowed to build on available land and may be required to conform to minimum size requirements. Or there may be residence requirements that do not permit free movement around a metropolitan area. The awareness requirement also seems less likely to be met because of the combination of lower educational levels, less environmental testing and regulation generally, and perhaps even control over the dissemination of "sensitive" information practiced by nervous regimes.

Even where markets are well functioning and individuals well informed, data collection may be much more problematic in developing countries. That is, there is likely to be relative scarcity of monetary land and property transactions in many cultures. And those that do occur may not be recorded in a fashion required for economic analysis.

Although these are certainly not all of the practical problems associated with hedonic analysis, they are the ones most relevant to developing country applications and should adequately convey the difficulties of applying the methodology in that context. Further, as pointed out in Chapter 7, hedonic models can provide only a partial measure of a change in environmental quality, because they capture only one aspect of the effect of environmental quality, that is, hedonic property models only measure WTP for the attributes of quality that are "captured" by choice of residence, while ignoring willingness to pay for environmental improvements at other points in the region, for example, in the work place, shopping districts, or parks and recreational areas.

Given these practical problems, it is little wonder that few hedonic studies have actually been carried out in developing countries, as is indicated by Table 15.1. Sim-

TABLE 15.1 Numbers of Studies Applying the Hedonic Property Pricing Method

Area of Application	In USA	In Europe	In Developing Countries
Agriculture	Few[a]		
Air quality	Many	Some	
Health risks	Few		
Hunting	Few		
Noise	Many	Many	
Parks, nature reserves, & wildlife	Many	Some	
Water quality	Few		
Water supply & sanitation	Few	Few	Few

[a] "Few" is not defined by Georgiou et al., but it seems safe to take it to mean one to three or four. "Some" is defined as up to ten and "many" as more than ten.
Source: Georgiou et al., *Economic Values and the Environment in the Developing World*, 1997.

ilarly, there are few examples of hedonic wage studies, for much the same reasons.[3] Nonetheless, the partial derivative of a first-stage hedonic price function has been used to produce an approximate benefit number for "neighborhood" or "local" effects of environmental change, such as might be introduced by the construction of a sewer:

> . . . simple versions of the technique may be (indeed have been) useful in establishing the effects on property values of improvements in neighborhood amenities such as water supply, rubbish collection, street lighting, etc. providing there is data on property values before and after the changes, and so give rough estimates of benefits. (Pearce et al., 1994, p. 147)

However, as has been demonstrated by William Vaughan (1988), even a "correct" application of first-stage estimation can generate estimates that are two to three times as large as the "true" benefits. As a result, even the reduced effort needed to generate first-stage estimates seems unlikely to be merited, given the quality of the results.

TRAVEL-COST METHODOLOGY

A second indirect observed method of measurement of nonmarket benefits is the travel-cost methodology (TCM). As described in Chapter 7, TCM values a recreational site or characteristic by using the value of the time and other cost incurred in visiting the site as a proxy or for what a visitor would be willing to pay to visit the site. The most basic version of TCM is a continuous demand model for a single site, in which individuals maximize utility by choosing the number of visits to the site subject to monetary and time constraints. This maximization generates the individual's demand function for the site, from which consumer surplus can be calculated and aggregated across individuals.

Although there have been some applications of TCM in developing countries,

TABLE 15.2 Numbers of Studies Applying the Travel-Cost Method

Area of Application	In USA	In Europe	In Developing Countries
Fishing: Recreational	Many[a]	Many	
Parks, nature reserves, & wildlife	Many	Many	Some
Water quality	Many	Some	Few
Water supply & sanitation	Few	Few	

[a] "Few" is not defined by Georgiou et al., but it seems safe to take it to mean one to three or four. "Some" is defined as up to ten and "many" as more than ten.

Source: Georgiou et al., *Economic Values and the Environment in the Developing World*, 1997.

as shown in Table 15.2, the focus of the TCM studies that value recreational sites is generally on international visitors and therefore, of limited use, because most applications to actual decisions confine attention to *domestic* WTP for the project being analyzed.[4] Unlike hedonic analysis, the essential problem in applying the methodology in developing countries is not so much an absence of external sources of data as it is an absence (or at least alteration) of the relationship between environmental quality and the recreational "market." That is, as already noted, where people are poorer and have less access to transportation, travel for any sort of recreation may be very limited. As a result, TCM may be of limited help in estimating the (domestic) benefits of water treatment projects as they accrue via water-based recreational sites, because so few nationals incur the kinds of travel costs needed for TCM to generate valid WTP estimates; and because these values, if estimated, are likely to be small in relation to other project benefits. In addition, the great majority of travel-cost studies value a recreational site *as it exists*. Valuing the introduction of a new site or proposed changes to an existing site, as would be required for analysis of a water quality improvement project, requires more sophisticated versions of TCM, and these are necessarily more data intensive and assumption sensitive.

AVERTING BEHAVIOR

The third type of indirect observed benefit estimation technique to be discussed here, averting behavior, infers a value for an improvement in environmental quality from changes in spending on ways to reduce the impact of the lower quality. Examples of averting behaviors used for studies include: boiling water for cooking and drinking, staying indoors during times of heavy air pollution, purchasing an air conditioner, and using bottled water for drinking. Averting behavior techniques provide a relatively straightforward route to estimating environmental quality use values when the environmental threat or harm is known and effective averting behaviors exist. Unfortunately, the results are often imprecise, because the averting measures cannot, in general, produce exactly what we are looking for—willingness to pay to reduce the effects of pollution. There are several interpretation problems here that can be illustrated by the air conditioner example. First, the physical amount of "averting" that is accomplished is far from clear because people do not and cannot live life entirely in their homes. But neither can the air conditioner's cost be confidently apportioned 100 percent to averting pollution, because these appliances produce other important (almost certainly more important) outputs as well. How much of the cost "ought to" fall in the averting "account" is probably impossible to tell. And, in any case, in dealing with the damage from ambient air pollution, people may well adopt other strategies as well. For example, we have all seen pictures of Asian city dwellers wearing surgical masks.

Attempts to value environmental quality changes using averting behavior suffer from at least four other problems or complications. First, if conditions get too bad, people are apt to simply relocate, thoroughly complicating the sampling and valuation processes. Second, the model depends upon people's subjective perceptions of the environmental deterioration and of the risk of harm to themselves, which do not necessarily correspond to actual environmental conditions. Third, the behavior often involves some form of discontinuous choice, such as a capital investment in the purchase of an air conditioner or water filter. Presented with this investment decision, people tend initially to resist the purchase, but when the decision to purchase is made, it is guided by long-term expectations as to future environmental conditions and therefore is difficult to interpret in relation to current conditions, even to *perceived* current conditions. Fourth, market imperfections, such as credit rationing, can constrain behavior. As a result of these problems, while values for changes in environmental quality based on averting behavior may be relatively easy to obtain, it is essentially impossible to know whether they understate, overstate, or correctly state the populations' WTP to reduce pollution loads.

Given these problems, it is not surprising that the averting behavior method has not been used with anywhere near the frequency of the first two methods in either developed or developing countries. However, the one area where the methodology may have the most to contribute is in the analysis of water quality improvement projects. There are a number of reasons for this assertion. First, the perceived risks from poor water quality and the behaviors that can avoid these risks are relatively easily known and understood. Second, these behaviors are often within the means of developing country residents. Third, the results may be more easily communicated to, and related to by, decision makers than estimates generated by more esoteric or hypothetical methods. Finally, it may often be the cheapest of the available methods.[5]

DIRECT, HYPOTHETICAL, OR "STATED PREFERENCE" METHODS

CONTINGENT VALUATION

Just a few years ago, the inclusion of a section on hypothetical methods in a review of benefit estimation in developing countries would have been pointless, even though the methods were being widely applied in the United States. However, the difficulties encountered in applying the data-intensive, revealed-preference methodologies and the successes achieved in using hypothetical methods—predominantly in estimating demand for water supply and sanitation—have so completely reversed this perception that hypothetical methodologies are now actually seen to enjoy an advantage over indirect methods in developing countries:

> Ten years ago only a handful of very rudimentary [CV] studies had been conducted in developing countries; at the time the conventional wisdom was that it simply could not be done. The problems associated with posing hypothetical questions to low-income, perhaps illiterate respondents were assumed to be so overwhelming that one should not even try. Today we have come full circle; it is now assumed by many environmental and resource economists working in developing countries that CV surveys are straightforward and easy to do. . . . Bilateral donor agencies and the international development banks are increasingly putting [CV] techniques to use in project and policy appraisal as part of their everyday operations work. . . . Moreover, in light of the controversy over the use of [CV] in the United States, most future applications of [CV] are likely to be in developing countries. (Whittington, 1998)

Table 15.3 summarizes the key advantages and disadvantages of the CV method. The survival and growth of CV in spite of the attacks on its validity probably have more to do with its advantages in being able to address almost any policy question asked and being able to measure total economic value (TEV) than in the effectiveness of the responses to these attacks. Although some authors have discounted the importance of nonuse values in the developing country context, and thus the importance of measuring TEV, there are developing country examples where nonuse values are clearly important—the symbolic value accorded to Rio de Janiero's Guanabara Bay by Brazilians seems to be such an example. In addition to nonuse values, some use values can be important and yet difficult to measure by revealed preference methods. And in any case, as pointed out in Chapter 7, trying to arrive at TEV by adding up the results of separate revealed preference methods applied to different routes to benefits is fraught with difficulty because of the near certainty of underlaps and overlaps. Finally, there is the problem of the "external data" required by the revealed preference methodologies and the advantages of conducting surveys in developing countries:

TABLE 15.3 Advantages and Disadvantages of Contingent Valuation Method

Advantages	Disadvantages
1. Is applicable to more environmental goods	1. Is based on respondents' stated intentions
2. Directly (but *not* separately) measures nonuse benefits	2. Places respondents in unfamiliar decision setting
3. Directly estimates correct Hicksian welfare measure if questions correctly phrased	3. Depends on creation of understandable, plausible scenario
4. Can incorporate reliability and validity checks	4. Is vulnerable to abuse in survey design
	5. Is sensitive to econometric specification when using yes/no or ranking questions

> There are some contingent valuation researchers (I count myself among them) that believe it is easier to administer high quality contingent valuation surveys in some developing countries than it is in industrialized countries. For example response rates are typically very high in developing countries, and respondents are often quite receptive to listening and considering the questions posed. Also interviewers are inexpensive relative to prices in industrialized countries. This allows CV researchers to use larger sample sizes and conduct more elaborate split-sample experiments. (Whittington, 1996, p. 28)

The use of CV in developing countries also presents a number of unique challenges, however. For one thing, many developing country economies may be only partially monetized, causing difficulties in translating values into monetary terms. This need not be an insurmountable obstacle when some other unit of value is appreciated by the population to be sampled—volumes of rice or grain, for example. A second challenge is presented by the translation of the survey instrument and responses into local languages or dialects. Third, considerable attention must be paid to local institutional and cultural issues. The survey designer must be sensitive to the attitudes of local people and their perceptions about local, national, and international institutions. Focus groups are a useful way to learn which payment vehicle, funding, and service delivery mechanism CV survey respondents are likely to trust. Also, respondents who are reluctant to say "no" to a question because of local mores pose interesting challenges for researchers using hypothetical methods. Finally, since developing country applications rely almost exclusively on personal interviews, asking face to face about what may appear to respondents or interviewers to be ridiculously high or low numbers may lead to distorted responses.

One observer has suggested the overall evaluations shown in Table 15.4 as a starting point for choosing a benefit (damage) estimation technique in the developing country context. The overall effect of these perceived advantages seems to be

TABLE 15.4 Evaluation of Nonmarket Benefit Estimation Methods[a]

Methodology	Validity and Reliability	Comprehensiveness	Completeness	Ease of Implementation
Dose response	✓	⊖ ⊖	✓✓✓	
Hedonic market	✓	✓	⊖	✓
Travel cost	✓	✓	⊖	✓
Averting behavior	✓	✓	⊖	✓
Contingent valuation	✓	✓✓✓	✓✓✓	✓✓

[a] Where ⊖ ⊖ represents a very low score, ⊖ a low score, ✓ a moderate score, ✓✓ a high score, and ✓✓✓ a very high score.

Source: Ruud Hoevenagel, "A Comparison of Economic Valuation Methods," 1994, pp. 251–69.

TABLE 15.5 Number of Studies Applying the Methodologies in Developing Countries

Area of Application	Hedonic	TCM[a]	Averting Behavior	CV[b]
Fishing: Commercial				Zero-Few
Fishing: Recreational				Zero-Few
Parks, nature reserves, & wildlife		Some		Some
Water quality		Few	Zero-Few	Some
Water supply & sanitation	Few[c]			Many

[a] TCM, travel-cost methodology. [b] CV, contingent valuation. [c] "Few" is not defined by Georgiou et al., but it seems safe to take it to mean one to three or four. "Some" is defined as up to ten and "many" as more than ten.

Source: Georgiou et al., *Economic Values and the Environment in the Developing World*, 1997.

making CV the method of choice in developing countries, as illustrated in Table 15.5 compiled from Tables 15.1 and 15.2 plus information from the cited source on CV applications.

SOME EVIDENCE ON CONTRASTS BETWEEN DEVELOPING AND DEVELOPED COUNTRIES

The first part of this chapter stressed differences between developing and developed countries in the likely importance of various routes by which benefits accrue to society from an improvement in environmental quality. Both because of the imprecision of the notion and the lack of appropriate data, any exploration of this assertion must necessarily be impressionistic.[6] Nonetheless, even an impression may help us gain some insight into the development and environment problem more generally. Let's look at two areas: measuring and valuing the health effects of air and water pollution, and estimating WTP for water quality improvement at recreational beaches.

THE HEALTH EFFECTS OF AIR AND WATER POLLUTION

We might well expect that in developing countries, water pollution would take a greater health toll than air pollution, while the opposite would be true in developed countries. These are expected *relative*, not absolute, rankings. In developed countries, both types of pollution may be responsible for fewer deaths and disabilities. The reason for this hypothesis about relative deadliness is that, while everyone is more or less equally vulnerable to similar levels of air pollution, citizens of wealthier countries are much better protected against ambient water pollution. In particular they almost always have piped drinking water that has been treated to reduce disease transmission to close to zero, even if upstream wastewater treatment is less than perfect. It is also almost never necessary for them to come in contact with polluted water, while in developing countries not only may drinking water be withdrawn individually, *untreated*, from polluted water courses, but other basic household functions such as bathing and doing laundry may be accomplished in ambient water, not in the house with piped water. All this vastly increases exposure to pathogens.

This expectation is borne out by the data presented in Table 15.6, in which estimates of deaths, years of life lost, and disability-adjusted life years lost are shown for developing and developed countries, as attributed to water and air quality problems. Thus, the damage measures attributable to water pollution are vastly smaller in the OECD world, both in numbers and as percentages of the corresponding aggregate (deaths, YLLs, etc.). And while the air pollution *numbers* are also smaller, air pollution-related damages account for much larger percentages of the corresponding aggregates.

Another way of examining relative importance is to look at monetized damage estimates. To this end, in Table 15.7, the results of studies in six developing countries and two in the United States are compared, with the results having been transformed into 1996 U.S. dollars per capita.

Because the studies in Table 15.7 reflect different assumptions, not to mention different techniques, and seek to answer different questions (what are the benefits of x? versus what are the damages suffered in the absence of any change?) it is hardly surprising that the numbers reported are all over the lot. To the extent there seems to be a pattern, it is that the air pollution-related numbers are smaller in developing countries. This is consistent with the evidence in Table 15.6 that the physical burden of air pollution on health is not hugely different between the two categories of countries and with the observation that, because WTP is related to income, the valuation of those physical burdens should raise the relative money damages for the developed world.

TABLE 15.6 Health Effects of Air/Water Pollution in Developing and Developed Countries

Risk Factor	Deaths (000s)	% of Total Deaths	YLLs[a] (000s)	% of Total YLLs	DALYs[b] (000s)	% of Total DALYs
Water, sanitation, & hygiene						
Developing	2,665	6.7	85,436	10.4	93,163	7.6
Developed	3.5	0.0	83	0.1	229	0.1
Air pollution						
Developing	293	0.7	3,995	0.5	4,828	0.4
Developed	275	2.5	1,630	1.9	2,426	1.5

[a] Years of life lost. [b] A DALY (disability-adjusted life year) is one lost year of healthy life, either due to premature death or disability "of specified severity and duration" (Murray and Lopez, 1996, p. 6).

Source: Christopher Murray and Alan D. Lopez, "Quantifying the Burden of Disease and Injury Attributable to Ten major Risk Factors," 1996, pp. 295–324.

TABLE 15.7 Some Evidence of Per Capita Environmental
Health Damages and Benefits

Source	Country	Nation/Region/ City as Applicable	Damages or Benefits	Air Pollution Related	Water Pollution Related
Margulis (1992)	Mexico	Nation	Damages	$15	$50
World Bank (n.d.)	Chile	Santiago	Benefits	24[a]	[b]
World Bank (1996)	Brazil	Rio de Janiero	Benefits[c]	72	–
Maimon (n.d.)	Brazil	Rio de Janiero	Damages	–	2
Serôa da Motta et al. (n.d.)	Brazil	All urban areas	Damages	–	6
Albernini et al. (1996)	Taiwan	Three urban areas	Benefits[d]	$9.80–39.60	–
Freeman (1982)	USA	Nation	Benefits[e]	259	11[f]
Public Interest Economics Foundation (1984)	USA	Nation	Benefits[g]	147–402	–

[a] Benefits of reducing but not eliminating particulates less than 10 μ in diameter, ozone, NO_2, and SO_2 by an average of about 10%. [b] The study provides an estimate of the benefits of avoiding the irrigation of locally consumed fruits and vegetables with typhoid-contaminated wastewater. [c] These are referred to in the study as damages but seem to have been calculated as damages avoided by decreasing air pollution (particulates less than 10 μ in diameter) by about 40%, from 83 $\mu g/m^3$ to 50 $\mu g/m^3$, the desired ambient standard. [d] These are the benefits of 50-percent reductions in PM_{10}, SO_2, and O_3 based on work in three urban areas in Taiwan. [e] Freeman estimated the air pollution control benefits of 20% reductions in ambient levels of total suspended particulates (from 106 $\mu g/m^3$) and SO_2 (from 23 $\mu g/m^3$) and a 30% reduction in carbon monoxide, all in annual average terms. [f] On the water side, Freeman estimated the benefits of going from the 1970 status quo to the technology-based treatment standards of the original clean water legislation (see Chapter 2). These included recreation prominently. The health benefits, reported here, were estimated to be about one-tenth of the total. [g] Freeman's work updated to reflect other studies and considering also reductions in lead.

There is both less to compare and higher within-category variation where water damages and benefits are concerned. The developing country numbers on the water side differ by a factor of 25 from highest to lowest, while on the air side we see a factor of about 7. That said, I would expect the developing country numbers to show up as substantially larger than those from the United States for the reasons already suggested, *even after* the reflection of higher U.S. WTP to avoid health effects. The Brazilian numbers are very low compared even with Freeman's U.S. number, even allowing for Rio's status as a cosmopolitan world-class city.

RECREATION VALUES IN DEVELOPED AND DEVELOPING COUNTRIES

Turning from health to recreation (with some associated nonuse value), there seems every reason to expect these values to be more important in developed countries than in developing countries because they are likely to be luxury "goods."

> One could imagine a hierarchy of values which emerge in response to and as a result of economic growth. Initially people are willing to pay for environmental improvements that yield increases in real money income. These are the environmental

effects which influence productive capacity. Then they become willing to pay for improvements in quality which enhance the utility of nonmarket activities. Finally, as their expanded budget constraints allow them, they are willing to pay for the presence of environmental quality, regardless of its direct impact on them. (McConnell and Ducci, 1989, p. 3)

Other authors have taken this argument a step further, asserting that CV surveys are not appropriate for use in developing countries because questions about nonuse values are not relevant to developing countries. They criticize efforts to apply the CV and travel-cost methodologies to developing countries because they believe that, in those countries, environmental functions and components are much more important as inputs to production processes than as environmental amenities generating recreation or nonuse values.

It does not seem, however, that this claim is supported by the small empirical literature that exists. For example, the results from six CV surveys regarding water quality improvement at local beaches—summarized in Table 15.8—seem to indicate that respondents in both developing and developed countries are likely, on average, to be willing to contribute less than 1 percent of their incomes to such causes. Two points about this table need to be made, however. First, the dollar amounts are not stated in terms of a common base year, because few of the studies disclose the year in which the data were gathered. Second, comparability problems related to the degree of water quality change are even more relevant in CV studies such as these, because, while it is difficult to measure the extent of change in water quality (and the size of the area in which the change will occur) envisioned by the surveyors, it is impossible to measure the extent of change envisioned by the respondents. As a result, it is not clear if these studies are comparable in any meaningful way. However, what can be said with some degree of certainty is that there is no indication that the use of CV for measuring environmental improvement in recreational resources is any *less* useful or appropriate in developing than developed countries. On the contrary, as discussed above, there are reasons for thinking it to be *more* useful.

TABLE 15.8 Willingness to Pay for Water Quality Improvement at Local Beaches

Study	Area	Mean Annual WTP (per household)	% of Income
McConnell and Ducci (1989)	Uruguay	$14	0.4%
Darling et al. (1993)	Barbados	$11	NA
Choe et al. (1996)	Davao, Philippines	$12–24	< 1%
Bockstael et al. (1989)	Baltimore/Washington	$9–183	< 1%
Hayes et al. (1992)	Rhode Island	$80–187	< 1%
Georgiou et al. (1997)	East Anglia, UK	$21	< 1%

BENEFIT ESTIMATES FROM LATIN AMERICA SPECIFICALLY[7]

Local Sewers

A review of documentation in twenty-six project loan applications approved by the Interamerican Development Bank (IDB) since 1989, and having water quality improvement as an explicit goal, uncovered useful benefits estimates in eighteen cases, almost all of which involved CV estimates of national resident WTP.[8] With only a few exceptions, a referendum question format was employed by the analysts, consistent with the NOAA Blue Ribbon Panel's recommendations on CV protocols (see Chapter 8). The projects being financed usually include potable water supply, household sewer connections, and drainage via collector and interceptor sewers; followed by wastewater treatment, or some subset of these components.[9] Given the design characteristics of the projects, two categories of benefit predominate: the neighborhood effects of sewering and the more general ambient water quality improvement in the river or coastal water to which the sewage is discharged.

Construction of a combined sanitary sewer system (household connections with storm drainage) produces a cost savings for connected residents who no longer have to maintain and eventually replace more expensive individual wastewater disposal solutions like cesspools and septic tanks. Moreover, it provides a greater level of what one might call "desirability" attached to the absence of clogged piping and foul smells in the vicinity of the home, the avoidance of flood damage to personal property, and the alleviation of transportation delays in rainy periods. Other benefits include the reduction of health risks through the elimination of pools of polluted standing water in the neighborhood and even some localized improvements in the quality of watercourses (creeks, ravines) that formerly received the polluted domestic, commercial, and industrial discharges and storm runoff flows that sanitary sewer projects collect and channel elsewhere, usually to a consolidated downstream outfall. CV estimates of the WTP for sewer connections (sanitation and drainage) appear in Table 15.9. On average, households in this small sample of projects claim to be willing to pay 3 percent of their income each month (a recurrent, not a one-time, charge) to have a sewer connection and drainage service.

The sample average WTP of almost U.S. $20 per month (U.S. $240 per year) is influenced by the underlying distribution of income levels across the project sample. The relation between income and stated WTP implies a positive and highly statistically significant income elasticity of WTP of 0.54. While one should not make too much of the magnitude of the elasticity, the fact that it is positive and significant across a sample of independently produced expectations of WTP in different projects provides at least a consistency check on the pattern in the data generated via CV. The existence of no relationship between WTP and income would be cause for concern about the plausibility of the method. The income levels in the sample are generally low, however, since IDB projects are often focused on low-income beneficiaries in the client countries, so the WTP elasticity cannot be taken to be a global estimate across all income levels in all countries.

TABLE 15.9 Inter-American Development Bank Contingent Valuation Estimates of Willingness to Pay for Local Sewer and Drainage (1996 U.S. dollars)[a]

Country	Mean WTP (per household)	Household Monthly Income	WTP as a Percentage of Income
Argentina	$21.01	$721	2.9
Argentina	47.27	1,471	3.2
Bahamas[b]	16.82	NA	NA
Brazil (excludes drainage)	28.96	1,094	2.6
Brazil (sewer plus drainage)	15.95	399	4.0
Brazil	12.70	343	3.7
Brazil	16.36	343	4.8
Brazil	16.75	558	3.0
Colombia	2.32	NA	NA
Colombia	15.60	233	6.7
Ecuador	12.15	NA	NA
Uruguay	26.69	348	7.7
Uruguay	21.50	NA	NA
Average:	$19.54	$612	3.2%
Standard Deviation:	$10.67	$416	NA
Median:	$16.75	$399	4.2%

[a] Converted using the exchange rate of the period and the U.S. Bureau of Labor Statistics Implicit Price Deflator. [b] Includes sewer benefits plus benefits of ensuring water at beaches is safe for contact recreation.

Benefits More Generally

CV estimates of WTP for ambient water quality (AEQ) improvement are even more of a mixed bag than sewer benefits, mainly because the no-project AEQ baseline and the extent of AEQ improvement to be provided by the project are often unclear in the documents reviewed. Table 15.10 provides fifteen estimates culled from eleven different project documents. Since very few of the documents clearly report the average income of the beneficiary population, the table does not risk stating an income level,[10] and no income elasticity estimate for the value of ambient water quality improvements is possible with these data. However, it is possible to hazard a guess about what level of improvement is being valued. On the basis of the current AEQ status reported, it is safe to assume a very poor initial level of water quality, with only a few exceptions. Ignoring differentiated levels of AEQ achievement and taking a crude sample average in Table 15.9 suggests that, in contrast with the Table 15.8 results, households are WTP only about 30 percent as much for the more amorphous and distant (in both time and space) AEQ improvements in major watercourses ($5.78) as they are for the more concrete and immediate utility gains from having sewers. It does not seem at all implausible to find this relationship among respon-

TABLE 15.10 Inter-American Development Bank Project Estimates of Willingness to Pay for General Ambient Water Quality Improvements in Rivers, Lakes, and Coastal Waters (1996 U.S. dollars)[a]

Country	Method	AEQ Target	Mean WTP/ Household/Month
Bahamas	CV[b]	Beaches—swimmable water	$1.04
Brazil	CV	River pollution control–no specifics	7.85
Brazil	CV	Beaches—swimmable water	7.74
Brazil	CV	Beaches—swimmable water	5.40
Brazil	CV	Beaches—swimmable water	7.28
Colombia	CV	Odor elimination	3.24
Colombia	CV(Direct)	Odor elimination	3.28
Colombia	CV(Direct)	Odor elimination & aesthetics	7.14
Colombia	CV (Direct)	Swimmable water	11.34
Colombia	CV	Swimmable water	3.72
Ecuador	Hedonic	Property "affected" by pollution	4.20
Mexico	CV	Clean river—no specifics	6.30
Nicaragua	CV	Odor elimination & aesthetics	4.00
Paraguay	CV	Improvement in water quality	13.38
Uruguay	CV	Beaches—swimmable water	0.74
		Average:	$5.78
		Standard Deviation:	$3.50
		Median:	$5.40

[a] WTP expressed in constant 1996 U.S.$ by application of the U.S. Bureau of Labor Statistics Implicit Price Deflator.
[b] CV means referendum question format unless otherwise noted.

dents of limited means, who, of necessity, give greater weight to interventions providing a higher relative portion of use than of nonuse values.[11]

CONCLUSION

This chapter has looked at environmental quality damage and benefit estimation in developing countries with two goals. The first was to assess the usefulness of the techniques that are available. The second was to provide some feeling for the sizes of the relevant numbers, both within the developing world and in comparison to analogous numbers from the developed countries.

The executive summary in the matter of technique seems to be that, contrary to early expectations and pronouncements, the direct survey methods are taking over the field in developing countries. A major reason is that it is even harder to apply the data-intensive indirect techniques in developing countries, where the required data are often just not there. A second reason is that, given care and sensitivity to local language, customs, and "world views," the survey technique is useful even in (or perhaps because of) the absence of a history of public opinion and market polling.

Where the numbers are concerned, the lessons are somewhat less clear-cut. It does seem that the really big environmentally created public health problems in developing countries arise from lack of sanitation services and involve contact with contaminated ambient watercourses. These problems have all but disappeared from the developed world after about a century of investment in sewering, wastewater treatment, and provision of extensively treated potable water to homes. Where air pollution is concerned, the two categories of country look much more alike. This must be in large part because the sources and routes of exposure are very similar. When the physical effects are valued, however, the developed world seems to have a relatively larger problem on its hands because the (income-related) WTP to avoid the effects is much greater. This is *not* to say, I hasten to add, that developing countries can afford to ignore the air quality problems of their biggest cities. Some of these, such as Mexico City, São Paulo, Bangkok, and Beïjing live with truly appalling air, and major local efforts at cleanup are likely to be economically justified. It is to say that, as a general proposition, fixing the water sanitation problem is probably where the next dollar of environmental investment ought to go in most of the lowest income developing countries.

NOTES

1. "More or less directly" refers to the contrast between what we may call traditional contingent valuation (describing a change or condition and asking directly for a WTP number to ensure it happens), and some version of the vector ranking or rating approach in which an inference about the WTP value being sought is derived statistically (see Chapter 8).

2. For example, it was not so many years ago that almost no one was aware that radon gas, a by-product of the natural breakdown of trace radioactive elements in rocks of the earth's crust, could seep into and accumulate in homes, raising cancer probabilities for the inhabitants. The quantity of radon and hence the size of the increased cancer risk depends on the type of underlying rock and soil and the design of the house. Today, most people have at least heard about radon, so its inclusion in an hedonic equation would be less problematic than it would have been two decades ago.

3. "Labour markets in developing countries are likely to be highly imperfect, often having an excess supply of labour. People may even disregard risk in the search for a job and income if they are poor. Furthermore, risk perceptions are unlikely to be high, and the returns to a job may depend on caste, class, etc. Data requirements make the approach prohibitively expensive and so few uses in developing countries are envisaged" (Pearce et al., *Project and Policy Appraisal: Integrating Economics and Environment*, 1994, p. 150.

4. In the context of major national parks and preserves, a measurement of the producer surplus generated by international tourism would be appropriate. Another area of application of TCM in developing countries is to projects improving conditions of fuel-wood

and drinking water supply where consumers of these goods must spend substantial time and effort to collect and transport them.

5. The common practice of crediting wastewater treatment plants with reducing either the costs of downstream intake treatment of municipal drinking water or the costs associated with treating water for reuse in irrigation are aggregate applications of the averting behavior method.

6. The imprecision has, in turn, several sources. One is the vast differences, already cataloged, among the developing countries. A second is the aggregation problem, where the measure of improvement will usually be very location specific and its value will depend on the characteristics of the specific population affected. Such local values can vary hugely across a single nation.

7. These estimates come from loan application documents submitted to the Interamerican Development Bank.

8. In two or three cases, producer surplus estimates were produced for tourism effected by improvement in marine coastal waters, but they were not firmly grounded in survey data and are not discussed. Similarly, estimates of medical costs avoided were undertaken a few times, but they too do not appear reliable. One hedonic analysis was done and is included.

9. Potable water supply benefits are obtained for these purposes by integrating under statistically estimated demand functions, and are not of concern here.

10. It is dangerous to presume that the expected value for general AEQ improvement reported in Bank documents is independent of income, or that the same average income applies that was used for sewerage (if both elements are present). The scope of beneficiary population for AEQ benefit evaluation is often the population of the entire city, not just a neighborhood.

11. It would probably be a stretch to try to read anything more into the limited information in Tables 15.8 and 15.9. In particular, no test is done of the statistical significance of the roughly $14/household/month difference between average WTP for sewerage and improved AWQ. Nor is any effort made to translate the description of the AWQ target in likely categories of improvement "size" in order to see if there is any relation between that size and the stated WTP.

REFERENCES

Albernini, Anna, Maureen Cropper, Tsu-Tan Fu, Alan Krupnick, Jin-Tan Liu, Daigee Shaw, and Winston Harrington. 1996. "What is the value of reduced morbidity in Taiwan? In *The Economics of Pollution Control in the Asia Pacific*, edited by Robert Mendelsohn and Daigee Shaw. Cheltenham, U.K.: Edward Elgar.

Bockstael, N.E., Kenneth E. McConnell, and Ivar E. Strand. 1989. "Measuring the benefits of improvements in water quality: The Chesapeake Bay." *Marine Resource Economics* 6(1):1–18.

Choe, KyeongAe, Dale Whittington, and Donald T. Lauria. 1996. "The economic benefits of surface water quality improvements in developing countries: A case study of Davao, Philippines." *Land Economics* 72(4) (Nov.):519–537.

Darling, A., C. Gomez, and M. Niklitschek. 1993. "The question of a public sewerage system in a Caribbean country: A case study. In *Environmental Economics and Natural Re-*

source Management in Developing Countries, edited by M. Munasinghe. Committee of International Development Institutions on the Environment (CIDIE), World Bank. Washington, D.C.: The World Bank.

Freeman, A. Myrick III. 1982. *Air and Water Pollution Control: A Benefit-Cost Assessment.* New York: John Wiley.

Georgiou, Stavros, Dale Whittington, David Pearce, and Dominic Moran. 1997. *Economic Values and the Environment in the Developing World.* Cheltenham, U.K.: Edward Elgar.

Hayes, Karen M., Timothy J. Tyrrell, and Glen Anderson. 1992. "Estimating the benefits of water quality improvements in the Upper Narragansett Bay." *Marine Resource Economics* 7(1):75–85.

Hoevenagel, Ruud. 1994. "A comparison of economic valuation methods." In Rudiger Pethig (ed.), *Valuing the Environment: Methodological and Measurement Issues.* Dordrecht, the Netherlands: Kluwer Academic Publishers.

Maimon, Dalia. n.d. "Health impacts of chemical pollution and domestic wastewater in Rio de Janeiro metropolitan region." Report to the Environment Department Policy and Research Division of the World Bank.

Margulis, S. 1992. *Back-of-the-Envelope Estimates of Environmental Damage Costs in Mexico.* Working Paper Series, No. 824. Washington, D.C.: The World Bank.

McConnell, Kenneth E., and Jorge H. Ducci. 1989. "Valuing environmental quality in developing countries: Two case studies." Paper presented at a session of the American Economic Association Meeting, Atlanta, Georgia.

Murray, Christopher J. L., and Alan D. Lopez, 1996. "Quantifying the burden of disease and injury attributable to ten major risk factors." In *The Global Burden of Disease: A Comprehensive Assessment of Mortality and Disability from Diseases, Injuries and Risk Factors in 1990 and Projected to 2020*, edited by Christopher J. L. Murray and Alan D. Lopez. Cambridge, Mass.: Harvard School of Public Health, pp. 295–324.

Pearce, David W., Dale Whittington, Stavros Georgiou, and David James. 1994. *Project and Policy Appraisal: Integrating Economics and Environment.* Paris: Organization for Economic Cooperation and Development.

Public Interest Economics Foundation. 1984. "The aggregate benefits of air pollution control." Prepared for the Office of Policy Analysis, Environmental Protection Agency.

Serôa da Motta, Ronaldo, Ana Paula Fernandes Mendes, Francisco Eduardo Mendes, and Carlos Eduardo Frickmann Young. n.d. "Environmental damages and services due to household water use." Working Paper No. 258. Rio de Janeiro, Brazil: Instituto de Pesquisa Econômica Aplicada.

Vaughan, William J. 1988. "Empirical issues in the estimation of hedonic rent or property value equations and their use in prediction." OEO working paper, OEO/WP-02/88. Washington, D.C.: Inter-American Development Bank.

Whittington, Dale, 1998. "Administering contingent valuation surveys in developing countries." *World Development.* 26:21–30.

World Bank. 1996. *Brazil: Managing Environmental Pollution in the State of Rio de Janeiro. Vol. 2: Technical Report.* Report No. 15488-BR. Washington, D.C.: The World Bank.

World Bank. n.d. *Chile—Managing Environmental Problems: Economic Analysis of Select Issues.* Washington, D.C.: The World Bank.

16

Choosing Instruments of Environmental Policy in the Developing Country Context

In chapters 9 and 10, the available alternatives for implementing chosen environmental goals—policy instruments—were described and categorized. Criteria relevant to choosing among them were set out and some important but often overlooked results were derived. Most important, I think, the static efficiency property of so-called market-based instruments was shown to imply a need for (1) substantial information about the cost functions of the parties to be regulated; (2) a model of the relevant natural system connecting human actions (most often discharges of pollution) to the points at which damages accrue or at which ambient standards are enforced by monitoring; and (3) an optimizing algorithm operating on the information to find a solution minimizing costs (or the sum of costs and damages) of meeting the chosen standards. I say "most important" because appeal to this property, without qualification or explanation, is part of the "boiler plate" of too many papers purporting to deal with instrument choice or the design of implementation systems. Seeing this property in a more realistic light, one in which the *institutional* costs of achieving static efficiency are made explicit, is a good foundation for shifting to the developing country situation, in which institutional capability, broadly defined, is often the limiting resource.

Further preparation for shifting venues was provided by Chapter 11, in which the institutionally demanding business of monitoring and enforcement was analyzed. That chapter emphasized the need for a match between problem setting and measurement technology, for maintaining "surprise" in visits to monitor, and for credible penalties and a workable system to impose them on discovered violators.

To these observations from earlier chapters I would add a few others to set the stage for the rest of this chapter. First, any implementation system that involves transfers of money—as do emission charges—increases the temptation to, and ease of, corruption via side payments to bureaucrats. While developing nations hardly can be said to have a monopoly on corruption, one does get the impression that, in many such countries, supplementing low civil-servant salaries in this way is seen as quite a reasonable thing to do. Second, it is not only public institutional capabilities that may matter. If a marketable emission permit system is to function to equalize marginal costs of discharge reduction, the private players in that market must be "good at" trading in markets.[1] This may seem a trivial observation and a requirement that could hardly not be fulfilled. But we have to remind ourselves that many nations in the developing and "transition" (from communism) worlds have lived for decades under systems of state control of production and distribution. The players in these economies were not autonomous deal makers but rather manipulators of centralized rules and of the agencies imposing and adjusting them. This is not to say they could never become successful free-marketeers, but it is to say that it might be better to let them practice on private rather than what amounts to public goods.

Finally, a system that involves establishing new property rights, as does a marketable permit approach, also requires functioning institutions for protecting such rights. To the Western economist, at least, this means a court system with well-defined rules and procedures, delays in obtaining judgments measured in tens of months rather than tens of years, and the ability to make those judgments stick. Even our own (OECD) court systems seem to have trouble meeting these requirements consistently, in the face of determined manipulation. But almost any randomly chosen issue of *The Economist* will contain at least one story about the horrors of the civil justice system in a country that qualifies as developing.

Let us begin, then, with a closer look at developing country institutional capability.

THE INSTITUTIONAL SETTING IN DEVELOPING COUNTRIES

Within the question of public sector capacity there are again two types of questions to consider. The first type are by their nature messy, politically delicate, and difficult to answer in straightforward legalistic or quantitative ways. These may be called the "awkward" questions. The second question type is cleaner and neater, involving documents, organization charts, and matters of legal reasoning. If the first set of questions produces answers that point to inadequacies, there is little the outside world can do, even the multilateral aid agencies with their massive resources of money and expertise. If, however, any problems seem to be with the second set of questions, providing assistance is fairly straightforward. It is possible that institutional failures of the first sort are at least as common as those of the second sort; but institution-building assistance seems designed as though only a few documents and organizational arrangements need to be tidied up.

SOME "AWKWARD" QUESTIONS

Most general and least easily answered is the question: Does the country have the political will to impose current costs, often concentrated on a few large enterprises or municipalities, in return for much more diffuse benefits, some of them postponed, and most of them not routinely monetized? Asking the question in these terms, however, might be said to betray a sort of democratic assumption—that it makes sense to think of each country as operating under a process that reveals something that can reasonably be called a collective "will." But if the great mass of the population is not really consulted—if, for example, the country is an oligarchy run for the convenience and enrichment of the owners of industry and property—then this assumption will not be valid. As important, for the purposes of this discussion, such a government is unlikely to be environmentally activist. In voting democracies, in which legitimate governments peacefully succeed each other, the above question of political will has more meaning, but the answer may still be no. No one is obliged to believe the local version of the assertion that some environmental protection will always make sense. And believing it does require a certain amount of faith in complex chains of causality, as from more expensive, unleaded gasoline to better health, smarter children, and higher incomes.

A second question is: Even if the formal institutions of government seem to have opted for a considered environmental policy, are there informal and disruptive institutions that prevent full discussion and effective action in environmental matters? These might operate by punishing individuals who speak out, by controlling neighborhoods or entire regions de facto, or simply by buying off the "legitimate" decision makers (e.g., the Colombian guerrilla groups and their informal military opponents who range across the entire country).

The last possibility above suggests a third fundamental question: Is there an ethic of public service in the country that makes bureaucratic or legislative rent-seeking (corruption) something that must at least be covered up by the participants? Or is every public policy hostage to a culture of bribery or of nepotism? When corruption is endemic, again the formal arrangements written into laws and regulations, the sizes of fines or charges, the terms of permits, and even the requirements for best management practices may mean very little.

A final question is: What sort of information sources are accessible to the population? Are these sources free to report pollution incidents? To tell what is known about effects of the chronic exposures experienced by parts of the population? To reveal which organizations, public or private, are responsible for the incidents and the chronic exposures and who stands to profit? Or do state censorship, strict libel laws, or more informal and violent sanctions keep the media tame?

If the answer to any of the above questions runs counter to the notion of a transparent, accountable governing structure, then environmental management, because of the incidence of its costs and benefits, is very likely to suffer along with other, analogous, programs such as rural health care and primary education. And such fundamental institutional problems are, unfortunately, far from rare in the world. Consider the characterization of "Third World Countries" by Fola Ebisemju as displaying:

> . . . a low level of awareness of the environmental hazards of modern, large-scale development projects, political instability, intense promotion of ethnic rather than national interests, pervasive corruption, and abuse of power . . . also lack of political will on the part of the government. (Ebisemju, 1993)

In such situations the comparison of policy instruments on the basis of their efficiency properties may well seem beside the point. A prior pair of questions will be whether any serious policy can be said to exist and whether any policy instrument can operate in a predictable and consistent way. These questions are returned to in the section below on recommendations.

SOMETHING EASIER: LEGAL ARRANGEMENTS AND ORGANIZATIONAL STRUCTURE

Having the general political will and lacking powerful informal obstacles to imposing that will may be necessary conditions for sound environmental policy design, but they are by no means sufficient. To translate will into action on the ground requires writing detailed rules and regulations (even when economic incentives are to be used); acquiring and deploying technical skills such as those for monitoring ambient conditions and the contributions to those conditions of regulated parties; coordinating the actions of different levels and sections of government—central and provincial, the environmental agency and the prosecutorial and judicial systems—and keeping records that document problems and progress and that can form a basis for new recommendations or midcourse corrections. Here are some questions that probe these areas of what might best be called formal institutional capacity.

First, and perhaps too obviously, do the necessary laws exist? For example, do laws cover the forms of pollution discharge, renewable resource damage, and overharvesting that are to be policy targets? Do these laws make the connection between development projects (roads, dams, ports, power stations) and the environment? Are these laws internally consistent so that, for example, account is taken of the conservation of mass and energy in production and treatment processes? Are the laws enforceable in that they specify the duties that may be placed on private parties or subordinate government units?

A second set of questions involves the institutions of environmental management themselves. How unified or how fragmented is the structure that will turn the laws into specific rules (or economic incentives) and then enforce the rules (or collect the charges, or record the permit trades, or whatever)? There is nothing that says that success requires complete integration, but the realities of bureaucratic behavior are such that if, for example, air pollution control in urban areas is assigned to municipalities, while rules for gasoline composition are made by an energy agency or state oil company, and power stations are designed and built under the direction of a planning agency with no environmental remit, the results are likely to be less than satisfactory. A minimally promising structure would seem to be one in which there is a pollution control agency (with full sectoral and geographic coverage); a natural resource management agency; and some sort of coordinating body that brings these agencies together with the development planning agency. To get a feel for inadequacies and recommendations for improvements in specific countries we can consult a set of institutional assessments prepared by consultants to the Interamerican Development Bank on Latin American countries. Examples include:

- Bahamas: discussing fragmentation and sheer lack of enforceable regulations and proposing to help develop a national commission that would in turn develop environmental policy as well as an environmental impact assessment system

- Colombia: strengthening regional "corporations" responsible for natural resource management

- El Salvador: proposing both general (information and environmental assessment systems) and specific (wastewater and solid waste regulations and pricing or incentive systems) improvements to existing environmental management system

- Guatemala: proposing a program to strengthen the institutional capacity of the national environmental management agency (CONAMA) and its regional offices and to promote legal reform and regulatory redesign

- Jamaica: documenting the shortcomings of this country's existing system (inadequate rules and regulations, poor planning, inadequately defined property rights) and recommending an ambitious program of reform.[2]

The third test of capacity involves skills. Do the agencies have the skilled people available to implement the laws? This means having everything from lawyers who write regulations to technical specialists in the field who can operate ambient-quality and discharge-monitoring equipment, or interpret aerial photos for signs of overharvest or slash and burn agricultural encroachment.[3]

Finally, given laws, institutional structure, and skills, it is still necessary for the system to be set up to ride herd on the details of implementation.[4] For example, if discharge standards are to be the enforceable duties laid on industry and municipalities, is there a system in place for writing them? Is it a system that guarantees consistency with whatever basis has been chosen for these standards, be it a simple percentage roll-back model or an effort to meet given ambient quality targets at something approximating least cost? Is an effort made to do the necessary enforcing?[5]

ARE MARKET-BASED ENVIRONMENTAL POLICY INSTRUMENTS THE BEST ANSWER FOR DEVELOPING COUNTRIES? OBSERVATIONS AND SUGGESTIONS

The economic cautions from earlier chapters and the institutional discussion of the previous section bring to mind the following observations and suggestions.

To set the stage, I first assume that the "awkward" questions asked in the previous section have reassuring answers. That is: The phrase "political will" has meaning beyond referring to the desires of an autocrat or oligarchy. That will embraces some level of environmental effort. There are no insurmountable problems posed by parallel, informal institutions bent on frustrating the legitimate authorities. The public service ethic is at least strong enough that inevitable efforts at personal enrichment must be concealed from public view, because there is a price to be paid for discovered corruption. And there is at least some approximation to a free and critical mass media.

CAPABILITIES

The key questions under these general conditions concern the capabilities of the legitimate government institutions and the current and aimed-for configurations of the commercial/industrial and rural sectors. Of the very large number of possible combinations of specific conditions in these sectors, let me concentrate on three, which I will label "traditional," "transitional," and "modern." The features ascribed to each sector in each setting are summarized in Table 16.1, where the reader will see that a roughly consistent path of evolution for each of the three sectors is assumed. That is, as formal government organization improves, so do the available skills and information and so does the revenue-raising capacity of the public sector. Correspondingly, the enterprise sector is also advancing toward large numbers of competing firms and facing less intrusive economic regulation; and, in the rural areas, large estates (if there are such) are becoming skillful global competitors, while subsistence farmers are transforming themselves, almost certainly with public help on the technical and credit fronts, into producers of cash crops for local and regional markets.

INSTRUMENTS

To parallel these settings it seems to me reasonable to suggest an evolution of instruments from the most easily defined and enforced (although the least closely connected to ambient quality goals) toward those involving more difficult definition tasks and closer connections to desired ambient results, aiming at tradable permits in the long run. Such an evolution is set out in Table 16.2 for the three institutional settings and three problem types: pollution control, agriculture, and renewable resource management (forestry and fisheries principally).

Thus, in the traditional setting the emphasis is on simplicity of demands on both government and the regulated parties, and the specification of technology figures large. The advantages of this approach lie in the type and source of the information required: for example, about the technology already developed by industrial countries, and about the actual performance of the regulated parties. While installation does not guarantee operation, at least it is possible more easily to begin establishing norms of compliance when what is at issue is the presence or absence of pieces of equipment. There is no link required to any particular ambient quality (or fish population or rate of timber harvest).

This last feature is, of course, a double-edged sword. It greatly simplifies the government agency's definition problem, and that is one justification for using these instruments here. But it also makes discussion of static economic efficiency beside the point. Said another way, the target proposed here is the technology itself. Some improvement in ambient quality will follow (unless the specification process goes

TABLE 16.1 Three Alternative Developing Country Institutional Settings

Sector	Government	Commercial/Industrial Enterprises	Rural
Traditional	Highly centralized but lacking experience and skills. Laws still primitive and management structure primitive. Revenue generating ability limited largely to the borders (import/export taxes).	Industry and commerce dominated by state-owned enterprises. Relative prices distorted by vestiges of import substitution and urban subsidy strategies. A thriving gray economy operating in the lacunae of state control.	Rural society and economy divided into traditional estate and subsistence farming. Neither involved in competition and efficient production, with large estates discouraged by export taxes or managed relative prices favoring urban interests; small farmers involved in bare subsistence operation. Natural resource exploitation often in hands of state enterprises.
Transitional	Highly centralized, with well-crafted laws but still gaps in skills and experience to make sophisticated translations from, e.g., AEQ stds to discharge results. Some information about newly privatized enterprises. Management structure more integrated. Revenue-raising capacity includes in-country sales taxes or VAT.	Privatization well under way but often producing private monopolies or at least single-firm-dominated oligopolies. More external competition and threat of internal competition pushing prices closer to marginal cost. Gray economy much smaller and concentrated in minor services.	Reforms of internal and export price policies, of arrangements for rural credit availability, in some cases of land ownership arrangements, and provision of technical advice ("extension" service) begin to change the incentives and opportunities facing both types of farms. Privatization in logging and mining under way, but ability to regulate concentrated industry not developed. Vestiges of state control, as over labor use and rules, complicates problem of competing globally.
Modern	Less highly centralized, with considerable technical skills at every level. Information-gathering machinery consistent with environmental program needs in place. Management structure reasonably integrated both vertically and horizontally. Government revenue sources diversified and well administered.	Generally competitive economy. Natural monopolies regulated under rate of return or CPI + X pricing rules.	Large farms modernized and mechanized and competing in global commodity markets. Small farms producing surpluses of staples and other cash crops that can be sold in local or regional markets to provide cash income. Extraction industries competing globally. Open bidding for access to state-controlled resources such as forests and mineral deposits.

TABLE 16.2 Recommendations for the Evolution of Policy Instruments in Parallel with Institutions

Sector	Pollution	Agriculture	Fisheries and Timber
Traditional	Treatment technology specification	Simple best management practices (BMP) • terracing • tree belts • animal types	Gear restrictions: boat size, net mesh
	Banning certain products (e.g., leaded gasoline)	Formalization and enforcement of small-holder property rights	Allowable logging equipment; road building rules
	User charges for publicly owned facilities, such as wastewater treatment plants		Adoption and reinforcement of traditional rules, as for quasi-property rights in times and places
Transitional	Technology-based discharge standards embodied in permits	More complex and difficult-to-monitor BMPs (e.g., animals per acre, pest control practices)	Limits of harvests • Tree cuts • Catches per boat and fishery
		Taxes on inputs esp. pesticides and fertilizers	Stumpage or landing fees charged on harvest
	Technology demonstration projects	Challenge regulation	Challenge regulation
	Taxes on pollution-related inputs		
	Challenge regulation to take advantage of fears that stricter rules may be coming		
Modern	Tradable discharge permits	Tradable rights to apply fertilizer or pesticide	Tradable rights to catch fish or cut trees
	Charges on, e.g., energy sources where demand elasticity is low, substitutes uncommon, and link to environmental quality close (gasoline)		Requirements on forest condition after X years
			Definition of geographic/seasonal rights to fish
	Providing information on polluter performance to the public		Providing information on performance of harvesting firms to the public

horribly wrong). But once it is known what that improvement amounts to, it would (almost) always be possible to specify another route to its achievement that would be cheaper. One other danger exists—that these technology specifications will become frozen through political paralysis. These suggestions assume that antidotes are available for this disease, and that evolution of goals and techniques will be possible as well as desirable.

One final note on the traditional-phase instruments: charges are proposed in a few very simply organized and monitored settings. For example, if a public agency builds a wastewater treatment plant and requires that local industries be connected to it via sewers, it becomes quite straightforward to calculate a cost-recovering charge per unit of contribution to the plant's load.[6] In addition, as long as the sewering requirement is enforced, the accurate metering of the charged components of source contributions is itself quite straightforward for industrial users. (Whether domestic dischargers are or are not charged in any way approximating a per-unit charge will, as a practical matter, depend on whether their water use is metered. If it is, a wastewater treatment charge can be added to the water bill, again using well-established formulae.)

In the transition phase of institutional evolution, the array of potential useful policy instruments grows wider. In the pollution control area, the responsible agency may move first from technology specification to technology-based permits, as used, for example, in the U.S. Clean Water Act system. These permits do not require installation of any particular technology, but rather require each source to achieve what it is calculated *could be* achieved by installation of a technology defined by its relation to the state of the art, using such phrases as "best available technology" or "reasonably available control technology." Such permits could become the basis for a tradable permit system in the next institutional phase.

It is important to note once again that the connection between these permit terms and ambient quality is, in effect, the reverse of what is required for any claim of efficiency. That is, the technology-based permits will, if enforced, result in some level of ambient quality. But except by the luckiest sort of accident, it would never be cheapest to achieve that ambient quality, considered now as a target, by imposing the particular set of permits implied by the technology definitions. Once again, the recommendation is based on the judgment that the scarce resources of most concern here are related to institutional capacity—available information and computation sophistication capacity. (The monitoring problem for a technology-based permit system is the same as that for any other system in which quantities of pollution discharge per unit time must be checked up on, whether that system involves ambient quality-based permits, tradable permits, or emission charges.)

In the agricultural sector, the major instrument suggestions for the transition setting are roughly more of the same as for the traditional—best management practices—with the introduction of environmentally justified taxes on polluting inputs. For fishery and forestry management, the transition setting is the time to begin using more-difficult-to-monitor instruments, such as permits to cut so many board feet on so many hectares; or to catch so many tons of particular fish species over specified periods. (Such requirements are clearly the analogs to discharge permits expressed in weight of pollutant per unit time. The reason for avoiding such permit types in agriculture is the monitoring problem for nonpoint sources, a problem that has not yet been solved satisfactorily in the industrial world.)

Note also that as the transition toward the modern setting proceeds, experiments and demonstrations may be carried out in all the sectors. Examples include adding taxes on polluting inputs and introducing stumpage fees in forestry and catch landing fees for fisheries. One other possibility in this regard is "challenge regulation." In this technique regulated parties are challenged to do better than the current requirements in return for a promised reward under the anticipated (threatened) next phase regulatory regime.[7] (For example, go to 70-percent discharge reduction now instead of staying at 50 percent in return for a postponement of the new requirement to go to 90 percent, anticipated in five years.)

In the modern setting the instrument of my choice is some version of a marketable permit—to discharge a pollutant, to apply fertilizer or pesticide in agriculture, or to take fish or cut trees. The rationale for this choice—the determining property of the instrument—is flexibility on the face of exogenous change. As pointed out in Chapter 9, this flexibility reduces the recurring computational and political burden on the regulatory agency because it does not have to readjust permit terms or charge levels just to maintain some required ambient result.[8]

Once again it is necessary to point out that where location matters, a simple tradable discharge permit system will not, except by lucky accident, produce the lowest cost allocation of discharges consistent with a given ambient quality standard. The dynamic property of flexibility (or self-adjustment) seems worth trading off what would necessarily be a temporary cost advantage. Where location does not matter, as it often does not with fish catches, static efficiency will accompany flexibility. The forestry case might go either way, but the ambient effects of agricultural input application will almost always be location sensitive.

The tradable rights notion brings up a facet of political and social organization about which little has so far been said: the courts and their role in private dispute resolution.[9] Thus, for example, one extension of the notion of "rights" creation could be over time so that, for example, a defined group of fishermen would be made "owners" of a defined fishery resource (a particular species in a particular location) in perpetuity. This could allow government to avoid specifying allowable annual harvests. But if such arrangements are to survive, the group must be able to make and enforce (through courts) rules for what would become a common property resource rather than an open access one.

From rights that operate over time in a narrow resource context it is another leap, and in some ways a very large one, to liability rules. These create general rights, which apply to entire populations, to be free from certain kinds of harm.[10] Enforcement of those rights in the environmental area involves difficult matters of proof and valuation. This seems the most institutionally demanding way of attempting to affect environmental quality, and may not be worth pursuing, even in the modern phase of institutional evolution. This is also partly because its efficiency properties are much attenuated in real situations of multiple victims and sources of harm.

Finally, in the modern phase, the government will be in a position to experiment with the provision of information to the public, as is now done in the United States with the Toxics Release Inventory (TRI). As discussed in Chapter 10, it appears that this instrument can have powerful effects, particularly where there are environmental NGOs and a vigorous, free press ready and more than willing to amplify the message that some firm is the worst source of toxics in the country or region.[11]

Let me backtrack here and consider what, if any, options exist when the "awkward" questions of the institutional sector do not all have good answers. For example, assume that a hypothetical country's leadership has decided that environmental conditions do demand improvement, so there is at least the minimum necessary political will. But further assume lack of full control over what goes on in the countryside, a bureaucratic "ethic" that institutionalizes corruption, and mass media that are under the thumb of the ruling group. These are grave obstacles to effective action, even granting the assumption that some action is desired.

- Lack of full control of parts of the nation make field work and monitoring difficult or impossible, so that putting out information or checking on compliance with regulations or best management practices may be possible only in urban areas.
- Pervasive corruption means that payments to or from the government can too easily be turned into rent payments to agency "landlords."
- Controlled media imply that efforts to use information provision as a tool will not be pursued because of the open-ended and uncontrollable nature of the potential effects.

What to do? Two possibilities are: first, direct government investment in pollution control facilities; second, apply technology or technology-based standards to sources of urban water and air pollution. These steps could actually be enforceable and would offer relatively small or at least inconvenient opportunities for bribery. Beyond this, very few notions sound promising. For example, even technical assistance coupled with challenge regulation, with the implicit threat being the arrival of a new regime with a more serious commitment to good administration generally, seems problematic because of a credibility gap. A new regime may be considered unlikely, and any one that does replace the status quo may also be unlikely to honor the promise part of the challenge. On the other hand, technical assistance can at least be based on internationally available knowledge and involves small opportunity for corruption unless adoption of new technology is subsidized—something that would seem unwise in these circumstances.

It may also be tempting to think about attacking imported environmental hazards, such as pesticides or solvents might be in a developing country. This could be sold as an exercise in regaining sovereignty. But it is not clear that in general much could be gained this way, both because the purposes served by the imports will usually have to be accomplished in any case and because smuggling or illegal internal production may simply provide a new source of revenue to the informal challengers of government authority.

SOME EVIDENCE ON THE ACTUAL CHOICES OF ENVIRONMENTAL POLICY INSTRUMENTS BEING MADE IN LATIN AMERICA

Keeping up with evolving environmental policies (and attendant instrument choices) in developing countries would be a full-time job even if this were only done in a formalistic way. If one wanted to know how the language of laws, regulations, and court decisions translated into action on the ground, the task would become truly immense. In the circumstances, to pretend to completeness in this section would be foolhardy. On the other hand, a brief compendium will allow a first, very rough cut at comparing actual policy choices with the recommendations commonly found in the literature (for market-based instruments) and above (for a more conservative, step-by-step approach).

Accordingly, a table of experience has been constructed for one developing region from a variety of sources of policy "news" and institutional commentary. It summarizes what has been learned about the adoption of environmental policy instruments in Latin America. The arrangement of the countries in the table is, itself, worth some comment and explanation, however. To make the table useful, especially in the context of institutional capacity, it would be desirable to arrange the countries in an order that parallels the traditional/transitional/modern categorization used above. Unfortunately, but not surprisingly given the massive simplification effort lying between those categories and the multiple dimensions inherent in the notion of institutional capacity, there is no perfect ranking of Latin American countries for this purpose. Instead there are many possible different imperfect ordering systems including the UNDP *Human Development Index*, the Interamerican Development Bank's (IDB's) country groups used for project lending share allocations, and a ranking based on IDB staff perceptions of country environmental capacity and problems. Putting these three together leads to Table 16.3, the last column of which lists a composite classification using the same labels as the text proper: traditional, transitional, and modern.[12] Table 16.4 reports information about country choices of policy instrument, with the countries grouped according to the Table 16.3 result.

What expectations might one have a priori for this table? If the region's policymakers have been reading and believing the literature on development and environment, the expectation would be for economic instruments to appeal to each group. If there is skepticism about those recommendations, then the instruments might be found only in the "modern" countries.

Table 16.4 shows more evidence of adoption of economic instruments by the modern and transitional countries than by the traditional ones. But it is impossible

TABLE 16.3 Rankings of Latin American Countries by Institutional Capacity

Country	U.N. HDI[a]	Rank by U.N. HDI	IDB Group[b]	IDB Staff Ranking[c]	Composite[d]
Uruguay	0.905	1	C	III	Trans
Chile	0.878	2	B	II	Mod
Costa Rica	0.876	3	C	I	Mod
Argentina	0.854	4	A	III	Trans
Venezuela	0.842	5	A	II	Trans
Mexico	0.838	6	A	II	Mod
Panama	0.796	7	C	V	Trad
Suriname	0.792	8	C	III	Trans
Jamaica	0.761	9	C	I	Mod
Brazil	0.759	10	A	II	Mod
Colombia	0.757	11	B	II	Trans
Belize	0.711	12	D	Not Ranked	Trans
Paraguay	0.667	13	D	V	Trad
Ecuador	0.655	14	D	III	Trans
Peru	0.644	15	B	III	Trans
Dominican Rep.	0.622	16	D	IV	Trad
Nicaragua	0.612	17	D	III	Trad
Guyana	0.589	18	D	IV	Trad
El Salvador	0.524	19	D	III	Trad
Honduras	0.492	20	D	II	Trans
Guatemala	0.488	21	D	IV	Trad
Bolivia	0.416	22	D	III	Trad
Haiti	0.296	23	D	V	Trad

[a] United Nations Human Development Index. U.N. Environmental Program, 1991. Environment Data Report. Blackwell Reference, Oxford. Reported in Manuel Winograd, n.d. Environmental Indicators for Latin America and the Caribbean. GASE Ecological Systems Analysis Group. [b] Used as basis for project lending share allocations (A largest to D smallest)—a sort of capacity-to-absorb-funding index. [c] Based on IDB staff appraisals of country capabilities. These seemed to divide naturally into five groups from V, least institutional capacity, to I, most institutional capacity. [d] My own summary judgment. Mod, modern; trans, transitional; trad, traditional.

to tell whether this is because these countries actually adopt them more or simply because these countries are the ones covered well by the available sources of information. The other side of this coin, as it were, is that these two groups of countries do more of everything, experimenting with a range of instruments, not confining themselves to economic ones. The traditional countries do (or are reported to do) very little. It may be that these nations are waiting for ideas that seem likely to work in their institutional situations. Or they may be suffering from the maladies probed by the "awkward" questions of the institutional section above. Or possibly the compilers of tables and newsletters may simply not pay any attention to whatever it is that these countries do. Some of each would be a reasonable bet.

TABLE 16.4. Evidence on Adoption of Environmental Policy Instruments in Latin America (from a variety of sources)

	Modern Institutions	Transitional Institutions	Traditional Institutions
Charges per unit of pollution or other environmental insult	*Brazil*—Effluent charges in 4 states, with revenue earmarked for environmental agency. Presumed discharge levels; proof required to get lower charges. *Mexico*—Effluent charges for discharges exceeding certain standards. Revenues earmarked for agency.	*Colombia*—Pollution fees on organic discharges to water in Valle de Cauca. Air and water discharges subject to charges, at least in principle.	*Bolivia*—National Environmental Law "encourages" use of "financial instruments."
Marketable permits	*Mexico*—Tradeable permits in ozone-depleting substances.	*Chile*—Tradable point-source air pollution discharge permits in Santiago. Tradable bus route permits in Santiago.	
Taxes per unit of input or output	*Mexico*—Gasoline tax with revenue earmarked for service station upgrades.		
Standards (however derived; often embodied in permits)	*Brazil*—Emission standards negotiated on case-by-case basis though ambient standards exist. Emission standards for automobiles.	*Bahamas*—Permits embody conditions of lawful discharge. *Colombia*—Water pollution discharges require a permit. *Venezuela*—Standards required by Environmental Penal Law.	*Guatemala*—Permits governing what may be built in historic district of Antigua.
Technology specifications		*Colombia*—Solid waste management subject to best-available-control-technology requirements.	

TABLE 16.4. Evidence on Adoption of Environmental Policy Instruments in Latin America (from a variety of sources) (*Continued*)

	Modern Institutions	Transitional Institutions	Traditional Institutions
Government investment in environmental infrastructure	*Chile*—Vina Del Mar/Valparaiso WWTP (wastewater treatment plants).		
User charges	*Brazil*—Charges based on pollutant content to cover costs of wastewater treatment plants. *Chile*—Wastewater user chargers based on water use.	*Colombia*—Sewage charges based on water volume not pollution load.	
Land use controls	*Brazil*—"Green area" zoning in Curitiba to protect quality of life and of groundwater and to lower flood damages. *Costa Rica*—Control of shoreline development.	*Colombia*—Parts of sensitive environments protected by environmental laws, e.g., Amazon watershed.	
Environmental impact assessments	*Brazil*—EIA requirements contained in fundamental environmental law. *Chile*—EIA required for large projects.	*Argentina*—EIA required for new plants.	
Challenge regulation or volunteerism	*Brazil*—Air pollution reduction in Victoria, Espirito Santo via "voluntary agreement" with major emitters.		

Liability-type provisions	*Brazil*—Joint and several liability for pollution damages or cost of cleanup. *Jamaica*—Common law tort rights. *Mexico and Brazil*—Rights to petition government agencies for correction and compensation.	*Argentina*—Approximation to common law, tort rights in pollution cases. *Bahamas, Barbados, Jamaica, Trinidad & Tobago*—Common-law tort rights. *Colombia*—Government agencies liable for environmental damages from their operations. Action of *tutela* (protection) available, i.e. government investigation and action based on citizen complaints. Technical assistance offered to polluters by autonomous regional corporations. *Peru*—Right to go to court to demand environmental protection, even without proof of harm.	*Guyana*—Common-law tort rights.
Other	*Mexico*—Driving restrictions on Mexico City residents.		

CONCLUDING COMMENTS

Economic incentive instruments for environmental management, like all real-world alternatives for intervening in markets for public purposes, have both advantages and disadvantages. The most significant of the former, in my opinion, relate to dynamics:

- Charges on every unit of an environmental insult create the largest incentive among the available alternatives to search for less polluting technology.
- Marketable permits self-adjust to exogenous growth and change.

The disadvantages of these instruments revolve around what might be called their information intensity. This intensity is greatest when an effort is made to achieve static economic efficiency. Either a charge system must be tailored by the agency to the circumstances (costs, discharges, location) of each source, or an ambient quality permit system must be adopted, requiring sources to do and keep updated quite complex modeling calculations to determine the desirability of purchases or sales.

It is much simpler to institute a uniform charge (or its dual, the straightforward, tradeable discharge permit system), but there is no reason to expect such a choice to lead to lower cost of meeting a given ambient quality target than would some other quite arbitrary regulatory scheme.

If one believes that institutional capacity is likely to be among the scarcest resources in developing countries, there would seem to be good reason to seek less institutionally demanding approaches, recognizing that there will be other costs to taking these routes. Very roughly, I suggest that countries with the least sophisticated institutions—both government and market—should begin by focusing on technology. This allows the importation from the industrial world of directly useful knowledge (but does *not* necessarily imply the importation of developed country standards). It promises to pose a simpler monitoring problem. Though what can be easily monitored (installation) is not what counts for continuing compliance (operation), there may be a substantial long run payoff to "practicing" the whole monitoring and enforcement game as part of institutional growth. Finally, concentrating on technology seems to reduce somewhat the opportunities for corruption, compared with instruments that involve money transfers.[13]

As public institutions grow in skill and reliability, and indeed, as part of the process of fostering such growth, the specification of technology can evolve into the use of technological capability as the basis for writing permits that require particular discharge levels to be attained however they are achieved (technology-based standards). Such evolution could start in the metropolitan areas and be expanded to the hinterland as resources permit.

Finally, and again both leading and following growth in institutional capacity, these permits can gradually be made marketable among sources. Such an evolution might begin with a requirement that every proposed trade require a special request to the agency for authorization. At a later stage, approval might be assumed if no objection were made to a reported trade within some deadline. The agency might originally be responsible for doing (or overseeing) the modeling to check for hot spot creation. Later the sources could be required to have or buy the skills necessary to run the regional model(s).

Countries can, of course, enter this proposed sequence at the stage appropriate to their institutional capacity. This is not a rigid, all or nothing training program. At each stage undertaken the responsible agency(ies) should be challenged by the chief political executive's office and by international lending agencies to demonstrate that it (they) has (have) the current system under control and is (are) ready to move on to the next phase of effort.

Thus, in brief, my position is *not* that economic incentive instruments are bad or useless. It is that their use demands a high level of institutional capacity, especially if it is intended that the effort will be aimed at finding the least-cost (statically efficient) regional allocation of effort. Short of this target there is no second-best result to appeal to, and the institutional costs might, in effect, be paid in vain. Better to start with less demanding instruments, paying the price in other ways, such as some loss of innovation incentive, but looking at the process of environmental management in the long run and aiming at institutional evolution. This evolution could both be encouraged by the requirements of the instruments chosen and be aimed at the next level of sophistication.

─────────────── APPENDIX **16.1** ───────────────

INSTITUTIONAL CAPABILITIES AND MARKET CONFIGURATIONS IN LATIN AMERICA

The conventional arguments from static efficiency used to support market-based instruments (MBIs) rest upon a special or ideal view of interaction between private and public agents. In this model, economic transactions occur in perfectly competitive markets where firms maximize profits. The role of government is limited to that of fine-tuner. Since the market can adequately maximize social welfare, except for a few limited market failures, such as those that occur with pollution, any intervention beyond using pollution charges equal to the marginal external damages created by that pollution imposes unnecessary costs on society.

Competitive markets and passive governments are not characteristic of developing economies, however. Take Latin America, for example. The economic history of the region is better described in terms of state monopolies, distorted markets, and interventionist or dirigiste governments.[14] The good news is that the habit of over-regulation and overcentralization has recently begun to yield to a new wave of reform and restructuring actions that include privatization, market pricing, and removal of barriers to competition. With these reforms, markets in Latin America may evolve into those assumed in theory. When this occurs, MBIs may be able to reach their potential for inducing cost-effective policy through market manipulation, because firm owners, farmers, and industrial managers will have become skilled in responding to market signals rather than at lobbying government sources of privilege and cash.

Admittedly, there is no general relation that says environmental policies can only work in competitive settings. Indeed, the suggestions I make in the body of the chapter rely on the notion that competent government can achieve much via such instruments as product or process specification, technology requirements, and performance standards (as for discharges) that lack a marketability dimension. But when policy instruments involve administered prices or created markets, the general level of private sector skill does become an issue. A low level of skill will at least make it unlikely that the potential efficiency gains of the instrument will be realized. At worst, one could see an entire line of policy development discredited through, for example, widespread business failures.

The choice of environmental policy instruments may, therefore, usefully be thought about in terms of matching the evolution of instruments to the evolution of private institutions. A basis for discussing such evolution is provided by the notion of market (and nonmarket) "configurations." A configuration is defined principally by market structure but also reflects the nonmarket relationships among households, the government, and the productive enterprises, be they private firms or appendages of the government. Such relationships include both current rules, such as those involving enforcement of contracts, and expectations, such as whether or not the government will rescue a failed private enterprise.

Discussion of environmental policy in any developing country setting involves considering two configuration trajectories. The first describes the path of industrial and commercial development, usually in urban settings. This development is linked to problems of air quality, sanitation, and solid waste management that plague most cities. The second trajectory describes the unique path of rural markets. The pattern of land tenure, the extent of rural poverty, and the importance of export production determine configurations within the agricultural economy, and therefore will influence which environmental policies seem most promising at a particular time.

INDUSTRIAL AND COMMERCIAL
CONFIGURATIONS IN LATIN AMERICA

Between the Second World War and the early nineties, Latin America followed a strategy of import-substituting industrialization (ISI). Intense government intervention protected state-run monopolies with price controls and import taxes. This approach produced unbalanced growth in inefficient industries, and its short-lived success relied almost entirely on government engineering of relative prices. As noted above, ISI had its roots in a long tradition of symbiosis between state and enterprise that traced itself back to Spanish colonial policy. In the Spanish system, the state had control over resources and production. Property rights were seen as a political instead of contractual creation. Therefore, the state instead of the market was seen as the principal mediator of ownership transfer. Informal market configurations developed parallel to state monopoly configurations, however. ISI in Latin American countries generally concentrated development in one or two major cities. Growth in the urban sector led to massive migration from the rural areas. Formal labor markets in the cities absorbed only a small portion of these migrants. Unemployed and underemployed households settled in shantytowns on the urban periphery. To generate subsistence income, households established small enterprises that were unregulated and often illegal. When government controls cause significant distortions in market prices, as ISI commonly did, opportunities exist for those who can escape bureaucratic scrutiny and sell goods or services at something closer to a free market price. The informal sector in Latin America filled this niche effectively, and in some cases developed new microindustries.

The duality of state monopolies and unregulated informal market industries creates two distinct environments for the implementation of pollution reduction policy. In state monopoly configurations, the regulatory agency typically faces a small number of polluters concentrated mostly in industrial areas. A small number of potential polluters can mean it is easier to link environmental insults with their sources. However, with the market concentration enjoyed by monopolies typically comes significant political strength; and in this case, the monopolies were often part of the government itself. Political opposition can mute efforts to enforce "official" environmental statutes.

Informal market configurations create different challenges for environmental policy. Since the informal sector comprises numerous microindustries, production, and therefore pollution creation, is highly decentralized. It is also often concealed, insofar as possible, because of its illegality. These features make it difficult to pinpoint polluters. Unlike the state monopolies, these industries, because of their small size, rarely have sufficient political capital to challenge the authority of the regulatory agency. While the power of the agency can go uncontested, the limited financial resources of these industries restricts the set of environmental improvements that can be mandated without public subsidy. And the sheer numbers make it impractical to think of standards or charges tailored to the situation of the individual firm. Easily monitored requirements applying very broadly are much more likely to be practical.

By the late 1980s a variety of forces had pushed several Latin American countries into moves designed to change this "traditional" configuration, in particular its reliance on state monopoly as the form of organization for the production of goods and services. Sometimes private monopolies were used as intermediate steps toward competition. For example, Teléfonos de Mexico was granted a six-year monopoly so that it could expand service without threats from long-distance competitors. After six years, though, no protection from competition was guaranteed. Temporary monopolies were also granted in Argentina's privatization of Empresa Nacional de Telecomunicaciones. The state's telecommunication conglomerate was split geographically into two corporations to foster an immediate "competition by comparison" between two private monopolies. This, it was claimed, would enhance a competitive spirit already created by uncertainty of continued monopoly status.

Vestiges of the economic culture dominated by state intervention remained, however. Producers still expected public agencies to bail them out of bad business decisions; and government bureaucrats continued to be pessimistic about the ability of unregulated markets to produce economic improvements. Nonetheless, when markets move beyond monopoly to display some level of competition, they are said to enter a transitional configuration. Within this configuration, prices tend to move freely, production is typically less centralized, and global markets exert some unregulated influence.

The endpoint of market development and the restructuring process is seen as a mature competitive configuration. In this configuration, government ownership of production capital is very small, and private firms survive domestic and foreign competition without government support or protection. Entrepreneurship drives innovation, and market entry and exit are fluid. Market prices reflect the marginal costs of production. These are institutional market characteristics that are theoretically necessary for the successful operation of MBIs. However, since most of Latin America began restructuring in the late eighties and early nineties, the region offers few examples of this configuration.[15] For most industries and governments it is a goal for the future, though whether it is ever even approximated will depend on currently unknowable political forces and events.

RURAL CONFIGURATIONS

Whereas restructuring has produced some growth and competition in Latin American industrial and commercial markets, rural institutions have experienced little change. This is consistent with the area's history of static economic structure outside of urban areas. There are two reasons for this rural inertia. First, at least in Latin America, agriculture has not often been seen as a sector that created significant growth stimulus for a developing economy, and it therefore has not been a priority in development policy. Preoccupation with ISI following the Second World War, and with privatization in the late eighties, reflected this bias. With less public attention and fewer resources agriculture was not even as dynamic as industry or commerce. Second, because of a strong centralist tradition in Latin America, institutions at lower jurisdictional levels outside of large urban areas are inadequate in their representation of rural community concerns and their ability to administer public policy. This void in local leadership weakens the ability of policy actors to improve economic performance in rural areas.

Rural production is divided between latifundios and minifundios. Latifundios are large estates that specialize in commercial agricultural production. These configurations sometimes comprise as little as 10 percent of all farm units (Guatemala, Ecuador, and Peru), but they typically control 50 to 80 percent of the land, using it for the large-scale production of primary exports. There exists an historical alliance between latifundios and the central government so that, to the extent Latin American governments have taken an interest in agriculture at all, they have worked with latifundios to develop the capacity of agriculture to earn foreign exchange. This alliance gives the latifundios significant political power, which contributes to the previously mentioned weakness in independent municipal institutions in rural areas.

On land not controlled by latifundios, poor rural households, or minifundios, engage in subsistence and small-scale commercial agriculture and sell labor to larger estates. These households typically crowd marginal land at the periphery of latifundios, and sometimes their production is not enough to meet even basic needs. Reform in the 1960s and 1970s transferred more land to minifundio control, but it did little to raise per capita output on these holdings above subsistence. The role of government has always been limited in the minifundio context. Since latifundios dominate the political process, they typically siphon available public resources for their own development. This hinders integration of small farmers into the market process.

In the context of land and resource policy, government interaction with latifundios will contrast with the interaction with minifundios. A lot of land concentrated among a handful of latifundio owners creates a situation paralleling that described for state and private monopolies in industry, and exhibits similar advantages and disadvantages for environmental agencies. If there is cooperation between the agency and the latifundios, then the costs of negotiating initiatives in forest management, soil conservation, and nonpoint source pollution control can be low, because in order to manage large tracts of land, the government only has to deal with a small number of private decision makers. Cooperation, of course, may be hard to achieve due to the history of effectively unchallenged political power wielded by latifundios in the rural areas. Policies that require latifundio owners to answer to newly formed environmental agencies may, indeed, be extremely hard to implement.

Minifundios may not have the political power to raise the transaction costs of imposing regulations, but they still present two important challenges to the effectiveness of land management policy. First, many poor rural farmers occupying marginal land and producing just enough to meet basic subsistence needs typically have access to no alternative farming strategies that can decrease land degradation without decreasing food output. Even if such alternatives exist, policymakers must overcome the second challenge of limited rural knowledge. Few minifundio owners know even simple strategies for commercial agriculture and livestock management that minimize agricultural runoff. Governments will have to surmount this obstacle before even BMP (technology specification) policies can successfully be implemented.

NOTES

1. Remember, also, that equalizing marginal costs of discharge reduction does not equal attaining the least-cost solution to a regional problem involving meeting ambient quality standards in the general (nonmixing bowl) situation.

2. It is worth noting that several of these reports mention economic incentive policy instruments with approval (El Salvador, Guatemala, Jamaica in particular) though without any evidence that the documents' authors had considered the heavy institutional demands posed by use of such instruments.

3. "In the field" is not used here casually. One of the common criticisms of developing country government structures is that they are so centralized that field assignments are looked on as career death sentences, and much effort goes into avoiding or cutting them short.

4. It is interesting to note that some observers seem to think that widespread use of personal computers, possible in developing countries because of price declines, can substitute for all manner of institution capability.

5. Monitoring for continuing compliance is a big problem even in industrial nations; and by the logic of the situation, it is difficult to determine how successful any effort is without essentially duplicating it. But anecdotal evidence, albeit for other social standards, suggests poor prospects in developing countries. See, for example, *Wall Street Journal,* July 3, 1995, on labor law and agreement enforcement.

6. To say that this is a straightforward task is to say that there are well-established formulae available. It is not to say that these formula solve the fundamentally unsolvable problems of joint cost allocation over the hydraulic and pollutant load components.

7. Note that for challenge regulation to be effective in the long run the government must remain credible, both as regards the later arrival of stricter standards *and* the exemption for those who meet the challenge from those later standards.

8. The problem of spatial hot spots will remain for pollutant discharge systems, however. A practical if computationally intensive and bureaucratically annoying way to keep an element of control is to certify a regional air quality model as official and to require that all proposed trades be "run through" the model and produce no ambient quality violations. This could be done by consulting engineers, in-house by each party to the trade, or by the agency. (See the concluding section.)

9. For the enforcement of regulations, such as those requiring technology installation, administrative bodies may be sufficient to hear evidence of violations and assign fines. If criminal violations are created, as they have been in certain areas of U.S. environmental law, courts will probably have to be the venue for trial.

10. The enforcement of this general right is effectively in the hands of those who suffer, or claim to suffer, a violation of their right.

11. The World Bank is already experimenting with such an approach and has reported on results of its application in Indonesia. The approach there involved reporting publicly on the general environmental performance of firms, using a summary, color-coded categorization from bad to excellent.

12. This "composite" represents my informal combination of the implications of the other three rankings, with the internal IDB perceptions weighted most heavily. The Bahamas and Barbados are not in the table but are listed as transitional.

13. A similar rough sequencing to what follows could be sketched for fishery and forestry management, and, with modification to take account of special monitoring problems, for agriculture.

14. For an assessment along these lines see the *Wall Street Journal* of August 16, 1995, describing overcontrol in Venezuela. For a literary but telling version of this diagnosis see the V. S. Naipaul novel, *A Way in the World* (1994).

15. Chile spearheaded privatization and deregulation in the region and today offers some examples of healthy competitive markets. In Santiago and other large cities, municipal transportation was deregulated in 1980. With the disappearance of price controls, fares rose and converged across different transportation modes (buses, minibuses, taxis, etc.) in instances where these provided similar service. The quality of service improved, and most importantly, competition between a large group of private carriers was sustained. A year previous to transport deregulation was the privatization of Celulosa Arauco and Celulosa Constitución, two firms involved in industrial timber. This removed the state completely from an industry that already had little regulation. With competition and openness to external trade, timber price and production were determined by the market. At the other end of the institutional scale, Bolivia has been selling off state firms and putting the proceeds in retirement accounts for its citizens, as described in the *Wall Street Journal* of August 15, 1995.

REFERENCES

Ebisemiju, Fola S. 1993. "Environmental Impact Assessment: Making it work in developing countries." *Journal of Environmental Management* 38:247–273.

Naipal, V. S. 1994. *A Way in the World*. New York: Knopf.

Wall Street Journal. 1995a. "Conduct codes garner goodwill for retailers, but violations go on." July 3:A1.

Wall Street Journal. 1995b. "Populist disaster, Venezuela is suffering: Its economy strangled by too many controls. Aug. 16:A1.

Wall Street Journal. 1995c. "Money transfer: Bolivia is selling off state firms to fund its citizens' future." Aug. 15:1A.

17

DEVELOPING COUNTRY ENVIRONMENTS AND OECD COUNTRY TASTES
An Asymmetric Relation

The developing nations are the custodians of many environmental assets deemed to be of global significance by scientists and by ordinary citizens—often citizens of OECD countries who, by definition of citizenship, have no direct or obvious way of making their interests heard in the countries in question. Examples of such assets include:

- the great tropical rain forests of the Amazonian Basin and the large islands of Southeast Asia
- the unique and exciting ecosystems of the East African savannahs
- the mangrove wetlands along the ocean coasts of low-lying tropical nations
- the great, free-flowing salmon rivers of northern Russia[1]

The values held by OECD citizens may arise for a variety of reasons: directly through use as tourists; indirectly as they are part of the world population affected by the storage of carbon in LDC forests, or potentially by the discovery of new drugs or other chemicals in the plants and animals of those forests. There may also be nonuse values held, as in the willingness to pay to protect the great mammals of the East African ecosystems even in the absence of any notion of ever traveling to see them up close and personal.

This complex of interests in how developing countries manage parts of their environments is not matched by anything like the same interest flowing in the opposite direction. This asymmetry is clearly a very important cause of the tense dialog about environmental policy generally that continues sporadically between developing and developed nations. Further, if one buys into the high value given those assets, it follows that devising acceptable ways of making those values heard is of great and increasing importance for the future of the world at large.

SOME POSSIBILITIES FOR CROSS-BORDER INFLUENCE

The range of means that have been and are being tried to affect environmental policies in poorer countries is a wide one.[2] Some of these involve carrots, such as aid tied to particular policies (or, often, to *absence* of policies or projects); some are inherently stick-like, as when one nation refuses to import some product from any country that fails to produce or harvest or process that product in a particular way. Some involve third parties, such as the multinational lending agencies (the World Bank, for example) or environmental groups with international reach. And some have been generated at the grass-roots level, though these often do take advantage of favorable tax laws in the host OECD nation. A fuller discussion of some of these efforts follows, but to anticipate a conclusion I think you will agree with—taken together they present a most ad hoc face to the world; and a natural follow-on question has to be: Can we imagine doing better? I will speculate about that at the close of the chapter.

UNILATERAL IMPOSITION OF RULES VIA TRADE POLICY

A quite direct, though not widely applicable, way of trying to make an impact on another country's environmental policies is to make and enforce rules about how certain products can be produced or harvested. The United States has used this technique to try to force on tuna and shrimp fishing nations, the latter especially in Latin America, rules about acceptable harvesting techniques. In the case of tuna, the goal was to cut porpoise (dolphin) mortality, since dolphin are often "fished on" because of their association with tuna. Somewhat similarly, shrimp harvesting at sea can apparently result in sea turtle deaths that appropriate net technology can prevent. That such efforts are not confined to OECD/LDC relations is demonstrated by the European Union's ban on the import of U.S. beef because of the hormones given to U.S. cattle to promote growth.

The record of successful challenges of such policy initiatives by the excluded countries before international trade tribunals suggest that they do not constitute a winning option, at least under current trade agreements. The fact that the EU continues to defy the rulings and that the United States retaliates through penalty tariffs on EU products does show that with sufficient economic strength and determination, the technique can be used, albeit illegally, for a long time. But by itself, and in the absence of wider trade treaty change, it is certainly not an example of laudable policy.

An example of a developed nation fiat applied to developing countries that has had an effect and has not been challengeable is the 1990s international ban on trade in ivory. This was imposed under terms of a treaty dealing explicitly with trade and endangered species, so did not fall afoul of general international trade rules. Nevertheless, it clearly reflects an OECD perspective: that poaching of elephants had reached really dangerous levels and was not being suitably attacked by countries hosting the elephants, Kenya especially.[3] By cutting off all legal markets globally, the policy was expected to reduce the incentive for poaching.

EFFORTS AT IMPOSITION OF RULES OR POLICIES VIA THE MULTINATIONAL LENDERS

This particular stick has generally been wielded in situations involving major projects with environmental implications seen as bad by the OECD nations. An example is the Three Gorges Dam project currently under construction in China. Funding for this was ultimately refused by the World Bank under pressure of the richer nations, which in turn were being pressured by their environmental constituencies. The weakness at the heart of this approach is also illustrated by Three Gorges: There is so much private capital available around the world now that multilateral lending is of much less importance than even a decade ago. The refusal of World Bank loans did not stop the project.

In connection with the multinational lenders and their role in pushing OECD tastes onto developing countries, we should recall that the cost-benefit analysis done for loan applications is supposed to refer specifically to domestic willingness to pay. This is reasonable, given that the applying country has to service the debt via charges or taxes that will usually fall on domestic customers or taxpayers. But it does suggest also that a different rule might apply to projects for which a chance of tapping visitors' WTP exists. An obvious example would be loans for rain forest or wildlife conservation.

GIVING TECHNICAL ASSISTANCE THAT ENCOURAGES DESIRED BEHAVIOR

Just as with the provision of technical assistance *within* an OECD country, the notion here is that a lack of information about possibilities (technological or institutional) is preventing desirable actions from being taken or desirable policies followed (Chapter 10 contained a brief discussion of this instrument). By analogy, we might expect that this would have greater applicability the smaller, poorer, and more isolated the client nation. But further, we ought to expect that there would be a greater chance of such advice finding application if such an application were in the client's best interest. Thus, for decades, aid agencies of the OECD countries have provided international analogs of domestic agriculture extension services. An environmentally relevant target has been irrigation and particularly the prevention of soil salination, which at least prospectively seems in the self-interest of the irrigating countries. (The fact that costs will be borne immediately with benefits necessarily postponed means this is not a no-brainer, however.)

An example of an institutional innovation arriving via aid is apparently the CAMPFIRE program in Zimbabwe. This involves the sharing of wildlife-related tourist receipts with the localities on the edges of the great game parks. The idea is to make the locals take a positive interest in the wildlife, rather than viewing elephants, rhino, and other species as simply giant nuisances or as poachable tickets to higher incomes. It is very difficult to find data on the actual operation of CAMP-FIRE, and certainly it would be difficult in any case to attribute any observable change in poaching to that operation. But a priori the idea makes sense. It might be argued that providing collective rewards (e.g., to a village via the head man) might not do much to change the behavior of individuals, who might free ride, in effect, on the tolerance and honesty of their neighbors. If this is not happening it could be the result of the small and closely knit village societies involved; free riding may be very difficult.

FORGIVING DEBT IN EXCHANGE FOR ENVIRONMENT ACTIONS: DEBT-FOR-NATURE SWAPS

This type of transaction was pioneered in 1987 by the U.S.-based environmental organization Conservation International and the government of Bolivia. The idea behind it was to take advantage of the big discount at which much developing country debt trades on world money markets, buying the bonds and giving them back to the issuer in exchange for conservation-related promises and associated spending. According to Deacon and Murphy (1997), in the first five years of such exchanges almost $100 million in dollar-denominated developing country debt was purchased by foreign, private (nongovernmental) organizations at an average price of $0.26 per $1.00 of face value. This was exchanged for the creation of promises to spend almost $80 million, but in local currency terms, on conservation projects. The figures for these privately negotiated transactions have been, however, dwarfed by government-to-government deals of the same sort. Deacon and Murphy list $1.365 *billion* as the face value of the debt retired by such "public" transactions.

The quid pro quo is the agreement of the debtor country to spend money (not to say effort and political "chips") on agreed-to conservation projects. The mechanism of choice has been for this government to set up a trust fund or endowment, using local currency bonds, with the income pledged to the projects. The conservation work itself may be overseen (monitored or even performed) by a local nongovernmental conservation organization. The nature of this "work" varies from contract to contract but generally aims at making real and enforcing the host government's nominal rights over forested lands within its borders. This may involve developing management plans, demarcating boundaries, training and equipping "rangers," even buying equipment such as vehicles.

As you might expect, monitoring and enforcing the substance of these agreements is not easy, especially if one understands "substance" to refer to results on the ground. But the terms are often devised to make monitoring easier, as by specifying inputs to be provided rather than outputs or results to be achieved. Thus, it is easier to check that 100 forestry personnel have been trained for antipoaching work than it is to check up on the actual extent of poaching before and after such an agreement. There are other pitfalls as well, including local ambivalence or even hostility to apparently being dictated to by representatives of the "rich" countries;

and resentment that debts created, sometimes by discredited regimes, are the instrument for this dictation. Nonetheless, debt-for-nature swaps are important as another example of the translation of OECD conservationist impulses (willingness to pay for conservation actions) into real incentives for developing country action.

OTHER PRIVATE INITIATIVES: CHARITIES AND NONGOVERNMENTAL ORGANIZATIONS

Other efforts, beyond debt-for-nature swaps, to affect developing country behavior in matters environmental have arisen in the private sector. One of these involves harnessing OECD, especially U.S., tax laws to make it attractive for citizens to contribute to charities devoted to protecting specific resources overseas. An example mentioned earlier in the text is the U.S. organization founded to channel U.S. tax-deductible contributions to Lewa Downs in Kenya. This was once a "white settler" cattle ranch and is now an elephant and rhino sanctuary of 40,000 acres and a tourist destination, with an airstrip, accommodation, and a wide range of wildlife-related activities available.

The prerequisites for this model to succeed include having dedicated, skilled, and honest people on the ground running the supported activity; and operating in a country in which destruction or expropriation of the activity seems unlikely. Since both these conditions are nearly impossible for the randomly chosen OECD citizen to verify, the set of likely donors may be confined to the group that has visited the place in question and come away with strong positive impressions.

A more general but still private channel of influence is the set of internationally active environmental NGOs, such as the Environmental Defense Fund, Greenpeace, and the World Wildlife Fund. While these groups cannot generally themselves pursue policy change via lawsuits or lobbying in developing countries, they can and do form alliances with in-country groups. These groups can benefit from both the experience of the outside groups in such areas as public relations and fund raising, and the resources they can make available. (However modest these might be, they probably hugely increase the resources available to the local groups.) Again, the cards must be played with care and discretion, for the charge of being in the pocket of some rich-country group could be a disastrous public relations blow and might even lead to charges of subversion in especially closed and suspicious countries.

WHERE DOES THIS LEAVE US?

Pretty clearly there is no really satisfactory way for interested OECD citizens to try to influence developing country environmental actions. And, in a sense, there never can be. In a world of nation-states, transborder externalities, especially those that involve nonuse values, will always be extremely difficult matters. But several observations are suggested by the efforts to date, and these lead at least to a suggestion for some experimentation with alternatives.

First, international carrots are likely to be more use than sticks. For one thing, they are at least a bit less likely to generate serious resentment. For another, they allow a shift in the burden of proof, as was observed in the discussion of domestic policy instruments and the monitoring and enforcement problem. And, for a third, they imply that the concerned citizens have somehow been forced to put their money behind their stated concerns.

Second, while there may be a place for both government-to-government and private-to-private transactions, the bulk of the action seems bound to be in the former arena. Look back, for example, at the debt-for-nature-swap data; almost fourteen times as much public as private activity. This reflects both the greater revenue raising power of the government and the greater possibilities one government has for taking enforcement actions against another.

Third, it will often be necessary to try to affect the attitudes and behaviors of individual citizens at the site of the problem—poachers and those who tolerate them; illegal loggers and miners; peasant families collecting firewood or running too many sheep, goats, or cattle. This means that prohibitions, and rules generally, promulgated from the center are unlikely to do the trick unless the enforcement effort is very serious. Again, carrots may be the ticket, as in CAMPFIRE.

Fourth, the possible roles for international institutions have been only very lightly explored, but such successes as we can see tend to result from institutional arrangements made to attack quite specific problems. This seems inefficient but may be a necessary part of the world as it is.

If there is a general direction suggestion by all this it seems to me to be the encouragement of multilateral treaty negotiations aimed at a series of fairly specific problem areas and with carrots built in. That is, in return for agreements to adopt particular policies, to not build particular types of projects, or to create and manage particular sorts of preserves, the treaty would promise appropriate assistance.

How to get this assistance to the people at the appropriate place(s) in the environment is a second, and at least as difficult, problem as negotiating agreed-on goals and amounts of assistance. It may well be that experiments with government/NGO cooperation are a promising route, at least in nations that are not paranoid about losing political control. If the NGOs were brought into the process of negotiating the original agreement—as U.S. groups routinely are, using "observer" status, but also having sympathetic officials on the actual negotiating team—a role for the local groups in the developing countries could be written in. Something rather like this has been done in some of the debt-for-nature swaps. The local groups could act as the local or perhaps regional administrators of the carrots, bypassing as much of the official, centralized bureaucracy as possible.

Monitoring and enforcement would still be necessary to see that the carrots reached the intended targets in return for the desired behavior. But the checking up might be done by a "partner" NGO from the OECD, which would make the whole process less threatening to delicate sovereign sensibilities. The penalty for maladministration could be removal from the process, with loss of prestige, overseas contact, and, not least, overhead payments.

In any event, experimentation will be necessary, if we are to find ways to make greater progress in dealing with this globally significant preference asymmetry.

NOTES

1. However one might be prepared to classify the Russian heartland on the development scale, its current struggles don't seem to leave it much energy for environmental concern.
2. Some of these techniques apply equally well (or poorly) to relations among OECD countries.
3. South Africa, and to a lesser extent, Zimbabwe and Botswana, felt hard used by this agreement as they were doing a better job of protection, partly paying the bill through culls of excess population.

REFERENCES

Deacon, Robert T., and Paul Murphy. 1997. "The structure of an environmental transaction: The debt for nature swap." *Land Economics* 73(1):1–24.

INDEX

Access, monitoring, 243
Acid rain sources, 97
Actions, monitoring and enforcement, 241–42
Advection process, 78
AEQ. *See* Ambient environmental quality; Ambient
    water quality
Aesthetics, 102, 135–36
Africa, 307, 311
Agricultural production methods, 227–28, 360–61
Air pollution/quality
    cost shifts and, 150
    Environmental Kuznets Curve for, 317–19
    health and, 152–53
    in less-developed countries, 312–13, 331–32
    multi-sources of pollution and, 87–88
    plume-type models of, 83–84
Algal densities
    constraints on, 113
    dissolved oxygen and, 108
    in regional water quality optimization model, 101
Allais Paradox, 273–74
Alternative policy instruments, 9, 190
Ambient environmental quality, 92
    calculation of, 74–77
    and discharge reduction charges when location
        matters, 197–99
    standards, benefit-cost tests and, 118
Ambient water quality, 106–9
    benefit routes and, 134–35
    constrained cost minimization, 112–18
    Latin American contingent valuation studies,
        335–36
    Tennessee Dept. of Environment use
        classifications, 114–16
Appliance purchases
    as averting expenditures, 150–55
    efficiency ratings and, 228
Arora, Seema, 234
Asia, 308, 311
Audits of self-reporting, 211, 243–44
Averting behavior techniques, 150–55, 326–27, 329,
    330

Bankruptcy, penalties and, 244
Baumol, William, 196
Bayes' theorem, 265, 268
Beneficiaries, diversity of, 128
Benefit estimates, 8, 13, 94–96, 121–87
    damages and, 52–55, 135
    direct methods, 137, 166–87
    economic approach to, 129, 131–34
    economics misunderstandings, 126–28
    ethical objections/qualifications, 124–26
    general comments, 159–62
    hypothetical responses and, 141
    indirect methods, 137, 140–65
    Latin America, 334–36
    in less-developed countries, 314, 316, 323–27
    observed behavior and, 141
    practical arguments, 121–23
    risk and, 259
    routes review, 134–37
    valuation bases for, 128–29, 130–31, 132–34
    See also Direct benefits estimates; Indirect
        benefits estimates
Benefit-cost tests, 118
Bequest values, 136
Biochemical oxygen-demanding organics (BOD),
    79–84, 92, 97–98, 101–2, 104
Biological/biochemical reactions, 78
Bishop, Richard, 279, 292–94
Bohm, Peter, 167–71, 172–73, 276
Bolivia, Conservation International debt relief
    program and, 367–68
Boundaries, ecosystem, 89
Burden of proof. *See* Proof, burden of

CAA. *See* Clean Air Act
CAMPFIRE program, Zimbabwe, 366–67, 369
Capacity utilization, 104
Capital goods designs economic growth model,
    302–3
Carlin, Alan, 122
Carson, Rachel, 18
Carter, Jimmy, 20

Cason, Timothy, 234
CBA. *See* Cost-benefit analysis
Central America, 308, 311
    See also Latin America
Certification, product or service, 226, 227–30
Challenge regulation, 233–35, 236
    EPA's 33/50 program of, 234–35
Charitable contribution incentives, 368
Chemical transformations, 78
China, 312, 366
Clean Air Act (CAA, 1970 and amendments), 21–22,
    95–96
Clean Water Act (CWA, 1972), 19, 21–22
    benefits estimates of for freshwater recreational
        fishing, 158–59
    ratcheting down under, 220
    technology-based standards under, 160–61
Climate change
    predictive natural system model limitations, 91
    See also Global climate change debate
Clinton, Bill, 121
Coase, Ronald, 46
Coase theorem, 46, 49
Cobb–Douglas economic growth form, 300–301, 304
Coliform bacteria (CO), 101, 102, 107, 113
Command and control (CAC) instruments, 190,
    191–92
Common land, deforestation of, 2
Common Stream, The (Rowland), 16
Compartment models, 79, 84–88
    assumptions, 84–85
    complications, 85–87
Compensated demand function, 59, 142
Competitive price, 47
Complementarity, 140–50, 163
    description of, 142
    hedonics and, 145–46
    weak, 141, 142–44
Complementary regulations, to liability rules, 223
Compliance
    decision calculation, 246–49
    as decision under uncertainty, 250–55
    inference errors, fine sizes and, 255
    outcomes of inference with imperfect monitoring,
        252
Compliance testing, initial and continuing, 243
Comprehensive Environmental Response, Liability,
        and Compensation Act (CERCLA), 22–24
    liability provisions in, 221–22
    See also Superfund
Conjoint analysis, 176–78
Conservation International, Bolivia and, 367–68

Consumer surplus. *See* Surpluses
Consumers
    product or service analysis/certification for, 226,
        227–30
    public goods and, 48
    Toxics Release Inventory and, 231
Consumers Union, 227, 230
Contingent choices, 176–77
Contingent ranking, 177
Contingent rating, 177
Contingent valuation methods, 141
    advantages/disadvantages of, 328
    versus conjoint analysis, 177–78, 182
    in developing countries, 327–30
    in Latin America, 334–36
    for recreation in developing countries, 333
    referendum version of, 179–82
    trade-off of, 182
Controllable sources, 100
Corner solutions, 324
Corruption, 212, 340, 344–45, 350
Cost shifts, 150–55
Cost-benefit analysis (CBA), 8, 94–120
    biochemical oxygen-demanding organics removal
        benefits, 97–98
    hydrocarbons removal benefits, 98–99
    less than basin-wide net benefit maximization,
        112–18
    multinational lending agencies' requirements for,
        320
    optimization equations, 94–96
    politics of distribution and, 57
    potential Pareto criterion and, 52
    regional model, 95, 100–112
    sulfur dioxide removal benefits, 96–97
    See also Benefit estimates
Costs
    CAA and CWA implementation and, 21–22, 26
    discharge reduction, 94–96, 103–6, 200
    monitoring and enforcement, 245–50
    private marginal, 45
    TSCA and FIFRA balance of benefits against,
        24–25, 26
Credit rationing, 327
CVM. *See* Contingent valuation methods
CWA. *See* Clean Water Act

Damage estimates, 13, 94–96, 121–39
    benefit routes and, 134–37
    benefits relation to, 52–55, 135
    court rulings and, 129
    direct, 137

economics misunderstandings, 126–28
Environmental Kuznets Curve (EKC), 317–19
ethical considerations, 124–26
indirect, 137
irreversible decisions and, 286–87
in less-developed countries, 314, 316, 320,
    322–39
MWTP and, 129–34
practical arguments, 121–23
See also Direct benefits estimates; Indirect
    benefits estimates; Marginal damage function
Davis, Bob, 166
Dawes, Robin, 273
Deadweight loss (DWL)-producing taxes, 215
Debt-for-nature swaps, 367–68, 369
Decision analysis, 10–11
    multiobjective, 118
    present decisions and available future decisions,
        70–72
    rain forest loss estimation, 287–88
    See also Risks
Decision group, relevant, 131–32
Decision tree, monitoring and compliance, 250–55,
    256
    inference errors, 251–55
Decision weight, 267
    subjective probabilities estimates and, 269
Decisions, irreversible. See Irreversible decisions
Deforestation
    and debt-for-nature swaps, 367–68
    Mediterranean, 2
Demand function, 32–38
    empirical finding of, 39
    growth of, 290–91
    hedonics and, 146
    identification problem with, 39
    shifts in, 140–50
    willingness to pay and, 59–61
    See also Compensated demand function;
        Marginal willingness to pay (MWTP)
Democratic governments, efficiency in, 28, 51
Deposit-refund (D-R) system, 204–5, 206, 211
Detection probability, 248–49
Developing countries, 297–321
    basic comparisons, 305–8
    benefits estimates, 322–39, 334–36
    capabilities, 345, 346
    contingent valuation studies in, 328–30
    courts and private dispute resolution of, 349
    damage estimates, 320, 322–39
    descriptions, 304–14
    versus developed countries, 322–23, 330–36

economic growth models, 299–303
economic perspective of, 314, 316
environment, OECD interests in, 364–70
environment, sustainability issues, 303–4
governing structure, 341–43
health and sanitation, 308–12
hedonic price analysis, 323–25
human impact on environment, 312–14
hypothetical benefits estimates in, 327–28
imported hazards to, 350–51
institutional setting, 341–44
institutional settings, 346
Latin American policy choices, 351–55
legal structure, 343
market-based instruments for, 344–51
modern phase policies, 349–50
national income accounting, 315
organizational structure, 343–44
policy choices for, 340–63
policy instruments, 345, 347
rising income factors, 316–19
skilled people to implement policy, 344
state monopolies and informal markets, 359
static efficiency of market-based instruments, 340
technology-based standards, 350
traditional phase policies, 345, 348
transition phase policies, 348–49
travel-cost methodology, 325–26, 333
    See also Economic growth; Latin America
Development effects, 11–13
Dewees, Donald, 221, 223
Dichotomous choices, 176–77
    contingent valuation and, 178
    versus open-ended survey questions, 174
    See also Referendum contingent valuation
Diffusion, of material or energy, 78
Direct benefits estimates, 137, 138, 166–87
    Bohm's TV experiment, 167–71
    conjoint analysis, 176–78
    hypothetical bias in, 170–71
    improvements for, 183–84
    incentive-compatible mechanisms, 171–72
    inferences from, 178–82
    nonusers, WTP surveys and, 175–76
    open-ended versus dichotomous survey
        questions, 174
    practical problems of, 182–83
    for public goods, 166–67
    response prediction and, 173
    strategic responses in, 167–73
    surveys difficulties and, 173–75
    uncertainty and, 172–73

Direct use values, 136
Discharge information. *See* Toxics Release Inventory
Discharge reduction
  charges when policy goal is AEQ and location
    matters, 197–98
  costs, 94–96, 103–6, 200
  damage function separability and, 195–96
  Latin American standards, 353
  optimal standards for, 109
  ratchetting down standards for, 219, 220
  response allocation, 194
  See also Permits, tradable discharge
Discounted sum of net benefits, 62
Dissolved oxygen (DO)
  algal growth and, 108
  constraints on, 113
  in regional water quality optimization model, 101
  water quality ladder and, 108
Dissolved oxygen deficit (DOD), 79–84
Distance, contaminant effects and, 82, 83
Domar, E., 299–300
Dose-response function, 153, 329
Double dividend, 235–36
  emission charge revenue and, 214
  high marginal damages and, 215–16
Dynamic model, 201
  efficiency of, 207

East African savannahs, noncitizen interests in, 364
Ebisemju, Fola, 341–43
Ecological systems, pollution and, 78
Econometric methods and dichotomous choice CV,
  178–82
Economic growth, 297–304
  Cobb–Douglas form, 300–301, 304
  endogenous models, 301–3
  environment, sustainability and, 303–4
  environment quality and, 322
  Harrod–Domar model, 299–300
  understanding, 298–99
Economic incentives (EI) instruments, 190
Efficiency
  in democratic governments, 28, 51
  distribution and, 51–52
  of policy instruments, 50–51
  and voting, 130–31
Embedding effect, in direct benefits estimates, 174
Emergency Planning and Community Right-to-Know
  Act (1986), 230
Emission charges system, 26–27, 193–99, 207
  for developing countries, 348
  discharge reduction when location matters, 197–98
  Latin America, 353

  monitoring, 211
  problems, 194
  as replacement for tax revenues, 213–16
  use of, 28–29
Endogenous economic growth, 301–3
  human capital investment model, 302
Energy use, Environmental Kuznets Curve for, 317
Enforcement, 240, 244–45
  See also Monitoring and enforcement
England, integrated environmental agency in, 27
Environment, 74–93
  AEQ calculation, 74–77
  compartment models, 79, 84–88
  economic growth and, 303–4
  ignorance factors and, 91–92
  plume-type models, 79–84
  pollution and, 77–79
  randomness effects, 90–91
  space considerations, 88–89
  time considerations, 89–90
Environmental Defense Fund, 368
Environmental degradation
  causes, 4–5
  historical, 2–4
  solutions, 5–6
Environmental Economics (Mäler), 142
Environmental Kuznets Curve (EKC), 317–19
Environmental legislation, U.S., 18–19, 30
  1970s, 19–25
  citizen input into, 27–28
  economics concerns in, 25–26
  efficiency prospects for, 28
  national jurisdiction of, 46
  versus OECD environmental regulation, 29
Environmental performance by firms, 230–33
Environmental Protection Agency (EPA)
  CAA tradable discharge permits, 22, 26, 28–29
  contingent valuation method development and, 122
  NAAQS efficiency justification investigation, 117
  Toxics Release Inventory and, 230–31
Environmental quality, 94–96
  averting behavior techniques and, 150–55, 326–27
  buyers/sellers awareness of, 324
  rents, 304
  WTA/WTP and, 132–33
  See also Ambient environmental quality
EPA. *See* Environmental Protection Agency
Ephemeral actions, 242
Equilibrium models, 144
  Cobb–Douglas economic growth form, 300–301,
    304
  general, 110–11
  partial, 110

Errors of inference, 251–55
    See also Uncertainty
Europe
    citizen input into environmental quality
        improvements, 27–28
    economic development in, 307–8
    emission charges system in, 26–27
    health and sanitation in, 311
Event tree
    life/death, 282
    two-period, 281
Events, independence of, 267–68
Ex post rules/regulations changes, 220–21, 225–26
Executive orders, on economic legitimacy of
        environmental standards, 117, 121–22
Existence benefits, 136
Expected money value, 263
Expected penalty, 247
Expected utility, 261–65
Expected value criterion, 65, 66, 258–59, 260–61
Experts
    confidence expressions by, 266–67
    subjective probability formation and, 270
Externalities, 4–5
    market failure and, 44–48
    monopoly and, 67–68
    negotiation and, 46
    socially correct prices and, 57
    transborder, 364–70
    transparent, accountable governing structure,
        341–43
Extinction, irreversible decisions and, 285, 286
Exxon Valdez grounding and oil spill, 122, 123, 166

Fairness
    of challenge regulation, 235
    of liability provisions, 225–26
    perceived, 216–17
False positives/negatives in monitoring, 255
Feasible space, and social welfare frontier, 42
Federal Insecticide, Fungicide, and Rodenticide Act
        Amendments (FIFRA), 24–25
Fines, as penalty, 244
First order conditions (FOCs), 55–56
    for cost minimization, 197
    discharge charges schedule and, 194–95
"Fish," in regional water quality optimization model,
    101
Flow, river, 100–101, 106–7
FOCs. *See* First order conditions
Footprints, market, 137
Ford, Gerald, 20
Fraas, Arthur, 103

Framing problems, 273, 274–75
Free riding, 166
Freeman, A. M., 160
*Freshwater Recreational Fishing: The National
        Benefits of Water Pollution Control* (Russell
        and Vaughan), 158
Freudenburg, William, 266–67
Future
    averting behavior techniques and, 327
    bequest values and, 136
    bias against, 127
    for development economics, 318
    ignorance of, 64–65, 124
    present decisions and available decisions, 70–72
    standards, influence on, 235
    value of, 8, 125–26, 136–37

Gasoline, leaded, 313
General equilibrium model, 110–11
General Theorem of the Second Best, 67–68
General valuation functions, 66–67
Global climate change debate, 7, 49, 75, 91, 124
Global problems, trial and error approach to, 197–98
Goals, environmental, 7, 8
Government intervention, public goods and, 49
Government investments, Latin American, 354
Government revenue, 9
Graded pair rating, 177
Green accountants and accounts, 315
Greenpeace, 368
Grether, David, 275, 276
Gross domestic product (GDP), 305–6
    average per capita income, damage estimates
        and, 316–19
Gross marginal abatement cost (GMAC) function,
    214

Hanemann, Michael, 175
Harrod, Roy, 299–300
Harrod–Domar economic growth model, 299–300
*Has Environmental Protection Really Produced
        Productivity Growth?* (Repetto), 316
Hassle factors, WTP and, 154
Health
    air pollution and, 152–53
    benefits route, 135
    cost shifts and, 150, 151
    in developing countries, 308–12
    in developing versus developed countries,
        330–32
    dose-response function measurements, 153
    in regional water quality optimization model, 102
Heavy-metal poisoning, 3

Hedonic price function, 141
  complementarity and, 145–46
  in developing countries, 323–25, 329, 330
  MWTP and, 145–50
  studies in developing countries, 325
Hell's Canyon dam proposal, 289–92
Hicksian demand functions, 59
Hot spots, 200, 207
Human capital investment
  and capital goods design economic growth
    model, 302–3
  economic growth model, 302
Human Development Index, UNDP, 351
Human exposure to ambient environmental quality
    conditions, 94–96
Human impact on environment, 312–14
  Latin American assessments, 354
Hydrocarbons, reactive, 98–99
Hypothetical bias, in direct benefits estimates,
    170–71, 173
Hypothetical (survey) responses, 141

Identification problem, 39, 148
Ignorance, 4
  economic policy and, 30, 127–28
  of future, 64–65, 124
  knowledge and, 5
  lack of environmental data, 91–92
  of less-developed countries, 316
  lottery irreversibility game, 292–94, 295
  risk analysis and, 280, 285–94
  sensitivity analysis, 291
Impact
  human, on environment, 312–14
  Latin American assessments, 354
  of services or goods, 228–29
Import-substituting industrialization (ISI), Latin
    American, 358–59, 360
Imprinted actions, 242
Incentive-compatible mechanisms, for direct benefits
    estimates, 171–72
Incentives, open-ended, 7
Independence axiom, 273
Independence of events, 267–68
Indifference curves
  preference relations and, 58–59
  prices and, 38
  surpluses and, 57
Indirect benefits estimates, 137, 138, 140–65
  cost shifts, 150–55
  hedonics, 141, 144–50, 323–25
  overlapping/underlapping, 160, 164
  policy-related questions and, 160

technology-based standards under CWA, 161
travel costs, 155–59, 325–29
Tuolumne River preservation study, Calif., 160,
    162–63
weak complementarity, 141, 142–44
Industrial Revolution consequences, 17–18
Inference errors, 251–55, 284
Information intensity, of market-based instruments
    (MBI), 199, 205, 356
Information provision, 226–33, 236–37
  in developing countries, 350
  environmental performance by firms, 230–33
  product or service analysis/certification, 226,
    227–30
  technical assistance, 226–27
Institutional capacity
  in developing countries, 341–44, 356–57
  transparent, accountable governing structure,
    341–43
  weakness or failure of, 4, 5
Insurance irreversibility game, 292–94
Insurance premiums, 263, 267–68, 271–72
Integer-valued bids, in direct benefits estimates, 170
Inter-American Development Bank, 320, 334, 343,
    351, 366
Interference effects, 267
Interval method, in direct benefits estimates, 169
Intransitivity of preferences, 59
Intrinsic importance of natural systems, 125
Investors, Toxics Release Inventory and, 231–32
Irreversible decisions, 285–94
  damage estimates, 286–87
  payoff (lottery/insurance) games, 292–94
  rain forest loss estimation, 287–88
  Snake River dam proposal, 289–92

Jail-time, as penalty, 244
Joint and several liability, 223–24, 225
Joint damage function, 225

Kahneman, Daniel, 269, 274
Killer fogs (smogs), 2, 18
Kneese, Allen, 193
Knetsch, Jack, 166
Knowledge, nonuser benefits and, 136, 138
Krutilla, John, 279, 289–92

Lagrange Multipliers, 55
Lakes, 18, 87
Land use controls, Latin America, 354
Latin America
  benefits estimates, 334–36
  country rankings by institutional capacity, 352

economic development in, 308
health and sanitation in, 311
industrial and commercial configurations in, 358–60
institutional assessments, 343–44
institutional capabilities and market configurations in, 357–58
policy choices in, 351–55
rural configurations, 360–61
sewer/wastewater treatment project, 179–82
LCA. *See* Least-cost analysis; Life cycle analysis
LDC (Less-developed countries). *See* Developing countries
Lead-poisoning, 2
Least-cost analysis, 117
Least-worst result, risk and, 259
Less than basin-wide net benefit maximization, 112–18
Less-developed countries (LDC). *See* Developing countries
Liability provisions, 190–91, 236
in developing countries, 349–50
in Latin America, 355
perceived fairness of, 225–26
of policy instruments, 24, 220–26
several-party problems, 223–25
single-party problems, 222–23
Life cycle analysis, 228–29
Log-rolling example, 130, 131
Loss, in insurance/lottery irreversibility games, 292–94
Lotteries, Allais Paradox and, 273–74
Lottery irreversibility game, 292–94, 295
Lottery tickets
preference reversal and, 273, 275–76
risk-averse preferences and, 272
sales, 271
utility weighting and, 263
Lucas, Robert E., Jr., 302
Lucky feeling, 272

Mäler, Karl-Göran, 142
Mangrove wetlands, 364
Manifest system, for hazards tracking, 24
Man-made chemicals in nature, 91
Marginal abatement cost (MAC) function, 214
Marginal charge schedule, 195
Marginal cost function, 38–40
of discharge reduction, 202–3
of monitoring and enforcement, 249–50
for optimal discharge, 109
private versus socially optimal, 45–48
public goods and, 48–50

as sacrifice, 56
sources choices of, 217–19
Marginal damage function, 214
high, double dividend and, 215–16
shared liability, 225
sources choices of, 217–18
Marginal revenue (MR) function, 42
Marginal subsidies, 204–5
Marginal willingness to accept (MWTA), 129
Marginal willingness to pay (MWTP), 33, 56
externalities and, 47
hedonic price analysis and, 145–50
for public goods, 166
public goods and, 48
social, 57
valuation for environmental goods, 129, 131, 133–34
See also Demand function
Market, extent of the, 132
for nonusers, 162–63
Market bias, 126–27
Market configurations, 357–58
Market equilibrium, 323–24
Market failures, 44–45, 57, 67–68
Market price, 45–48
Market-based instruments
for developing countries, 344–51, 356–57
institutional costs of static efficiency, 340
political effects of tradable discharge permits, 213
types, 190–92
Markets, informal, 359
Marshallian demand functions, 59
Material damage, hassle factors and, 154
Maximum price, surpluses and, 40
MBI. *See* Market-based instruments
MC function. *See* Marginal cost function
MD function. *See* Marginal damage function
Measurement of Environmental and Resource Values, The (Freeman), 160
Media
controlled, 350
free and critical, 345
Mendelsohn, Robert, 279, 287–88
Methodology choices, 191, 192
See also Econometric methods and dichotomous choice CV
Microeconomics, 32–73, 67–68
basics, 57–67
correcting market failures, 67–68
demand function, 32–38, 59–61
efficiency and distribution, 51–52
extensions, 67–72

Microeconomics (*continued*)
    future decisions changed by present decisions, 70–72
    ignorance of future, 64–65
    optimization in, 52–56, 68–70
    rationality, 57–59
    risk and uncertainty, 65–67
    social welfare, 41–50
    supply/marginal cost, 38–40
    surpluses, 32–38
    time and uncertainty, 61–64
    willingness to pay, 32–38, 59–61
Minimax loss, in insurance/lottery irreversibility games, 293
Minimax-regret choice, 260
Mixing-bowl model, 84, 197–98
Monitoring and enforcement, 7, 9–10, 240–56
    actions, 241–42
    characteristics of, 241–44
    compliance decision calculation, 246–49
    compliance decision under uncertainty, 250–55
    definitions, 240
    detection probability, 248–49
    developing country policy instruments and, 340, 356
    economics of, 245–50
    elements of, 244–45
    information from, 230
    instruments for, 242–43
    marginal costs of, 249–50
    nongovernmental organizations and, 369
    policy instruments and, 210–12, 235
    variations in, 30
    See also Risk analysis/management
Monopolies, 42–44, 67–68, 359–60
Moral negligence, environmental degradation and, 4, 5, 6, 26
Moral suasion, environmental improvements and, 234
Moveability of pollutants, 241–42
MR (marginal revenue) function, 42
Mullahy, John, 152
Multilateral treaties, 369
Multinational lenders, OEDC/LDC relations and, 366
Multiobjective decision analysis, 118
Munley, Vincent, 103
Muskie, Edmund, 19
MWTA (marginal willingness to accept), 129
MWTP. *See* Marginal willingness to pay

National Ambient Air Quality Standard (NAAQS) levels, 21–22, 95–96

National economy, water quality optimization model for, 110–11
National Health Interview Survey (1979), 152
National income accounting, 315, 319
National Rivers Authority, England, 27
National Sanitation Foundation Water Quality Index, 98
Natural disasters, probable recurrence of, 268
Natural resource damage assessments (NRDA), 24
Negligence standard
    liability provisions and, 225
    several-party liability and, 224–25
    single-party liability and, 222–23
Negotiation, externalities, policy and, 46
Net marginal abatement cost (NMAC) function, 214–15
Net returns, time and, 62–64
New information, incorporation of, 268
Nitrogen, 102
Nitrous oxide, 312
Nixon, Richard M., 20
Nongovernmental organizations (NGOs), environmental, 368, 369
Nonpoint sources, pollution, 22
    in developing countries, 349
    monitoring, 212, 235
    variations in monitoring/enforcement of, 30
    See also Point sources, pollution
Nonuse values, 175–76, 328, 332–33
Nonuser benefits (NU), 102, 136, 160, 162–63
Null hypothesis, burden of proof and, 284

Oates, Wallace, 196
Observed behavior, 141
OECD (Organization for Economic Development and Cooperation), 11–13, 305
    developing country environments and, 364–70
    economic development in, 308
    environmental regulation versus U.S. environmental regulation, 29
    health and sanitation in, 312
    trade policies of, 365–66
Open access, 2
Open-ended versus dichotomous survey questions, 174
Optimal policy equation, 94, 96–99
    See also Regional optimization model, water quality
Optimization
    constrained, 55–56, 112–18
    with inconveniently shaped functions, 68–70
    open-ended requirement, 95
    unconstrained, 52–55

Option value, 137
Ordinary demand relations, 59
Outcomes, utility weighting of, 261–65
    probabilities, 263–65
    risk-averse utility function, 261–63
    in uncertain situations, 270–72
Outer Continental Shelf Lands Act amendments
        (1978), 221–22
Oxygen sag curve, 80–84
Ozone, 99
    cost shifts and, 150
    respiratory illness and, 152–53
    skin cancer, pain and suffering costs and, 153

Packaged food container recyclability, 228
Pain and suffering, WTP and, 153
Pairwise rating, 177
Pareto, Vilfredo, 41
Pareto optimality, 41, 42, 51–52
Partial equilibrium model, 110
Parzen, Emanuel, 268
Penalties, 7
    credibility of, 244, 245
    'encouraging the others' and, 249
    expected, 247
    process from violation to, 245
Per capita benefits, 102–3, 108
Perceived fairness, 216–17, 225–26
Perceived risks, 210, 217–20
    to the agency, 217–19
    for the public from instrument choice, 219–20,
        327
Permits, technology-based, 348
Permits, tradable discharge, 22, 26
    in developing countries, 349, 356–57
    in dynamic model, 202–3
    economic uses for, 28–29
    Latin America, 353
    as MBI instrument, 190–91
    monitoring and, 211
    political dimensions of, 212–13
    sources problem, 212
    static efficiency and, 199–200, 206–7
    technical advances and, 218–19
Phosphorus, 102
Plott, Charles, 275, 276
Plume-type environmental models, 79–84
Point sources, pollution, 22, 30, 235
    See also Nonpoint sources, pollution
Policy choices, 7–11
    ambient environmental quality and, 74–77
    cost-effectiveness of, 117
    history of, 16–18

incentive-compatible mechanisms and, 172
indirect benefits estimates and, 160
monitoring and enforcement and, 255–56
OECD versus LDC, 364–70
perceived risks for public from, 219–20, 327
unconstrained optimization, 52–55
unidimensional goals and, 117
Policy instruments, 8–9, 188–239
    ambient environmental quality and, 74–77
    bases for judging among, 192, 193
    challenge regulation, 233–35, 236
    for developing countries, 343
    economic development and, 13
    efficiency of, 50–51
    ethics and, 212–16
    implementation costs in, 21–22
    information provisions, 226–33, 236–37
    institutional demands, 210–12
    liability provisions, 220–26, 236
    narrowing range of, 188–92
    perceived fairness of, 216–17
    perceived risks, 210
    perceived risks of, 217–20
    politics and, 210, 213–16
    prices and, 212–13
    static efficiency, 192–201, 205–7
    static versus dynamic cases and, 201–3
    subsidies, 204–5
    See also Developing countries
Political dimensions of policy instrument choice,
        212–13, 255
Political/regulatory process, 95
Pollution. See Nonpoint sources, pollution; Point
        sources, pollution; Sources (pollution)
Pollution charges, 190–91
Pollution reduction, 96–99
    benefits, unconstrained optimization and, 52–55
    of biochemical oxygen-demanding organics,
        97–98
    removal efficiency costs and, 104–6
    of sulfur dioxide gas, 96–97
Pollution sources. See Nonpoint sources, pollution;
        Point sources, pollution; Sources (pollution)
Population, 4, 5–6, 108
Population Explosion, The (Ehrlich and Ehrlich), 5–6
Portney, Paul, 152, 233
Potential Pareto criterion, 51–52
Poverty, relative, 13
Preference relations, 57–59
Preference reversal, 273, 275–76
Preferences, revealed versus stated, 140
Present decisions, available future decisions and,
        70–72

Present value of net benefits, 62
Presumptive charges, 211, 212
Price failure, 47
Price line, 37, 59
Prices
    market, 45–48
    policy instrument choice and, 212–13
    quality and, 144
    versus values, 121
    WTP and, 33–38
    See also Demand function
Principal-agent problem, 13–14
Private goods (X_S), 45–48, 340–41
Private marginal costs (MC_{PR}), 45
Probabilities, 263–65
    estimating subjective, 269
    problems with, 267–70
    risk analysis and, 280
    time and, 281–83
Product analysis/certification, 226, 227–30
Production function, 38
Production possibility frontier, 41
Productivity, discounting and, 62
Proof, burden of
    compliance decisions and, 252
    liability provisions and, 225
    monitoring and, 243
    null hypothesis and, 284
    as risk management strategy, 283–85
    shifting, 285
    TSCA and FIFRA on, 25
Public goods, 48–50, 166
    market failure and, 44–45
    private aspects of, 49–50
Purchasing power parity, 306

Quality of life costs, 150–51, 154–55
Quantity, socially optimal, 45
Quantity changes, WTP and, 37–38
Quasi-option value, 137

Radioactive waste, irreversible decisions and, 285, 286
Rain forests, tropical, 91, 287–88, 364
Randall-Stoll WTP bids for public good quantity
    changes, 175
Randomness, 90–91
Ratchetting down, discharge standards and, 219, 220
Rationality, 57–59
Ready, Richard, 292–94
Reaeration, 80
Reagan, Ronald, 121
Recreation, 102, 134–35, 166, 332–33
    See also Travel-cost methodology

Referendum contingent valuation, WTP inference
    and, 179–82
Regional optimization model, water quality, 100–112
    ambient water quality and, 106–9
    cost-of-reduction functions, 100–103
    discharge reduction costs, 103–6
    dynamics of, 109
    interacting river basin models and, 111–12
    national economy considerations, 110–11
    Tennessee Dept. of Environment use
        classifications, 114–16
    uncertainty considerations, 109–10
Regret matrix, 259–60
Regulatory agencies, challenge regulation and,
    233–35
Relevant consumers, 137
Relevant decision group, 131–32
Removal efficiency costs projections, 104–6
Rents, environmental quality, 304
Repetto, Robert, 316
Requirements, enforceable, 7
Resource Conservation and Recovery Act (RCRA),
    22–24, 221–22
Resources for the Future (RFF), water quality ladder,
    98–99, 108, 134–35
Results specifications, 191, 192
Returnable bottles, 204–5
Revealed preferences, 140, 328–29
Rewards, 7
Risk analysis/management, 279–96
    burden of proof and, 283–85
    irreversible decisions, 285–94
    payoff (lottery/insurance) games, 292–94
    probabilities and time, 281–83
    rain forest loss estimation, 287–88
    risk analysis and, 279–85
    risk management and, 279–85
    Snake River dam proposal, 289–92
Risk-averse utility function, 261–63, 264
Risks, 257–78
    Allais Paradox, 273–74
    decision analysis and, 10–11
    decisions on, cognitive limitations of, 265–77
    expected value criterion, 258–59, 260–61
    framing, 274–75
    least-worst result and, 259
    not-so-rational models, 265–67
    observed judgments and, 273–76
    outcomes weighting, 261–65
    outcomes weighting in uncertain situations, 270–72
    perceived, 210, 217–20, 327
    preference reversal, 275–76
    probabilities problems, 267–70

rational models for, 258–65
regret matrix, 259–60
uncertainty and, 65–67
varying definitions of, 65, 257
River basin conferences, 19
River basin models, 111–12
Rivers, 2, 3, 5, 286
DOD/DO plume-type models of, 82–83
European policies for, 26–27
Russian, 364
Snake River dam proposal, 289–92
Tuolumne River preservation study, Calif., 160, 162–63
See also Flow, river
Romer, Paul, 302
Rosen, Sherwin, 145, 146
Ruhr River basin, Germany, emission charges system, 26–27
Rural configurations, Latin American, 360–61
Rural sanitation, 16
Russell, Clifford, 158
Russia, salmon rivers of, 364

Safety, definitions of, 23
Salinization of soils, 2
Sample size, 182
Sampling method, 182
Samuelson, Paul, 166
Sanitation
in developing countries, 308–12, 313, 337
Latin America benefits estimates of, 334–36
urban, 16–17
Saturation value, 80
Scientific analysis, 95
Second best policy instrument choice, 201, 207
General Theorem of, 67–68
Second dividend. *See* Double dividend
Self-reporting, audits of, 211, 243–44
Sensational information dominance, 270
Sensitivity analysis, 291
Service, environmental analysis and certification of, 226, 227–30
Several-party liability problems, 223–26
Shadow prices, 118, 199, 314
Silent Spring (Carson), 18
Single-party liability problems, 222–23
Smoking, costs of, 151, 152–53
Snake River dam proposal, 289–92
demand function growth, 290–91
irreversible decisions and, 292
sensitivity analysis, 291
Social welfare, 41–50
Coase Theorem, 46

frontier, 41–44
market failure, 44–45
MC, MWTP, prices and, 56
monopoly problem, 42–44
public goods and, 44–45, 48–50
Socially correct price, 47
Socially optimal quantity, 45
Solow, Robert, 301
Sources (pollution)
challenge regulation and, 233–35
influence on general reputation of, 244
monitoring, 245
moveable in time or space, 241–42
perceived risks of environmental change, 217–19
See also Nonpoint sources; Point sources, pollution
Source-specific coefficients, 77
South America, 308, 311
See also Latin America
Space, environmental pollutants and, 78–79
Spaces, ecosystem, 88–89
Species
accidental introduction of, 91
loss, irreversible decisions and, 285, 286
Standard apportionment rule, 221
Stated preferences, 140
Static efficiency, 192–201
dischargers' marginal costs and, 205
emission charges, 193–99
hot spots, 200, 207
institutional costs of, 340
marketable permits, 198–200, 206–7
model revisions/updating, 206
second-best choice of policy instruments, 201, 207
Static model, 201–3
Stavins, Robert, 162–63, 200
Stock market values, Toxics Release Inventory and, 231–32
Storage/storeability of pollutants, 78, 242
Streams. *See* Rivers
Streeter-Phelps DOD/DO model, 87
See also Plume-type environmental models
Subjective probabilities estimates, 269
Subsidies, 190–91, 204–5, 211
Sulfate (SO_4) aerosols, 18
Sulfur dioxide (SO_2) pollution, 2–3, 96–97, 312
Superfund, 22–24, 217, 218, 225
Supply function, 38–40
Surface roughness, of rivers, 101
Surpluses, 32–38, 57
demand/supply and, 39–40
market failure and, 44

Surveys
    cognitive difficulties with, 173–75
    conjoint analysis, 176–78
    format of, 182
    inferential stage of benefits estimation and,
        178–82
    nonusers responses to, 175–76
    types, 182–83
Suspended solids, in rivers, 102
Sustainable environment, 124, 303–4
System, state of the, 70–72

Taxes, 47–48, 353
    See also Emission charges system
Technical analysis, 95
Technical assistance, 226–27
    desired behaviors and, 366–67
Technology
    capital-to-output ratio and, 299–300
    for developing countries, 345, 348
    development, 4
    environmental standards and, 26
    monitoring using, 24, 245
Technology-based standards
    challenge regulation and, 233
    Clean Water Act and, 21–22
    in developing countries, 350, 356
    for discharges, 218–19
    versus technology specification, 191
Television WTP experiment, Bohm's, 167–71
Temperature, of rivers, 101
Tennessee Dept. of Environment, water use
    classifications, 114–16
Tennessee Environmental Council (TEC), 231
Time
    cost shifts and, 150, 154
    discounting, 62–64
    environmental change and, 89–90
    environmental pollutants and, 78–79
    optimization calculation and, 108
    probabilities and, 281–83
    in regional water quality optimization model,
        101, 102
    uncertainty and, 61–64
Total economic value (TEV), 137, 328
Toxic Substances Control Act (TSCA), 24–25
Toxics Release Inventory (TRI), 23, 24, 230–33,
    350
Trade policies, OECD/LDC relations and, 365–66
Trading ratios, for discharge permits, 200
Transfer coefficient, 92
Travel, technology and, 304

Travel-cost methodology (TCM)
    demand curves for, 156–57
    developing country studies, 325–26, 329, 330
    hedonic, 141, 155–59, 163
    inappropriateness for developing countries, 333
Trial and error, discharge reduction costs and, 195,
    197–98
Tropical rain forests, 91, 287–88, 364
Tuolumne River preservation study, Calif., 160,
    162–63, 176
Turbidity, of rivers, 101, 113
Tversky, Amos, 269, 274

Uncertainty, 7, 10–11
    direct benefits estimates and, 172–73
    framing alternatives under, 274–75
    liability provisions and, 225
    of monitoring and enforcement, 250–55
    in optimization equations, 95
    outcomes weighting and, 270–72
    in regional water quality optimization model,
        101, 109–10
    risk and, 65–67, 279–85
    single-party liability and, 222–23
    subjective probabilities and, 65
    time and, 61–64
    See also Ignorance; Risks
Unconstrained optimization, 52–55
Unfamiliar problems, surveys and, 183
Urban sanitation, 16–17
"Use of Standards and Prices for Protection of the
    Environment, The" (Baumol and Oates),
    196–97
Use values
    benefits route and, 136, 138
    in Latin America, 354
User benefits, of rivers, 102
Utility-weighting function
    feeling lucky and, 272
    for gains versus losses, 270–71
    risk-averse, 261–63, 264

Value versus prices, 121
Vaughan, William, 158, 325
Voluntary agreements, Latin America, 354

Warm-glow effect, 174
Water Authorities, England, 27
Water quality
    benefits estimates of for freshwater recreational
        fishing, 158–59
    ladder, 98–99, 108, 134–35

in less-developed countries, 330–32
multi-sources of pollution and, 87
parameters, 98
regional optimization model, 100–112
Waterways contamination, 3
Welfare frontier. *See* Social welfare
Wildlife poisoning, 3–4
Willig bounds, 175
Willingness to accept (WTA), 37, 132, 175, 183–84
Willingness to pay (WTP), 32–38
  to avoid sickness, 153
  in Bohm's TV experiment, 168–71
  difficulty in answering predictive questions on, 173
  environmental quality improvements and, 145
  hedonics and, 145–46, 324
  inferences, referendum contingent valuation and, 179–82
  Latin American contingent valuation studies, 334–36
  level allowing for 100–percent acceptance, 181
  MWTP contrast with, 132–33
  for public goods, 166
  in regional water quality optimization model, 101
  valuation challenges, 183–84
  See also Surveys
World Bank, 320, 366
World Resources Institute (WRI), 316
World Wildlife Fund, 368
WTA. *See* Willingness to accept
WTP. *See* Willingness to pay

Zimbabwe, CAMPFIRE program, 366–67, 369